SITTING ON TRETIAK

The 1972 Summit Series-Play by Play.
Volume One-The Canadian Games

Grant Douglas Pennell

Amazon KDP Publishing.

D1529119

Dedicated To the Game of Hockey.,,, for being so Awesome.

Thank You.

CONTENTS

1965-1970

SITTING ON TRETIAK

THE SUMMIT SERIES PLAY BY PLAY

GRANT DOUGLAS PENNELL

FOREWARD

For 30 years the story of the 1972 Summit Series was limited to books, newspaper articles, player and fan recollections, and statistics that could never be questioned, cross-checked, or denied. However, the release of the 1st DVD set containing all 8 games in 2002 helped show what happened on the ice during those games revealed new truths that completely changed our understanding of the series in ways we never expected.

I was able to reveal a bounty of those in my 2012 book: 1972 – and further expand on that in my 50th Anniversary Edition to show that what we thought we knew was not always true, and what we didn't was perhaps just as important. My good friend, Grant Pennell, has now done his own deep dig into who did or didn't do what in the '72 Series, and the results will no doubt add to the legacy of the series that has continued to interest and thrill fans for a half century, and beyond. Congrats Grant, and hope fans will enjoy reading about your discoveries and insights as much as they did mine!

Richard J. Bendell Author:
THE SUMMIT SERIES: Canada vs. USSR, Stats, Lies and Videotape, The UNTOLD Story of Hockey's Series of the Century

When I wrote my book EPIC CONFRONTATION on the Canada-Soviet hockey rivalry, I felt it was time to tell the true, complete story. From the perspective of both sides, based on what was being said at the time, rather than on faulty decades-old memories that served mostly to reinforce legend rather than fact.

Meeting Grant while I promoted my own book in Canada, I could tell he has a very deep knowledge of the game. His father was an outstanding NHL prospect in the exceedingly top notch pre-expansion era, who, despite losing his chance of distinguishing himself in the NHL due to injury, had an outstanding professional career in the high-level American Hockey League, retiring to coach junior hockey in Manitoba for many years. Having a father who played the game at a high level does not in itself ensure children will inherit the same knowledge of, and instinct for, the game. However, in this instance this is what happened.

Grant developed an interest in hockey by playing game and being witness to the wonderful, European focused, WHA club Winnipeg Jets in the late 1970's. Grant witnessed this with an interest and enthusiasm that was ahead of its' time among his fellow Canadians. It was an era where it was one thing to voice admiration for the new style of play, but quite another to appreciate it to the extent where it became central to one's understanding of the game.

Grant possesses something rare among Canadians: The ability to look objectively at this story that is so emotionally close to many Canadians who recall it or have learned of it since. Canadians are close to, and invested in, the story that it is impossible to separate themselves from the passions involved to tell the truth. I know no one more capable of approaching the task with the needed objectivity to do it justice.

In any sport, it's impossible to take in everything that's happening in real time. Until someone is ready to analyse and isolate everything in context, in much the same way a coach does in preparing for the next game, there is too much happening, multiple games within a game, to keep track of what everyone is doing at once.

This volume covers the four games in Canada which turned hockey on its' head in a week. On the fiftieth anniversary of those games, I had a taste of what the process to write this book was like when I endeavoured to break down the games in a manner like what Grant had done, though still in far less detail. Even so, doing it this way required 6-8 hours to watch each game. The result is that I learned fascinating things I hadn't previously noticed in a dozen or more viewings.

Grant Pennell watched and analysed the games in great depth so his readers won't have to, but as a result, they will reap the benefit of a much greater knowledge of - as the title of my book termed it, "the greatest sports drama of all time." I came away with a greater awareness of many aspects of the Canadian half of the series than I had had before, a greater appreciation of the monumental task Grant undertook in researching and preparing this book.

Greg Franke Author "Epic Confrontation"

Author's Foreword

"No one would have believed in the last years of the nineteenth century that this world was being watched keenly and closely by intelligences greater than man's and yet as mortal as his own; that as men busied themselves about their various concerns they were scrutinised and studied, perhaps almost as narrowly as a man with a microscope might scrutinise the transient creatures that swarm and multiply in a drop of water."
H.G. Wells, The War of the Worlds

You might wonder why I am talking about a book from 1897. What would that have to do with international hockey? As a boy this was my favourite book. While It might be a stretch to compare classic science fiction about an alien invasion to a hockey series, there are some similarities.

In H.G. Wells' book, humankind was unaware they were being watched, studied, and strategized against, naive and arrogant until it was almost too late. Like the oblivious mankind in HG Wells' novel, the Canadian hockey establishment, media, and NHL players were also oblivious to the growing talents and abilities of European hockey. Abilities that threatened the Canadian perception that they were the top hockey nation on earth. When the games started, Canada was shocked, unprepared. One difference was that in War of the Worlds, the aliens were a surprise, unknown. In the 1972 Summit Series, the Soviets had been around for twenty-five years. The Canadian hockey establishment had plenty of warning but yet, were still seemingly caught unawares.

This always puzzled me. How could the NHL not see

how good the Soviets were? Why was everyone shocked by game one in Montreal? The mystery of it added glamour to the series. The NHL, familiar to all in Canada, was now playing a team from another part of the world, in an era before the internet and thousands of television channels.

Yet that wasn't the real truth. They weren't unknowns. The Soviets had made numerous Canadian tours since 1957. They had dominated the World Championships and Olympic Games. While impressive, the Canadian hockey establishment felt that level of play was certainly not the equal of the NHL. This may have been true up to the mid-1960's, but it was certainly false by 1972. This Soviet team was not supposed to be good, but good they were. Canada was supposed to be much better, but they weren't. What was going on? The Soviets may as well have been Martians, coming to conquer.

For myself, as a seven-year-old in Winnipeg, Manitoba, the Soviets were exotic. They looked different. They skated different. They played different. They were from a different part of the world. They were beating out the best, the heroes whose hockey cards I collected and traded with my friends. That was all it took. I was fascinated and hooked by the unknown of international hockey. Worlds colliding. **A War on Ice**, to rephase my favourite book on the Summit Series by Scott Young, or **a War of the Worlds,** hockey wise.

As I played minor hockey, that mysteriousness the unknown brought stayed in my subconscious every time I played a team from another city, province, or country. Who were they? How good were they? How did they play? The few times we travelled to the USA, I always felt pride that I was representing Canada in my own way.

When I was a midget-aged player, I played a team from Sweden in a game. I wasn't a top player; I wasn't going to play professionally. I knew that. I was a kid playing minor hockey in Winnipeg. I knew this would be the closest I would come to facing a foreign invader. This was it! These weren't the Americans, players I was used to playing, these were the Swedes. They looked different, skated different and even wore the Tre Krona yellow sweaters. It was a surreal moment when I hit the ice, knowing I was facing a team from Europe. In my teenaged mind I was in as important moment as those players on Team Canada in 1972. It was my turn to represent my country. As it turned out, the Swedes were really good. We didn't win that game, but I don't know if I ever tried harder. It's a memory I cherish to this day.

While I loved playing hockey and still play fifty years later, (just much slower), learning about hockey history has always been my true love. I was more interested in sports history, statistics and reading about hockey than my friends, or anyone I knew. I spent hours reading hockey books as a boy, learning about Eddie Shore, Newsy Lalonde, or the Rocket. Glamourous stories about driving through snowstorms to get to a game, carrying players on your back to score an overtime goal. I studied statistics, numbers, evaluating careers and impact the players had. At the same time, I was reading about hockey, ingesting all the knowledge and history I could, I was learning about the game at the deepest, most strategic, analytical level possible. I had a real-life hockey expert living in the same home.

A member of the Manitoba Hockey Hall of Fame, my father Gord Pennell started as a local junior star. Soon after, he played in the Montreal Canadiens organization with the Barrie Flyers, then spent several years playing in the very high level 1950's AHL for the Buffalo Bisons. He was a very good player, making the all-star team for the first ever AHL all-star game. He was a future NHL player until a broken leg shattered that career. He went on to be a top Senior A player for the Warroad Lakers, and then a long-time coach in Winnipeg junior hockey. As a coach, he helped several players make the NHL becoming a well revered hockey expert. Long-time WHA and NHL player Paul Baxter called him the most knowledgeable hockey man he had ever met.

My dad coached me for a few years in partnership with his good friend Ab McDonald, a long-time NHLer. I learned much during those years but teaching about the marvellous game of hockey began years before.

My father spent hours teaching me the strategies of hockey, positional play, decision making. It was our thing. Every time we watched a game together or I skated with his junior team at late night practices, staying out of their way so they didn't run over the coach's 10-year-old son, he pointed things out. Why a player did this or that. Why the team played a certain why. Why players acted a certain way. How one play developed into another. I was getting a master's degree in hockey strategy that was as much osmosis as parental bonding and my own innate curiosity and love of the game. I didnt know it at the time, but as I wrote this book, that knowledge helped me break down the plays as I studied each Summit Series game, providing my analysis.

Growing up in Winnipeg, I was blessed to be able to attend many of the WHA Winnipeg Jet games. This was a team built on speed and the European game. This allowed me to observe in real time the differences in the Canadian game versus the European one. I watched how the hot line of Anders Hedberg, Ulf Nilsson and the legendary Bobby Hull flowed together seamlessly. The Jets had one of the world's best defencemen, the diminutive, highly skilled Lars Erik Sjoberg. I could, even, on special occasions, watch the Martians themselves, the Soviet National Team.

I saw the Soviets in person, without their hockey uniforms, as regular people, once, as a young boy. At my oldest sister's wedding in 1974, her reception was at a Winnipeg hotel called the International Inn. It was the same time that the Soviets were playing the WHA Team Canada in Winnipeg and were staying at the hotel. I caught glimpses of the legendary Soviets players. They looked like giants to me, athletic, stoic. Wearing blazers and turtlenecks, uniforms showing the collective mindset even away from the rink.

The memories of them speaking amongst themselves in Russian is still imprinted on my brain.

That love for international hockey, especially Canada versus Russia, carried over. I watched the dramatic, inconclusive Super Series 1976. The dominant victories by the Flyers and Sabres matched only by the New Year's disappointing Montreal tie with the Red Army. I watched the conclusive Challenge Cup, shocked how easily the Soviets could best the NHL all stars. In 1980 I cheered for the Americans, probably for the only time in my life, against the Soviets in the Olympic Miracle. I was almost brought to tears watching Team Canada embarrassingly lose the Canada Cup in 1981. The unappreciated Canadian victory in the 1984 Canada Cup was another milestone for me, but it was the culmination of 15 years of best on best that became the 1987 Canada Cup that solidified my bucket list to write a book about Canada-Russia hockey history.

The question, was, of course what to write about? There were so many books on the 1972 Series, what could I possibly add? That question answered itself during the Covid pandemic as I read and digested Richard Bendell's excellent book "Stats, Lies and Videotape". This was a new look at the Summit Series, a book in which Richard corrected the statistics given out (goals and assists) to the players. He also questioned decisions the coaches made, player selections etc. That piqued my curiosity, there was obviously more to the series than the usual quotes from Paul Henderson or Phil Esposito.

Next up was Greg Franke's well researched book "Epic Confrontation". From Greg's writing I learned there may be entirely different viewpoints and history leading up to the series. Perhaps the Canadian viewpoint was myopic and one sided. Having won the series, the saying history is written by the victors seemed to be applicable. I reached out to both authors, developed cherished friendships with both, friendships that led to countless hours of discussion on international hockey.

Spurred on by readings and conversations, I started to watch the first game of the Summit Series, game one in Montreal. Using modern technology, I slowed each play down. Growing up, I was a huge fan of Howie Meeker's traditional "stop right there, back it up" on Hockey Night in Canada telecasts. Howie's expert analysis enlightened me on what happened during each play. I decided to do that for game one. As I did that on each play in game one, many things became clear. ***There was a story there***. All that was needed was to break down and describe every single play for every game, and countless revelations would surface. Easy enough. It would only take hours upon hours! Yet, as I did, things started to be revealed: Who played well? Who made mistakes? Why were goals scored? Who were the players who scored or contributed to the plays? Why did they happen? From revealing these moments, a pattern formed. I could go back in history, a virtual time machine and see the reasons for what happened and maybe, just maybe, some previous myths would be dismissed, and new revelations would appear.

My favourite sports book was by political writer **Richard Bradley.** Titled **"The Greatest Game"**, it tells of the one game, sudden death playoff baseball game between historic rivals the New York Yankees and the Boston Red Sox at Boston's Fenway Park on the afternoon of October 4, 1978. Bradley's approach was to describe the game in its' entirety, pitch by pitch, play by play, with information about players, the rivalry, and the moments in which they find themselves. It's a wonderful book taking the reader to each moment. It gave me the foundation for this book. I would try to take the reader back to the moment of each game in the Summit Series in Canada. Describing what went on. Analysing the goals. I would tell the story of what happened, who made it happen. Giving insights on those players from both teams.

Those insights might appear negative. However, in

analysing the games and the plays, I'm not trying to be critical in a derogatory way. These were the best players in the world, I respect their abilities immensely. I understand, and appreciate, the pressure both teams were under. This was an event that was never seen before in hockey or sports history. I call it as I see it. If Brad Park or Alexander Gusev made a poor defensive play, I mention it. I don't think it's reflective of Brad Park as a Hall of Fame level hockey player or Gusev's great Soviet career, it's what happened in that moment, my interpretation. No offence is intended.

I also wanted to tell the historical stories of the participants in the Series. How did hockey develop in Canada? In the Soviet Union? Who were the great international teams and players? Rivals? Victories, losses, tragedies? The stories rarely told? Stories that weren't Canada versus the USSR, but the Czechs, the Swedes, everyone else. How did it lead up to the glorious hockey and culture clash that was the Summit Series? I felt there were so many stories to tell, so if the reader didn't know who the Warwick brothers were, or Rudi Ball, Anatoli Firsov, even Carl Brewer, they would now.

This book is the first of two volumes. This volume analyses the Canadian games. Those games were powerful, ground-breaking, and dramatic in their own way that they deserved their own volume. Those four games affected the way Canadians viewed the NHL players, reflected the way Canadians view themselves. The shocking defeat of game one, the bounce back of game two, the stalemate in Winnipeg and the utter collapse both of play and character in game four, culminating in the speech by Phil Esposito, is unmatched in Canadian sports drama.

The Soviets were unsure if they could compete; once they realized they could compete with the NHL pros, defeat them, it was a shocking reversal. Combining that with Canadian crowds, pressure and unseen western freedom and opulence, it was a life changing series of games for the

Soviet players. On a quick note, I generally only refer to the **Russians** as the **Soviets** in the book. At that time, Russia did not exist as a country; it was the Union of Soviet Socialist Republics, or Soviet Union.

The Summit Series was one of the greatest dramas in the history of sports. The end of the story is known, but I hope you will enjoy the breakdown of the first part of this classic series, the stories that I thought were worth telling, that you might feel the same excitement that I did reviewing these amazing games moment by moment.

Enjoy!

Grant

(P.S. No Martians were hurt in the writing of this book).

SITTING ON TRETIAK

PART ONE: IN THE BEGINNING…

CHAPTER 1: YOU WANNA GO, RUSSIA? LET'S DO THIS....

"We had watched the professionals play; we knew the level of play was very high. We were the world champions, the Olympic champions, we wanted very much to play against them. Our coach Tarasov had been dreaming of it for years. We were the best in Europe and the world, but cross the ocean, there were other hockey players who considered stronger. The strongest in the world. They would say they would defeat us by a double-digit margin, and they would destroy us physically to the point that no players could come out for the second period! Generally, there was this kind of mocking attitude and that's why such a series of games couldn't be arranged for many years. When it was finalized, we knew how important these games would be. We didn't know the results. We knew we had trained three times a day for 9 months. We knew how to play hockey, so we went there to show our game".

Boris Mikhailov Hockey Time Machine.

Strong words from the great Soviet player Boris Mikhailov. The clash of cultures, of styles, training styles and abilities would finally take place. Like the first Frazier Ali fight, the showdown was years in the making. It was time for the best to face the best. The world watched and marvelled as the greatest drama in team sports history took place. The games in Canada were incredibly fascinating to the Canadian public. Myths were shattered and eyes were opened as a country went through shock, disdain and redemption in a short period of time. **There was, never will be again, anything like the 1972 Summit Series.**

How did the series evolve? It wasn't a single moment in time. There had been some discussions in 1969, but an agreement seemed difficult, impossible, to reach. One of the main events allowing things to progress was the changing international hockey landscape.

Canada's withdrawal from international hockey early in 1970 created a gap in competition for the Soviet Union. While they had their traditional rivals, the Czechoslovak National Team, a motivated skilled group that often gave the Soviets all they could handle, there was no other legitimate challenger left. Sweden was improving and certainly gave the Soviets a game, but they were not a country who could defeat them with any realistic consistency. Finland was also improving but they were not even close to challenging the Soviets in 1970. After peaking in 1967, the Canadian National Team had been unable to take its program to the next level, and as the Soviets rolled out new star after new star in the late 1960's, the Canadians continued to lose repeatedly. The reality of world hockey in the early 1970's? The Soviets sat atop the international hockey totem, and they needed a greater challenge. **There was only one foe left to face**.

It's hard to determine the exact moment where the Soviets felt they were truly ready to play the best Canadian professionals. There was typical on and off Soviet bluster and grandstanding, but for many years the Soviets seemed respectful to the NHL level of play. In 1957, Soviet hockey coach Anatoli Tarasov felt his team skated faster than the NHL, an assumption backed by Canadian fitness guru Lloyd

Percival who measured both teams' skating speed in a game. Tarasov didn't go as far as claiming they were as good as the NHL at that time, which would have been unrealistic, but the seeds were planted. That was their eventual goal: progress until they could defeat the Canadian professionals, becoming the best hockey nation on earth. As Soviet hockey progressed, Tarasov believed his teams were ready to test the NHL professionals by the mid-1960's, boldly asking the 1964 New York Rangers for a game. He had claimed by 1968 that his team could defeat any professional team, a statement backed by the Swedes National Team coach proclaiming the 1968 Soviets were better than any other team in the world.

The reality was the Soviets had progressed faster than anyone expected, except perhaps the Soviets themselves, in a very short time. They went from a team in the mid-1950's that was often unable to defeat a top Senior A team, to fielding a National Team that by the late 1960's would have been more than a match for any NHL team. That is an advancement that was unprecedented in sport. This progression was motivated by not only a love for the game, but **the Soviet political goal of showcasing sport as a political statement.** The message to the world was that the Soviet system of government and life was superior and reflected in sport achievement. Those ambitions in the sport of hockey were based on two key things: developing internal processes, structure and teaching that would create the foundation of the Soviet game. **Their own unique style of game**. The second goal was to face the best competition, on a consistent basis, testing themselves and developing from that test. By 1970, that second goal was seemingly impossible, as long as the "best" were not accessible.

That potential test of playing the NHL was also potentially problematic for the Soviets. They could and would state it was about learning and developing, but the reality was, if they did play the NHL they could not afford to lose badly. This would minimize their world championship and Olympic victories. A significant defeat would be a disaster for their sports program and shed a negative light on their communist way of life. If they could not field a team using their collective methodologies that would at the very least match the capitalist professionals, then their entire sports programs would seem questionable. There was also the debate about Olympic eligibility for any teams that played the professionals, especially when the IOC weighed in with a hypocritical statement that playing the NHL could possibly taint them for amateur status and Olympic eligibility. The Soviet players were not amateurs per se. While some studied and took university programs, they did not have other jobs. Their role in Soviet society was to play hockey, supported by the state. Another issue was that in many ways a series against the best professionals in Canada was less a hockey decision than a political one. It would take **political buy in** internally in the very complex Soviet ecosystem to arrange.

Canada started the process. In November 1970, Hockey Canada sent a letter to the IIHF challenging the winner of the 1970 World Championships to compete in a tournament in Canada in 1971 against a team of Canadian professionals. Gordon Juckes of the CAHA and Charles Hay of Hockey Canada followed up with a trip to Moscow for discussions. The Soviets turned down the proposal for technical reasons, whatever that meant, but left the door open by suggesting a Canadian professional team could visit the USSR in the fall. The Canadians went back to the drawing board proposing a fall tournament to the IIHF involving the USSR, Sweden, Czechoslovakia, and a Canadian professional team with no restrictions on play selections. IIHF president Bunny Ahearne chimed in, responding with a ridiculous counter proposal that would only send the Soviets and the Swedes to Canada, for seven exhibition games but only four against professionals, the other three would be against Canadian amateur teams. Ahearne also wanted three Canadian tours to the Soviet Union, Sweden, and Czechoslovakia, with the obvious intent to fill the IIHF pockets with European revenue much like historic Canadian tours of Europe. Ahearne wanted Canada to return to the World Championships in 1972 but with only pure amateurs and to enter the B pool, further humiliating Canada. **This was rejected with the best-on-best tournament that became the 1976 Canada Cup was several years away**.

It was at this time the legendary Soviet hockey patriarch Anatoli Tarasov started to make significant noise about playing the Canadian professionals. Tarasov approached Aggie Kukulowicz, a Russian speaking former NHL player who worked in Moscow for Air Canada about arranging a series of ten games between the Montreal Canadiens and Tarasov's Central Red Army team. Five games would be in Canada and five in the USSR, ideally in May 1971. When Canada responded that they were already negotiating with the IIHF, Tarasov tried a very North American strategy, which in hindsight hurt his problematic relationship with Soviet authorities; **he went to the media**. Using a Soviet sports publication, Tarasov went on a tangent. He chastised Canada for always sending second rate amateurs to play the Soviets, subtly hinted that the Canadians feared losing to his National Team, that Canada's withdrawal from international hockey was for fear of losing and set up his view that the Soviets were more than able to defeat any professional team sent his way. Canadian officials viewed this with interest, but nothing more. He was not speaking officially; nothing would get done without official political involvement.

Tarasov's rant may have motivated the internal Soviet hockey authorities to reach out to Canada with a proposal. On November 18th, 1971, the Canadian Department of Internal Affairs was contacted by the Soviet embassy with an offer of the Central Red Army club playing the three Canadian NHL clubs, Montreal, Toronto and Vancouver in Canada, January 9th, 12th and 14th 1972. The proposal was turned down because of the NHL schedule, but it was progress.

The seeds of Tarasov's rant had roots in Canadian-Soviet political developments three years earlier. In 1968 Canada newly elected Prime Minister Pierre Trudeau was only a casual hockey fan as he preferred outdoor individual activities. Trudeau had enough passion for the game, along with political acuity, to realize that something needed to change regarding Canadian participation in international hockey. He also knew that there was a large political advantage to focusing on helping Canadian success. Trudeau oversaw the creation of Hockey Canada, an organization funded by the government. One of their main mandates was to focus Canadian success in international play. Trudeau's unprecedented May 1971 tour of the USSR opened the door for a reciprocal tour of Canada by Soviet Premier Alexei Kosygin in October 1971. The tour was a difficult one for Kosygin as anti-Soviet protestors dogged him across the country. Kosygin, a former hockey player, decided to accept an invitation to a Vancouver-Montreal NHL game in Vancouver. As Kosygin dropped the puck for the ceremonial faceoff, the applause from the Vancouver crowd was the warmest welcome he had ever received outside Russia:

> *"The light went on for Alexei Kosygin that October night in Vancouver. If the Soviet Union wished to improve its relationship with Canada and enhance co-operation, the way to do it was through hockey."*
> *Gary Smith*

As Kosygin returned to Moscow an agreement was made between both governments to continue to explore cultural and sporting opportunities. This was an important development, as talks prior to that had not resulted in any real progress to arrange a true best on best matchup. In fact, groups of Canadian delegates from the CAHA, Hockey Canada and even Clarence Campbell, the NHL president, had gone to the 1969 World Championships to discuss a global tournament between the NHL professionals and the top countries, which the Soviets had been reluctant to discuss. They did not view Hockey Canada as legitimate and would only deal with the CAHA or their amateur counterparts. That included Alan Eagleson who they viewed as representing the capitalist owners. Eagleson would later rectify that situation by explaining he represented the workers, not the owners, but still found himself stonewalled.

While these developments in Moscow moved the Soviets slowly towards a showdown with the NHL, facing the Soviets or top European teams wasn't a major priority to the NHL. The mindset of the NHL franchise owners especially was hardly focused on international hockey. North American hockey in the late 1960's and early 1970's was still in a **financial growth mindset.** The league had expanded to 12 teams in 1967, a business decision to target markets previously untapped. With air flight modernized, teams could travel easily between coasts. Hockey was growing as a business. The only real team competition for winter consumer dollars was basketball with the NBA struggling, battling a rival league, and often playing in smaller cities. For an NHL owner, international hockey was unimportant. There was money to be made in North America.

That internal focus only increased as expansion increased, with Vancouver and Buffalo bringing the NHL total to 14 teams. Even the myopic NHL decision makers had to notice that the modern sports landscape was changing. Slowly but surely the players themselves were becoming independent, no longer content with the status quo as paid indentured servants using a "reserve clause" which bound a player to his team indefinitely. The AFL had gotten to a point where they could challenge the NFL and defeat them in the Super Bowl. The ABA had started in 1967, stealing stars such as Rick Barry away from the NBA. In 1972 baseball player Curt Flood challenged the traditional reserve clause and, while unsuccessful, the gauntlet had been laid. Players, agents, unions, and new leagues were changing modern sports by challenging the status quo and it wasn't going to stop. By 1972 the NHL was not looking overseas for any challenge that needed to be answered. They had their own issues domestically. **The World Hockey Association.**

Dennis Murphy and Gary Davidson were not hockey men. They were entrepreneurs from the USA heavily involved in starting the rival American Basketball Association in 1967. Hockey was the lowest paid major team sport in 1971, with an average salary of $25,000. Bound by the reserve clause, the NHL had a monopoly over the talent and control over the players' livelihood. As a result, Murphy and Davidson saw an opportunity to disrupt a major sport. They recruited Bill Hunter, a bombastic showman currently the president of the Western Canadian Junior league and started recruiting potential franchise owners. The new venture grew quickly; by November 1971, 12 franchises were announced.

A key offering for the new franchises would be the lack of a reserve clause. The new league would challenge the NHL clause in court. The league started recruiting NHL players, successfully recruiting star players Derek Sanderson from Boston, JC Tremblay from Montreal and others. While those hurt the NHL it wasn't until Chicago's Bobby Hull signed with the Winnipeg Jets for an unheard of $2.7 million that the NHL realized there was a war for players starting. Clarence Campbell, the NHL president, a former lawyer at the Nuremburg trials, went to a United States federal court to prohibit the signings. In Chicago, the Black Hawks were successful in having a restraining order filed against Hull and the Jets, preventing their star from playing for the new league. The WHA responded by legally challenging the reserve clause in court.

In November 1972, a federal judge in Philadelphia placed an injunction against the NHL, preventing it from enforcing the reserve clause and freeing all players who had restraining orders against them, including Hull, to play with their WHA clubs. The decision ended the NHL's monopoly on major league professional hockey talent. This wouldn't be the only impact the WHA had on hockey as the league would welcome European talent, changing the game completely throughout its' seven years of existence. **The new league's formation would have a dramatic effect on the Summit Series; once the series was announced, the war between players bled out to affect team Canada's player personnel**.

In 1971, Gary Smith was a young Canadian diplomat stationed in Moscow working for the Canadian embassy. He and his wife had extensive Russian language training, becoming fluent in the language. Gary was a hockey player growing up. He was quickly recruited by local former NHLer Aggie Kukulowicz to play in regular fun games against Soviet media and political staff as part of the Moscow Maple Leafs. During these games, Smith would quickly learn that the Soviets could be duplicitous. When the two teams were supposed to meet for an important game, two regular Soviet players were suddenly replaced by two players from Moscow Dynamo, ideally to counter Kukulowicz and ensure a Soviet win even for a fun game, which they did.

Part of Smith's role at the embassy was the responsibility to be aware of sport and cultural exchanges, anything that might involve and strengthen Canada-Soviet relations. One part of Smith's assignment was to read the Soviet state paper Izvestia, getting a feel for the direction the Soviet government was taking on issues, at least in a public sense for the local readers. Smith was shocked to read an article in December 1971 by sports editor Boris Fedosov indicating that the Soviet hockey program needed a new challenge. As a diplomat, Smith understood anything printed in Izvestia was reviewed by the state, thus legitimate rather than Fedosov's opinion. Perhaps spurred on by Alexei Kosygin's upper-level approval, the Soviet appetite for games against the NHL had increased.

Smith followed up, meeting with Izvestia sports editor

Boris Fedosov, verifying the information. A second meeting was arranged, this time with Soviet hockey boss Andrei Starovoitov. The Soviets divulged they were officially ready to play in a series between its National Team and the best Canadian professionals. The Soviets suggested their traditional Izvestia tournament or their Sovetsky Sport tournament in September 1972. After the meetings, Smith's boss, the Canadian ambassador Robert Ford, forwarded the information to Ottawa. The Soviets were ready to negotiate a series, but Canada was given the task to nail down terms.

In April 1972, a Canadian delegate consisting of Lou Lefaive (Sports Canada Director), Charles Hay (Hockey Canada Director), Douglas Fisher (Board member) along with CAHA President Joe Kryczka, a lawyer who spoke Russian, and CAHA secretary Gordon Juckes, attended meetings with the IIHF during the World Championships in Prague. Andre Starovoitov handled negotiations from the Soviet end. Alan Eagleson arrived late to negotiations, and as a result was not party to the terms set. **He disagreed with the September timeframe and the use of international rules and officials**. This became an area of contention later, as Team Canada struggled in the series. Eagleson, true to his nature, was the first to report the Series having been agreed upon, contacting well respected sports journalist George Gross to announce the news.

IIHF President Bunny Ahearne would sign the agreement, presenting a hypocritical face to the press that he had always been supportive of a proposed series. NHL president Clarence Campbell released a statement that the NHL supported the series. The Soviets also announced the agreement via state media to great excitement amongst the populace. After years of speculation, negotiations and rabble rousing, the series was set. Eight games between the USSR and Canada. Canada could use an open roster, including NHL players. There would be four games in Canada, Montreal, Toronto, Winnipeg, and Vancouver chosen as host cities.

The final four would take place in Moscow, with the Canadians agreeing to two exhibition games in Sweden and one in Czechoslovakia. Training camps would officially begin August 13th, 1972. Officially being the key word.

CHAPTER 2: CONSTRUCTION SALES, A FIGHTER AND THE FATHER GETS REPLACED

The Soviets had a huge advantage over Canada in preparation. Firstly, they had had a National Team program in place since the early 1950's. That meant that getting a team together for an international series was nothing new. Secondly, the players on the National Team were familiar with each other. Thirdly, the continued focus on conditioning in Soviet hockey meant the players were in excellent shape. Vladislav Tretiak mentions the constant training and focus Tarasov had implemented on the Soviet team,

> *"He managed to deceive time and outplay Canada thanks to our summer camps. We had intensive training sessions three times a day. Almost nine months per year we didn't see our families. He told us that we needed only victories, only gold, silver medals were a loss for us."*
> *Vladislav Tretiak*

Many of the players played together on club teams and had grown up in the Tarasov model of hockey, playing the same style. This would be a theoretically give them a significant advantage over a hastily put together group of NHL all-stars.

There had been a shocking development for the National Team that caused a stir in Soviet hockey. On February 24, 1972, after the Soviets won gold at the 1972 Winter Olympics, long time coaches Arkady Chernyshev and Anatoli Tarasov were replaced by Spartak coach and former star player Vsevolod Bobrov and former goalie Nikoli Putschkov from Leningrad. Both new coaches had more individual styled personalities who had clashed over the years with Tarasov. There were no reasons given at the official announcement by news agency TASS, just that Chernyshev and Tarasov would continue coaching the club teams Moscow Dynamo and Central Red Army. On February 25th, Chernyshev was interviewed with TASS and said the strain of coaching had been too much. He also mentioned that together he and Tarasov were 110 years old, meaning it was time to retire. He then lauded the skills and experience of Bobrov. It was an odd statement as Bobrov was only slightly younger at 47. In June, only a few months since he had been named and seemingly without reason, Putschkov would be replaced by Boris Kulagin in June as assistant coach on the Soviet National Team. This was hardly a stable environment to prepare for the greatest challenge in Soviet hockey history.

For years, a change from the Chernyshev and Tarasov duo seemed unlikely. They had been so successful. Yet, the signs were there. Tarasov had often ruffled feathers with senior Soviet hockey officials. In 1969 he pulled his Central Red Army team off the ice to protest a decision about a non-goal. With Soviet leader Brezhnev present in the audience, Tarasov refused to obey senior officials and bring his team back on the ice for forty minutes. The Soviet authorities were furious and stripped Tarasov of his **merited coach** title. Adding to his fall from the party graces was his recent rant in the media regarding playing the Canadians. He had become a thorn in the side of the autocratic Soviet hockey authorities, so a change was decided. Chernyshev was much less bombastic but was seemingly forever paired with his counterpart.

One of the first consequences of this coaching change was the omission (injury?) of long-time supporter of Tarasov and star player **Anatoli Firsov** from the National Team roster. To emphasize the regime change, Firsov wasn't chosen for the World Championships in March despite being among the leading scorers at the Olympics and Soviet league MVP as recently as 1971. The move didn't pay off. Bobrov and assistant coach Boris Kulagin would start off their National Team coaching experience by losing the World Championships to their Czechoslovakian rivals.

In Canada, the process of building a team from scratch began. The name **Team Canada** combined with the unique Maple Leaf uniform was presented to Eagleson and the Team Canada staff by advertising agency Vickers and Benson. Modelled after Team McLaren auto racing, they convinced Eagleson to discard the original preferred name "The NHL All-Stars" and go with a national identity. **Team Canada was born**.

Canada's only prior experience in forming a National Team had been Father David Bauer's program. Building a team of professionals? Getting the necessary work done for the biggest series in hockey history? This was uncharted territory for the Canadian hockey authorities. They needed a coach. Names such as Toe Blake and recently retired Montreal Canadiens star Jean Beliveau were tossed around as potential coaches, but Alan Eagleson only had one name in mind. **Harry Sinden**.

In 1972, Harry Sinden was 40 years old and had never played a game in the NHL. He was also not currently employed by an NHL team, having quit the Boston Bruins after winning a cup in the 1969-70 season and not getting a raise. Sinden was blackballed by the Bruins as they put his status as voluntary retired which prevented him from working in the NHL for a year. Sinden went to Rochester, New York and accepted a high paying job in the construction industry and turned down future coaching roles with the Toronto Maple Leafs and expansion New York Islanders. Sinden had a strong personality, having shown the ability to successfully coach superstars Bobby Orr and Phil Esposito. Sinden possessed a unique background that was not present in other coaches: he had played international hockey against the Soviets. He was the captain of the 1958 World Championship winning Whitby Dunlops Senior A squad, and also played in the 1960 Winter Olympics, winning a silver medal as an add on to the Kitchener Waterloo Dutchman. He finished his playing career in the minor leagues, as playing coach of the Oklahoma Blazers in the Central Professional league, a team he coached to a championship in 1966.

Eagleson arranged for Sinden to meet with the Hockey Canada/CAHA committee for interviews, but his mind was already made up. Sinden was the only choice, the right choice. On June 7th, 1972, Harry Sinden discovered he was going to coach Team Canada. Sinden decided to add only one assistant coach. In a surprising move, Sinden asked recently retired Montreal Canadiens forward **John Ferguson** to fulfil a dual role as both player and assistant coach. Ferguson was a weak skater as a player, but he had one special quality: he had an incredible will to win. He could, would, fight most anyone in the league, but he also could score goals. Twice, he had 20 goals in the NHL, topping out with 29 in the 1968-69 season. An intelligent, thoughtful man, Ferguson knew his skill set as a player wouldn't have been useful against the fast skating, skilled Soviets, so he wisely turned down the offer of a playing comeback but agreed to become Team Canada's assistant coach.

Coaching set, the two men started work on who they wanted on Team Canada. Sinden tasked Ferguson to come back with his own list of players. They would then sit down together to review to decide a final list. A decision was made to invite 35 players to camp, the thought process being that this would allow intense scrimmages of team versus team, players battling for ice time. The Summit Series agreement was for 30 players. The Soviets made an exception for Bobby Orr if he was able to play, so Sinden supplemented the invitation list by adding several junior players for training camp only. Those players were the 1972 first overall draft pick, Billy Harris from the Toronto Marlboros, not to be confused with former Maple Leaf and 1974 WHA Summit Series coach Billy Harris, John Van Boxmeer from Guelph junior hockey and goalie Michel Larocque from the Ottawa 67's. All went on to solid NHL careers, Harris topping the thirty-goal mark for the New York Islanders in 1976 and Larocque as Ken Dryden's capable backup on the Montreal dynasty from 1976-79.

When Sinden and Ferguson compared lists, they were surprised they had picked most of the same names. The goal had been to pick a team of different parts rather than an all-star team. A team that would play well together, but also a team that could grind and play the **NHL style** which if things went as predicted, overwhelm the Soviets.

Below is the **original list** of players with their traditional NHL positions (with author's selection of potential lines and defence partners):

Bobby Hull Chicago   Phil Esposito Boston   Yvan Cournoyer Montreal

Vic Hadfield NYR   Jean Ratelle NYR   Rod Gilbert NYR

Frank Mahovlich MTL   Peter Mahovlich MTL   Mickey Redmond Detroit

Jean Paul Parise Minnesota   Red Berenson Detroit
Bill Goldsworthy Minn

Ron   Ellis   Toronto   Bobby   Clarke
Philadelphia   Paul Henderson Toronto

Dennis Hull Chicago   Gilbert Perreault Buffalo
Wayne Cashman Boston   Walt Tkaczuk NYR
Derek Sanderson Boston   Marcel Dionne Detroit

Defence

Dallas Smith LD Boston   Bobby Orr RD Boston
Gary Bergman LD Detroit   Brad Park RD NYR
Jacques Laperriere LD Mtl   JC Tremblay RD Mtl
Pat Stapleton LD Chicago   Bill White RD Chicago
Don Awrey LD Boston   Rod Seiling LD NYR
Brian Glennie LD Toronto   Serge Savard RD Montreal
Dale Tallon RD/RW Vanc.   Jocelyn Guvermont RD Van

Goalies

Ken Dryden Montreal Canadiens
Tony Esposito Chicago Black Hawks
Gerry Cheevers Boston Bruins
Ed Giacomin New York Rangers

Phone calls and letters went out offering spots on the team, rejections soon coming back. Walt Tkaczuk, a solid two-way centre from the Stanley Cup finalist New York Rangers declined due to hockey school obligations. His teammate, top goaltender Eddie Giacomin, also declined as he was recovering from off season knee surgery. Bobby Orr's traditional defence partner Dallas Smith, from the Stanley Cup Champion Boston Bruins, had to focus on his family farm. The final refusal was big rangy defensive defenceman Jacques Laperriere from the Montreal Canadiens whose wife had just given birth. While those names stung, none of these players would be considered crucial.

Boston Bruins Bobby Orr, Phil Esposito and Chicago Black Hawk Bobby Hull were considered the three best players in the NHL, consequently all of hockey. The three would have been the obvious choices on any coaches list. Yet Canada had a big problem. **None of them were guaranteed to play in the series.** The issues? One was recovering from major knee surgery, another didn't want to go because of hockey school commitments, and one had just signed the largest contract in sports history, with the WHA's Winnipeg Jets.

In 1971 Clarence Campbell celebrated his 25th year as NHL President. He had faced internal challenges, from star players like Rocket Richard and Ted Lindsay, yet during his tenure Campbell had never faced the challenge of a rival league. The last league to rival the NHL, the Pacific Coast Hockey Association, had struggled financially, before merging with the Western Canada Hockey League, before selling their players to the NHL in the mid-1920's. The World Hockey Association was the first time in Campbell's time at the NHL that another league had challenged the status quo. **The president was not happy**.

Campbell had few avenues for retaliation with the new league. He could belittle them in the media, make bold statements about the reserve clause that might scare potential defectors from signing with them, he could fight them in court, and he could ensure they didn't play in the Summit Series. The last thing Campbell wanted to do was showcase the other league in any way or give the WHA an ounce of legitimacy by allowing them to join his NHL players in an expected win over the Soviets.

CHAPTER 3: COMRADE, WHERE IS BOBBY HULL AND DAVEY KEON?

On July 12th, 1972, Douglas Fisher of Hockey Canada formally announced that any player not signed to an NHL contract (WHA players) were deemed ineligible for the series. While names were not included in the announcement, four players who were expected to be key members of Team Canada were now deemed ineligible: **Bobby Hull, Derek Sanderson, JC Tremblay, and Gerry Cheevers**. Hull was the biggest shock, but the other three players would also be a significant loss for the Canadians. Derek Sanderson was a feisty two-way centre, a superb penalty killer and face off man, although also a known night life lover. JC Tremblay was a superb puck carrying defenceman and Gerry Cheevers was known as a money goaltender who played his best under pressure.

How significant was the loss of these players? Bobby Hull was one of the greatest players in hockey history. He was a fantastic explosive skater, strong as a bull, excellent hockey sense and had the world's best slap shot. Hull would terrorize Vladislav Tretiak in head-to-head matches, with Hull scoring 7 official goals in 8 games in the 1974 WHA Summit Series (one goal was disallowed in game 7 that would have given Hull 8 goals in 8 games). He would score another on Tretiak in the 1976 Canada Cup match, a 3-1 win for Canada. Finally on January 5th, 1978, aged 39, in perhaps Bobby Hull's last great game, he would pound three more goals past the Soviets in a surprising Winnipeg Jets 5-3 win over the Soviet National Team. Tretiak would admit Hull's shot intimidated him. With Hull there was the possibility of a Team Canada super pairing as Hull had played with Phil Esposito in Chicago, they were good friends. Hull would have certainly added to Canada's powerplay unit, which struggled throughout the series. **It was a big loss**.

Derek Sanderson was a wild card. He had the skillset to help Canada from a defensive centre standpoint, but that role was performed superbly by Bobby Clarke, with Red Berenson and Peter Mahovlich adding wonderful penalty killing when required. Sanderson was bad tempered and was known more for his social life than his fitness and focus. JC Tremblay was an excellent puck control player, a smooth skater and good outlet passer. He would play well in the 1974 WHA series, and in other future international games for the WHA Quebec Nordiques. The issue that he was a right defenceman, and that position was stacked with Brad Park, Bill White, and Serge Savard, plus Bobby Orr. Even if Tremblay had been allowed to play, it would have been a battle for him to get in the line-up.

The second greatest potential loss in this group was goalie Gerry Cheevers. Cheevers would play in the 1974 WHA Summit Series. He was exceptional in a losing cause, leading to Boris Kulagin calling Cheevers the best goalie the Soviets had ever faced. Sinden was familiar with Cheesy (as he was often referred), and most likely would have used him in game four instead of Ken Dryden. Whether that would have changed the result of that game is unknown, but it certainly creates an interesting alternative discussion.

After Douglas Fisher's startling announcement, Harry Sinden took the stand and announced the final list of

Team Canada players. The players who had declined were dropped from the potential list, and the WHA players had been replaced. **Stan Mikita** had been chosen to replace Derek Sanderson. Mikita, who was Czech before coming to Canada at age 10, was no longer the best centre in the NHL as he was in the 1960's. He was a veteran at 32 years old, and now suffered from back issues that left him playing in pain, unable to play at the high pace of his youth. He was still a clever, smooth player, feisty and a potential team leader.

Young **Richard Martin** of the Buffalo Sabres was chosen to replace Bobby Hull at left wing. Martin had many of the qualities that Hull possessed. He was an excellent skater, with a heavy shot and the ability to score goals. Martin had burst onto the NHL scene with one of the greatest rookie seasons in NHL history, scoring 44 goals in 1971-72, but losing the Calder Trophy as rookie of the year to Ken Dryden. Martin formed a young dynamic duo with Gilbert Perreault in Buffalo. The downside was he was only 21, and like Perreault he had a large youthful ego that led to a growing disenchantment with playing time as the series progressed. On defence Montreal's **Guy Lapointe**, a mobile defender with some offensive instincts was picked to replace JC Tremblay. Perhaps the biggest surprise was Cheever's replacement, his former backup goalie Boston's **Ed Johnson**. Johnson was much more than a backup which Sinden knew. He was an excellent goaltender, who had been a workhorse for the weak Boston teams in the mid-1960's. Johnson was the last goalie to play every minute of every game in a season, a feat he accomplished in 1963-64. He was coming off a superb season with the Stanley Cup Champion Bruins, with a season win loss record of 28-7 and then a sparkling playoff record of 6-1 with a miniscule 1.86 goals against average. Johnson was good enough to be called upon if Dryden or Tony Esposito faltered, and Eddie was a likeable fun guy to have around. Johnson would only play in one game in the Series, a 4-4 tie against Sweden, but he would be sparkling in that game, holding the Swedes to a tie.

While Team Canada's player announcement covered the majority of the NHL's best players, there were some surprise omissions. **Toronto's Dave Keon** was a wonderful skater and two-way centre, whose omission was probably the biggest surprise. If it wasn't Keon, then it was probably **Montreal's Jacques Lemaire**. John Ferguson had played with Lemaire and would have known how talented and defensively responsible he was. Lemaire had centred a line in 1971-72 with Frank Mahovlich and Yvan Cournoyer. **That would have given Team Canada a set Montreal unit with which to work.** This would have majorly helped with the cohesion lacking in the Canadian games, possibly stemming the decline of Frank Mahovlich. Another full line potential would have happened with the inclusion of Toronto's **Norm Ullman**. Ullman partnered with Paul Henderson and Ron Ellis as a strong two-way line in the 1971-72 season, but at 37 he was considered at the end of his career. Ullman would play another six seasons scoring 31 goals at age 40 for the WHA's Edmonton Oilers. **Garry Unger** was a good offensive centre who scored 42 goals in 1970 for Detroit, and 36 with St Louis in 1971-72. Despite the bevy of riches at centre for Canada, Unger would not have been a shocking choice.

On the wings, Boston's Ken Hodge not being selected was the biggest surprise. Hodge was a big strong winger who played on one of the best lines in the NHL with Phil Esposito and Wayne Cashman. On the downside, Hodge was a moody player who didn't get along well with Harry Sinden when Sinden coached the Bruins. Hodge scored a very impressive 105 points in the 1970-71 season, but his inconsistent play surfaced the next year as he dropped to 56 points in 1971-72. That off season and his personality conflict with Sinden was probably reason enough for him to be left off the roster. Continuing with the Stanley Cup champion Bruins, team captain **Johnny Bucyk** was a very good player, scoring 83 points in 1971-72, but like Norm Ullman, being 37 would have been kconsidered too old for the series. Boston's two-way player **Fred Stanfield** was an excellent utility player who could produce points, but Team Canada already had players selected like Red Berenson and Pete Mahovlich to fill those roles.

On defence there were very few notable omissions. In hindsight, perhaps smooth skating **Carol Vadnais** who was toiling in obscurity with the California Golden Seals could have been considered, but generally the NHL's best defencemen had been selected. Goalies were a similar situation, New York's **Gilles Villemure** was an excellent goalie in tandem with Ed Giacomin, but Sinden knew Ed Johnson and had coached him. Any other potential goalie picks like **Jacques Plante or Gump Worsley** would have been considered too old, and future Canada Cup 1976 MVP **Rogie Vachon** had not yet established himself with Los Angeles. Another future Hall of Famer, Toronto's **Bernie Parent** had signed with the WHA eliminating his selection.

The Sinden Ferguson duo had tried to put together a group of players that could be coached, could play in different situations, and would fit in well with a team concept. At the time, they had no idea of the challenges they would face with some of their selections as the series progressed.

CHAPTER 4: BOBROV AND CHUCKLES, THE GAMBLING DUO: SOVIET PREPARATION

The Soviets had a set team already, with set processes, so there was no grand announcement of players or ongoing media debates on who would and wouldn't be playing against the Canadians. The exception to that rule may have been long time star Anatoli Firsov. Firsov was a legend in the USSR, but he had been dropped for the 1972 World Championships with long time National Team defensive stalwart Vitali Davydov. While both players were reported as injured for the Summit Series, they were most likely excluded due to their history of closeness to Tarasov. Both players were also in their thirties, which gave a built-in reasoning to test younger players against the professionals. Going younger was exactly what Bobrov and Kulagin decided, starting with the bold move of adding an **entire line from the Soviet Wings (Kryyla Sovetov) of 21-year-old players**. Vyachislav Anisin, Alexander Bodunov and Yuri Lebedev would all get their first international games with the National Team in the series.

Two more surprises were added to the Soviet forward

lines. One of Bobrov's players on Moscow Spartak, **Evgeny Zimin**, was brought back to the National Team, allowing Bobrov to put together **a full Spartak line** with Alexander Yakushev, Vladimir Shadrin, and Zimin. Long-time veteran player **Vyacheslav Starshinov** was also added to the squad. Starshinov was the Soviets answer to Stan Mikita. He wasn't the player he had been in the 1960s, but he was well revered. His selection may have been a reward for his service to the National Team, a chance to finally play against the best professionals, at the twilight of his career. This was something Tarasov supporters Firsov and Davydov would be denied. The other players named to the team that hadn't participated in the World Championships were **Alexander Volchkov**, a 20-year-old from the Central Red Army club and another player from Bobrov's Moscow Spartak squad, **Alexander Martynyuk**. Martynyuk usually played on a line with Yakushev and Shadrin, so **Bobrov was looking for familiarity**. Martynyuk was a solid point a game player in the Soviet league but was talented enough to set a Soviet National Team record by scoring eight goals in a game against the East Germans in 1973.

On defence the biggest name missing was **Vitali Davydov**. A small defenceman at 5'8, he was a wonderful skater, but at 33 was at the end of his career. A long-time National Team player, he wasn't directly linked to the Tarasov as he played domestically for Moscow Dynamo, but he was certainly bonded to long-time National Team coach Arkady Chernyshev who was also the coach of Dynamo. National Team stalwarts **Alexander Ragulin** and National Team captain **Viktor Kuzkin** were named to the team, adding a direct link to the great Soviets teams of the mid-1960s. They were joined by regulars **Gennady Tsygankov, Alexander Gusev** and **Vladimir Luchenko**. This group would be joined by the physical **Valeri Vasiliev** as the backbone of the Soviet defence core in the 1970's. **Yuri Lyapkin**, 27, was not a regular on the National Team. He had not been selected to play in the 1972 World Championships. Lyapkin had two unique aspects as a Soviet player; firstly, he was Jewish, secondly, he played for one of the lesser club teams Khimik Voskrenensk, a rare occurrence for a player to become a National Team member. Bobrov had noticed the Khimik player, however, as not only was Lyapkin named to the National Team for the series, he had been transferred to Bobrov's club team Moscow Sparktak for the 1972-73 season.

The defence corps were rounded out by two more additions to the National Team, **Evgeny Paladiev** who Bobrov was familiar with on Sparktak and **Yuri Shatalov** from the Soviet Wings. Dropped from the team was 32-year-old defenseman **Igor Romishevky** who had been with the National Team since 1968. Igor had played with Tarasov's Central Red Army club and may have been dropped because of the age and allegiance. An interesting note was that Romishevsky was probably the smartest man in hockey, getting his PhD in physics in 1974. Doctor Romishevsky would become the head of the Moscow sports physics and technology division that same year, before moving into coaching with SKA Leningrad.

In goal, the Soviet team was led by twenty-year-old **Vladislav Tretiak**. Tretiak was the offspring of a fighter pilot father and an athletic mother. He was a top swimmer and athlete as a boy, taking up hockey at 11; once he did, he quickly became noticed by the Central Red Army program who moved him to their children's school. Tarasov worked hundreds of hours with the young goalie, obviously seeing the immense athleticism in his young protégé. His development was unprecedented as Tretiak made his debut on the National Team at 17. The Soviets would put all their hopes against the professionals on the shoulders of the young goalie. Bobrov would add **Viktor Zinger** from his Spartak club as Tretiak's main backup. Veteran journeyman **Alexander Pashkov** was also named to the roster. Pashkov's career had gone back to the early 1960's. He would make a tour of the Soviet Elite league, eventually playing for seven teams in a twenty-year career. Soviet Wings goalie **Alexander Sidelnikov** was also added to the squad. He would have a winning record with the Wings in the 1976 Super Series versus the NHL but would get absolutely lit up by the Buffalo Sabres in the famous 12-6 loss.

Bobrov and Kulagin certainly put their stamp on the revised National Team, with eight Spartak players matching the 13 from the Red Army club. They had seemingly cleaned house by dropping players that were aligned to the previous coaches. That tactic included the best Soviet player of all time, at that stage, Anatoli Firsov. It was a gamble and combined with the fact that the coaching duo had already lost the World Championships in 1972, they were in deep to ensure their selections performed well against the NHL. Any other result would indubitably be the end of their coaching careers in the USSR.

While the official start for training camps was August 13th, the date was a moot point for the Soviets. **The Sovetsky Sport tournament** was a club team tournament held in late summer or early fall. The tournament traditionally involved all the top Soviet teams, adding teams from other countries, Sweden, Finland, Czechoslovakia etc. While the official records show many of these games taking place in August, the club teams were certainly practicing and dry land training by mid-July. That was the traditional start date for those teams as they prepared for the tournament. As the tournament officially started in August 1972, reports show that most of the Summit Series players participated in the games for their clubs, with teams like Spartak and Dynamo playing in several games.

These games were an opportunity to ensure game readiness that the Canadian team didn't have. The Soviet club teams tended to keep the same lines together that allowed for synergy once they played for the National Team.

Examples included the Spartak line of Shadrin, Yakushev and Zimin/Martynuk, or the Wings Kid Line of Anasin, Lebedev or Bodunov. Vladislav Petrov, Boris Mikhailov and Yuri Blinov played together with the CSKA team, but the Army's top line of Valeri Kharlamov, Anatoli Firsov and Vladmir Vikulov would be changed on the National Team, with Alexander Maltsev replacing Firsov.

The Sovetsky tournament would be playing at the same time period that Canada would be sending over two scouts for a four-day period to analysis the Soviet players. The results of this scouting trip would fill Canada with further confidence. In one key area the scouts would get it completely wrong with dubious results for Team Canada. John McLellan and Bob Davidson were scouts for the Toronto Maple Leafs and as part of the original agreement for the series, were to be given full access to Soviet practices and games.   The first problem was the Sovetsky tournament games that were still going on, so the Leaf duo had the difficult task of determining who were the National Team players, on which teams, when would they play, and with whom? They certainly were not familiar with any of the players. This had to be done by navigating in a foreign language neither understood, and in a Soviet system where cooperation was not always what it seemed.

One player stood out for the Canadian scouts, was the big and talented Alexander Yakushev, a player they felt could make Team Canada. In face he was the only one they felt could make Team Canada. (Valeri Kharlamov anyone?) Yakushev's linemates Shadrin and Zimin were also noted as strong players. The scouts were also bang on with some of their other reflections. They noted **the conditioning** of the Soviet players, mentioning that some had played a dozen games since July. They noted that **team passing** stood out, especially finding the open man and they had **a flexible game plan**, switching easily from a strong forecheck to a defensive zone seamlessly. Another strategy was using the international rule for two line passes where a forward stays out near the red line waiting for the puck to cross ahead of him, and then gets **a quick break**. These were accurate observations that the Soviets would use in the coming games in Canada. Team Canada should have listened more intently to the feedback.

The scouts dropped the ball in their analysis of goaltender Vladislav Tretiak. The scouts watched one game Tretiak played, where he played badly, letting in multiple goals. Instead of a prodigy, he looked like a 20-year-old junior goalie. Tretiak was getting married the next day and his mind was elsewhere. The other option was that Tretiak was told to not play up to his standards, something Tretiak cleverly admits today is possible, having mentioned in interviews slyly that *"Maybe it was a trick, a very good trick."*

The final impressions were inaccurate. Davidson and McLellan left the USSR with the impression that the Soviets had not improved much over the years. They felt Canada did most everything better than the Soviets. Their goaltending was weak, Canada shot the puck better and would not have too much trouble winning the series.

When the preliminary Sovetsky games finished for the National Team players on August 18th, the candidates for the Summit Series gathered for practices and training on August 20th. They would not do so in the Luzhiniki arena where the Moscow games were to be played, because the arena lacked ice in August. While they would have one week to get organized, they had been training and preparing since early July, and would come to Canada, for the biggest games of their lives, in very good physical and mental condition.

CHAPTER 5: LONG JOHNS, LAUGHTER, PREDICTIONS. THE TEAM CANADA TRAINING CAMP

"All through training camp. I don't think we really put enough emphasis on defence. All the time, it was goals... goals..."Serge Savard

On August 14th, 1972, Team Canada opened its training camp at Toronto's Maple Leaf Gardens. The training sessions included 37 players adding the three junior players and Bobby Orr testing his knee with light skating. Since Team Canada didn't have a Sovetsky tournament in which to participate, three intrasquad full game situations games were planned. These would be with two teams, a red and a white, one coached by Sinden, the other by John Ferguson with the games to be played in front of fans at Maple Leaf Gardens. **Two a day skates would lead up the games, with line-up spots up for grabs.**

The habit of Canadian professional players showing up at training camps to get themselves into condition was standard practice in 1972. NHL seasons were much more a grind than European players experienced, with the NHL cramming in close to 100 games, including exhibitions and playoffs. Training camps would start in September, with exhibition games and scrimmages. Those games and scrimmages could be very intense as players jousted for roster spots. Even the best NHL players were never secure in their jobs, as the age-old fear of being sent to the minors was ever present. The majority of the players attending Team Canada's training camp came to Toronto's Maple Leaf Gardens having only skated as instructors for hockey schools, if at all. The exceptions were three young players who were not considered star players nor players that were expected to be impactful, Ron Ellis, Bobby Clarke, and Paul Henderson. All three players were fit, athletic, and had trained in the summer by running and exercising.

Before training camp, the NHL's leading scored Phil Esposito had already told his brother Tony Esposito that he wouldn't play for Team Canada, as he had a hockey school in Sault St Marie Ontario and didn't want to lose the income or disappoint the young players who had signed up. It took a phone call from Bobby Orr to convince Phil to play, who subsequently cancelled the hockey school and came to Toronto with his brother. As the camp opened, journalists were asking Phil about his training methods, making a joke about how the Russians are probably up training while the NHL players are just coming in from a night on the town. Phil would remark that he went to Sweden to teach in a hockey school and was shocked that players kept fit all year round by swimming and doing weights. The concept seemed foreign to him, and in a case of dramatic foreshadowing, the jocular Bruin star would jokingly dismiss the significance.

When training camp opened, the Team Canada doctors were concerned about the following players:
- Jean Ratelle: fractured his ankle in the Stanley Cup playoffs
- Pat Stapleton: recovering from knee surgery
- Stan Mikita: ongoing going and debilitating back

issues
- Dale Tallon: major knee surgery at the end of the 1971-72 season
- Don Awrey: ankle fracture during the 1971-72 season
- Bobby Orr: reconstructive knee surgery

All the players including Orr would arrive at camp, with the Bruins superstar agreeing to light skating to test his knee as the camp progressed. Sinden, well aware of the traditional late summer fitness level of the NHL player, implemented two a day practices combined with stretching and basic fitness exercises in the hallways of Maple Leaf Gardens. As recorded on CBC television, those exercises were not always taken seriously. The players looked semi-ridiculous exercising in full length white long johns. In the players' minds, hockey fitness would happen on the ice, only on the ice. Also, as the media had been saying nonstop the series would be easy. Why would they need to get into mid-season shape?

After the first easy day of pictures and interviews, the competition began on August 15th with a Red versus White scrimmage game. The game was a low scoring one with the new Clarke-Henderson-Ellis line combining for two Paul Henderson goals, leading Team Red to a 3-1 victory over Team White. Rod Gilbert scored the other Red goal and Marcel Dionne added Team White's goal. The next day the two teams met again with different line ups as the coaches moved players around looking for chemistry. The Clarke line would again strike for two goals, this time by Ellis and Clarke as the White team won 4-1. Red Berenson and Peter Mahovlich added singles, while Jean Ratelle scored the only marker for Team Red.

This game had a potential major calamity for Team Canada as New York Ranger star defenceman Brad Park was hit and knocked out cold by a Dennis Hull slap shot. Park spent the night in the hospital for observation, but with concussion protocols very minimal in 1972, Park was released, and would take August 17th off, missing two scrimmages. To add to Park's distress, his wife Gerry was hospitalized as she was pregnant and overdue. Hull's shot was one of the hardest in hockey, but the accident was a result of a deflection off Yvan Cournoyer's stick, with the puck ricocheting to Parks cheek. Park himself would remark that,

"His brain didn't feel functional, and he had trouble focusing when reading."

In retrospect, Park certainly had a concussion. Combining that with the stress of having a child, the Ranger star's somewhat substandard level of play, for him, in the Canadian games could be understood.

Scrimmages three and four on August 17th had left wingers Frank Mahovlich scoring three times and Vic Hadfield twice. The Esposito brothers did not participate as they had to sort out their hockey school issues. Mahovlich was part of the second surprise line in training camp so far partnering with Stan Mikita and Yvan Cournoyer. More impactful than the Big M's (nickname) play was the players seeing Bobby Orr out on the ice for over an hour, skating lightly but able to participate in some shooting and skating drills. The Soviets in a show of both sportsmanship and sincerity about wanting to play the best, had allowed Canada to add Orr as a separate 31st player to the roster if he became available.

On August 22nd, 6000 fans paid NHL regular game ticket prices to watch Harry Sinden's White squad defeat John Ferguson's Red team 8-5. Sinden had told the players to keep the games clean, as he didn't want anyone being hurt, but also used getting into the line-up for game 1 in Montreal as motivation. Set lines and defensive pairings had started to form. Phil Esposito scored two goals and an assist playing with regular Boston linemate Wayne Cashman and Minnesota North Star energy player Jean Paul Parise. New York Rangers Ratelle, Gilbert and Hadfield line was intact, while Bobby Clarke's trio with Henderson and Ellis continued to play seamlessly together. A newly created line had also shown some potential. Detroit's two-way centre Red Berenson had two goals and an assist playing on a line with teammate Mickey Redmond and Peter Mahovlich. On defence, Brad Park and Detroit's Gary Bergman were meshing despite never playing together before, as did a surprising duo of Boston's Don Awrey and New York Ranger Rod Seiling.

The two a day skates and practices continued, leading up to the second full scale intersquad game on August 26th. Perhaps due to the limited fitness level most players reported to camp in, injuries were beginning to pile up for Canada. Wayne Cashman had a badly swollen ankle after getting nailed from a slapshot from Dennis Hull. Big North Star winger Bill Goldsworthy was hooked from behind from the gentlemanly Jean Ratelle, fracturing Goldsworthy's nose. Ron Ellis pulled his groin, and Stan Mikita's back issues were compounded by a pulled groin muscle. On the positive side Vancouver Canucks young star Dale Tallon was seemingly recovered from his off-season knee surgery and had replaced Goldsworthy at right wing. Tallon had the helpful ability to play both defence or wing. Bobby Orr had also continued to test his knee, albeit gingerly yet without negative ramifications. Despite the positive results to date, he wouldn't be ready to play in the Canadian games.

Saturday August 26th was the second full scale intersquad game, with another low attendance of 6734 fans. Sinden put together what he hoped would be a power line of Phil Esposito centring Frank Mahovlich and Yvan Cournoyer, but they lacked chemistry and Esposito went back to original linemates Cashman and Parise. The power line did get together for a power play goal in the first period. The star of the game was Jean Ratelle who bagged three goals in a 4-2 win for the white team. A surprise offensive output was had by defensive defenseman Bill White who scored twice. Paul Henderson and Wayne Cashman playing on the bad ankle, also chipped in goals. Tony Esposito and Eddie Johnston shared the win as each let in one goal. **Ken Dryden however had let in six goals in the first game and had another weak outing with four goals against and a second straight loss.** Reviews stated that the game was better played than the first one, with the players showing stronger positional play and hustle.

With the first game of the Summit Series looming the following Saturday September 2nd, players needed to perform in the final intrasquad game on Tuesday August 29th. The game itself would have an interesting aspect to it: each period was officiated by a different pair of European referees. This would include the West German team of **Josef Kompalla and Rudolf Bata** that would cause Team Canada so much consternation in Moscow. Sinden would commend them for doing a fine job by in this game.

The game would be a 6-2 win for Harry Sinden's white team, which had the NYR line, the Clarke line and Red Berenson line with Redmond and Peter Mahovlich. All played well. Ken Dryden and Ed Johnston split the game, with Dryden finally showing some form as he shut out the red team for the first half. John Ferguson's Red team struggled as Phil Esposito Frank Mahovlich and Cournoyer were put together again but struggled. Harry Sinden would remark they weren't shooting enough. The hoped-for power line ended up scoreless in the game. Brad Park appeared to have recovered from his head injury, adding three assists to give him six assists in three games. Reporter Frank Orr for the Toronto Star felt the only bright spot in an otherwise lacklustre game was the Clarke line:

"In last night's overall team laced with listless performances, this line stood out with its quick breaks on the attack, persistent forechecking and strong defensive play".

With the three intrasquad games completed, the plan was to have one or two more severe scrimmages before setting off to Montreal to prepare for game one. The players themselves were feeling the effects of a harder than regular training camp. Brad Park gave a summary of his thoughts on Team Canada's camp in Robert MacAskill's 1972 Series:

"We're training the best that we can. We're doing the little things like in most training camps, little variations because Harry Sinden is coaching, and he has his way of doing your skating drills and everything like that. But the guys were suffering. The guys took the time off like normal in the summer, and like all training camps, some guys were throwing up, some guys are pulling groins, some guys are getting hits, bruised, they got ice packs on..."

Historians have debated whether Team Canada was in good enough physical condition at the start of the Summit Series. Had three weeks been enough to get the players in game shape? Possibly. The players were skating twice a day, with scrimmages and intrasquad games catalysts to get the timing back. The conditioning may have been enough to start an NHL season, what the players were used to; they would play themselves into game shape in a month of training camp. They would slowly work off the beers, hot dogs etc from summer cottage life, allowing the old injuries, both major and nagging to heal. **A deeper question might be whether the players took the training camp as seriously as they needed**. To a man, the Soviets were probably in better physical condition than any player on Team Canada. The Canadians had no idea of the calibre of team they would be facing, nor the relentless pace of the games they were about to endure. If they had, the physical and mental focus would have been greater during training camp.

The other issue was that a short training camp, nor matter how intense, **would not be enough time for the players to bond, gel and form an actual team**. One of the biggest issues for the coaches was team building. They had the inevitable task of attempting to get players to forget the past, forget age old rivalries, forget hating each other, to go and form a brand-new team. In three short weeks. This was certainly an uphill battle as most of the players not only had issues with each other from years of on ice rivalries, they didn't even know each other. Players sat and socialized with their regular teammates. They hung with the guys they knew, looking suspiciously across the dressing room at players they had spent years hating. It was a key element that the Soviets had, but Canada did not at that stage. **They were not yet a team.**

As part of the original agreement preluding the series, scouts or observers were allowed from both sides to attend each other's camps. As mentioned, Canada had sent the Toronto Maple Leaf scouts for a short visit to Moscow; in return the Soviets had long-time National Team coach Arkady Chernyshev and newly named National Team assistant coach Boris Kulagin journey to Canada. In the Hockey Hall of Fames legends book, the Soviet news agency TASS printed some of the feedback from Chernyshev, which was translated by author and contributor to Legends Magazine, Alexander Braverman.

Chernyshev starts by mentioning Brad Park as a great player who jumps into the offence. He was also impressed by the duo of Pat Stapleton and Bill White, especially White's defensive ability. Up front he liked the Esposito Cashman Parise line. He spent a lot of time praising Phil Esposito. The soviet coach regarded Esposito as unstoppable, very gifted, skilled, and physical. He talked about Esposito's shooting ability, but then remarked how *"of course today, after summer vacation, Esposito is not in the best physical condition"*. Chernyshev continued discussing the conditioning aspect, explaining how the Canadians wouldn't be able to maintain the high temp through a full game. A very wise analysis in retrospect considering Canada's late third period collapse in game one and losing a two-goal lead in game three.

The Soviet team would arrive in Montreal on August 30th. The next morning, they would be on the ice for 10:30 am and for a second practice that evening at 8pm. Those practices would be attended by Canadian media, coaches, and players. In 1972 Canadian hockey, practices were fairly basic. There would be skating drills used for cardio, up and down the rink, blue line to red line etc. The players would partake in shooting drills with the dual purpose of goaltender practice and shooting practice. Game situations would be worked on, three on two breakouts, two on ones, one on ones, and specialty team practice such as penalty kill or powerplay. These were useful yet basic preparations in retrospect.

The Soviets showed up to practice wearing old equipment, tattered sweaters, and skates. They did drills that were completely foreign to the Canadian observers. They were constantly moving, never standing around waiting for their turns, instead everyone on the ice was involved. Individual drills were challenging and involved balance, twisting, turning, edging, jumping over obstacles, almost always with a puck. The players skated differently than the Canadians, more upright, hands in front, head up, sometimes the arm swinging like a speed skater. This was foreign to the Canadian players, and as a result they didn't view the Soviets as equals. Pat Stapleton elaborates on watching the Soviets that first practice:

"I remember going to the forum and watching the first practice. They had these funny jerseys on like army vests. You expected that they could turn around and have parachutes on their backs."

The Canadian players would lose interest in watching the practices, opting to spend time talking to themselves, making jokes and laughing in the stands. The Soviet players seeing this, felt that laughter was directed at them. A lack of respect. That would add further motivation to prove themselves to the arrogant professionals. Looking at the situation analytically, it would be difficult to imagine a group of Canadian professional hockey players, laughing at another group of hockey players, no matter where they were from. The more realistic conclusion would be that the Canadian players were interacting, making jokes amongst themselves rather than being so obviously disdainful of their opponents. Either way, it added to Soviet motivation.

The Media and "Experts" Predict

The impact of the media predictions on the Canadian populace cannot be minimized. For several months there was a consistent, arrogant tone to the message. Canada would win and win easily. The Soviets would be overwhelmed, put in their place.

"I don't think Canada will lose a game," said well-respected hockey scribe Red Fisher from the Montreal Star

"6-2 for Canada." Author and Hockey Night in Canada commentator Brian McFarlane

"The NHL team will slaughter them in eight straight," predicted Gerald Eskenazi from The New York Times.

"Eight to nothing Canada — and that's the score of the first game," Fran Rosa Boston Globe.

"Canada will win in eight straight, the toughest one will be the opener" Long time respected hockey official Red Story

"Canada 6-2." Former National Team player and Summit Series commentator Brian Conacher.

The most outlandish prediction came from Globe and Mail columnist Dick Beddoes:

"Make it Canada eight games to zero. If the Russians win one game, I will eat this column shredded at high noon in a bowl of borsch on the front steps of the Russian embassy."

The Soviets themselves were aware of Dick Beddoes' opinion as Boris Mikhalov remembers:

"A main thing that affected game 2 is that we were waiting for that journalist to eat the newspaper which he promised

he would do if we won! They made borscht for him."

There was one Canadian journalist who went against the grain and predicted a Soviet victory. Writing for The Montreal Star, John Robertson took a position at odds with the general consensus in the Canadian media.

Robertson felt Canada had taken 100 years of hockey tradition and put it on the table yet allowed for the odds to be stacked against them. He predicted a 6-2 win for the Soviets as a result. Robertson himself claimed his prediction was garnered from personal observations of the Soviet team, challenging the opinion of the Canadian experts, and also validating the reports of Canadian players laughing at their opponents:

"Before the series started, I remember sitting in the stands with a bunch of the

> *Canadian players. I loved these guys, but they were sitting there ridiculing the Russians' equipment and laughing at them. Nobody wanted to give them a chance. The column was half serious and half frivolous. But I'd been to Russia and done stories on their hockey program. And I really felt they were a better team than anybody thought," Robertson "Paying the Bills".*

In two more days, on September 2nd, 1972, all the predictions would be tested. Canada's preparation would be tested. After years of speculation, the question of who is better would be tested.

On the ice.

PART 2: GAME ONE. MONTREAL

CHAPTER 6:
MONTREAL, WHERE
IT ALL BEGAN

"I don't wish to upset any other city in Canada, but in my opinion, Montreal is a true hockey city. Hockey was born here. The Canadiens have won the most Stanley Cups, fans understand hockey, and the whole city lives through its team. Some of my best games were in Montreal." Vladislav Tretiak

Montreal, Canada is one of the oldest cities in North America. A metropolis on the banks of the St. Lawrence River, it's the home of the most successful NHL franchise of all time, the Montreal Canadiens. This made the beautiful city a perfect choice for the first game of the Summit Series, but there is a secondary reason. Montreal is considered the birthplace of hockey. **It's the city that had the greatest impact on the roots of the game.** A city unmatched in the history of hockey, unmatched in the glory that has taken place on its' ice surfaces.

Why is Montreal considered the birthplace of hockey? Historians have debated the actual origins of the game of hockey. European claims go directly to a painting called "Hunters in the Snow" by Dutch painter Pietr Bruegel the Elder. The painting was done in 1565, showing multiple people enjoying skating around a frozen pond. Looking closer, there is an exception. One skater, off to the side, is carrying what appears to be a curved hockey like stick. The skater is trying to hit a puck like object on the ice. This shows some form of stick and ball game was practiced in Europe centuries ago. In Canada, both Nova Scotia and Kingston, Ontario laid claim to being the birthplace of hockey. There were reports that games were played on the frozen Nova Scotia ice in the mid-1800's with a stick and ball. Kingston was, for years, referred to as the birthplace of hockey, because of a claim that the Royal Canadian Rifles played a game of hockey in 1855. Kingston authorities have now rejected that claim, stating the game was played in 1886.

The reality is, none of these non-Montreal claims have enough validity to stick, because they didn't have **the first acknowledged organized hockey game.**

That game took place at Montreal's Victoria Rink on March 3, 1875, between an assortment of McGill University students. Sides were nine a piece, score was kept, rules were enforced, and a flat square piece of wood was used instead of a ball. A Montreal resident, McGill law student **James Creighton**, organized the game, participated in the game and was responsible for publishing the rules of the game in 1877. No earlier descriptions of any full-fledged game of hockey, including a recorded score, have ever been found. Strengthening the Montreal claim is another game at the same rink two weeks later. The formation of the Montreal University based McGill Hockey Club in January 1877 was the beginning of the first organized hockey team. This led to the publication of Creighton's written rules in February 1877; a staging of a highly publicized tournament at the Montréal Winter Carnival in 1883 and the founding, in Montreal, of the Amateur Hockey Association of Canada in 1886. If other places dabbled with hockey-like games on outdoor ice, the game itself was refined, organized, and launched as a team sport in Montreal. It can be safely called the birthplace of the game.

A team from Montreal was also the first hockey

team to participate in an international game. The Montreal Carnival was a big, extravagant winter festival that started in 1883. The festival brought people from all over Canada and the United States, that included skating competitions, curling matches, tobogganing, and sleighing. In the evenings, there were fancy dress balls and dinners under the patronage of luminaries such as the Governor-General of Canada. One of the showcase events was the burgeoning sport of hockey. In 1885 the event was won by the Montreal AAA, the Amateur Athletic Association. The tournament had included the top Montreal teams, with entries from Quebec City and Ottawa, and was strictly a Canadian affair. Although the game had started to grow in the northern United States, there had yet to be an international game between teams from Canada and the USA. This would soon change.

A smallpox outbreak caused the cancellation of the 1886 Montreal Carnival. Situated 150 kilometres away from Montreal, on Lake Champlain, Burlington, Vermont had been discussing hosting its own version of a winter carnival. When they heard about the cancellation of the Montreal Carnival, the town decided to move forward, with the blessing of their Montreal neighbours. As part of the Montreal cooperation, they would send the two best hockey clubs, the Montreal AAA and the Montreal Crystals. The Ottawa Hockey Club was scheduled to participate in Vermont, but poor weather cancelled their plans. In need of a replacement team, a local Burlington hotel, the Van Ness House, formed a team to compete. The games would be played outdoors on wind-swept Lake Champlain.

When the tournament began, the weather was horrible. The two Montreal teams would battle in the blizzard-like conditions, with the Montreal AAA getting a hard-fought overtime win. While not the level of the Summit Series opener, where the entire hockey world watched, the second game of the tournament was significant in its' own right. **The Burlington Vermont local squad would face off against the Montreal AAA in the first ever international hockey game**. Playing in the merciless wind, the teams agreed to play two short 15-minute periods. The Canadian team would defeat the Americans 3-0, winning the tournament. The Crystals would grind out a close 1-0 victory over the competitive Van Ness House team to end the tournament. Despite the snowstorm, and the short games, the first ever international hockey games were a huge success. The Burlington Free Press noted the immediate love of the game from the cold frozen spectators.

> Observed the Free Press: "Hockey at once leaped into popularity on the part of those Burlingtonians who witnessed the game."

The city of Montreal would be deeply involved in the growth of the game. The Montreal Wanderers were one of the great teams of the early era of hockey. They rose out of the Montreal AAA team, becoming professional in 1903. They would win 4 Stanley Cups and, along with the Montreal Canadiens, would be two of the original four teams composing the beginning of the NHL in 1917. The Wanderers rink, the Montreal Arena, would burn down on January 2, 1918, and they disbanded shortly after. In 1924, another team would rise in the city to play in the NHL, the Montreal Maroons. The Maroons were created to appeal to the English-speaking populace and were successful in their 14 years of existence, winning the cup twice. The team ceased operations in 1938 because of depression era financial trouble folding for good in 1947. The lasting legacy of the Montreal Maroons, despite multiple Hall of Famers, was the arena. Often associated with the Montreal Canadiens, **the fabled Montreal Forum**, home to game one of the Summit Series, was built in 1924 as the home of the Maroons. The Maroons had the Forum to themselves for two years before they were joined by the Canadiens in 1926, who become the dominant team of the 20th century.

Prior to September 2, 1972, game one of the Summit Series, the Montreal Canadiens had won 17 Stanley Cups, including 11 in the years from 1952-1971. They had been blessed with some of the best players in hockey history, including Newsy Lalonde, Howie Morenz, Maurice" Rocket" Richard, and brother Henri Richard, Jean Beliveau, Doug Harvey and Vladislav Tretiak's idol, Jacques Plante. Montreal fans had been privy to many Stanley Cup playoff games and Cup wins, that in 1972, the Canadians rivalled baseball's New York Yankees and basketball's Boston Celtics as the top sports franchises in North America. They were the most successful hockey club in the world. Despite those great games and moments at the Forum, they were NHL moments. International hockey? Not so much. **Before September 2, 1972, there had been only a handful of international hockey games played at the Montreal Forum.**

The first, in 1957, occurred when **the Moscow Selects**, a group of National Team players travelled to Canada and were playing seven games against Senior A competition and Junior A teams. After going winless in their first three games, the Soviets had beaten both the Sudbury and North Bay Senior A teams. The next game on the tour was in Montreal against the Ottawa-Hull Junior Canadiens. The Junior Canadiens were a very strong team that had future Montreal Canadiens stars JC Tremblay, Ralph Backstrom and Bobby Rousseau. They were managed by Sam Pollock, who went on to build the Montreal Canadiens 1970's dynasty. The coach of that same 1970's powerhouse dynasty was also the Junior Canadiens head coach, Scotty Bowman. This junior team would get all the way to the Memorial Cup final that season, losing in 7 games to the Flin Flon Bombers. Despite this, the Soviet Select team made easy work of the Juniors, winning 6-3 in a game that was 6-1 before a couple of late Canadians goals. The two teams would face each other again a few days later in Ottawa. The Junior Canadiens would get reinforced by players from the Junior Toronto Marlborough's, but lost even worse this time, **a 10-1 thrashing by the Soviets**.

Seven years later, the Soviet National Team embarked on one of their many North American tours of the 1960's. On December 11, 1964, after a 20-hour flight, the Soviet National Team arrived in Montreal to play the Montreal Junior Canadiens. The Junior Canadiens was still coached by Scotty Bowman and had future Summit Series stalwart Serge Savard on defence. They also had future Hall of Famer Jacques Lemaire up front, and one of the better offensive defencemen of the 1970s, the smooth skating Carol Vadnais, on the back end. The Junior Canadiens were a middle of the pack junior team that season, so a decision was made to supplement their roster with professionals from the Quebec Aces. These would include one of the greatest defensemen of all time, **Doug Harvey** and Montreal Canadien great **Gump Worsley** in goal. Red Berenson was another Quebec Ace who would play in this game and provide the same elite penalty killing he showed in Moscow during the Summit Series. **The caveat would be that the game would be played under international rules, which meant no bodychecking in the offensive zones**. The Soviet team would include 1972 defencemen Ragulin and Kuzkin. They also included Anatoli Firsov and Vitali Dayvdov; two outstanding players who helped the Soviets dominate international hockey throughout the 1960's.

The game was a tightly contested **3-2 victory for the Soviets** in front of 16,000 fans. The consensus was that the Soviets dominated the junior players but had trouble against the professionals. The reviews on the Soviets were mixed, but mostly negative. The players complained about the international rules that limited forechecking, as well as how the Soviets often skated with their heads down, unused to mid-ice hitting. Doug Harvey was especially harsh on his opponents as quoted in the Montreal Gazette,

"They have a fair system of hockey, but it's not very

exciting. I didn't see any top players on their team. Some could possibly make an American league team, but I didn't see any NHL prospects" Harvey continued *"under those rules (international) they would make a good intermediate team."* Then with some astute foreshadowing of what would come eight years later, Harvey added the following *"The rules make it tough; NHL players would be in the penalty box until they adjusted." Montreal Gazette Dec 12, 1964*

NHL president Clarence Campbell declared about the Soviets,

"They have greatly improved since their last visit. They have uniformly high calibre skating, probably better than ours. They are overpassing less now, but they don't know how to shoot and are a long way from NHL calibre." Montreal Gazette, December 12, 1964.

Red Berenson seemed to agree.

"They have improved on individual play (Berenson played against them in the 1959 World Championships), now take a chance once in a while, but they are a long way from the NHL".

Berenson then seemingly contradicts that statement by saying, *"On any given night they could beat an NHL team but lose the next night to a junior team".*

Future 1974 Summit Series stalwart Ralph Backstrom would remark,

"I think an American league squad would beat them easily. You notice they didn't do much when the defence played the man".

The most condemning quote came from coach Scotty Bowman. *"The Montreal Canadians would be 8-10 goals better using any rules".*

Soviet head coach Arkada Chermenshev had the last word, with a nice built-in defence against any criticisms,

"It was a very gratifying win. We had great difficulty in

playing after a 20-hour flight from Moscow".

A year later at the Forum, the Junior Canadiens would meet the Soviets in a rematch. The Junior Canadiens would have most of the same line-up as a year earlier, but this time had two additional reinforcements. **Five players from the Central Hockey League Houston Apollos** would join the team and legendary goaltender **Jacques Plante** came out of retirement to play goal. Plante had been the netminder of the 1950's Montreal Canadiens dynasty but had retired from the New York Rangers prior to the season. This game would be one of Plante's great career moments as he backstopped the team to **a 2-1 victory**. Norm Dennis from the Apollos scored with 29 seconds remaining. The night belonged to Plante. The 15,000 fans stood and applauded the great goalie for over a minute and a half. Plante himself told the Montreal Gazette how deeply the ovation impacted him,

"I've never had anything like this in the Forum, but this" he said, groping for words, "this comes right at home...and its wonderful".

The reports of the game were not favourable for the Soviets. The Junior Canadiens coach would mention how the Soviets were more physical a year later, but less precise in their passing. Plante would say the following,

"They are a good junior club. They shoot the puck well, but not very hard. If they played in the Junior league, we would soon get used to their back passing. We began catching onto it in the third period."

While the Soviet coach would remark that Plante was the best goalie they had ever faced, defenceman Alexander Ragulin would adhere to a consistent Soviet tradition of excuses when they would lose.

"We are tired, that's our seventh game in thirteen days. "

Ragulin wanted to say more, but the translator left the room. It was the Soviets' fourth game since arriving in Canada December 10, but in fairness, they had played the night before in Toronto against Bobby Orr and the Toronto

Junior League All-stars, where they won a hard fought 4-3 victory.

Montreal hosted other international games at the Forum in the 1960's. Both the Swedish and Czechoslovakian National Teams played exhibitions. The last big international game, before September 2, 1972, involved another game between the Montreal Junior Canadians and the Soviet National Team. This was a different Montreal junior team, as they were **one of the greatest junior squads of all time**. The Canadians won back-to-back Memorial cups in 1969 and 1970. They were led by the best junior aged player in the world, **Gilbert Perreault**, with a supporting cast full of future top NHL players. This included Summit Series teammates Buffalo sniper **Richard Martin**, and Vancouver's **Jocelyn Guevremont**. 1970's Toronto Maple Leafs all-star defenceman Ian Turnbull was only 15 but already playing on Canada's top junior team. The Junior Canadiens were enhanced by **eight minor-pros** for the game, including future Team Canada 1972 defenseman Guy Lapointe and '74 Summit speedy defensive forward Rejean Houle. Other notable future NHL players were Jim Rutherford in goal, the versatile Guy Charron at forward and the physical Andre Dupont on defence. Dupont would make himself quite known in the Philadelphia Flyer rout of the Central Red Army in the 1976 Super Series.

An interesting incident in January 1969 could have been a precursor to the difficulties in dealing with the Soviet Hockey Federation. The Soviets arrived for a tour of Canada to playing the Canadian National Team. On January 17, the first game versus Canada at Montreal had to be cancelled. The Soviet team had arrived late on their flight and refused to play in Montreal on the 17th. They also threatened to cancel the whole tour. The Canadian Amateur Hockey Association managed to straighten everything out, but not in time to save the Montreal game. The Montreal Forum officials were furious and refused to reschedule the Soviet game.

The following year, on December 29th, 1969, a sold-out Montreal Forum watched the Soviets face the enhanced Memorial Cup champions. This was the same Canadian tour where Ken Dryden was humiliated with the Canadian National Team in Vancouver. For several years now the Soviets had been beating the amateur Canadian National Team regularly and had often talked about challenging the NHL. They were a team in transition. The Soviets only had seven players on this squad that had won gold in 1968. This Soviet team had new young players, who using the seven games to experience playing against Canadian opposition for two weeks across Canada. The tour was a baptism of sorts for their new, powerful group of young players. Players named **Kharlamov, Petrov, Shadrin, Maltsev** and **a young Vladislav Tretiak**, much of the same group who would challenge Team Canada three years later.

The junior champions shocked the crowd and the well-travelled Soviets, winning 9-3. The winners were led by Perrault, who had two goals and three assists. Rejean Houle of the AHL's Montreal Voyageurs added another two goals and two assists. The lightning-fast Houle would face the Soviets again in the 1974 WHA Summit Series. He would play well in a checking role. The juniors outshot the Russians 36-30. Viewer accounts mention the Soviets were playing tired, perimeter hockey, not engaged physically. The IIHF had instigated checking in all three zones in 1969. As a result, these games in Canada were a learning experience against players who were used to hitting, especially on the forecheck.

To the Soviets, these were learning games, not championship games. They were looking at the future of Soviet hockey in their young players and at the same time, learning to adapt to the new IIHF rules, adding a greater physical element to their game. This was obviously a game where the young Soviet players were obviously not able to adapt to a pumped up physical Canadian team, probably from both inexperience and exhaustion at the end of the long trip.

Future NHLer Bobby Guindon would remark after playing the Soviets about their lack of hitting,

> *"They're good stickhandlers but they don't hit at all. They make too many passes, short passes and back passes."* Montreal Gazette Dec 30th 1969

While this game was a great victory by one of the greatest junior clubs of all time, this game had the opposite effect on the Canadian hockey "expert" mentality. **If the obviously overrated Soviets could lose to a junior team, how badly would they lose to an NHL all-star team?** Roger Bedard, the coach of the Montreal Junior Canadiens had this to say about the Soviet level of hockey compared to the NHL,

> *"I have said that an NHL team could spot the Russians five or even eight goals and still win and I think we proved the point. I think we also proved that we in Canada play the best style of hockey. The Russians are tough, but they play parlour hockey. I'll tell you; any NHL team would kill them!"* Montreal Gazette Dec 30, 1969.

This would be the last important international game held at the Montreal Forum, ending a twelve-year period where the Soviets played the Montreal Junior Canadiens, six times, with the Soviets winning four and losing two. The Junior Canadiens would also play the Swedish National Team twice. They would beat the Swedes in 1963 4-3 and lose to them in 1966 3-2. The strong Czechoslovak National Team also played the junior Canadiens twice. They beat a combined Regina Pats, Montreal Junior Canadiens and Peterborough Petes team 3-2 in 1965 and beat a Montreal junior Canadiens team supplemented with minor pros 5-3 in 1967.

Overall, the junior team, with some help, had a record of 3 wins and 7 losses, albeit against the top European National Teams. Montreal would go on to host the revered New Year's Eve matchup between the Montreal Canadiens and the Central Red Army in 1976, along with the rematch in 1979. Canada Cup games starting in 1976 would be played at the Forum, but none of these games would match the hype and intrigue of the first game of the Summit Series.

CHAPTER 7: GAME 1, MONTREAL: SINDEN'S FOLLY PART 1

This series was uncharted grounds for both coaching staffs. While the Soviets were a set team at the national level, Coaches Bobrov and Kulagin were facing a test that **no Soviet team had ever faced**. Knowing the attention to details and due diligence the Soviet hockey brass tended to do for major events, they would have prepared to the best of their ability against how they perceived the professionals would play. The Soviets had been playing Canadian teams since the 1950's, so they had years of learning to adapt to the Canadian style. The professionals didn't play a different style per se than the top Senior A and Junior Teams the Soviets faced in the past. **The feeling was the top NHL pros just did it better.** The Soviets certainly expected a bigger, stronger, faster, more challenging opponent than they had ever faced before. Strategy wise, they anticipated that playing at home, with the entire nation cheering them on, Team Canada would be extremely motivated to start game one. This would result in a **sustained burst of pressure** from the amped up Canadians, that the Soviet team would have to withstand, diffuse, and eventually counterattack. The coaches knew the pressure would come in a Canadian style forecheck, with Bobrov having personally experienced it going all the way back to the Penticton Vees in 1955. As a result, they planned their line-up for game one accordingly.

The Soviet strategy for their forwards would be hanging high, watching the Canadian point men, positioning themselves for the **quick counter attacks** against the Canadian forecheck. Using their **superior fitness** to tire them out with their own version of sustained forechecking. The defence would hold the fort, playing positionally smart hockey until an opening came to set up the quick counter strike, disrupting the Canadian momentum. The line-up needed to be a combination of speed and strength, combined with some experienced veteran poise.

Anticipating the Canadian onslaught, the Soviets would **dress seven defencemen** in game one, pairing experience with youth. It would be a veteran group led by team captain Viktor Kuzkin, 32, paired with 25 year old Alexander Gusev. The second pairing would be another long-time National Team veteran, 31-year-old Alexander Ragulin paired with Gennady Tsygankov who had just turned 25. The third pairing would be 27-year-old Yuri Lyapkin with Evgeny Paladiev who was 24. The seventh, youngest defenceman was the more offensively oriented Vladimir Luchenko, 23. Not dressed for this game would be the talented Valeri Vasiliev, and extra defenseman Yuri Shatalov, rounding out the nine Soviet defenseman for the series. Missing from the line-up was the small but extremely mobile veteran Vitali Davydov who would have been the team's oldest player at 33.

Up front, the Soviets went with three set lines and one extra forward. The top line for the USSR at the 1972 Olympics had been Valeri Kharlamov with Anatoli Firsov and Vladmir Vikulov. With Firsov not selected for the Summit Series, the coaches moved slick center Alexander Maltsev between the two high scoring wingers. Big and versatile center Vladmir Petrov would center Yuri Blinov and Boris Mikhailov. The third line would be all from Spartak

Moscow. Alexander Yakushev on the left side with center Vladimir Shadrin and small quick winger Evgeny Zimin. Strong, aggressive left winger Evgeny Mishakov would be the extra forward. The line-up had depth, with a small skilled Maltsev line, a versatile line centred by Petrov and finally a set line from Moscow Spartak. The Spartak line would have been the biggest surprise. They were not yet regular "go to" players on the National Team at that stage. They were obviously chosen for their chemistry and in Yakushev's case size and potential ability to win battles against the tough Canadians. Forwards not dressed for the USSR in game one including the young trio of Vyacheslav Anisin, Alexander Bodunov and Yuri Lebedev. A line that had dominated as juniors. Soviet legend Vyatcheslav Starshinov, and fringe players Alexander Martynuk and 20-year-old Alexander Volchkov would also not dress for game one. Anatoli Firsov would be reported as injured and did not make the trip overseas with the team.

Young Vladislav Tretiak would start in goal. The Soviets had three other potential goalies for the series starting with veteran Viktor Zinger from Moscow Spartak. Zinger had been a long-time National Team goalie, mostly in a backup role to Viktor Konovalenko. Zinger won a couple of championships with Spartak in the later 1960's and would remain a long-time coach for the organization after his playing days were done. He seemed by all accounts to be the designated backup for Tretiak. Alexander Sidelnikov was a goalie who would get playing time against the professionals throughout the 1970's, but generally with poor results. He was 22 at the time of the Super Series and wouldn't have been considered a serious candidate to play. Finally, there was the long-term National Team veteran Alexander Pashkov. Pashkov was the Soviet version of suitcase Gary Smith, as he would play for sixteen seasons in the Soviet League, with stops at Lokomotiv Moskova, Krylia Sovetov Moscow, Central Red Army, Moscow Dynamo and finally Khimik Voskresenk.

A 32-year-old veteran at the time, Pashkov was a part time National Team player, and would only have been seen as a possibility if major injuries had happened to the other goalies. A final goaltender named Vladmir Shepovalov was not available due to injury. Shepovalov was a goalie with SKA Leningrad (St Petersburg) but had been on the National Team radar leading to dressing for four games at the 1972 World Championships. The Soviets lacked the goaltending depth that Canada had, and **they would go to the series staking their hopes for success on the 21-year-old Tretiak.**

Team Canada, on the other hand, had some obvious choices on who to start game one, as well as some difficult choices. With eighteen forwards, eleven defencemen and three goaltenders in camp, plus Bobby Orr, Sinden and Ferguson knew that there would be some disappointed players each game. NHL mega stars Phil Esposito and Brad Park would be guarantees in the line-up, but the rest of the team would be up to the coaches, including what goalie would start. **The Canadian coaches decide to focus on offensive pressure**, especially on the suspect Soviet defence and even more **suspect young goalie**. As a result, Sinden makes the fateful decision to dress four lines and five defencemen. The assumption being that the extra forward line would wear down and help to overwhelm the Soviets.

The forward lines reflected the offensive strategy. Even though Frank Mahovlich and Yvan Cournoyer have been playing with Stan Mikita in training camp, **Sinden decided to start them on a line with Esposito**. His hope was that the line would become a super line of three high level players. The trio had played one of the three Red White Intersquad games as a line but **lacked chemistry**. A line that did have immediate chemistry was the second line selected. Bobby Clarke, Ron Ellis and Paul Henderson had been the best line in the training camp and were well set up to be a dynamic checking line for Team Canada. The New York Ranger GAG line (goal a game line) with Jean Ratelle centring Vic Hadfield and Rod Gilbert would be the third line. The final forward spots would be a bit of a surprise, but like the Clarke line they had gelled in the intrasquad games. Detroit's speedy sniper Mickey Redmond would be the winger on a line with St Louis centre Red Berenson and big Peter Mahovlich from Montreal on the left side. Redmond had experience playing in Montreal and added more offense to the line-up. Red Berenson was more of a two-way centre and an excellent penalty killer. He also had some international experience playing against the Soviets. Finally, Pete Mahovlich was used to playing in Montreal and was a very skilled, adaptable player who could kill penalties if Canada got into some penalty trouble.

Forwards not dressed for game one included Esposito's Boston usual linemate Wayne Cashman, Minnesota North Stars Bill Goldsworthy and JP Parise as well as Chicago's Stan Mikita and Dennis Hull. Young future NHL stars Marcel Dionne, Richard Martin and Gilbert Perreault were also watching from the stands for game one.

On defence for Team Canada, coach Sinden decided to **only go with five defensemen** at the back end. Brad Park had played well in training camp with Detroit's Gary Bergman, so they will start as Team Canada's first pair. The second pairing of Boston's Don Awrey and New York's Rod Seiling would have had to be a huge surprise. These were serviceable NHL defensemen, who had solid if unspectacular all-around games. **They were not star level players and had never played as a pair before training camp**. However, they had, by all reports, gelled, in the three-week training period, to the point that the coaching staff felt this was Team Canada's top pairing. The fifth spot was taken by Montreal Canadien Guy Lapointe. Lapointe was an energetic player, a good skater, with some offensive potential. He was inexperienced, having only completed two prior seasons as a regular with Montreal. Lapointe did have some experience against the Soviets and that may have been a determining factor in his selection over his more notable teammate Serge Savard, although Savard had also played a game against the Soviets. Savard was a more seasoned player at that stage of his career, having won a Conn Smythe trophy as the most valuable player in the playoffs in 1969. He had been injured for much of the 1971-72 season, and **Sinden felt he had only started to show form at the end of training camp**. Also, surprisingly not making the first game line-up, were the Chicago duo of Pat Stapleton and Bill White. They had been second team all stars in 1971-72, and were a set pair, used to playing together. They would have been the expected choice to be in the top four instead of Awrey and Seiling. Other defensemen in training camp, Vancouver's Dale Tallon and Jocelyn Guevremont, as well as Toronto's Brian Glennie were not considered strong candidates for the line-up. The strategy of using five defence with three intersquad games as warmups would be a big ask of the players. However, with the strategy of offense first, and **the theory that the play would be in the Soviet end, Sinden and Ferguson were gambling that the defence would have an easier time out there.**

Ken Dryden got the starting nod for the Montreal game. **He had not played very well in camp**; he was used to playing at the Forum and had some experience playing internationally with the Canadian National Team. Dryden was a big man, intellectual, and cool as a cucumber in net. Sinden certainly felt confident with Dryden, although he hadn't coached against him personally. While Dryden had played a large role in the upset defeat of the Boston Bruins in the 1970-71 Stanley Cup playoffs, leading Montreal to the cup, Sinden was not the coach of the Bruins that season. Sinden could have chosen Boston's backup Eddie Johnson, but Johnson was not considered an elite starting netminder. As a result, the only other real choice for the coaches was Chicago's Tony Esposito. Esposito had once briefly played for the Montreal Canadiens but was picked up on waivers from the Chicago Black Hawks in 1969. Esposito had thrived on the Hawks, winning the Calder Trophy as rookie of the year and setting an NHL record with 15 shutouts. In the 1971-72 season Esposito had a league low 1.77 Goals against average and was the NHL's first team all-star goalie. He had won the Vezina trophy as the NHL's best in two of the last three seasons. Despite Dryden's playoff success, Esposito had to be considered the NHL's penultimate goalie. Those numbers combined with his extremely competitive personality would have been serious considerations for the coaches in choosing the starting goalie for the game. Despite those qualifications, the decision was made to go with Ken Dryden. **Dryden now had the pressure of an entire country as well as carrying the reputation of Canadian hockey on his back, as he prepared for the biggest game of his short career.**

With the starting line-ups set, the pre-series training camps and practices completed, the most anticipated series in the history of hockey was set to take place. The question whether the Soviets could compete with the best professional players in North America was about to be answered. The predictions from the media and other hockey "experts" were all moot points at this stage. After years of speculation, the answers would finally be revealed on a brutally warm evening, September 2nd, 1972.

The game almost didn't start. Officials had discovered that **the Soviet equipment had been seized over a lawsuit.** A local Montreal resident sued the Soviet government over the loss of a vehicle during the Soviet invasion of Czechoslovakia in 1968. He had gone to court and got a successful injunction against the Soviet team, allowing authorities to seize their equipment. Alan Eagleson intervened and resolved the issue a few hours before game time by paying the $1600 himself, out of his own pocket. Eagleson would go to jail himself many years later for embezzling money from the players he represented and other infractions, so the chances the $1600 was his own pocket money were probably rare. With that drama resolved, the game could continue as planned.

CHAPTER 8: GAME 1, PERIOD 1. THE MYTH OF THE UNBEATABLE

With the Soviet team sitting nervously in the Montreal Forum dressing room for the start of the game, goalie **Vladislav Tretiak is informed he has a visitor.** He looks up to see the handsome, confident face of Goaltending legend **Jacques Plante**. Plante was still an active player for the Toronto Maple Leafs, and at age 43 was still a very good goalie. Plante was doing the French-language TV analyst for the Summit Series and came to the Russians' dressing room with an interpreter to brief Tretiak on a blackboard about the shooting tendencies of Team Canada. The two had met for the first time a year earlier in St. Louis, when Tretiak was hustled away from the showers by his coach to watch Plante practice. For his attention, Plante gave him a goalie stick. **Tretiak sits and listens to Plante explain Canadian players habits and strategies.** The student listens eagerly, lapping up the information, building his confidence. Tretiak is in shock that this is happening to him. He pays attention and soaks up the advice.

To this day Tretiak really doesn't know why Plante came to the room. He believes that Plante didn't want a member of the goaltending fraternity humiliated in what most everyone believed would be a Canadian rout. Plante never revealed why he decided to sit with the young goalie and explain the shooting habits of NHL stars such as Phil

Esposito and Frank Mahovlich, but **the prevailing opinion was that he felt bad for the young netminder and wanted to help**. Tretiak relayed the appreciation and help that Plante provided him:

> "Jacques Plante came into our room with an interpreter and amazed us by sitting with me and explaining in detail how I should play against the likes of Mahovlich, Esposito, Cournoyer and Henderson. I am still puzzled by what motivated him to do that. I will always be very grateful to Jacques Plante, whose suggestions helped me very much."
> Tretiak Autobiography "I would like to ask Jacques Plante, but it's not possible. Maybe he felt sorry for me?"

As the players get introduced, Canadian coach Harry Sinden accidently walks out when they announce the Soviet coaches, but scurries back to the Canadian bench to a chuckling John Ferguson. The Soviet players get introduced first, with the Montreal crowd giving the same polite applause for each player. Favourites had not been set by the Canadian public. The Canadian players, on the other hand, all received loud ovations with the loudest going to the hometown Montreal Canadian players, Cournoyer, Lapointe, Peter and Frank Mahovlich and goalie Ken Dryden. Assistant coach and former Montreal Canadiens enforcer John Ferguson also gets an appreciative welcome. Canadian Prime Minister Pierre Trudeau comes out to centre ice to drop the ceremonial puck. An exchange of small flags happens between the Soviet captain Viktor Kuzkin and Assistants Ragulin and Vikulov with the three Team Canada co-captains, Phil Esposito, Jean Ratelle and Frank Mahovlich. **As the ceremonial puck drop is about to happen, Soviet captain Kuzkin defers the draw to Vikulov.** He would remark afterwards that because he was a defenceman, it would seem silly for him to take the draw against Esposito. **Esposito takes the draw seriously** and easily wins the puck back to his Canadian teammates. The crowd roars in approval as a bemused Vikulov skates back to his group.

Esposito goes and grabs the puck and brings it back to the laughing Prime Minister, giving him the puck as a souvenir.

After the national anthems, the crowd is murmuring in anticipatory excitement. Team Canada sends out the Ratelle, Gilbert, Hadfield line to start the game, but then suddenly pulls them off and goes with the hoped for "power line" of Esposito centring the Big M and Cournoyer. Brad Park and Gary Bergman start on defence. Soviets go with Petrov, Mikhailov and Blinov. On defence is Gusev and team Captain veteran Kuzkin. An overexcited Cournoyer jumps ahead before the puck is dropped. The Canadian players are antsy, obviously very pumped to start the game. **That excitement leads to a sudden, shocking, first goal.**

Goal 1: Esposito Canada 1 Soviets 0

In 1972, Phil Esposito was the greatest scorer the NHL had ever seen. In 1970-71 he scored 76 goals, shattering Bobby Hull's 58 goal mark. He had added another 76 assists for an unheard of (pre-Wayne Gretzky) 152 points. In the 1968-69 season, Espo had been the first player to reach 100 points, winning his first of five Art Ross Trophies as scoring titles. He also won the Hart Trophy that season, as the NHL's most valuable player. His offensive production had helped his Boston Bruins team win two cups in the last three years. He had a big, loud, jovial personality, one of the most recognized hockey players in the world. Despite all of that, **Phil was not truly respected in the hockey establishment.** He was often portrayed as a garbage collector, someone who just stood in the slot and scored goals. He wasn't a beautiful skater nor did he possess the handsome elegance of Jean Beliveau. Esposito also played with the best player on the planet, Robert Gordon Orr. Orr's brilliance and dominance over his opponents led to a mindset that Phil was the beneficiary of Orr's passes and greatness. His high goal and point totals were a result of Orr's dominance, with Espo seen as a finisher, more than a truly great player in his own right. A younger Esposito had also been overshadowed by Bobby Hull when they played together on Chicago.

Despite all the records Phil set, there was always that thought that he was possibly not quite good enough or even capable enough **to lead a team on his own**. That would change with the Summit Series. In the crease area, using his great hand eye coordination to bat a puck out of the air past Tretiak, Phil Esposito would start that amazing month off with the historic first goal of the Series.

The goal starts immediately after the opening faceoff. The puck goes back into the Canadian zone, where Gary Bergman shows some good speed as he blows by a fore checking Boris Mikhailov. Bergman then makes a little flip pass to centre where Frank Mahovlich does a Soviet style behind his back pass to a streaking Esposito. Esposito flies into the Soviet zone with Blinov pestering him along the boards. The NHL scoring champion who normally shoots left, **switches hands to send a shot right-handed**. This was an old Gordie Howe trick that Esposito mastered. The shot misses and goes around the boards on the left side blue line. Here Bergman is in position to send the puck up to Mahovlich (referred to as the Big M) in the corner. The Big M misses the puck as it goes around the rink to the right side where Yvan Cournoyer and then Esposito lay down body checks, firstly on Gusev and then Blinov, the latter resulting in a turnover. Cournoyer gets control and drops it back to a pinching Brad Park who fires a clever pass to the left side of the Soviet net, attempting to get it to Mahovlich. Tretiak stacks the pads and makes a good first save off Mahovlich, a sign of things to come. The Big M's shot hits Tretiak's pads, bounces out mid-air, where Esposito with some nice hand-eye knocks it into the net.

What is shocking about this first goal and sequence of events is that **the Soviets barely touch the puck since**

the beginning of the game. They were overwhelmed. There wasn't a poor giveaway or lack of Soviet effort, it was all Canada. Canada looks like a hockey machine in total synchronicity. The goal itself must have seemed to both the Soviet players, and the fans watching, a testament to the early predictions of complete Canadian dominance. Vladislav Tretiak recounts the goal and Esposito's reaction,

"There was so much noise. I remember the crowd going crazy; people were roaring, laughing, whistling, yelling. Esposito patronizingly tapped me on my shoulder and said, 'OK.' It was a clear message: 'Don't forget who you are playing against."

Twenty-one seconds into the game, Canada has already scored. The anticipated rout has begun. **All the pre-series predictions coming to life**.

On the next shift after the Canadian goal, Alexander Maltsev carries the puck behind his own goal. He makes a quick pass and then suddenly gives a fore checking Bobby Clarke an introduction to Soviet stick work with a **nasty, uncalled for cross check** to what appears to be Clarke's face. For once, Clarke was the innocent on the play, and he must have been shocked to be eating lumber so early into the game. Clarke gets his revenge on Maltsev later. Soviets demonstrate their transition game with a pass from the right corner to centre ice. This would be a play they would continue to use effectively throughout the series.

With the action in Canada's zone, a ramped-up Paul Henderson trips Maltsev. The Soviets go on the first powerplay of the Series. The Canadian players are still amped up and the Pete Mahovlich/Red Berenson tandem do a great job preventing the Soviets from getting any cohesive play started. This power play is the first shift of Valeri Kharlamov and immediately **his speed is unlike anyone else on the ice**. During the entire 2-minute powerplay, the Soviets switch personnel three times, yet the Canadian Pete M-Berenson duo was still out there during this entire time. **Long shifts by**

Canada would be one of their weaknesses in this game and series. As they would learn, the Soviets are too fit, too strong and play at too high of a pace for the long luxurious shifts some of the NHLers are used to as stars of their respective teams.

Soviets have their first real good chance with a tired Pete M weaving at centre with his head down resulting in a quick Soviet turnover. Vladmir Shadrin gets a good shot and Dryden makes his first real save of the night. The Soviets keep it in the Canadian zone where Paladiev makes a nice move over **a flopping Rod Seiling**, and then sends a nice pass to Evgeny Zimin at the right post. Zimin tries to slip it across to big Alexander Yakushev, but Dryden reads the play and stacks his pads. Two notes from this play, Canadian defenders are already trying to block shots and taking themselves out of the play and the **Soviet "back door" passing play is dangerous**. It will soon take its first bite out of Canada. After a Canadian clearing goes into the Soviet zone, Zimin carries the puck through the neutral zone. He slips into the Canadian zone but is hit with a perfectly executed hip check by Brad Park, sending Zimin somersaulting to the ice.

The New York Ranger line of Jean Ratelle, Vic Hadfield and Rod Gilbert was known as the GAG Line. In the 1971-72 NHL season, they had become the highest scoring line in Rangers' history. They also finished 3-4-5 in League scoring just behind the Bruin duo of Phil Esposito (133) and Bobby Orr (117). Jean Ratelle led the New York Rangers in scoring during the 1971-72 season despite playing only 63 games before breaking an ankle. He scored 46 goals with 63 assists finishing with 109 points and won the Lester B Pearson trophy for the best player in the NHL voted oby the players. Team captain Vic Hadfield became the first New York Ranger to hit the revered 50 goal number. He finished the season as the NHL's top left winger with 50 goals and 56 assists for 106 points. Rod Gilbert was the third member of the GAG line who fell just 3 points of 100 points scoring 43 goals and 54 assists for 97 points. This was amazing considering the severe back injury Gilbert suffered early in his career. A smallish, skilled player, he had shown great perseverance overcoming the debilitating injury of a broken back. This line was the only set line selected for Team Canada, and there were high hopes for the trio.

The GAG line gets their first shift and quickly has two chances, but the game is already ramping to a faster pace as the Soviets counterattack, showing off some quick puck movement down the ice leading to a Boris Mikhailov shot off a drop pass. Canada comes roaring back, but Gilbert starts the Canadian habit of **stick handling at the Soviet blue line**. He loses the puck and resulting in an offside, losing any temporary momentum. Ratelle wins the faceoff, throwing it back to Don Awrey. Awrey decides to try and dump the puck into the Soviet zone, but his pass gets blocked leading to some pressure in the Canadian zone. Canada recovers, but Awrey again loses the puck in centre ice and the puck goes back into the Canadian zone. The Ranger line has been on the ice for over two minutes, and it starts to show. Alexander Maltsev bumps the much bigger Vic Hadfield into the boards, an early sign that they will not be outmuscled this evening. The exhausted Ranger winger freezes the puck for a whistle.

On the next shift, Frank Mahovlich makes a nice pass to the Roadrunner who almost gets clear on Tretiak. Cournoyer gets slightly hooked from behind by rangy defenseman Alexander Gusev with no call on the play. Soviets immediately counter again with long pass to a streaking Boris Mikhailov. This leads to a good shot on Dryden, but it should be noted that Awrey backs up almost to his goalmouth letting Boris have plenty of room to fire a dangerous shot.

On Canada's next foray into the Soviet end. The puck gets behind the net where **Esposito gets speared by Mikhailov** behind the net. The big Bruin gives him a high whack towards Mikhailov's face in return. The Canadian players would continually react that way to Soviet stickwork. A spear or hook would lead to a Canadian high stick, a seeming **overreaction**. Nevertheless, these two will continue to battle for the next 8 games.

As the puck gets dumped back into Canada's zone, Brad Park makes a smooth rush, deking out a forechecker and then head manning the puck to Cournoyer, but as they have done several times this period, Canada goes offside.

Goal 2: Henderson Canada 2 Soviets 0

Clarke, Henderson, and Ellis are out on the faceoff in the Soviet zone. This line was the surprise of camp as none were considered locks to make the team. It's been theorized that had Bobby Hull been eligible to play it was Paul Henderson who lost a spot at left wing on the team. Considering Richard Martin had just turned 21 and was the replacement named when Hull was deemed inadmissible, Henderson most likely would have been on the team. The line of Bobby Clarke, Ron Ellis and Henderson gelled instantly and their performance in the training camp turned heads. Sportswriter Milt Dunnell of the Toronto star remarked about how well Henderson and Ellis were performing during Team Canada's training camp:

> *"The two Leaf wingers have never looked better than they have with Clarke, Philadelphia Flyers workhorse between them." Toronto Star 1972*

Bobby Clarke was another debatable choice when Sinden and Ferguson were making their decisions. The choice came down, in hindsight, between Dave Keon and Clarke. Dave Keon was 32 in 1972, coming off a poor season by his standards with 18 goals and only 48 points in 72 games. He had been hobbled by ankle issues caused by trying new skates out at the start of the 1971-72 season. Keon was a wonderful two-way player, a truly great skater, and a determined checker. Never a big scorer or point producer, his career high in goals was 38 in 1970-71; it was also the only season where he had a point a game with another career high with 76 points in 76 games. Keon was a tireless worker. Consistency was his trademark. He was always on the move, checking, digging, eliminating guys from the play after they got rid of the puck. He created countless opportunities for line mates and killed penalties while also almost never taking a minor penalty himself. He won two Lady Byng sportsmanship trophies, the Calder for top rookie in 1961 and the Conn Smythe in 1967 when the Leafs last won the Cup. Keon was the heart and soul of the Leafs Cup dynasty in the mid-60's that, even the Soviets were shocked he wasn't picked for Team Canada.

Robert Earle Clarke (Bobby) was a product of Flin Flon, Manitoba, 23 years old in 1972. Clarke was a tireless worker like Keon, had wonderful hockey sense and passing ability with an edge unlike few players in history. He was extremely competitive, a leader and very nasty when needed. He wasn't as anywhere near as good as skater as Keon (who was?) or as respected throughout the league, yet, but it was still a tough decision to make for Sinden and Ferguson, youth versus experience, grit versus smooth skill.

One would think this was a detailed, deep thought process on behalf of the coaching staff. After all Canada's hockey reputation and image was on the line, correct? No. The decision was a stalemate between Sinden who wanted Keon and Ferguson who wanted Clarke. What did they do? **They asked Alan Eagleson, who simply asked who had more points last year**. That was Clarke who had a breakout year with 81 points compared to Keon's 48. The final spot choice was Clarke's.

> *"But going back to the choices, the only choice I remember a lengthy discussion about was what I remember as the final pick. Players that were picked at the bottom without any doubt. Probably three of the last four, five players picked who ultimately played in the tournament were probably*

Henderson, Ellis and Clarke. And I know that Henderson and Ellis were on the team ahead of Clarke and they were down to the last center man, and Harry Sinden was very partial to Dave Keon. John Ferguson who just retired that previous year was very partial to a young player named Bobby Clarke. They wanted to know my views, it's tough for me. I just said well, why don't we look at the stats? And my recollection is that Keon had 58 points (actually 48) and Clarke had 85 (actually 81). And I think that was the reason Clarkie was chosen for the team. And in retrospect, who knows, I mean Clarke was a very important part of our team, but Davey Keon's the type of player who on the large ice surfaced might have shone as well."

Alan Eagleson NHLPA Director 1967-1992. Robert MacAskills 72 Series 1997 transcripts.

Much like the first Canadian goal, the second was a much shorter series of Canadian passing where the Soviets really didn't touch the puck. After a Soviet icing, the faceoff was in the Soviet end to Tretiak's right. Canada would go on to win 62.5% of the face-offs this game and this draw was won cleanly by Clarke over Shadrin. Canada was set in a standard offensive faceoff position for this era with Henderson having moved from the boards to the top of the circle anticipating a Canadian faceoff win and a resulting quick shot. Clarke a left-hand shot wins it cleanly over to Ellis who is at the hash marks, he quickly drops it back to Henderson who drills a snapshot to the lower right corner. Tretiak comes out slightly but misses the angle. Shadrin had a moment to block the shot, but his reaction time was slow, and he was hesitant getting to Henderson too late. This goal was a well set up, lightning quick strike by Canada and the Soviets must have been thinking it was going to be a very long night and an even longer series. The organist at the Forum started playing the Funeral March in further anticipation of impending Soviet Doom.

After the Henderson goal, Ron Ellis gets tripped,

falls, colliding with Paladiev at the blue line and appears to be hurt. A tripping penalty is called against Yakushev on the play.

The Ranger GAG line come out for the powerplay with Esposito and Park on defence. Esposito on the point is an odd choice as his game was much more slot based and off the rush bull like strength combined with extremely accurate and quick shooting ability. Canada struggles for puck control throughout the power play as the Soviets are playing very aggressively on the penalty kill. Rather than a stationary box, the Soviets attack the puck, constantly skating and disrupting the puck carrier. Without a clear Canadian chance, the GAG line is replaced with the Canadian fourth line of Red Berenson, Pete Mahovlich and Mickey Redmond for the end of the power play. Brad Park and Phil Esposito are still on the points. Esposito makes a dangerous rush into the Soviet zone, but his pass out front is blocked. Soon after, Vladimir Luchenko knocks Redmond flying and tries the long pass to hit a streaking Mikhailov at centre. The pass almost works just as Ragulin gets out of the box and you have to wonder if this is **a set Soviet play** at the end of a power play to spring the penalty taker for a breakaway. Pete Mahovlich makes a good defensive stop on the resulting 2 on 1, however a Soviet trailer comes in, firing a hard shot on Dryden. Just when a play looks dead, the Soviets will move other players up, **Canada will have to learn to never give up on a play.**

Having killed the penalty, the Soviets come to life. Tsygankov pinches in from the point but runs into a man mountain named Peter Mahovlich who flattens the Soviet defender. Mahovlich was not a physical player, but this was a glimpse of the player he could have been if he had added that element and edge to his talented game. Mickey Redmond tries a solo rush, and fires it awkwardly wide, falling on the shot. The Soviets recover as Alexander Yakushev unleashes a "what the heck was that "powerful slap shot from a distance at a seemingly shocked Dryden. **Yes, Ken, the Soviets could**

shoot.

On the next shift, Bobby Clarke comes out with Cournoyer and Frank Mahovlich. Immediately Clarke is all over the puck, battling at the blue line tenaciously with four soviet players. Ragulin gives Clarke a push from behind but suddenly swings his stick carelessly at Cournoyer who has joined the fray. The puck goes to Valeri Kharlamov. Kharlamov goes wide on Don Awrey, gets around him but falls on the play, as does Awrey. **One could theorize that this play allowed Kharlamov to know he could beat Awrey wide now**. The game becomes end to end, wide open action and the stick work and contact increases. Yvan Cournoyer flies down the ice in pursuit with another speedster, Valeri Kharlamov, and Cournoyer aggressively grabs Kharlamov, trying to get around him, pulling him from behind before falling and sliding into the Soviet zone. Kharlamov wins this battle showing excellent balance, and Canada easily could have been called for two straight penalties now with Awrey hauling down Kharlamov and then Cournoyer. Kharlamov is already causing the Canadian players all kinds of issues every time he is out.

Phil Esposito gets a fantastic chance alone on Tretiak after a nice feed from the corner from the Big M. Tretiak comes out and stones him. **If Espo had deked him, it would have been 3-0 and perhaps a different end result.** The pace has increased in the hot rink and the Soviets seem to be gelling after their nervous start, a bad sign for Canada.

One of the key issues Canada would have for this game was bench management, especially for the 5 defensemen dressed. As the agreement was for 19 players dressed per game, both teams were left to figure out a strategy that allowed for the odd number of 17 skaters and 2 goalies dressed per game. That left a decision, do you dress four complete lines and five defence or do you dress an odd number of forwards and the standard six defenseman or three pairs? For this game, Canada decided to dress five defensemen. The logic was that with four complete lines the pressure would be in the Soviet end and Canada would be able to manage with only five on defence. That might have been the right decision if a few things were different. If Canada was in better condition. If it wasn't a very hot day and the resulting steamy sticky Montreal Forum. If the Soviets weren't such great skaters, and having played a two man fore-check this game, they were constantly putting pressure on Canada's tired, hot, five defensemen. **One more issue was the new stylish Team Canada jerseys which were tightly woven, allowing for poor air flow**. These jerseys were restricting in the sleeves and poorly fitting. That had to have added to the exhaustion Team Canada would face as this game continued.

A valuable lesson Canadian defenseman should have learned from this game was **not to over-commit, drop down and block shots**. The Soviets simply held up on shooting and walked around the prone Canadian player(s) or made a pass putting them out of position. This standard NHL play where players shot more often was poorly adapted to the Soviet game. Guy Lapointe makes this mistake, and the result was a historic goal; the Soviets first goal on the "legendary" Canadian professionals.

Goal 3: Zimin Canada 2 Soviets 1

Guy Lapointe was the fifth defenseman selected to play the opening game. He was thought of as an offensive defenseman for the powerful Montreal Canadians but for some odd reason he wasn't put out for the early power plays nor seen any ice time to this point as Sinden rolled two sets of defencemen, Brad Park, and Gary Bergman and then Rod Seiling and Don Awrey. As a result, a pumped up anxious Lapointe comes out and is full of pent-up energy, running all over in Canada's end. The puck comes to Paladiev at the Soviet point and Lapointe rushes to the Soviet player, completely out of position now, and drops down to block a shot. Paladiev doesn't bite moving the puck goes from one side of the ice to the other. Canada now appears to be in pure panic mode, all positioning lost. The puck comes back to Paladiev on the right boards near the hash marks and again Lapointe inexplicably attacks the Soviet defender and attempts a body check, but the puck has already moved to the corner to an open Yakushev. This is a player that should not have been open if Lapointe had been playing more positional. Jean Ratelle attempts to cover up for Lapointe by going towards Yakushev, but before Ratelle can get close the Big Yak makes a great cross crease "back door" pass to a wide open Evgeny Zimin who had snuck behind Rod Seiling. In fairness to Seiling, he was already tying up Shadrin near Dryden's left post and would not have been able to see Zimin sneak in. Dryden moves quickly but Zimin was faster and roofs it upstairs.

In review, if Lapointe had been in better positioning for a left defenseman, he would have certainly been able to prevent Yakushev's superb pass, but all credit to the Soviets who as Canada would learn, will take advantage quickly and ruthlessly of any Canadian positional error. The reality is, the Soviets looked for that pass, and often snuck a trailing player to the far post. This sneaky move not only took the defenseman out of the play as his back would be turned to the player sneaking in, but often fool the goalie. The goalie would be looking at the puck carrier and traditionally standing at the opposite post, closest to the puck carrier but a difficult distance from the trailing player. The Canadian players would have to learn to adapt to this play as the series continued, especially on the deadly Soviet power play.

Yevgeni (Evgeny) Zimin was a solid Soviet winger standing only 5'8 and weighing a very solid 185 pounds. He was a young star in the Soviet Elite league in the mid-60's playing for Spartak Moscova (Moscow Spartak). This team was coached by Bobrov who of course was also the head coach for the Soviet National Team for this series. Zimin himself scored 34 goals in only 41 games at 19 years old in 1966-67 and another 32 in 43 games the next season. This landed him a spot on the gold medal winning 1968 Soviet squad. He also played in the 1968-69 World Championships but only scored 1 goal in 10 games.

Zimin's game seemed to decline as he got into his 20's, and in 71-72 only had 12 goals, dressing in only one Olympic game in 1972. However, with Bobrov being named the head coach, he included his former young star on the roster and played him in games 1 and 2 on a very effective line with Shadrin and Yakushev.

What happened after Game 2 with Zimin has always been a mystery. The Soviets claimed he was injured, but in a 2002 article by Dave Shoalts in the Globe and Mail another possible reason was explained. Zimin was a high risk for defection. This theory is explained in Shoalts article by Gary Smith who was the Canadian Government Liaison officer with the Soviet team in 1972,

"People focused on Kharlamov, but Zimin matched him. Head Coach Bobrov said he was injured but I never saw any evidence he was hurt. I always found it a bit strange because of all the players and I ate and swam with them, I thought he was the guy who was the most interested in the capitalist world. It's hard for me to document but I always thought Zimin did not play because they thought he was a risk." When Shoalts reached out to Zimin about the different theory regarding his not playing after game 2, Zimin hesitated and then avoided the reporter's calls afterwards. It would be interesting that the Soviets would bench a player who was so effective in the first two games, but this was the height of the cold war and a possible defection of an athlete must have been seen politically in the USSR as a danger to their reputation internationally." Dave Shoalts Toronto Globe and Mail 2002

Zimin would go on to have a long career in hockey,

coaching Spartak, and the Soviet Under 18 team in the 1980's. He later became a scout for the Philadelphia Flyers and was a TV commentator in Russia. Zimin understood the significance of that first goal against the Canadian professionals if not the exact details.

"Before the match in Montreal, we were very worried. Canadians took advantage of this and took the lead in the first minutes. Surprisingly this calmed us down and we began to show our hockey. In one of our attacks, Shadrin won the fight in the corner against the Canadian defender, made the transfer to Yakushev. I was open and received a pass that was amazing in its accuracy and scored almost into an empty net."

Another curious aspect of the Zimin disappearance is that if he was a flight risk, why not play him on the return to Moscow? Eugeny played in the first two games in Canada. The reality was probably not as exciting as potential international espionage. Zimin did not return to his Moscow Spartak club team until December 3, 1972, solidifying the injury claim.

Zimin died suddenly of a heart attack in December 2018, aged 71. The KHL had a moment of silence to honour him; even Vladmir Putin reached out to Zimin's son honouring his father's career. As Foster Hewitt said after the opening Soviet goal,

"This Zimin is a top notcher!"

Canada continues with the Berenson line who look lifeless, barely skating, missing passes. The Soviets continue to pressure the Canadians, as their weaving fore-checking energy seems to be confusing Canada. The crowd starts to murmur in discontent. A bad pass by Gusev is intercepted by Mickey Redmond, who gets subsequently tripped by Boris Mikhailov. Canada will get another power play try.

On the power-play, Phil Esposito's defence experiment seems over as he is back at centre, Frank M and Cournoyer come out, with Seiling and another surprise in forward Red Berenson on left defence. The power play looks better with Espo getting a goalmouth chance and then the Big M having a clear shot which he fires wide. Espo also makes a nice backhand pass to Henderson who breaks behind the defence, but Tretiak anticipates the play and makes an excellent save. The Soviets are again skating and pressuring the Canadian power play and they really can't get set up at all in the Soviet end.

Brad Park was a very confident player. He had the high skill level to make quick dekes as he carries the puck, getting past forechecking with his slick hands. He uses those skills here as he makes a nice individual rush up ice, just as Mikhailov 's penalty ends. Park enters the Soviet zone at the blueline where he draws a tripping penalty from Ragulin. Canada will remain on the power play. A quick TV scan of the crowd shows many people fanning themselves in the stifling heat of the Forum. The Canadian team would start to feel heat of their own, as this next power play turns into disaster.

Goal 4: Vladimir Petrov Canada 2 Soviets 2

The New York Rangers GAG line starts the power play with Park and Seiling on the points. The Soviets counter with Petrov and Mikhailov up front and Viktor Kuzkin with Alexander Gusev on the back end. The faceoff is in the Soviet end to the right of Tretiak. While Jean Ratelle would win 70% of his face-offs in this first game of the series, this would be one he loses to Petrov with a disastrous result.

This second Soviet goal is a combination of poor Canadian defensive positional play countered by Soviet speed, skill, and opportunism. After the draw, Ratelle turns away, doesn't tie up his man which allowed Petrov to rocket up the ice unencumbered. The puck goes to Rod Gilbert who loses it to Boris Mikhailov as Gilbert just turns away rather than pursuing. Brad Park, having backed up, now chases Boris but he was a step behind as he was caught flat footed. Park does a diving sweep check that takes him out of the play at mid-centre ice as the puck goes to the trailing Petrov. Petrov headmans it to Mikhailov who is now streaking down the left side and only Rod Seiling is back for Canada. Seiling is able to keep Boris from making a pass by skating hard and diving on the play, but the shot on Dryden handcuffs the big goalie who surprisingly doesn't seem ready. The rebound comes directly out to Petrov who slams it underneath the flopping Dryden. Rebound control for Dryden was a big issue against the Soviets in this game. If he had been able to clear a shot into the corner or if a Canadian player had reacted quicker to the breakout, Petrov would not have been open, but full kudos to the Soviets who broke out with such speed Canada always seemed to be a step behind.

The Soviets would continue to show throughout this series and their history that they were very dangerous when killing penalties. Why? While they were in excellent shape, skating constantly, putting pressure on the team with the power play, it might also be a result of differing rules between international hockey "amateurs" and the North American professional game.

Into the 1960's international rules required players assessed with a minor penalty to serve the full two minutes in all circumstances, while a professional player charged with a minor penalty could return to the game as soon as the other team scored a goal on the power play. The NHL adopted this rule because the 1950's dominant Montreal Canadiens team were scoring so many power play goals when given the full two minutes, that just one or two power plays per game could enable them to build an insurmountable lead. In addition, amateur hockey did not change the "icing" rule for a team short-handed because of a penalty, while professional hockey permitted short-handed teams to ice the puck.

These two rule differences made penalties significantly less punitive in professional hockey than in Soviet or European hockey. The Soviets countered that by having an aggressive mentality shorthanded. Rather than just use a stationary box format to keep the puck on the outside, they would use constant movement to disrupt the attacking teams play counter attacking when given the opportunity. It was a mindset and style Canada would struggle to adapt to throughout the series, and certainly one of the reasons Team Canada's power plays were not very effective.

Despite the shorthanded goal against, Ratelle's line stays on the power play and applies a bit of pressure. The Esposito line replaces them soon after, with Gary Bergman and Red Berenson on the points. Frank Mahovlich gets a great chance, taking a powerful slap shot with which Tretiak stops without any issues. The previous theory that Tretiak would be weak and overwhelmed by the powerful Canadian slap shots seemed to be dying a slow death with every save he made. Cournoyer makes a wonderful pass to Esposito who has a clear shot in the slot, but again Tretiak stonewalls him, and the Soviets clear the puck down the ice. Soviets get one final shorthanded dangerous two on one break using the long break out pass, but Ragulin takes a harmless shot into Dryden's pads. Gary Bergman again shows some offensive wheels with a rushing foray into the Soviet zone just before the siren goes for the end of the first period.

Game 1. First Period Analysis

The first period of this game was a series of contradictions. The Soviets came out nervous and tentative, perhaps influenced by the years of hearing how the professionals were unbeatable. Those nerves showed for the first 10 minutes of the period. On the other side, Canadian players had been hearing about how they were going to win all 8 games. The early goals only reinforced that belief, as they encountered a nervous soviet team seemingly overwhelmed by the moment.

There was also the case of national pride. Very few of these players had played any sort of international hockey before. In fact, on the starting line-up only Ron Ellis, Paul Henderson, and Bobby Clarke in single one-off games as juniors and Rod Seiling, Guy Lapointe and Ken Dryden on the Canadian National Team had played against a Soviet team. For the rest of the starting line-up, it was a chance to represent their country. This was a new concept to most of these pros, and many were filled with excited pride at the chance. It seems that national pride won out over pregame over-confidence and in period one Canada came out flying. The first two Canadian goals were excellent plays with great passing and teamwork. However, it became apparent by midway through the period that the Soviet players were not only able to compete with the Canadians, but they could also take the game to them. Canada had a strong period, with several point-blank chances on Tretiak, and with **a lesser goalie the score might have been 4 or 5-2**. However, the Soviets seemed to gain confidence from their stellar twenty-year-old net minder and by the midpoint of the period were pressing the Canadians in their own end for longer and longer periods of time. The Soviet fitness level and strength shocked the Canadians.

"I remember walking into the dressing room after the first period and talking to Yvan Cournoyer," Marcel Dionne said in The Days Canada Stood Still. "He just looked at me and said, 'You can't believe their strength and conditioning."

Combining this pressure with the poor defensive ice time management by Sinden/Ferguson, it became a slowly losing test of fitness and will for Canada. The "not yet in mid-season shape" Canadian team must have been quite happy for the first period intermission,

"I didn't play the first game, and I remember going into the dressing room after the first period seeing the defensemen. They'd had it. Everything was moving so much faster than we'd thought. It was conditioning and there was nothing we could do about it. And the Russians, of course, just kept coming." Bill White

Notable players in period one for the Soviets: Yakushev, Kharlamov, Maltsev and Mikhailov, their four top forwards all showed glimpses of their significant speed and skill. Tretiak was simply excellent. For Canada, Phil Esposito was skating well and was dangerous every shift. Frank Mahovlich had several excellent chances, playing with energy and passion. Gary Bergman was a rock on defence with his skilled partner Brad Park making some nice rushes and organizing the power plays. Bobby Clarke was Canada's energy player, hustling everywhere, introducing the Soviets to unique brand of hockey.

CHAPTER 9: GAME 1. PERIOD 2: HELLO WORLD, I'M VALERI KHARLAMOV

For the start of period two, the ice is starting to get foggy as the building heats up internally. Canada starts the Esposito, Mahovlich and Cournoyer line with Bergman and Park while the Soviets counter with Petrov, Blinov, Mikhailov and Kuzkin. The play is scrambly to start, with neither team making any real offensive forays. Yvan Cournoyer makes a rush through the neutral zone, **stick handles at the Soviet blue line and loses the puck**. Canada keeps repeating the same mistake, they are stickhandling in the neutral zone and losing the puck. However, the next shift Clarke does the opposite, dumps the puck into the corner, where a streaking Paul Henderson forechecks Lyapkin forcing a turnover. Clarke retrieves the puck and creates a good chance by driving towards Tretiak. Clarke then digs for the puck behind the net with Paladiev, who takes offense to Clarkes stickwork in Paladiev's stomach. On the same shift Henderson dumps it in the right Soviet corner to a streaking Ellis who fires a low quick snapshot that completely handcuffs Tretiak. It doesn't appear to go in, but in today's game that would probably be cause for a video review.

The Ranger line of Hadfield, Gilbert and Ratelle come out with Awrey and Seiling. The first half of this shift is scrambled play by Canada who seem out of sorts, lacking in energy. Awrey loses the puck trying to stickhandle out of the Canadian zone and then Seiling completely misses an easy pass to Gilbert, instead firing it 10 feet in front of him. The Ranger line seems lifeless. On one play Gilbert gets the puck at mid-ice and is quickly and easily caught by Kharlamov who makes a clever between his legs pass to Maltsev. The Soviets are gaining confidence and disaster is about to strike for Team Canada.

Goal 5: Kharlamov Soviets 3 Canada 2

If Zimin's first goal of the game for the Soviets was historic, **this goal was the one that woke up the Canadian hockey world**. Fans, historians, and players still recount this goal as the first sign the Soviets were not only ultra-skilled and cohesive as a team, but they also possessed dynamic individual stars. The goal happens on a very poor shift by the 5 Canadian players on the ice. As the puck goes into Canada's zone Don Awrey attempts to skate and stickhandle it out; over stick handling was a major issue for Canada in this game instead of head manning the puck or simply getting it out of Canada's end. He ends up getting checked by Kharlamov who tries to send a pass to the right point.

Rod Gilbert intercepts Kharlamov's pass, and **lazily** starts to skate to centre ice with the puck. Kharlamov accelerates, catches Gilbert easily, strips him of the puck and makes a slick between his legs pass to Maltsev. Canada is able to get the puck back and Ratelle carries the puck deep into the Soviet zone, but his weak backhanded effort is deflected behind the Soviet net by Maltsev. As Maltsev goes for the puck, in the far corner, both Gilbert and Hadfield him attempt to body check Maltsev. **Maltsev jumps out of the way, keeps his balance, and flies up the ice head manning it to Kharlamov, trapping the two New York Rangers' forwards deep.**

Why was Maltsev able to get out of the way of

the body check? The answer goes back to the father of Soviet hockey, Anatoli Tarasov, his teaching and preparing the Soviets to face and defeat the best Canadians. In 1957 Tarasov was interviewed at a Toronto Maple Leaf's versus Chicago Black Hawks game regarding Canadian body checking. His response?

"We are not learning how to do it. We are learning how to avoid it." Anatoli Tarasov

While the Soviets could hit and would hit, when necessary, their game was founded and perfected on **quick puck movements and counter strikes**. Rather than play the Canadians at their own game, they worked on a system to use their opponent's aggression against them. While that included the Soviet players delivering body contact when required, the actual Soviet goal was to use the opponent's physical play against them by being able to anticipate and shrug off body contact, **leaving the opposing player out of position**. The training of the Soviet players to have superior fitness and core strength allowed for superior balance and agility as demonstrated by Maltsev on this play. Their team play emphasized fast, accurate passing which allowed them to create quick strike scenarios. Like a boxing counterpuncher, the Soviet player would either take the hit and counterpunch by moving the puck very quickly, leaving their opponent out of position, or avoid the hit as Maltsev does and trapping the Ranger forwards deep.

When Kharlamov received Maltsev's pass, it should be noted that **he had two full zones to carry the puck uncontested.** This allowed the extremely fast Valeri Kharlamov to get to what was probably a very uncomfortable speed for the rapidly retreating Awrey and Seiling. In fact, they were already backing up into their own zone as Valeri was not yet at his opponent's blue line. This left **a large gap** between them that allowed for Kharlamov to blow by Awrey on the outside (Awrey's left). As Kharlamov gets closer, Awrey tries a poke check that fails as Kharlamov stickhandles the puck away from Awrey's stick without any drop in speed, a significant skill for anyone.

Awrey is in big trouble. Because of that gap, and with Kharlamov's speed, by the time the Canadian turned, Kharlamov was already a step past him. The gap between them **needed to have been closed at the blue line** as Kharlamov could have been angled into the boards with Seiling acting as a plan B for any Soviet players attempting to break to the net in anticipation of a Kharlamov pass.

Kharlamov goes quite wide on Awrey, just outside the Canadian faceoff circle, as Awrey does a last-ditch diving attempt for the puck, similar to Park's diving attempt on the Petrov shorthanded goal. Kharlamov was a fantastic skater and his edging as he turns towards the Canadian goal allows him to not only get a better angle to shoot on Dryden, but to move the puck to his forehand for the shot. Kharlamov is able to move to his forehand, but he was still at a sharp angle when he shot. **Dryden plays the shot very poorly** and it goes between his pads into the net. This was not an angle that any player should have been able to score from unless they were able to cut across the crease or shoot to the far post quickly and accurately. Kharlamov does neither of these things, and Dryden simply allows a shot from a bad angle through his pads.

This goal was a combination of a fantastic individual talent making a world class, legendary rush, and a full ice Canadian breakdown. While the two Canadian forwards Gilbert and Hadfield were trapped deep from the clever Maltsev manoeuvre, Ratelle is seen back checking through centre ice, but despite being a very strong skater, Ratelle never catches up to the play. **Awrey has poor timing on the rush and misplays the one on one, but the real issue on this goal was Ken Dryden**. A world class goalie simply does not let in a shot from a bad angle through his pads. Unfortunately for Canada, this would not be the end of Dryden's mishaps this game or for the Series. In a 2007 interview with Jay Moran, Awrey would reflect on both his style and the Kharlamov goal, putting the blame on Dryden, with maybe a bit of rose-coloured glasses.

Jay Moran: Serge Savard said that you liked to block shots but that wasn't the right style for the defensemen against the Russians. What was he looking for in a defenseman in that series, more offense?

Don Awrey: "Well, probably just that. I guess, they were very heady hockey players, very, you know, when they had the puck, their head was up. That was just the style that they played. And I guess with a shot-blocking defenseman I was waiting for them to put their head down and then I just, I would know that, I would go down and block the shot. But if you watch - and I've watched the games many times - the two games that I played, which was game one and four, was not the result of me going down and trying to block any shots. And even the one goal that they said that, I don't know who it was, walked around the outside of me and ended up scoring, I thought it was a bad, bad goal and he really didn't beat me to the outside. He didn't cut in and go to the net, but I thought it was a bad goal on Dryden."
1972summitseries.com

This goal more than any other introduced Canada to the talent that was Valeri Kharlamov and shocked the North American hockey world with the speed and individual skill Kharlamov showed. As Harry Sinden would comment on the goal,

"All of us were impressed, but none of us wanted to let on. I've seldom seen anyone come down on two NHL defensemen and beat them to the outside, go around them and then in on the net. It just isn't done." Richard Bendall 1972 The Summit Series

In 1972, North America fans and media really had no idea that the Soviet Union, and Europe overall, had such talented players. The feeling had always been that the best players were only in Canada, and the Europeans were amateurs (sham-ateurs) who were not NHL "level". This was more than Canadian hockey arrogance, there was some basis for these feelings at the time. The European teams had only played Senior A teams from Canada such as the Whitby Dunlops and Trail Smoke-eaters and until 1961 they often had trouble defeating the Senior Teams consistently. **The viewpoint was: If they can't defeat a group of Senior A players who worked at 9-5 jobs back in Canada, how could they compete with the NHL?**

By the early 1960's, the European hockey powers had improved past the Senior A level. The Soviets kept improving rapidly year over and from 1962-1972 where they won 9 straight World Championships. This success had little impact on the Canadian viewpoint. Even with the noted improvement and European teams regularly playing in Canada against the National Team and enhanced or all-star Junior teams, the Canadian hockey public refused to view the European game as anywhere near the level of the NHL. Why? In the Canadian view the Europeans were only beating the Canadian National Team or junior teams and besides a brief appearance by NHL star Carl Brewer, the Canadian National Team was full of players that the Canadian hockey establishment barely even viewed as NHL prospects.

As Brad Park would relay before the series,

"We've seen some of the guys come off the Canadian National Team or the US Olympic team and we've seen some European players come over. They haven't held off, they haven't had long careers. And we got the best of the best. So we probably, we definitely are not taking them as seriously as we should" Robert MacAskill's 72 Series 1997 Manuscripts

Who were the Europeans who had come over and in Park's mind not had long careers? Was that a fair analysis? The Boston Bruins of the late 1950's certainly had interest in Europe's best. According to European Hockey expert Patrick Houda, the Bruins had been interested in Czech stars

Jaroslav Drobny and **Vladmir Zabrodsky** as far back as 1949, however nothing amounted of the interest.

The Bruins' General Manager Lynn Patrick attended the 1958 World Championships and scouted several players. He was particularly interested in Soviet centre man **Veniamin Alexandrov** and believed there was a chance he could attend training camp in 1958. However, the year before that Patrick had invited one of Europe's dominant players **Sven Tumba** or **Tumba Johannson** as he was often known to the 1957 Boston Training Camp.

Tumba was a fantastic athlete, 6'3, weighing 210 pounds, a Swedish National Team member as well as the Swedish national soccer team and a world class golfer by the mid-1960's. He didn't start to play golf until he was 31 yet was voted Sweden's most influential golfer of the century, beating out Annike Sorenstam. Starting in 1951, Tumba played hockey for the Djurgarden club and won eight Swedish championships and three goal-scoring titles. He represented Sweden at fourteen World Championships and four Winter Olympics. He was honoured as the best forward at the 1957 and 1962 World Championships and was the top goal-scorer at the 1964 Winter Olympics. In 1999 he was voted the "best Swedish player of all time". He was the major sporting figure in Sweden in the 1950's.

How did Tumba do at the training camp? He played one exhibition game and scored a goal in a 2-2 tie against the New York Rangers. He was sent to the Quebec Aces farm club where he played 5 games with limited ice time and had 4 assists. The Bruins were impressed enough to offer Tumba a lucrative contract. However, Tumba was not getting along with the Bruins players after a practical joke on them (switching dentures around as he tried to fit in) and decided he wanted to remain an "amateur" so he could participate in the Olympics. He went back to Sweden to finish his outstanding career without signing a contract.

Was Tumba NHL level? Looking back at videos he

certainly looks like a powerful skater with an excellent shot and excellent lateral movement for such a big man. His reputation was that of a bit of an individualist, but the Bruins were confident he would have become a solid NHL player, perhaps even a star. In videos, he certainly seems to compare favourably to a player like Frank Mahovlich.

The second significant player to come to North America from Europe was **Ulf Sterner** in 1964-65. Sterner was not the dominant star that Tumba Johannson was, but he was still a good player in Europe. It was Sterner's debut for the New York Rangers in 1965 that made him the first European trained player to play in the NHL. Sterner played for Sweden in the 1960 Olympics at 18, won a gold medal at the 1962 World Championships, followed by a silver medal in 1963, the same year he was named Sweden's Player of the Year. The Rangers became interested in the 6'2", 187-pound centre in 1963 and invited him to training camp. Sterner came to camp and signed a five-game try-out contract but declined to play that season to preserve his amateur status for the 1964 Olympics where he led all scorers with 6 goals and 5 assists as Sweden earned a silver medal.

Sterner reported to the Rangers training camp in 1964 and was assigned to St. Paul of the CHL to become acclimatized to the North American game. Ulf did very well in St. Paul, scoring 12 goals and adding 9 assists in 16 games before being promoted first to Baltimore of the AHL and then to the Rangers. He made his NHL debut in a 5-3 win over the Boston Bruins. Sterner played well and had a goal disallowed due to an offside call. But as Borje Salming and other European trailblazers would learn, **the NHL was not a welcoming place for foreign players.** Sterner became the target of physical and verbal abuse from opposing players. This was a common feature as the NHL integrated with European players in the 1970's and 1980's; instead of matching skill, they would use intimidation.

After four games Sterner was sent back to Baltimore

where he recorded 18 goals and 26 assists in 52 games and helped the Clippers make the AHL playoffs. He returned to Sweden after the season, where he continued to star in international competition as well as Swedish leagues until his retirement following the 1977-78 season.

Whether Sterner had the talent to consistently play in the NHL was never proven. He was a trailblazer, though, and by watching videos of his game, it was clear that he had a high skill level and decent speed for a big man. The problem was in Europe until 1969 offensive zone checking was prohibited. **The physicality of the game and the players targeting him for the crime of being Swedish was foreign to him**. He struggled to adapt to the North American style game. In 1972, he would however play in the Exhibition games against Team Canada in Sweden and was ironically involved in two nasty, very physical incidents in the second game.

Former WHA and NHL Swedish star Ulf Nilsson had this to say about Sterner:

"Sterner was one of the best forwards that ever came out of Sweden. I talked to Fred Shero about him and he said that Ulf was one of the most talented players that he had ever seen. He was sort of unusual because he was a big guy for those days and pretty good on his skates for a player of that size. In those days the big guys didn't really move that fast. It must have been really hard to be on your own in a new country with a new style of play", Nilsson said when asked why he thought Sterner didn't try return to North America as a player. *"I think it was the loneliness, I think it was easier for Anders (Hedberg) and me coming to Winnipeg as teammates." Inside Hockey.Com George Grimm 2012.*

Looking back at these two trailblazers, Park's comment makes sense. Two of the best players in Europe didn't last in the NHL. While there were understandable circumstances in both cases, neither Tumba Johannson nor Ulf Sterner did anything to change the perception that

Europe's hockey was not the same level as North American, it didn't seem to matter that the North American hockey fans, scouts, coaches and even players could see the level of the European players when they came to North America for exhibition games, the perception was never changed.

Until Kharlamov's famous goal on that hot night in Montreal.

Despite the hushed, shocked Montreal crowd, Canada comes back hard after the goal. Peter Mahovlich has a solid chance with a long slapper from the wing that Tretiak seems to have trouble corralling as Redmond crashes the crease. It should be noted, however, that this shot takes place from the far-left hash marks as the Soviet veteran defenseman Kuzkin plays him beautifully on the one on one, angling the Canadian to the boards. A few minutes later, Guy Lapointe makes a nice rush, going wide and then cutting in on Tretiak but his clever deke misses the net. As the Soviets counterattack, Zimin looks like he loses an edge and gets knocked easily off the puck. To make matters worse for Zimin he makes a horrible drop pass that results in a 3 on 1 with Frank Mahovlich, Esposito and Cournoyer as the trailer. Inexplicably, **Mahovlich doesn't pass to the wide-open Esposito.** Frank decides to shoot the puck himself, taking a big slap shot from the off wing which goes right into Tretiak's pads. Frank had the top goal scorer in the league on a rush and decided to take a shot himself at Tretiak's pads. Whether this was because of Sinden's pre-game advice to take a lot of shots at the assumed weak Soviet goaltending or a case of an individualistic player not using his line mates, it was a wasted opportunity for Canada.

As mentioned earlier, on Bobby Clarke's first shift in the game Alexander Maltsev gave him a cross check to the face on an innocent play in the Soviet end. Now, halfway through the game, Clarke chases Maltsev from behind the Soviet goal to just before the Soviet blue line. **He hooks Maltsev, then slew foots his feet out from under him,** getting a tripping penalty. Clarke then gives him **a whack with his stick right over Maltsev's red Jofa helmet**. Foster Hewitt, perhaps unaware this was Bobby Clarke he was referring to, calls the infraction "accidental". This certainly was not accidental. Whether it was in retribution to the cross check in the first period or not, it was a dangerous, unnecessary play that easily could have cost Canada a five-minute infraction. The chop on his head could have also severely injured Alexander Maltsev as the Jofa helmet was very poor protection. Kharlamov comes over to Clarke and pushes him after the play angrily. **The Clarke/Kharlamov on ice feud was just beginning.**

The Soviet power play is surprisingly sloppy. Circling repetitively in their own zone, Kharlamov gives the puck up to Peter Mahovlich in the high slot for a shorthanded opportunity. Ron Ellis is everywhere during the penalty kill, taking a page from the Soviet shorthanded playbook and pressuring the Soviets. Boris Mikhailov gets the only real chance of the power play, off a pass by defenseman Vladimir Luchenko who made a rare rush by a Soviet defender. Phil Esposito takes a shift killing the penalty, something he rarely did in the NHL. His **surprising adeptness at the role** would lead to his being increasingly called upon, as the Series progressed, to help stifle the vaunted Soviet powerplay.

Canada, perhaps with a bit of a lift after the penalty kill, shows some life. Esposito gets it out of the Canadian zone with a nice pass to Frank Mahovlich. The Big M makes a slow rush into the Soviet end, stops, spins, and fires a beautiful pass across to Rod Gilbert, but Gilbert, perhaps through fatigue or rust, completely fans on the pass. The New York Rangers line has a couple of good opportunities with Hadfield getting stoned by Tretiak on a nice cross crease pass by Gilbert and then Gilbert and Ratelle getting a 2 on 1 break. Gilbert continues the Canadian habit of shooting first instead of passing and like the Big M before him, blasts a slap shot ineffectively at Tretiak's pads.

106

On the ensuing faceoff, Ratelle wins the draw clearly, pulling it back to Brad Park on the point. Park decides to stickhandle at the Soviet blueline, a dangerous play for a defenceman. Park makes a good first move fooling Yakushev but then tries again and loses the puck to Shadrin, who breaks down the ice on a potential two on one with Zimin. Lucky for Park, Gary Bergman read the play and used his speed to angle Shadrin off the puck. Hadfield seemed to get hurt on this shift and can be seen holding his hand gingerly as he skates out of the Canadian end. Foster Hewitt notes this and mentions Hadfield headed to the dressing room.

The game picks up pace as Clarke makes a bad pass to a streaking Yakushev who shows good speed for a big man, shooting as Seiling backs up almost to Dryden's crease. Dryden makes a good stop on the screened shot. An interesting moment happens soon after where Lapointe and Kharlamov go for the puck along the boards in the Canadian end. Kharlamov, who was a small player, shows the Soviet strength and balance by **knocking the much bigger Lapointe off his feet.** Clarke can be seen running into Kharlamov aggressively perhaps attempting to avenge his fallen teammate. This led to the strange half-truth commentary by Conacher that said,

> "...there are two things that Canada do the best. They skate better and shoot better. They should stick to that, because if they try to outmuscle them, the Soviets are too strong on their skates and they will take advantage of it because of that superb conditioning."

Halfway through game one, Canada appears to skate slower, shoot too often and yes not anywhere near as fit as the Soviets. Strange comment indeed.

After the next faceoff in the Canadian zone, Mickey Redmond shows some significant speed as he bursts up the ice unleashing a high hard shot that just misses the net. It's puzzling in retrospect that seeing Redmond's blazing speed, and as the series continued, a lack of offensive production from Team Canada's right side that he was only dressed for one game in the series.

Peterborough's Mickey Redmond was a junior star with the Peterborough playing on a legendary Junior line with 1974 WHA Summit Series star Andre Lacroix. Redmond made the powerful Montreal Canadians in the 1967-68 season, winning the cup in that season as well as winning again the following season with the Canadians. With two Stanley Cup rings under his belt, Redmond began playing more confidently. He broke out in the 1969-70 season with 27 goals and 27 assists, establishing himself as one of the Canadians' brightest young players. Redmond was however weak in the defensive aspect of the game and Canadians management decided to make changes midway through the 1970-71 season. Despite his lack of success and his reputation for not being very reliable in his own zone, he remained a highly sought-after prospect by other NHL teams when it came to trade discussion. After many rumours, Redmond was dealt in one of the biggest deals in hockey history - Redmond went to Detroit along with Guy Charron and Bill Collins in exchange for Team Canada teammate Frank Mahovlich.

"The trade was a shock because the Canadians told me I was in their plans for years

to come. It was a disappointment because I always wanted to play for them. But it   worked out. Detroit gave me the playing time I needed to develop. They needed me, while the Canadians did not. Being needed brings out the best in you," said Redmond.

Redmond's first full season with the Wings was a success. He pocketed 42 goals and 71 points playing on a line with the legendary Red Wing centre Alex Delvecchio. This led to his invitation to Team Canada at age 24. His 42 goals from the right side would be the third most on the team at right wing and with the first three spots seemingly locked up by Cournoyer, Rod Gilbert and Ron Ellis, the fourth spot seemed to be Redmond's to win or lose. Despite that, Mickey only played in game one in the Series, although he did play in Czechoslovakia. He returned to the NHL where he had two 50 goal seasons for the Red Wings in 1972-73 and 1973-74. Unfortunately, his All-Star career took a turn for the worse. In the 1974-75 season Redmond was limited to just 29 games due to a ruptured disc in his back. He was plagued by chronic back pain throughout the 1975-76 season, scoring 28 points in 37 games. After three years of stardom, his career was over at 28. Mickey went on to have a successful broadcasting career in hockey, doing colour commentary for Hockey Night in Canada and for the Red Wings for 30 years.

Goal 6: Kharlamov Soviets 4 Canada 2

One of the many preconceptions the Canadian hockey establishment had about Soviet hockey before the series was that **they were not great shooters**. Some of that was style based. As far back as the mid-1950's, Canadian observers would scoff at the Soviet style focusing on an assumption that they overpass. When Bob Davidson and John McLellan came back from their pre-tournament scouting trip to the Soviet Union, they remarked on their superior passing but at the same time showing a bit of a surprise at the improved Soviet shooting ability,

> *"Their passing is excellent. The Russians players seem to know exactly where their mates are at all times and get the puck to them. No team can afford to allow a Russian to be lose in their zone because they are deadly with passes to the open man. They use the slot area in front of the net well too. The Russian players have improved their shooting. Many of them are using the Slap Shot now a great deal". John McLellan Frank Orr Toronto Star August 24/72*

Perhaps defenseman Rod Seiling and goalie Ken Dryden had failed to read this report or perhaps after Kharlamov's first goal, the expectation was that the slick

Soviet player would attempt to beat Seiling on the one-on-one play. Perhaps Dryden wasn't expecting a quick hard accurate shot from a Soviet player in flight, believing they were always a pass first team. Either way, if Valeri Kharlamov hadn't fully introduced himself on his first skilful goal against Canada, **the hockey world certainly was introduced after his second goal in the period.**

The play develops quickly off the neutral zone faceoff in the Canadian half of the ice. Berenson loses the draw to Maltsev and both he and Redmond fail to tie up their checks off the draw. Testament to Redmond's one way game. Maltsev quickly gets the puck over to Kharlamov who bursts away from Redmond. Kharlamov's acceleration is outstanding as he separates himself from the slow reacting Redmond. Suddenly, Kharlamov is crossing over the red line as Seiling backs up over the blue line. In his apparent panic, Seiling pivots, but like his defence partner Awrey a few minutes earlier, Seiling makes a fatal error. He turns to his left which is **away** from the streaking Kharlamov. With a solid space between himself and Seiling, Kharlamov gets to the top of the faceoff circle where he unleashes a shortened slap shot (half snap half slap) that catches Dryden off guard. It's a similar style shot that Bobby Orr would use throughout his career, a shortened back swing slap shot that can be released quickly, often catching goalies unaware. It is possible that the shot was deflected, as Seiling did a last gasp reach for the puck, but even with slow motion video it's difficult to determine. In the TV telecast, Brian Conacher remarks after this goal,

"...that will nullify anyone who thinks the Soviets can't shoot. He catches Dryden back in the net. I don't think Dryden expected him to shoot that puck at that time."

Further analysis would determine that this shot went through Dryden's legs as Conacher continues,

"Dryden was expecting a high shot and it went down in between his legs."

Much like the Soviets' third goal in this game, this goal was a combination of Canadian defensive mistakes and Kharlamov's world class skill. As previously mentioned, the Canadian forwards are lax at the faceoff, and the resulting quick rush catches them flatfooted. **The defensive pair of Seiling and Awrey are almost too respectful of Kharlamov and back up quickly.** However, much like the first Kharlamov goal, the spacing between the Soviet forward and Seiling is a major issue as Kharlamov streaks to his left just over the blueline. Seiling makes a second mistake in pivoting away from Kharlamov, furthering the distance between them. Kharlamov seizes the open ice to fire a quick hard shot in full flight just over the faceoff circle. Not an easy task, but a testament to his high skill level.

Seiling's final mistake is attempting a last-minute poke check with may have slightly deflected the hard shot or may have slightly hidden the puck from Dryden at a crucial moment. Dryden himself plays the shot poorly and seems completely out of sync, awkward and surprised. If, as slow-motion shows, the puck went through Dryden's legs, it makes **Dryden's response to the shot a very poor one and much like the first goal, not the world class goaltending required against a team like the Soviet Union.**

Valeri Kharlamov may have been the most dangerous forward in the world in 1972. His game one effect can be summed up by noted Soviet hockey historian Arthur Chidlovski said Kharlamov made the Canadian defenders look like

> *"They were old-timers, minor-league wannabes or something. What he was doing to them was very intimidating. The Canadians were always looking at Kharlamov with their mouths open. But they just couldn't accept it," Chidlovski added. "He was just this skinny guy. But on the ice, a magician."*

The Montreal Forum crowd was completely subdued by the fourth Soviet goal, **stunned and in shock at the**

unexpected turn of events. The Canadian players seemed to be drained of energy and it shows with a few half-speed futile forays into the Soviet zone. The Petrov line on the other hand is flying, and Dryden is called on to make two great saves. The first one was on another cross-crease play to Blinov, Dryden flies across the net and stacks his pads to make the save. The second was on a nice drop pass from Blinov to Boris Mikhailov who fired a quick screened shot. It should be noted that on this second rush the puck goes from Kuzkin deep in the Soviet end to Petrov, back to Blinov, back over to the now streaking Petrov along the left wing, over the Canadian blue line, back to Blinov and finally dropping it to Mikhailov for the quick shot. **This sequence of quick, one touch passes take less than 7 seconds from the Soviet end to the shot, and the Canadian players fail to touch the puck even once.** This sequence of aligned, one touch passing had to be shocking to Canada, and completely foreign. It just wasn't done in the NHL. This one touch passing was a long-time strategy of Soviet hockey, and something Anatoli Tarasov was a huge proponent for. As a result, every player who played for Tarasov had been trained by the authoritarian coach to move the puck to the open man quickly with constant motion. Canadian hockey of course hadn't been paying attention. Even in 1957, on the first visit to Canada by a Soviet squad, Harold Cotton of the Boston Bruins had noted how well the Soviets broke from a standing start.

Why was this strategy such a key element of the Soviet offensive game? The goal was to catch their opponents flat footed and chasing the pass instead of the player or sometimes both. This would cause positional mistakes that the Soviet players would take quick advantage of. It would also tire their opponents out which of course would play right into the Soviet superb conditioning advantage.

As the second period was winding down, an exhausted Team Canada was learning first-hand the ruthless effectiveness of the Soviet game plan. The Soviet speed of execution whether it was passing or carrying the puck across the blueline, was **completely intimidating the Canadian defence.** They were being backed up and this blitz offense was often trapping the Canadian forwards behind the play.

Colour commentator Brian Conacher would sum this issue up in his bang on synopsis after the Soviet "one touch" passing display.

"They skate at you hard at the blue line. Team Canada is coming to the blue line, Esposito, Mahovlich, they are all waiting for the play on the blue line. The Soviets are skating down hard at the defencemen, they are pushing Team Canada's defence back into their end and it's leaving a grey area in the top of the slot, the top of the circles, and the Soviets are taking advantage of this.". He continued at the next break, "When a club does skate down at you hard, the defencemen have to back up a little faster, which gets them deeper into their end a lot quicker than normal."

With five minutes left in the second period, the Clarke/Henderson/Ellis line gets penned in their own end by the Shadrin line, and the crowd is heard murmuring their disapproval. Lapointe is still running around trying to hit players and Canada is really struggling with the pace the Soviets are playing at. At one time during this shift, Lapointe chases the puck to the Soviet defenseman Paladiev at the point and Henderson starts chasing the puck in the Canadian corner, a complete reversal of roles and responsibilities. This **horrible positional play by Canada** is highlighted when Paladiev has tons of free space and time to move in from the point and let a slap shot go that Dryden barely handles. Canada gets a quick breakout, but Ellis's pass to a streaking Clarke is too far ahead of him and Clarke makes a weak pass in return that is intercepted by Lyapkin. Yakushev picks up the puck in the Soviet slot area after the Clarke pass and circles quickly gaining speed. The **Soviets are breaking out uncontested now, setting up in the Canadian zone now with ease**. Lapointe continues his erratic play by taking a frustrated slashing penalty after a long, exhausting shift.

The Soviets start to get set up in Canada's end on the power play, but Park intercepts a Maltsev pass and slowly carries the puck up ice. **He stickhandles and loses the puck just before the Soviet blue line and is now caught up ice**. Canada will need to change this habit of stick handling in the neutral zone, rather than dumping it deep into the Soviet end, especially when shorthanded. Soviets recover and get set up in the Canadian zone a second time. The Soviets use a modern day set up on the power play with the wingers playing higher on the boards in order to feed the point man for the shot. The points are not spread out but positioned more towards the right or left posts so the shots can be deflected by the other winger who is positioned low by the far post. This set up and resulting play would cause Canada to give up two goals in game 4. Alexander Maltsev is flying during this power play, as the Canadian defence pairing of Seiling and Awrey back up, giving Maltsev easy access to the Canadian zone. In a momentary déjà vu moment, Maltsev goes wide on Seiling but fans on his attempted shot from the same spot Kharlamov scored his second goal from.

Canada is listless on the penalty kill and seems content to just have the Soviets move the puck around their stationary 4-man box. Frank Mahovlich makes a horrible clearing attempt that is intercepted by Petrov who takes a hard shot on goal. This same sequence of events would lead to a Soviet goal by Petrov in game 3.

The Soviets get sloppy on their passes as a pinching Gusev throws the puck blindly into the high slot area. Suddenly, with unexpected energy, Frank Mahovlich gets another 2 on 1 break with Phil Esposito. His speed is impressive, he flies up the ice leaving the back checking Petrov far behind, to no avail. **The terrible decision making of the Canadian forwards continues as the Big M decides again to just blast a big slap shot at Tretiak**. This one hits the side of the net. While Frank had scored 43 goals the season before, his line mate in this game, Phil Esposito had 66 goals and had set the NHL scoring record with 76 goals in the 1970-71 season. Why Frank would continue to not pass the puck to Espo on these rushes is puzzling and limits or even nullifies what should have been excellent scoring chances for Canada to get back into this game.

It should be noted that Guy Lapointe is seen fore-checking here deep behind the Soviet goal, seemingly playing the wing on this shift as he left the penalty box with Awrey and Seiling on the ice already. He rushes back, gets a good solid hit in on Boris Mikhailov and then Lapointe gets stuck in the Canadian end, seemingly lost or unsure where to play. He decides to stand in the slot area where defenseman Gary Bergman is already standing, further confusing an already beleaguered Canadian team.

Brad Park makes a nice pass to Esposito who easily walks around Gusev and cleverly tries to cut in and deke out Tretiak. The young goalie reads the play flops to make the save and Park just misses the rebound. Canada's best chance this period is foiled again by Tretiak.

The penalty successfully killed, Awrey tries a solo rush but loses the puck at the Soviet blue line, this time it wasn't a Soviet defender, it was the official who failed to get out of the way. The Soviets counterattack with the smooth skating Paladiev making a nice rush up the ice, passing to Shadrin who makes another quick one touch pass to the dangerous Zimin in the slot. Zimin fires in one motion and again Dryden has to make a good save. Despite the two weak goals let in by Dryden this period, he seems to have settled down and has made a couple of good saves keeping Canada within 2 goals. Hadfield is back on for Canada, seemingly ok from his previous injury and has a little skirmish with Shadrin in the Soviet corner.

Shadrin wins the ensuing faceoff against Ratelle and again Kharlamov takes off like a rocket down his wing with the puck. Since Canada was set up for a faceoff win back to

Gilbert for a quick shot, similar to the Henderson goal in period 1, Kharlamov had free ice to pick up speed. **He utterly blows by Brad Park** like he was skating past a Tuesday night men's league player. To emphasize Kharlamov's speed this game, the Rangers Rod Gilbert was an excellent skater and even he loses ground on the puck carrying Kharlamov as he tries to keep up on the backcheck. Fortunately for Canada, Gary Bergman makes a superb defensive play intercepting Kharlamov's pass to Vikulov in the high slot. Bergman, and later Bill White, would be one of Canada's defensive rocks in this series.

Gary Bergman, like his Soviet counterpart Alexander Ragulin, was a veteran defenceman in 1972. Despite winning a Memorial Cup with the Winnipeg Braves in 1959, it wouldn't be until 1964 that he would claim a full-time spot on the Detroit Red Wings blue line. He would keep that spot for the next eight seasons as the Red Wings would go from contenders, making the Stanley Cup Final in 1965-66, to last place by the 1970-71 season. He only played in one all-star game and the highest he ever finished in voting for the James Norris "Best Defenceman" was 6th in the 1967-68 season. That wasn't reflective of his skills or his value. He was an excellent skater, a very strong positional player and while not an overly big man at 5'11, he was strong and played with a bit of an edge, especially in front of his own net. A bit of a surprise choice for Team Canada, Bergman was paired with Brad Park by coach Harry Sinden, and they worked so well together that they were among only seven men on the 35-man roster who were used in all eight games.

"We hit it off really good for guys who didn't know each other very well," Park mentioned. "I was more of an offensive guy so we jelled very well together. "Right away I realized what a classy guy he was in how he handled himself on and off the ice, and what a great competitor he was. He had a lot of confidence in his ability and wasn't worried about how he was going to play. He just went out and

played. He was as solid a defenseman as has ever played the game." Brad Park

Harry Sinden added this about his selection of Bergman,

"I'm so happy when I look back on that series that we picked him. We thought he had the character, integrity and type of personality that would add to our team, and we were exactly right in our assessment. He was one of the biggest surprises in terms of contribution that we had. We felt he could be a regular member of the team but his contribution exceeded that. He was a terrific member of the team, and well respected." CBC Sports · Posted: Dec 08, 2000

In the first two periods of game one, Bergman would stand out as the best Canadian defenseman, if not overall player.

The GAG line has a final period shift against the Maltsev/Kharlamov line and while they are skating hard, the Soviets are working harder, faster, and smarter across all areas of the ice. Ratelle gets a puck deep in the Canadian end, slowly tries to get organized and yet gets swamped by Kharlamov who is everywhere this game. Ratelle, an elegant, clean player, appears shocked and frustrated by this, mixing it up with the smaller Soviet who semi strips Ratelle of the puck before losing it himself to Bergman. Bergman and Gilbert mount a rush, but Bergman loses it at the blueline to Tsygankov who like all Soviet defencemen this game, is in the right place at the right time, standing the Canadian defenseman up at the blueline. Bergman recovers the puck, sends a long breakout pass to Peter Mahovlich, who fires another hard slapper from a bad angle at Tretiak. **As he has been doing all game, Tretiak handles it easily.**

The Berenson line comes on to finish the period, and after Redmond goes offside, a quick pass from Tsygankov to Blinov allows for an excellent chance for Boris Mikhailov. Coming in on Seiling and Awrey, Blinov makes a nice feed to Mikhailov who easily steps around Awrey who falls, again, and Dryden has to make a good save. Peter Mahovlich has a nice view of the play watching it lazily as he semi-backchecks. Awrey trips Boris on the play with no call. Awrey to this point has really struggled with his timing and the Soviet speed. Almost immediately after the faceoff, Peter Mahovlich throws the puck away in the Canadian zone, right on the stick of Vladimir Petrov. **Canada looks completely exhausted**.

Sinden, having obviously seen enough of the Berenson line, sends the Clarke line out. The Petrov/Blinov/Mikhailov remain on the ice but for some reason Peter M stays on the ice instead of Henderson coming out. Seiling attempts a rush and for what seems like the 20th time a Canadian defenseman rushes the puck and loses it at the Soviet blue line, this time to Gusev. With seven seconds left in the period, Sinden puts out Esposito and Frank Mahovlich for some sort of last shot attempt. He keeps Clarke for the faceoff. Clarke was one of the NHL's best faceoff men, and Canada's second goal was a direct result of a clean faceoff win by Clarke. One final oddity from this sequence, as Frank M gets on the ice. Announcer Brian Conacher says,

"When Frank Mahovlich wants to play hockey there is not a better player in the world".

While Mahovlich had been one of Canada's better players so far in the game, it's an odd comment. Considering his linemate on this shift was Phil Esposito and considering that Valeri Kharlamov had completed dominated Canada this period, giving Frank such lofty praise seemed out of place. Unfortunately for Canada, the undisputed best player in the world, Bobby Orr was in the stands watching the game. The period ends without incident.

Game 1: Second Period Analysis

While Team Canada's players made positive comments about the abilities and speed of the Soviets after the first period, it was the second period of Game One that would be Canada's international hockey baptism by fire. It can be safely said that for the majority of period two, the Canadian players were outskated, outsmarted, out muscled. Completely overwhelmed by the Soviets. This was no doubt a result of several factors. Firstly, the Soviets gained confidence in the last ten minutes of the first period and realized not only could they keep up with the vaunted professionals, but on this day, they could outskate them and even outplay them. A viewer can almost see the Soviet confidence increasing with every shift in period two, sometimes to the point where they seemed to be toying with the struggling Canadian players. Secondly, the opposite seemed to happen to the Canadian confidence. They start to panic, run around out of position, back up quickly into their own zone and any counterattack seemed rushed or poorly executed, individual efforts. This was a complete opposite to the confident, high-flying Canadian team that started the game.

Fatigue seems to have been a large factor in this period for Canada along with the effects of the Montreal Forum heat, and the hot, restricting, Canadian uniforms. Sinden's strategy of going with five defensemen and his poor ice time management of those five all contributed to the resulting fatigue. Combine that with constant pressure by the Soviet forwards who swarmed the beleaguered Canadian defensemen, usually with a 2-man fore-checking scheme, it became too much. This was relentless, effective, and draining on the Canadian players. The Soviet fitness, strength and skating ability made the pressure appear relentless. Never ending. Shift after shift the Soviets pressed, pressured, and broke out of the defensive zone with lightning quick efficiency.

This period was the period of Valeri Kharlamov. He scored two high speed, high skill goals that shocked the Canadian crowd and his presence was everywhere, fore checking, back checking, chirping at Clarke, frustrating

Ratelle and even knocking the bigger Lapointe on his rear end. It was the Valeri Kharlamov show and Team Canada had front row seats. Canada was put on notice that he was a force to be reckoned with and stopping him was going to be very difficult. Kharlamov wasn't the only Soviet player flying that period, however, as Maltsev made some excellent rushes and offensive forays as did Yakushev. It should be noted that lesser-known players such as Blinov and Paladiev had strong periods and made some excellent plays. The Soviet game of puck control and speed, especially the one touch passing seemed to be too much for the Canadian players who were too often chasing the puck or worse, standing around watching.

The last noticeable difference between the two teams this period was one of hockey sense and positional play. Canada was sloppy at times defensively, with a lack of attention to detail at the faceoff circle, poor backchecking, often seeming exhausted or lacking intensity. Defensive timing and space was off for players such as Awrey and Seiling, and Lapointe, while energetic, was not disciplined or positionally strong. Offensively Canada was pretty ineffective, too much stick handling at the offensive blueline led to constant neutral zone turnovers, resulting in very little pressure on the Soviet defence. Bad angle slap shots, slap shots instead of passes on two on one breaks all made Tretiak's life easier.

It would be hard to pick any Canadian players who shone for this period as all four lines struggled. Dryden was weak on the two goals, although he also made a couple of good saves that kept it within 2 goals and four Canadian defensemen struggled with only Gary Bergman being the exception. The Soviet defence to their credit played excellent hockey, well positioned, smart, assertive, and energetic. Their defence stood the Canadians up at the blue line, cleared the front of the net efficiently, pinched and or jumped into the play when needed, angling the Canadian attackers to the boards effectively. The reality for the Canadians watching across Canada was not pleasant. Team Canada was getting a Hockey lesson and it would get worse for them before it would get better.

CHAPTER 10: GAME ONE PERIOD 3: WHAT? WE HAVE TO SHAKE HANDS? I'M TIRED!

The third period begins with the outdated international hockey format of two 10-minute halves. This was instigated for outdoor games where wind and sun played a part; thus, splitting the third period allowed for equal time in each end per team for the game. Dryden is still in goal for Canada. Sinden theoretically could have changed goalies for the 3rd period as he had All Star Tony Esposito on the bench. Dryden had let in 3 questionable goals so far, but he also made some excellent saves. In analysis, the goals so far were a result of team defensive lapses mixed with high level Soviet skill. Could Dryden have played better? Certainly, but he was only part of the problem, and he had made some good saves. As a result, Sinden decided to stick with Dryden, obviously not blaming him completely for the team being behind, assuming switching goalies was considered at all.

Both teams start the period with their original starting line-ups, the Esposito line with Park/Bergman for Canada and the Petrov line with Kuzkin/Gusev on defence. Canada gets the first real chance as Gusev gives up the puck behind his own net. Frank Mahovlich steals it, feeding it to Esposito in the slot. Tretiak makes another excellent reflex save keeping it 4-2. Clarke, Ellis and Henderson get outplayed by the Shadrin line, spending the entire shift chasing the Soviets around the ice. In an embarrassing moment for Ron Ellis, he tries to hit Lyapkin into the boards, but bounces off him, falling to the ice. Men against boys.

The Berenson line comes out and Mickey Redmond gets the second solid chance for Canada with a hard accurate shot from just off the right faceoff circle. Tretiak is again up to the task. The Soviets at this stage seem content with the two-goal lead and are not skating or forechecking like they were in the second period. Redmond makes a terrible pass to absolutely no one and Berenson makes another terrible pass a moment later. This causes Foster Hewitt to comment about the lack of team play for Canada. The crowd starts to rumble again.

Redmond continues the consistent yet seemingly fruitless pattern of stick handling at the Soviet blueline and loses it to Kharlamov. Quickly it's in the Canadian end (again). The Maltsev/ Vikulov/ Kharlamov line starts cycling the puck as Canadian forwards Peter Mahovlich and Red Berenson watch or attempt listless stick checks. Park flops to the ice, a move Don Awrey did several times already in this game, and Kharlamov simply dances around him, kicks the puck up with his skate and fires a dangerous backhand at Dryden who makes a good save. The Montreal crowd murmurs again, this time in shock and mumbled appreciation at Kharlamov's skill display. Conacher notes how Bergman is backing in on Dryden causing confusion. Canada's defence simply has no answer for Kharlamov this game, and the Canadian forwards seem content to be leaving the defencemen basically on their own in the Canadian zone. Foster Hewitt remarks using a Beatles song analogy:

"There is just no stopping this Kharlamov who is here, there and everywhere."

On the last Kharlamov chance, Mickey Redmond cannot be seen in the Canadian zone. Whether he had headed to the bench to change or was waiting above the blue line for a breakout, it had left Canada with only four players back to defend against the Soviet group of five. This lack of defensive awareness would be an obvious reason for Redmond not playing again in the series. Overall, just an awful, disjointed, lacklustre shift by the Berenson/Peter Mahovlich/Redmond line.

The Ranger line comes out, and the game has now slowed again to a very casual pace. Brad Park attempts to stickhandle out of his own end but has no one to pass to and loses the puck. The Ranger line is not skating and thus ineffective. Sinden quickly goes to the Esposito group. When the Ranger line is changing, you can Park speaking angrily to Ratelle. Possibly because the GAG line was just standing still and he had no one to pass to, or perhaps just frustration at how things have gone for Canada.

The fog on the ice is increasing, the sauna-like conditions have affected both teams. The Soviets are not skating hard and have completely stopped the swarming forecheck. Guy Lapointe gets the puck behind his own goal and has free ice to skate. Lapointe plays the puck deep and the resulting turnover from Paladiev ends up with an excellent chance for Phil Esposito right in front of Tretiak. Esposito tries to deke Tretiak, pulling it across the crease, but on this night the young Soviet tender was in the zone, reading Esposito's attempt and stacking the pads to stop it. The Soviets quickly counterattack with Yakushev barely missing Zimin for a long breakaway. The NHLers have never experienced such rapid counterattacks. They seem unprepared.

The Clarke line then gets matched against the Maltsev/Kharlamov/ Vikulov trio. Right off the faceoff, the Soviet line gets it quickly into the Canadian zone, and out of the blue the energetic two-man forecheck returns which the exhausted, hot, Canadians have no answer to. The Leaf scouts who went to Moscow did warm Team Canada about the sudden tactic changes of the Soviets. As the Soviets swarm, Maltsev has an excellent opportunity but just misses the top right corner on Dryden, after yet another nice Soviet passing play. The usual clean playing Ellis and Henderson are going into corners with sticks high, frustrated, and tired. Henderson whacks the giant Ragulin across the back, but as expected the Soviet veteran shrugs it off easily. Despite being three of the fittest Canadians, the Clarke line isn't skating. As a result, the Canadians end up trapped again in their own end with the Soviets peppering Dryden.

As Canada changes lines on the fly, the Soviets decide to slow the game down to a snail's pace, playing keep away with the puck. Kharlamov circles and takes his time, passing it around in leisure until finally Redmond steals the puck from Vikulov. He tries to stickhandle into the Soviet zone but is easily stopped by Kuzkin. Soviets change lines as Blinov flies around a sliding, flopping Brad Park in mid ice, leaving partner Gary Bergman alone. This leads to more pressure in the foggy Canadian end, and Blinov gets another point-blank shot on Dryden who makes a good save. Brad Park is again on the ice during the second attempt, having dropped down to try and block a pass ineffectually.

Red Berenson finally rushes it out of Team Canada's zone, but continues the Canadian pattern of individual play, stickhandling through the neutral zone and losing it. Canada will have to change drastically their offensive game at this stage in order to get some pressure in the Soviet end. The constant one-man rushes are failing at the Soviet blue line and shift after shift the Canadian forwards attempt the same foray with the same negative result.

Out of the blue the Soviets decide to turn up the pressure and pace again. The Petrov line with Blinov and Mikhailov are really flying, and all three chase down a one-man rush by Peter Mahovlich, leading to another Canadian turnover. The pace they are setting and swarming of the puck by the Soviet forwards, especially Boris Mikhailov is obviously something the Canadians weren't expecting nor used to. Brian Conacher mentions this issue when he says,

"One thing Canada has not been able to do is slow down the play. The tempo is simply too fast."

Canada gets a rare chance when a bad pass from Zimin to Paladiev on the point is missed and Cournoyer makes a nice play to the Big M, who is alone on Tretiak. Frank struggles with the rolling puck on his backhand and fails to get a decent shot on Tretiak who athletically slides across on his pads. Frank Mahovlich has certainly been one of Canada's best players, skating well and creating offense, despite some poor decisions with the puck. Canada keeps it in with Seiling getting a long blast at Tretiak who gloves and smothers it without an issue for a whistle.

Goal 7: Bobby Clarke. Canada 3 Soviets 4

After being completed outplayed for the last several minutes, Canada gets a faceoff in the Soviet zone, to the left of Tretiak. The Clarke line is facing off against the Maltsev line, with Tsygankov and Ragulin on the back end. The puck goes into the corner, where Henderson gets to the puck ahead of Ragulin. Rather than taking the body, **Ragulin stands motionless** allowing Henderson to turn towards the point and make a nice quick pass to Ellis in the high slot. Tsygankov drops to his knees anticipating a shot, but Ellis cleverly throws it to Clarke (half shot-half pass) who is waiting on Tretiak's doorstep, just to his left. Clarke easily deflects it under Tretiak for an unexpected Canadian strike.

This goal, much like the second Canadian goal by Henderson, was a more a result of clever Canadian passing than a massive Soviet defensive breakdown. Looking at the goal critically, Ragulin should have used his size and strength to prevent Henderson from getting out of the corner. Instead, Ragulin, after his early inaction, chases the much more nimble and quicker Henderson, leaving the area where Clarke would score from unattended. Maltsev being the centre, could have dropped back to cover the now empty crease area while wingers Kharlamov and Vikulov were up high covering the points but he also stood stationary watching the puck. Finally, Tsygankov skates away from the front of his net, and then drops down to attempt to block the Ellis shot, which left him out of position. **Ironically, this move by Tsygankov was the same type of mistake the Canadian defence had been making all game long with attempted shot blocking.** Tretiak really had no chance on the play as Clarke was all alone. It was a well-orchestrated goal by Team Canada that gave them some life in this game.

The goal motivates Team Canada, realizing they are now within a goal, come to life, smelling blood. The Montreal crowd also comes to life, loudly cheering them on. **Bobby Clarke is everywhere after the goal, chasing and rubbing out Tsygankov behind the Soviet goal, Henderson in hot pursuit.** This happens after an actual dump in by Canada, something rare this game so far. After stealing the puck, Clarke gets a good shot off on Tretiak, who makes a quick save. Another Soviet turnover at the blue line by Maltsev leads to Henderson dumping it in again. With the Ranger line being benched by Sinden, Red Berenson's line comes out. Mickey Redmond flies through the neutral zone, dekes out Tsygankov at the Soviet blue line, gains the zone, stops and makes a nice cross crease pass to Peter Mahovlich, who misses the puck in front on Tretiak. The Montreal Forum is alive, as the fans see Canada's resurgence, sensing the momentum change for their heroes. Anticipating a goal to tie the game. With the crowd egging them on, **Canada pressures, with the Soviets suddenly showing actual signs of panic.**

Unfortunately for Canadas momentum, the previously mentioned 10-minute mark siren goes off and the teams change ends. This gives the USSR a much-needed break from the revitalized Canadians.

The final ten minutes starts off with both teams icing their starting line-ups. Canada continues with their renewed energy and even though the Soviets get the puck deep but Brad Park bodies Blinov off the puck, allowing Canada to take off up the ice. Esposito just misses the pinching Bergman with a long pass and both Bergman and Espo deliver solid hits in the Soviet zone. **Esposito was never known as a physical player despite his size, so the bodycheck on Gusev shows his intensity on this shift**. In a rare display of panic, the Soviets ice the puck to the boos of the Montreal Forum crowd. The Clarke/Henderson/Ellis line comes on and immediately gets a great chance when Paladiev gives the puck away twice, once to Clarke and the second time along the boards. Clarke makes a great pass back to Henderson who is now free with the puck off the boards. This allows Henderson to come in for a great chance to tie the game as he tries a quick shot from the angle which Tretiak stops. Tretiak can then be seen handing a two-hand slash to Henderson in the goal crease after Henderson bumps into him. **The Canadians are hitting the Soviets at every turn now, who seem truly rattled by the turn of events**.

Jean Ratelle's line has not had much ice time since the second Kharlamov goal. Sinden seems to ignore the potential danger of putting them out after sitting so long but they have a very good shift. Vic Hadfield doing some good forechecking work and Gilbert flying all over the ice. **An interesting observation is how the Soviets have trouble with the dump in play**. Hadfield does a very standard NHL play of the **angled dump** in, into the corner. This was a play once perfected by Detroit's production line of Gordie Howe, Ted Lindsay, and Sid Abel. The puck comes straight out, rather than around the boards, of the corner area of the boards and the offensive wing will get to it first and play it out front. Hadfield gets over the blue line and sends it a perfect angled dump in.

The Soviet defender Luchenko is looking back and forth and seeing two forecheckers in Gilbert and Ratelle panics with the puck. He subsequently gives it away to Ratelle who throws it out front, where the always aware Tretiak makes the stop. **This offensive play must have been somewhat new to the Soviet players, and it shows that both teams could be surprised by some foreign tactics of their still unknown opponent.**

Luchenko, like Paladiev in the shift before, gives the puck away a second time, forcing he and his partner Tsygankov to tie up Hadfield behind the Soviet net. To show how well the Soviets play positionally, having both defencemen behind the net doesn't leave the front of the Soviet net open, as Kharlamov drops back down to the low slot area ensuring solid defensive coverage. After the whistle in the Soviet end, Tsygankov can be seen outmuscling the strong Hadfield along the boards freeing the puck to Maltsev. Maltsev makes a wonderful full-length rush, easily deking out Gilbert and then beating the exhausted Park outside. With Awrey covering the front of the goal Maltsev continued back of the Canadian net before being absolutely drilled by Hadfield. Hadfield follows up the heavy hit with a **welcome to the NHL elbow in the face** which stuns the surprised Maltsev. The Ranger line gets one final rush on this shift, again using the angled dump-in to great effect as Gilbert collects the puck and hits Pete Mahovlich streaking into the Soviet zone with a pass. Pete drills a slap shot high and wide as Canada is still thinking they can blast a slap shot past Tretiak. **A super shift by the Ranger line, (especially Vic Hadfield) which makes the future decision to break them up even more surprising.**

Canada seems to finally be taking shorter shifts as the full Berenson line comes back out. Redmond strips Maltsev (with a possible trip) after Maltsev carelessly stickhandles in the neutral zone. Canada now has puck possession again. Peter Mahovlich gets another chance right in front of Tretiak after a nice dump in by Lapointe and a good forecheck by Redmond on Luchenko. **Luchenko has made two give aways in a row as Mahovlich fires another slap shot blast at Tretiak.** For the first time since the first period, the Soviet defence looks panicky, and **Canada is outskating their opponents.**

Luchenko's second giveaway allows Peter Mahovlich to get a great chance with a shot from the slot. He fires a low shot to the corner, but the time put in with Tarasov working on his glove hand comes to fruition here as Tretiak snags it quickly with his glove. Mickey Redmond comes flying in, bumping Tretiak after the save. Tretiak takes offense pushing Mickey, chirping at the Detroit winger, obviously upset. Tsygankov gets involved and a still hyper Guy Lapointe comes flying in and pushes the Soviet defenceman away from the scrum. After the scrum Guy Lapointe makes a not very diplomatic throat cutting gesture to Tsygankov despite having Prime Minister Pierre Trudeau watching in the audience.

This is the most passion Canada has shown in this game which seems to have rattled the Soviets at this stage. **With less than eight minutes left in the game, it looks like Canada is a good bet to tie it up.** Canada has been dominating the face-offs this game and Esposito wins the next one cleanly against Petrov. He pulls it back to Cournoyer who accelerates through the face circle to get a point-blank shot on Tretiak. Another solid save as the young Soviet goaltender, who is denying chance after chance for a revitalized Team Canada.

Goal 8: Boris Mikhailov USSR 5 Canada 3

As often happens in hockey, one team is pressing for a goal, dominating the action and a sudden break turns into a goal for the team who was under the relentless pressure. **This is where great goaltending comes in.** Grant Fuhr of the

1980's dynastic Oilers is a perfect example of a goaltender who could make the save when needed. This happened often as his team was pressuring heavily in the other teams end and the tables turned on the Oilers with a quick breakout on Fuhr. Fuhr would then shut the door preserving the Oiler comeback or lead. Dryden did this later in his career playing for probably the best club team of all time: the 1976-79 Montreal Canadians. However, this was 1972 and **Ken Dryden in this game, for the surging Team Canada, failed to do that.**

Petrov, Blinov and Mikhailov are out against Phil Esposito, Cournoyer and Frank Mahovlich. The play begins in the Soviet end to Tretiak's left. Esposito wins the draw and pulls it back to Cournoyer who gets a quick shot on goal. The puck goes into the corner where Gusev gives the twisting and turning Cournoyer a solid two hander and two subsequent hooks which are not called. Esposito can be seen battling hard with Tsygankov in front of the Soviet net, and easily could have taken a penalty himself, but nothing is called. The play continues in the Soviet end as the puck goes to Frank Mahovlich who stickhandles and then gets poke checked by Gusev. The puck comes directly to Blinov near the Soviet blue line. Blinov carries the puck unencumbered through the neutral zone before passing to a streak Boris Mikhailov on the left win. As Boris gets close to the Canadian blue line Rod Seiling is backing up. As the play crosses the Canadian blue line, Seiling does a good job closing the gap and angles Boris to the boards. **Suddenly, Mikhailov changes direction** and goes back towards the middle of the ice. This turns a seemingly harmless situation into a suddenly dangerous one for Canada.

This sudden shift by Mikhailov was an early version of a move that Wayne Gretzky perfected. The Great One would come directly at a defenseman and then just over the blue line turn sharply and go in a vertical line towards the centre of the ice. The defenseman is skating backwards and cannot pivot at the same angle or speed that Gretzky could, and it freed him up for a shot or a pass. This change of direction took away the physical contact possibility that would have happened if he continued going wide on the defenseman. **This is exactly what happens on this goal.** Mikhailov shows excellent edging and athleticism with his sudden turn and subsequent drive towards the net. He can control the puck with his right hand, skilfully away from the Seiling poke check, but that put him on his backhand, as he was a left-handed shot like most Soviet players. Seiling was a decent skater, which was probably one of the reasons he was selected to the team. He pivots and tries to catch up to Boris, but he is a half second behind. Lapointe on the other side of the ice has Blinov tied up, out of the play. Dryden comes quickly out of his crease, assumedly to cut down Mikhailov's angle. Boris shoots a low hard backhand that goes directly through Dryden's legs. Dryden is probably a solid five feet outside his crease yet somehow the shot evades him. A back checking Cournoyer is seen attempting to catch up to Mikhailov but just misses before Boris fires home his shot. This is a good, skilful goal, and exemplified the Soviet ability for lightning-fast counter attacks.

This goal was also the introduction to the North American hockey world of another Soviet star: **Boris Mikhailov**. Boris would continue to be a thorn in Canada's side throughout this series, and the rest of the decade. Mikhailov shows excellent speed and skating ability, and like the Kharlamov goals earlier, he was able to stickhandle at full speed. This ability, especially so late in the game made a solid NHL defenseman fall behind on what must have looked like a typical one on one situation for Seiling. Seiling in this situation generally does everything right. He closes the gap, attempts a poke check, and angles Mikhailov to the boards. **He simply was not able to anticipate the sudden change in direction the clever Soviet player takes as the play develops.** The issue for Canada was: this is a goal that

Dryden should have stopped. While the shot is a good one, low and quick, again Dryden simply MUST make this stop. Letting a goal in through his legs on a simple one on one situation, especially from directly in front of him, in the slot area, wasn't good enough in a high stakes game like this. This must have been very deflating for the Canadian team as they had been dominating the play for the last five minutes and seemed ripe to tie the game up. Now Canada is behind 2 goals, in a very hot arena, with time running out. This is the first real game for any of the Canadian players since in five months. The Canadian revitalized pressure in the third period seems to have exhausted Team Canada. Brad Park, Gary Bergman, and Rod Seiling have received immense amounts of ice time and it is beginning to show. **Combined with the heat, the high fitness level (and skill) of their opponent, the NHL players have hit the proverbial wall.**

Canada leaves the Esposito line out there but changes the defence to Park and Bergman. The Soviets, who are quite jubilant on the bench after the Mikhailov goal, change to the Shadrin, Yakushev, and Zimin line. Right off the faceoff, an obviously exhausted Brad Park dangles dangerously in his own zone, and then makes a terrible giveaway to Alexander Yakushev. Attempting to pass across to his partner Bergman, Park instead gives the puck directly to Yakushev in front of Canada's goal. Dryden and Park both flop to stop Yakushev's backhand which flies over the Canadian net. Frank Mahovlich then gives up the puck to Zimin by over skating it near Canada's goal, for another Soviet chance on the beleaguered Dryden and then the Big M tries to lug the puck down the ice but is outskated by Shadrin. Suddenly the game is being dominated by the Soviets. The Esposito line seems completely gassed and they are about to be on the ice for a second straight goal against. One must wonder if Harry Sinden had put out the more rested New York Ranger line if a different result would have happened.

Goal 9: Zimin USSR 6 Canada 3

The play starts when the puck goes back into the Soviet end and Paladiev tries the quick Soviet breakout play by firing it up the ice attempting to hit a breaking Yakushev at centre ice. Shadrin deftly tips it to Yakushev just over the red line and the big Yak (Yakushev's nickname) carries it into Canada's zone. Yakushev now attempts to outmuscle Brad Park at the Canadian blue line. Gary Bergman moves toward the Park-Yakushev battle leaving his side of the ice open. Yakushev holds Park with one big arm, goes slightly around him, and does a lovely little one-handed dish to Zimin. Bergman now does a quick circle to get back into play as Zimin is wide open coming into the slot area. Bergman for some reason over commits himself towards Zimin which gets him badly out of position. He twists and half falls to the ice while Zimin says thank you very much and walks around him for a shot at Dryden. Dryden again comes quickly out of his net, but at the same time Park gets back into the play and reaches out to Zimin. **Zimin shoots but the shot is blocked by Park's stick**. Dryden has dropped to one knee making him completely immobile on the play. Luckily for Zimin **the puck deflects right back onto his stick**, and he fires it under the helpless Dryden. Esposito this time is the back checker on the play, but he seems exhausted and arrives to Zimin a half moment too late. it's a second Zimin goal of the night.

On this goal, and several of the others that night, Team Canada had major issues with the Soviet transition game and overall skating abilities. While this goal was a bit lucky for Zimin at the crucial moment, it was much more than that. It was a testament to just how big and strong Alexander Yakushev was, and how quickly the Soviet team could transition from the defensive end to an offensive opportunity. It was an eye opener to the Canadian players that the Soviets had multiple offensive stars of whom Canada would need to become aware.

Bergman unfortunately makes a couple of mistakes on this goal, firstly in coming over to aid Park against Yakushev, which leads the trailing Zimin wide open. Secondly, he then realizes his mistake, circles to catch up to Zimin but in doing that he over skates his positioning and that allows Zimin to get his shot away. Zimin does make a nice hesitation deke when he sees Bergman has overshot his target. The real issue for Canada on this goal was not just Zimin being open in the slot but again it **was the play of Ken Dryden and his decision making.** Dryden comes out of his crease quickly as he sees the action in front of him, but then commits by dropping to his right knee when he is expecting the Zimin shot. While he had no way to anticipate Park being able to stop that shot and the proceeding deflection back onto Zimin's stick, by committing on one knee, he was in a position that lacked the mobility to stop the second shot, or any potential rebound from the first. Unfortunately for Dryden, it was a little bit of a bad guess and a little bit of bad luck, combined of course with the unexpected high level Soviet speed and skill. That same skill and speed of execution was forcing excellent defensive defencemen like Gary Bergman to make **unexpected positional mistakes.**

Clarke's line comes out after the second goal against the Esposito line and immediately Clarke delivers a Flin Flon two hander to Luchenko who is circling harmlessly with the puck in his own end. Bobby Clarke always said if he didn't learn to give two handed slashes he would have ended up working the mines in Flin Flon Manitoba. Clarke's slash is so hard his stick breaks, but no call is made. As the puck goes into the Soviet corner, Valeri Kharlamov takes a run at Ron Ellis with his stick high. Ellis gets agitated and they get into a bit of a scrum. Clarke can be seen giving Kharlamov a little crosscheck afterwards. Kharlamov gets called for a high sticking penalty. No call on Clarke or Ellis. Jean Ratelle comes out with Frank Mahovlich and Yvan Cournoyer for the power-play.

Despite the previous lack of success, Phil Esposito is once again on the point with Rod Seiling. The faceoff is deep in the Soviet zone. Vladimir Petrov and Evgeni Mishakov on a rare shift are out killing the penalty with Ragulin and Tsygankov. Petrov wins the draw, and it goes into the corner where Ragulin again is not physical and loses the puck to Ratelle. This turns into an excellent opportunity for the Big M who gets a quick shot away on Tretiak. Tretiak fumbles with the puck a bit but it doesn't go in on what was Canada's first real chance in several minutes. Canada is listless on this powerplay, and you can see how exhausted they are, especially Seiling and Phil Esposito. Seiling falls behind the Canadian net, the exhaustion prevalent in his movements. Brad Park comes on, makes a nice, controlled rush, stickhandling his way into the Soviet end, but instead of stopping and setting up the powerplay, he simply shoots from a bad angle. **Canada is still not playing intelligent, positional hockey and it's made the Soviets tasks in this game much easier.**

Esposito has moved up from defence, without a break, now centring Hadfield and Gilbert with Bergman and Park. Espo stickhandles through the neutral zone and loses it, as Canada fails to get any shots or pressure on the power play and has obviously hit the wall of exhaustion. The Berenson line has one final shift and has some solid, sustained pressure on the cycle, which leads to another big slap shot blast from Peter Mahovlich that Tretiak handles easily. Mickey Redmond especially seems to still have a jump in his step, and he does some good work at both ends of the rink.

Kharlamov is out showing his stick handling ability and makes several nice moves, including a slick spin-o-ram at the Canadian blue line, before finally being stripped of the puck by Redmond. With 1:46 left in the game, Clarke's line comes out and Guy Lapointe gets an excellent chance on Tretiak after a nice give and go play with Henderson. Tretiak is up to the task, but seeing how Lapointe is still flying out there, **one has to wonder why he wasn't given more ice time in this game?** Lapointe's chance was on a 2 on 1 with Ron Ellis, yet Lapointe shot from an angle instead of trying to make the pass to Ellis. Canada has had several of these 2 on 1 breaks this game and **not once did they attempt to pass the puck**. Shocking really considering the offensive talent out there for Canada. Whether it was just a collective mindset of blasting the puck past Tretiak or a case where they lacked the confidence to make the pass is unknown. **What is obvious is that Tretiak had an easier time as a result with the angle blasts knowing the NHLers wouldn't make the pass to their teammate like the Soviets would.**

To put the nail in the coffin, the Soviets switch to the deadly Shadrin/Zimin/Yakushev line and score the final goal of this game.

Goal 10: Alexander Yakushev. Soviets 7 Canada 3

Immediately after the Lapointe/Ellis 2 on 1 rush, the back checking Shadrin banks it up the boards out of the Soviet end to an awaiting Evgeny Zimin. Zimin smoothly skates into the Canadian zone with Rod Seiling backing up accordingly. Zimin does a drop pass to open ice, which as Canada was learning, was never open for long with the Soviets. Yakushev reads the play and moves into the Canadian zone over the blue line, accepting Zimin's drop pass. A battle ensues along the boards just over the blue line. Yakushev quickly gets knocked down and loses the puck to Henderson, however Henderson loses it in turn to Shadrin who digs it off the boards away from him. While this has been going on Yakushev has gotten up and cleverly snuck behind Seiling who is, standing stationary, watching the scrum on the boards.

Ron Ellis, anticipating a pass up the ice from Henderson, has turned his back on the play and headed out of the Canadian zone. Seiling seemingly ignores Yakushev and attempts to poke check the puck off Shadrin from his current standing position. Lapointe has gotten back into the play after his rush and is near the Canadian slot area moving towards Shadrin. Shadrin reads the Seiling poke check and makes a highly skilled deke, moving himself and the puck quickly to his right towards Lapointe. Lapointe seems completely focused on watching Shadrin with the puck and seemingly **doesn't see Yakushev open behind Seiling** (or ignores him). Lapointe continues at Shadrin, lining him up for a body check, but Shadrin makes a wonderful backhand pass, through the prone Seiling and right onto Yakushev's stick. Lapointe hits Shadrin with a nasty elbow but is now **completely out of the play**. Yakushev uses his reach to pull Dryden across the crease and fires a beautiful backhand into the top left corner over the sliding Dryden. Seiling is in the crease and attempts to glove the puck haplessly. **Seiling stands in front of his net, head down. The frustration, the embarrassment, the utter dejection shows as he stands there, a symbol of this game.**

While it would be easy to point out the Canadian mistakes on this goal, Henderson losing the puck along the boards to Shadrin, Seiling not committing to either taking Shadrin or following Yakushev, Lapointe going out of position to hit Shadrin, or even Dryden for getting pulled across his crease by Yakushev. Those mistakes would only tell half the story on this seventh goal for the USSR. This was a goal that highlights two things: Firstly, the lighting fast transition game the Soviets possessed and secondly the extremely high skill level of the Soviet forwards, completely unexpected by the NHL. Much like several of the goals in this first game, the Soviets went from the defence to offense in rapid fashion. Shadrin's clever tip to Zimin gets the puck into the Canadian end within seconds. Shadrin especially shows wonderful skill not only with this tip pass, but when he anticipates Seiling's poke check, pulls the puck away from the poke, and **slides a world class backhand pass** through Seiling onto the tape of the waiting Yakushev.

As Canada would find out for the remaining seven games (and several other international contests) **Alexander Yakushev was the real deal**. A very large man in that era (6'3), he was a strong skater, clever with the puck with excellent hands and a physical force. Brian Conacher compares him to Frank Mahovlich after this goal, but that might be generous to the Big M as Yakushev was a better player at this time in their careers. Bobby Hull called the Big Yak the best left winger in the world after the 1974 WHA Summit Series and he was probably right. On this goal Yakushev shows great skill but also great patience, pulling Dryden across the crease, and getting his backhand up over the large goaltender and into the top corner. **Simply a well-executed, skilful goal**.

In retrospect, Rod Seiling might have been considered an odd choice for Team Canada. He was neither considered an all-star like his teammate Brad Park (although Seiling did play in the 1972 NHL All Star Game), nor a high point producing defenceman. What he was, though, was a solid defenseman for a very good New York Rangers team. He had put together five solid seasons in a row, where his plus minus rating was a cumulative +153. Seiling had a good junior career with the Toronto Marlboroughs (Marlies) winning a Memorial Cup in 1964. From there he played for Father David Bauer's Canadian National Team, including playing in the 1964 Olympics. This was the year that Canada was denied a Bronze Medal despite finishing tied with Sweden with ten points. This experience combined with such glowing reviews from Ranger General Manager Emile Francis as

"there isn't a better defensive defenceman, he gives our defence the steadiness it needs", led to his selection on Team Canada.

Unfortunately for Rod, he was as much of a victim of poor decision making and bench management by the coaching staff as he was his own play. While he ended the first game a miserable -6, he also played, according to Richard Bendall 1972 Summit Series, a total of 29.20 seconds of ice time in game 1, the second most on the team behind Brad Park. This included **over half of the second period**. In comparison his starting partner Don Awrey only played 12.25 mins and Guy Lapointe 17.36. Exhaustion both physical and mental was a natural, unstoppable, outcome.

Why was this the case? Firstly, when negotiating the Summit Series, it was agreed that each team would only ice 17 skaters per game. That meant if a team went with 4 full lines, as Canada did, they would only be able to use 5 defensemen. The coaches' reasoning for this was that Canada's powerful offense would keep the Soviets at bay in their own end, thus the five defensemen selected to play for Canada would have an easier time of it. This, however, isn't what happened. The Soviet forwards and transition game were quite simply too much for the 5 Canadian defence throughout most of the game. While the brutal heat inside the arena and hot restricting sweaters of Team Canada didn't help, there was very **poor bench management decisions** which surely over exhausted the three defensemen who played the most, Park, Seiling and Bergman. **This was coach Harry Sinden's major mistake**. His responsibility. In fact, once Awrey was victimized by Valeri Kharlamov on the third Soviet goal, the Bruins' defenseman's ice-time was severely reduced as Canada went with basically four men on defence. This led to the large amounts of ice time logged for someone like Seiling, who only had a three-week training camp resulting in his not being in peak, mid-season shape. Seiling himself explained, with some details incorrect, that he went to Sinden to convince him to dress six defencemen that night:

> "...before the series started, I went to Harry and asked him to dress six defensemen. They didn't in the first game in Montreal, Awrey and I played every other shift for the whole game and we simply weren't...the other three

rotated. And by the end of the game we were just dead". Jay Moran 199.

Rod would go on to play Game 4 in Vancouver and game 5 in Moscow, ending his Summit Series without a Canadian win. Perhaps his game one experience can be summarized with these thoughts:

"There was nothing we could do to stop the Soviets in game one. I felt like I was playing on my knees against Soviet speedsters like Kharlamov and Yakushev." Rod Seiling 1972 SummitSeries.com

The final minute of the game was not a great one for Team Canada. Another failed stick handling attempt by Yvan Cournoyer turned into a turnover where Shadrin takes a long slap shot from mid- ice at Dryden. Dryden makes the stop but suffers the humiliation of a Montreal crowd clapping at the simple save, a well-known crowd tactic to **show their displeasure at a goalie's performance.** The Soviets swarm Seiling in the Canadian corner, getting possession. Blinov makes a nice cross crease pass to Boris Mikhailov who barely misses the net on what might have been their eighth goal.

Yakushev gets two more close range shots as foster Hewitt remarks *"as the Soviets pour it on".* Canada is listless, Frank Mahovlich can be seen barely skating, seemingly already giving up. The Soviets' energy and pace is still very high, which seems to annoy Canada. Lapointe and Mikhailov start a bit of a melee in the Canadian end and a cross-checking penalty to Lapointe is called with 19 seconds left in the game. Esposito can also be seen giving a cross check to Petrov as well, for no apparent reason except frustration. Two final moments of shame for Team Canada were left. Firstly, Blinov carries the puck in a circle around the centre ice area and suddenly Bobby Clarke gives him a massive one-handed whack as he circles, running out the clock. The game ends with a jubilant Soviet squad congratulating Tretiak and the Canadian players walking off the ice **instead of participating in the traditional international hockey**

handshake, puzzling the Soviets, and creating a bit of an international furore.

Third Period Analysis

With 6 minutes and 28 seconds left in this game, the score was 4-3 and Team Canada had the Soviets on the ropes. During a roughly 7-minute stretch midway through the 3rd period, the Canadian team seemed to have woken up from a much of the game long slumber and were pressuring the Soviets intensely. However, the Boris Mikhailov goal, which put the game at 5-3 for the Soviets ended any hope of a Canadian comeback. **Canada was spent after that goal**, and the superbly conditioned, cohesive USSR ramped it up further scoring three more skilful, debilitating goals. Canada reacted with anger, cheap shots, and frustration.

The goal by Bobby Clarke that had made the score 4-3 showed that Canada did have another gear. **The Soviets would have done well to notice that**, even short lived as it was. During those moments, Canada had looked like a completely different team, passionate, skating, and intense. It was also the only time outside of the first shift of the game, where the Soviet team looked a bit panicky, especially at the back end where Paladiev and Gusev both have bad giveaways on the Canadian forecheck. Tretiak would have to be considered the star of those Canadian dominated moments, as he made save after save, frustrating Team Canada, ensuring the Soviet lead. Once the Soviet counter strike took over with the Mikhailov goal, the Canadian morale was broken. That was the end of any comeback hopes.

Notable players in the third period were Tretiak, Mikhailov who was a constant skating whirlwind all period, and Shadrin 's line with Yakushev and Zimin. For Canada, Bobby Clarke was the most notable player, hustling, making plays and causing disturbances. Mickey Redmond, Frank Mahovlich, the New York Ranger line and even Guy Lapointe showed some periodic energy but that all changed at the ten-minute mark. After that it was really an exhausted group that that was both outworked and outplayed by the Soviets.

CHAPTER 11: GAME ONE SUMMARY. A DICKENS NOVEL

Like the famous opening line of a Dickens novel, game one could summed up for both teams with **"it was the best of times, it was the worst of times."** For Canada, they couldn't have scripted a better start to the game and the series. They would come out and score two well-executed goals within the first six minutes. The world was as it should be, as predicted; they were going to win easily and often.

"When I got on the ice," remembered Rod Gilbert in Scott Morrison's excellent book 'The Days Canada Stood Still', "it was already 2-0. Before I played my first shift it was 2-0, so I'm sitting on the bench saying, 'Let me on. Let me score my goals.' I figured it was going to be 15, 17-0, and I wanted to score a few goals."

Things did not pan out that way. The Soviets started to play their game, one of speed, teamwork, and skill; at times Canada seemed to have little response. Why was this the case? For Canada, it seems that many factors came into play, overconfidence, fitness levels, the heat of the Forum, and a lack of team cohesion. However, in reviewing all the goals and plays throughout the game, it really came down to three factors.

Firstly, the Soviets were good. Really, really, good. Much better than Canada was anticipating.

"Before the series began, we were advised that their calibre of hockey would not be as high as ours. Boy - were we in for a shock." Vic Hadfield

Canada was not prepared for the speed, skill, and cohesiveness of the Soviets. This was obvious on several of the Soviet goals, when the Canadian defence struggled with timing, positional play and spacing. The Soviet quick transition from defence to offense, the one touch passing, the high-level skating and the two-man swirling fore check all caused Team Canada severe issues which would require some major adjustments moving forward. The depth and skill level of the Soviet forwards was another significant issue Canada encountered. On the original scouting trip by Team Canada's scouts, the feedback was that only Alexander Yakushev would have the ability to make Team Canada. After game one it was obvious that not only could most of the Soviet forward group make Team Canada, as a group, **their skill level might be higher than Canada's!** Combining that with their cohesive team play and the dynamic game breaking ability of Valeri Kharlamov, **Canada was in deep**.

The second main cause for the result in game one was **the poor preparation, bench management and strategy by Team Canada.** This has to come down to the coaching staff.

Harry Sinden had played against the Soviets in the 1959 World Championships for the Whitby Dunlop's Senior A team, winning the title. As a result, he knew the Soviet style, but it's entirely possible he wasn't truly aware how much they had improved since then. It was very difficult in 1972 to accurately judge just how good the Soviets had become in those 13 years. While an observer should have been able to determine that they were well beyond the Senior A level by the mid-60's, the fact was there was no barometer for Sinden to base his strategy on for game one. Their opponents had either been other European countries or Father David Bauer's Canadian National Team. Neither of those opponents were considered NHL level opposition as a result Sinden, like almost all hockey "experts" had felt that Canadian firepower would simply overwhelm the Soviets. They had simply never faced anything like the NHL stars before. The Soviets had a very young goalie Vladislav Tretiak who was unproven, only 20 years old. Sinden prepared his game plan accordingly.

As previously mentioned, Team Canada's strategy was to load up on offensive players who would stack four lines to wear down the Soviet defence and inexperienced goalie. They would shoot and shoot often, especially slap shots, as it was perceived that the Soviets rarely took slap shots, and certainly not to the level of power and expertise the Canadian shooters had. Tretiak would fold under this onslaught, allowing Canada to win easily. This of course would fail massively in game one. Tretiak, briefed by the legendary Jacques Plante before the game on the Canadian shooters, held fast the entire game.

"I will always be very grateful to Jacques Plante whose suggestions helped me so much," wrote Tretiak in his autobiography. Tretiak believes that Plante simply didn't want a member of the goaltending fraternity humiliated in what most everyone believed would be a Canadian rout. "I would like to ask Jacques Plante, but it's not possible," he said of the late goalie. "Maybe he felt sorry for me?" Dave Stubbs Montreal Gazette 2012

This focus on taking slap shots hurt the Canadian team, they missed several opportunities to pass on odd man breaks, and the shots they did take were often telegraphed and from bad angles. **The Canadian coaching staff needed to have the team adjust mid game, but that never seemed to happen**. While Tretiak did make several solid saves, it's fair to say that Canada made his night easier. The worst proponents of this were the Mahovlich brothers, especially Frank who wasted several solid opportunities on slap shots, ignoring his high scoring linemates Phil Esposito and Yvan Cournoyer in the process.

When Sinden decided to go with five defence and four lines, he needed to carefully manage the ice time of those five D-men. The reality is Canada had a three-week training camp with mixed reviews on how strenuous it was, and three White-Red inter squad games to prepare for the series. While these were professional athletes, they generally did not train in the summer, instead doing things like spend time with family, at the cottage, golfing and running hockey schools. Combine that with the previously mentioned heat in the Forum that day, and the high-level fitness and pace the Soviets played, going with a seemingly unmanaged, reduced defence would be disastrous.

In Richard Bendell's 2013 book "1972: The Summit Series", the author does the painstaking task of adding up the Canadian players' ice time in game one. The results were shocking. Brad Park plays over half the game with 30.31 mins of ice time. Rod Seiling was right behind his Ranger teammate with 29.20 mins and Gary Bergman was third with 25.33 mins. Guy Lapointe played 17.36 and then Don Awrey only hit the ice for a minimal 12.25 minutes, only 4 minutes a period, much of that was a benching after the first Kharlamov goal. This was coupled with a group of Canadian forwards who were inconsistent in their defensive responsibilities. While these statistics should in no way take away from the Soviet skill, speed, and ability, being on the ice for half a game, especially after not playing a real game since April, had to wear the Park/Seiling/Bergman trio down immensely. This led to mistakes with exhaustion, forcing them to miss that half step needed to stop their speedy opponents. **As coaches, Sinden/Ferguson were responsible for managing Canada's defensive ice time. Simply put, they didn't**. This coaching mistake seriously contributed to the end of game collapse.

The final area where bench/player management comes into question was the Canadian players selected for game one. While hindsight is perfect, a couple of choices seem questionable in review. Ken Dryden had played for the Canadian National Team and suffered one of their worst losses against the Soviets, a 9-2 beating in 1969 in Vancouver. Ken struggled during training camp letting in 6 goals in two periods in a losing effort in the first White-Red game, 4 goals in another losing effort in intersquad game 2, including a hat trick by Jean Ratelle, and then one scoreless period in game 3. While Tony Esposito struggled a bit in the intersquad games, he did have a better save percentage than Dryden and a bit of a point to prove for a game in Montreal. This was a result of being put on waivers by the Montreal Canadians after the 1969-70 season. Esposito had better statistics from the 1971-72 season than Ken Dryden, with a stingy 1.77 GAA (goals against average) compared to Dryden's 2.24. While history will never know if Canada competes better in game one with Tony O in goal, Dryden certainly didn't have a consistent strong game.

The decision to dress Don Awrey and Rod Seiling as Team Canada's second unit is a curious one. Neither were considered elite defensemen in the NHL at that time. While it could be argued that with players such as Bobby Orr, Jacques Laperriere, JC Tremblay and Dallas Smith not participating, that opened up roster spots for Seiling and Awrey, that certainly didn't guarantee starting roles in game one. Sinden had the Chicago pairing of Pat Stapleton and Bill White, who had familiarity with each other, they were 3rd and 4th in Norris (best defenseman) voting in 1972 and were selected as a pair for the NHL end of season second team all stars. Sinden's other option was to pair the Montreal Canadian defensive tandem of Serge Savard and Guy Lapointe together as his second unit. Familiarity with the Montreal Forum, and offensive ability of both players seemed to fit Sinden's offensive strategy more than the Seiling/Awrey group. Don Awrey even mentions this:

> "Rod and I had a terrific training camp," said the classic and classy blueliner. "But maybe things didn't work out in

the first game. We were two defensive specialists playing together." 1972 SummitSeries.com

Harry Sinden's thought process was flawed for player selection as he seemingly contradicted his own strategy! Sinden wanted offence yet went with these two defensive defensemen because of their strong training camp chemistry. He then seemingly ignored that logic by going with Ken Dryden **despite a semi-poor training camp**. He felt Dryden might play well at home, but he benched Montreal defenseman Serge Savard, a local player who provided offense and won the 1969 Conn Smythe for playoff MVP a few short years earlier. Sinden would settle down with a set line-up in Moscow, but the folly was not only bench management for this game, but his illogical roster decisions for game one, **severely impacted the final result**.

For the Soviets, coach Bobrov went with a line-up of 3 balanced, strong lines, and Mishakov as the extra forward. He also employed a strategy of 7 defensemen preferring to rotate them through the lines rather than going with set pairs. This was probably in the anticipation of Canadian heavy forechecking and pressure, thus having a group of 7 would prevent less fatigue. This strategy worked wonderfully as all three lines contributed at least a goal, and the Soviet defence played well as a unit throughout the game. **It was the Soviet transition game that played the biggest part in their win**. Paul Henderson remarks on facing it:

"We stayed with them for two periods, but by the third period, our poor defensemen were just sucking air. We turned it over in their end and they were gone like a shot. We had never seen a transition game like that. Their transition game was unreal. We'd be in their zone and have a good scoring chance, and the next thing we knew -- they were firing at our net. We weren't prepared for that kind of transition game at all. It just killed us."
Paul Henderson on Canada's Game 1 loss to the Soviets.

Bobrov seemed to have prepared his team for the

expected Canadian onslaught. He wanted them to remain calm if Canada scored a couple of quick goals and remember their training and skills. He felt that the Soviet fitness, skating, and puck control would turn the tide and make the game competitive. In fact, the Soviet win changed the perception of the Canadian team and brand of hockey as noted, rather harshly, in the Soviet State News Agency TASS:

> "...the defeat showed that Canadians, accustomed to competing in self isolation, play an archaic brand of hockey."

The third reason, which was perhaps the biggest differences between the two teams in game one was in **team unity and cohesion**. The Canadian players, both defence and forwards alike, kept attempting to stick handle through the neutral zone past the awaiting Soviet defenders. This failed time and time again, yet they continued the pattern. The Soviet forwards in this game were energetic back checkers, who were very good at using their sticks to hook the puck and the body. This would slow down and annoy the attacking Canadian forwards enough to allow the mobile Soviet defence to angle the Canadian forwards to the boards preventing any zone penetration. When Canada dumped the puck past the defence, especially the angled dump in, the Soviets struggled with the play and turned the puck over. However, this was a rare instance on this night as **Canadian player after player continued to stickhandle ineffectively through the neutral zone**.

The Soviets had no such issues, they would spring their forwards on quick lightening like breakouts with passes to the red line, and the Canadian defence, tired, hot and intimidated by the Soviet speed, backed up quickly into their own zone. This gave speedsters such as Kharlamov, Zimin and Maltsev time to cross into the Canadian zone and make plays. Once in the Canadian zone, the Soviets would start to cycle the puck, constantly moving to empty space and looking for their teammates. In return the Canadian defence often went out of position, chasing the puck. This had the dual effect of leaving a Soviet player open and exhausting the Canadian player further.

With the unexpected victory, the expectations for the Soviets had also changed, from a friendly series of knowledge exchange to a victory for the Soviet game and way of life. As Vladmir Petrov revealed after game one it was now the **players' "duty "to win the Series.** The giddy Soviet squad would head to Toronto full of confidence, joy, and excitement. That would all come crashing down as they would get their own hockey lesson this time, **NHL playoff style**.

PART 3: CANADA VERSUS THE DEVELOPING HOCKEY WORLD 1910-1954

CHAPTER 12: INTERNATIONAL HOCKEY BEGINS: FREDRICKSON AND WATSON? MUCH TOO MUCH

Game one is over. Canada has lost. The expectations of total dominance and eight straight wins is done. This was a real eye opener for Canadian hockey who had a long history of historical beat downs on European hockey nations (at least up until the mid-1950s). The reality was, that when the North American hockey world was shocked at the calibre of the Soviet team in the 1972 series, **much of that shock stemmed from an early history of Canadian total dominance, pitting Canada as the master and the European nations as the pupils**. This was a gradual process that included huge blowouts, demonstration exhibition tours and Canadian coaches developing European hockey. While the time would soon come when that would all change, the precedent was set. **Canada was the best. Always would be**. At least in the minds of the Canadian fans, players and hockey establishment.

Why was that the mindset? Part of that was because Canada had several decades of hockey development before any European nation started playing the game. While that gave Canada a significant edge, it wasn't as large of a gap as it appeared. That was because of another game played in Europe on large outdoor ice surfaces, the game of Bandy. Bandy had been played in many European countries, a skating game on a soccer field with a ball instead of a puck, since the late 1800's, mirroring hockey's development in North America at the same time-period. This included international bandy games between Sweden, Finland, and Russia in 1907 and a European Championship in 1913. The skill sets were very similar to hockey, which allowed for less of a learning curve for those nations when they started competition in Hockey.

How did hockey begin at a competition level in Europe? European/North American International Hockey competition was formulated out of the beginnings of the European/International Ice Hockey Federation that was founded on May 15th,1908 in Paris. The first countries participating were Belgium, France, Great Britain, and Switzerland with only Switzerland could be considered a strong hockey nation today. Later that same year the future world hockey power of Czechoslovakia joined, under the name Bohemia, as they were known at the time. A year later in 1909, a second meeting was organized, in which Germany became the sixth member of the International Ice Hockey Federation (the IIHF as it is still known as today). A small tournament was played in Chamonix France in conjunction with the second meeting, and a team from London England emerged as the winner.

The first European Championships, a precursor to the World Championships, were played in Les Avants, near Montreux, in Switzerland in January 1910. The participating countries were the four founding countries of Belgium, France, Great Britain, and Switzerland, plus Germany. What was significant about this tournament was not only was it the first official IIHF championships, but this was also **the debut of a team representing the Maple Leaf Emblem of Canada.**

When France declined to send a participating team, the organization asked England's **Oxford Canadians** to participate, but the games would be exhibitions only. English and European hockey at the time was more like bandy, the Soviet game would have similar roots and they allowed forward passing, something that was not implemented in the NHL until the 1929-1930 season.

The Oxford team was founded in 1905 and was composed of Canadian students from Oxford University attending on a Rhodes Scholarship. They were known for their physical game, **perhaps starting the Canadian reputation abroad that was prevalent in 1972**. The university students played what was becoming known as "Canadian rules" hockey which did not allow the forward pass and mirrored the rules in the various professional and amateur leagues back in Canada at the time. The Times of London reported that,

> *"...the chief objective in admitting them (Oxford) to the competition was to give spectators the opportunity to observe their method and style of play. "*

The Oxford Canadians' exciting and rugged style of play was instrumental in the LIHG formally adopting the Canadian rules of ice hockey on March 14, 1911. The tours embarked upon around Europe by the Canadians had played a crucial role in these rules being adopted. The Canadians would continue to field strong teams in comparison to the weaker European game throughout the 1920s and had alumni such as future Prime Minister Lester Pearson and future NHL president Clarence Campbell.

On January 10, 1910, wearing white shirts emblazoned with a red maple leaf, **the first hockey club representing Canada to do so**, the Oxford Canadians stepped on to the outdoor rink at the Swiss resort of Les Avants to play the host nation at the first European Championships. In doing so, they became the first team to represent Canada on the international stage. As what would become somewhat typical for the next forty years, the Canadian players had an easy time of it, winning 8-1 over Switzerland, and 4-0 and 6-0 over Germany and Belgium respectfully. This was truly the start of the long history of Canadian-European matches and in many cases **the birth of international hockey**. Canada would now start to participate with regularity, both as masters of the sport and teachers of the game to the hockey developing European Countries. Russia was not one of them.

With the breakout of World War II, it wasn't until the 1920 Summer Olympics in Antwerp, Belgium that Canada would first send a topflight team to Europe. This team was the Allen Cup Champion **Winnipeg Falcons**. The Falcons were a unique team at the time as they were comprised almost exclusively of players from **Icelandic backgrounds**, who had been banned from playing in the Winnipeg Senior Leagues until 1919-20 due to their "immigrant" status. They also had seven members participating who had fought in WW1 and had sadly lost two team members in the War. The team was motivated to win for their fallen teammates as they returned to Europe.

The Falcons were a powerful squad that were led by future Hall of Famer **Frank Fredrickson**. Although an amateur, at the time, Fredrickson was one of the world's best players. This was proven once he turned professional, as he led the Pacific Coast Professional League in goals in 1922-23 with 39. He then led his Victoria Cougars team to a Stanley Cup in 1925 and won another with the Boston Bruins in 1929. He would be elected to the Hockey Hall of Fame in 1958.

How did Fredrickson and his Allen Cup winning team do against the European teams? As expected, they tore through the overmatched Czechoslovakian team, generally considered the best in Europe, 15-0. The Falcons then had to face an American All-Star team that included future NHL player **Herb Drury**. In a surprisingly tight 2-0 victory over the USA that had people lined up on the streets to attend, the Falcons were matched up against Sweden in the gold medal game. The resulting 12-1 victory over Sweden in the final ensured Canadian gold. It should be noted that most of the Swedes, however, were bandy players **who had never seen a competitive hockey game**, let alone played in one. In fact, the Swedish goaltender wore a fencing mask and uniform for the game.

The tournament was played under IIHF Hockey rules, with 7 players on the ice including the Rover and no substitutions or forward passing. These restrictions were of little importance to Fredrickson who ended up with 12 goals in the 3 medal games. While this was the start of many years of easy victories for the top Canadian Amateur teams, European hockey had seen a top Canadian team, (and player), and **the process of constant improvement** had begun.

One final note on this ground-breaking tournament, Canada and the USA were added to the IIHF ranks at meetings taking place during the Olympics, in a sense replacing Germany and Austria who had been booted out after the conclusion of World War I. However, in what would turn out to be constant Olympic and international Hockey hypocrisy, four of the USA players were Canadians: Drury (who they claimed got American citizenship just before the Olympics), Frank Synott and the McCormick brothers. George Geran **was a professional** who had played in the NHA two years earlier, where he had played four games for the Montreal Wanderers. Despite these national and professional obstacles, **they were allowed to play for the United States in the Olympic Games**. This flexibility would be allowed for Soviet Bloc players in later years in sports like soccer, and seemingly turned a blind eye to Soviet hockey players who were amateurs in name only, yet always had strict standards for Canada in using professional players. That debate was to reach a boiling point 50 years later in 1970. In 1970, Avery Brundage from the IOC would state the concern that playing against professionals would taint that country from further Olympic involvement, yet as far back as 1920, a verified professional had already.

The gap between the European hockey playing countries and Canada and to a lesser extent the USA seemed to get wider after the 1920 Olympics. In the 1924 Olympic Winter Games **the Toronto Granites** were sent as Canadas's representative. The Granites were two-time defending Allen Cup Champions, with a team that was probably as good as a top NHL or PCHL team at that time. **Harry Watson** was the main star, a former World War I fighter pilot who was a fantastic hockey player. The Granites also had **Hooley Smith** who would go on to play 17 seasons in the NHL. These two great players were supported by **Albert McCaffrey** and team captain **Dunc Monro**, both who would also have long careers in the NHL. Harry Watson and Hooley Smith were eventually elected to the Hockey Hall of Fame.

To call the Toronto Granites dominant over their opponents in the 1924 Winter Olympics is understated. They were simply overwhelming, outscoring their opponents 85-0 including 30-0 over Czechoslovakia, a game in which the Czech players were unable to get a shot on goal. Watson would score 37 goals in 5 games and turn down a $10,000 offer to play for the Toronto St Pats when he returned to Canada. At this stage in hockey history, after a devastating war, and being new to the Canadian version of hockey, the European hockey playing nations were not competitive with a top Canadian team. The European nations were learning the game, and as many of them were still recovering economically from the first world war, they lacked the resources to build facilities. They had also unfortunately lost thousands of young men, which further stagnated any grass roots development in any sport, especially a new novelty one like Hockey.

The 1928 Olympics were another cakewalk for the Canadian representatives the Allen Cup winning Toronto Varsity Grads. The Olympics adopted the Canadian Amateur Hockey Association rules, one being the rink boards becoming 5 ft high instead of just one foot as in previous Olympics. The Varsity Grads, despite **Coach Conn Smythe** stepping down due to a nepotism debate with his two top players goalie Joe Sullivan and future Canadian House of Commons member Hugh Plaxton, were able to easily win gold in St. Moritz, Switzerland. Led by **Dave Trottier**, who would go on to star with the NHL's Montreal Maroons, the Canadians outscored their opponents 38-0.

With the worldwide economic crash in 1929, travel overseas became a more costly adventure than it might have been in the 1920s. In 1929, the IIHF decided in Budapest to organize, starting in 1930, a World Championship every year, whereby the best placed team from Europe should win the title of European champion and the overall winner would be crowned **"World Champion"**, ignoring that the best teams at that time were in the NHL. This gave Canada and the other participating nations yearly opportunities to send amateur teams to the World Championships. As a result, the 1930s decade would be one of continued Canadian dominance, but with a gap that was slowly closing. In fact, the 1930s was a decade that had a few shocking surprises for the justifiably confident hockey nation.

1930 was the first year that the World Hockey Championships were a separate tournament from the Olympic Games. Another Toronto team was chosen to represent Canada, but this time it wasn't a top Allen Cup winning squad. The Toronto Canadas were an "industrial or mercantile "league team, who were represented by the CCM Hockey Manufacture. **The Toronto CCMs** had won the Toronto and York Mercantile leagues and CCM decided to use them to promote the company on a European tour. The

CAHA decided that it was fiscally responsible to use the CCMs as Canada's representatives in the World Championships, since they would already be in Europe.

The CCMs had the unfortunate distinction of being the first Canadian team to lose a game to a European team when they lost 1-0 to the Austrian National Team in a rain-soaked outdoor rink. This loss barely registered a blip back in Canada, assumedly because the CCMs were a lower-level industrial team and not the Allen Cup Champs. The CCMs redeemed themselves by beating the winner of the European division of the World Championships, the reinstated Germans 6-1 in the final. Due to the one-sided victories in previous years, Canada had been given a bye right to the final game. A record 12 countries took place in the tournament, including a team from Japan.

The next year, **the Manitoba Grads,** a group of good players who had formed the nucleus of an Allen Cup Championship in 1928 went to Poland for the 1931 World Championships. The Grads won the tournament but **tied Sweden 0-0** and won the final against a strong American side, 2-0. These results were even more shocking than the CCMs exhibition loss to Austria. Sweden's 0 – 0 tie with Canada was the first time an Allen Cup winning team representing Canada failed to outright win a game in a World Championship match. The Swedes had certainly improved significantly from their first exposure to hockey in 1920. They had got to the point where they could tie a strong Canadian Amateur team. Much like the Soviets would discover in the late 1940's, having a bandy playing background, and resulting skating ability, gave the Swedes a solid foundation for future hockey success.

Canada would continue to somewhat struggle in the next Olympic games in 1932. Without strong European entries from Sweden or Czechoslovakia, who chose not to travel to Lake Placid NY, Canada won again, but this time they sent the Allen Cup champion **Winnipeg Hockey Club.**

The Winnipeg team went undefeated, but they narrowly won gold by a double overtime victory against the USA. Even more shockingly, the 1932 Allen Cup winning **Toronto Sea Fleas would lose to a strong Boston Olympic Club 1-0** in overtime at the 1932 World Championships! **This would be the first time Canada had failed to win either the Olympic Gold or the World Championship title.** While the Sea Fleas were coached by 1924 Toronto Granite Olympic star Harry Watson, in a bit of hockey bad karma, they were managed by the infamous, future Toronto Maple Leaf owner **Harold Ballard**. The Sea Fleas poor showing was not seen as a glimpse of the world catching up to Canada, but instead a blame on the team representing Canada. Sports editor and athlete Lou Marsh had this to say about the Sea Fleas loss:

"And as for the Boston Team, it was not even from the club which won the US amateur title last year. It was just a team which won on a Cooks tour around Europe. And that is exactly what the Sea Fleas were doing over there, on a sightseeing tour with hockey as an excuse!" Michael McKinley, It's Our Game

Canadian teams representing Canada had in a short 3-year span lost an exhibition game to Austria, tied Sweden to a scoreless draw, and lost the World Championships to the USA. In 1934 **the Saskatoon Quakers** who were Western Finalists in the Allen Cup, won the World Championship, but had to win in overtime against the USA and even Switzerland. The rapidly improved Czechoslovaks had two games against the Saskatchewan team and lost both, but they were tight 2-1 battles. While the teams Canada had sent were not the strength of the Winnipeg Falcons or Toronto Granites who had future Hall of Famers in their line-ups, these were still solid strong Allen Cup competing or winning hockey clubs, Toronto CCMs excepted.

Overall, the European countries were not yet at the level they would become in the 1960s and onward, but their improvement was certainly noticeable. Even countries like

Poland and Nazi Germany were no longer being blown out by large numbers. At the same time another future powerhouse was improving rapidly. Czechoslovakia was being guided in the mid-1930s by a Canadian who would have a large impact on Czechoslovakian hockey and international hockey as a whole. While that future adversary was developing, a non-hockey playing, bureaucratic adversary would cause Canada's first great international hockey crisis.

CHAPTER 13: BUNNY AHEARN AND A BALL AT THE 1936 OLYMPICS

While the Czechoslovakians were improving under Canadian tutelage, an Irishman named **John Francis Ahearn** (known as Bunny) had taken control of the British national hockey team. Ahearn would become a great thorn in the side of Canadian hockey, but in 1934 Ahearn had become Secretary of the British Ice Hockey Association and coach of the National Team. Despite never playing the game, Ahearn was successful as a coach, winning bronze at the 1935 World Hockey Championships. England had a thriving professional League and that had helped grow the domestic game throughout the 1920's and 1930's.

Crowds of 10,000 plus were common, and players were paid well even during the Depression. In fact, the circulation of Ice Hockey World, a British publication on hockey had peaked at a circulation of 50,000 a week! This financial success allowed for recruitment of foreign players, particularly Canadians who were considered the best players in the world. Ahearn understood a team of only British players would not be competitive with Canada or even the

USA. He also astutely decided that not having played the game himself, he needed to bring in a top-level coach.

Percy Nicklin had Scottish parents, but had grown up in Canada, played the game all his life and by the early 1930's had become a top Canadian coach. Nicklin led the Senior A Moncton Hawks to consecutive Allen Cup victories in 1934 and 1935. Once successfully recruited, he joined the British League Richmond Hawks. Ahearn and British Hockey executives quickly made him the Head Coach of the British National Team. Foreshadowing successful Soviet hockey leaders such as Tarasov and Tikhonov, Nicklin was a disciplinarian who trained the National Team players with ruthless efficiency and focus on defensive hockey. Daniel Harris wrote in Europesport in 2018 about Nicklin and his discipline:

> "Nicklin imposed a rigid discipline: Practice began daily at 7am, and during the 2 hours it lasted, players were forbidden from talking and he ordered about using a megaphone. Next came a team breakfast, chalkboard teaching on tactics and then off-ice fitness sessions. There was an 11pm curfew and cigarettes were limited to 2 a day max"

There have been unproven rumours over the years that someone at the CAHA was a "mole" for Ahearn as Bunny was able to get information on top Canadian players who would qualify to play for Britain. Ahearne went to Canada in 1935 with British team captain Carl Erhardt to find the best available players. The Canadian Amateur Hockey Association / CAHA reluctantly agreed to allow permission for any player wishing to transfer, as long as the BIHA would only use such players who were properly transferred. As a result, he put together **a powerful British team by recruiting players living in Canada who obtained British citizenship under the British nationality law, through ancestral linkages to the United Kingdom**. The key recruit? One of the best goalies in the world outside the NHL, **James**

"Jimmy" Foster from Winnipeg. Foster had been Nicklin's star goalie for the back-to-back Allen cup winning Moncton Hawks. Jimmy had once gone 417 minutes without letting in a goal and was known as a goalie who knew how to win. Foster joined Nicklin at his Richmond Hawks British League club and carried them to first place, earning all star status in the process. With Nicklin cracking the whip on the players and a world class goalie in net, the British were ready to take on the world at the 1936 Olympics in Nazi Germany.

The 1936 Winter Olympics in Germany have been somewhat overshadowed by the Summer Olympics and the exploits of Jesse Owens in front of the Nazi Germany leaders. While that is a true symbolic moment in sport, the 1936 Winter Games had its own drama playing out in the hockey arena. There were two main stories that played out in the Hockey aspect of the 1936 Winter games. The first being the British use of players from Canada, and the resulting protest and gold medal upset. The second was the legacy of German hockey star **Rudi Ball** who happened to be **Jewish in Nazi Germany**.

Rudi was one of two Jewish athletes representing Germany in 1936, the other being gold medal winning fencer Helen Mayer. The star of the German national hockey team, Rudi was a small player, standing only 5'4 and 140 pounds but like Aurel Joliat who was starring for the Montreal Canadiens at the time, Ball could really fly. He was a superb stickhandler and passer, who had been inspired to take up hockey at the late age of 15 when he saw Canadian star Harry Watson play in Europe. Rudi had been a star himself in the 1932 Olympics, **being the first European to score a hat trick**, leading Germany to the bronze medal. Ball, and his brother (who was a top European goalie) went to Switzerland to play for EHC St. Moritz in the 1933-34 season. In April of 1933, the ruling Nazi Party in Germany enacted a rule that made for "Aryan Only" in all sports. This effectively barred non-Aryan groups from playing for sport clubs or against sports clubs. **Despite the ban on Jews**, and the fact that Rudi was playing in Switzerland, Rudi was still invited to play on the 1934 German National Team in the World Championship where Germany finished 3rd behind Canada and the US. Rudi decided not to go back to Germany after 1935 due to fear of persecution, which left off the German National Team when it was named. However, another top German player, **Gustav Jänecke said he would not play without Rudi**. Soon after, the entire German National Team echoed Jänecke's stance and would refuse to play without Ball. The Ministry of Sport with Hitler's approval conceded and reached out to Ball to join the team for the Olympics. However, Ball had one condition before agreeing to play and represent Nazi Germany. **His condition was for his family to leave Germany** and escape persecution. The German government allowed for this stipulation and the Ball family left for South Africa, probably saving their lives in the process.

Ball and his German team would play well in the Olympic tournament, beating Italy 3-0 in their opening game. Ball would then score a goal and an assist against the Swiss in a 2-0 German win, and they gave the strong Americans a much closer than anticipated in a narrow 1-0 USA win. The next game against arch-rival Hungary would include a Rocket Richard like moment for Ball, one that is forever etched in the history of German hockey. In front of 10,000 German supporters, **including Adolf Hitler**, Ball would be injured in the first period after setting up teammate Janecke for the opening goal. Ball would miss the entire second period and then as described by Noah Caplan in the website Brotherlypuck,com:

> *"He didn't play the whole 2nd period and watched as the Hungarians tied the game up. Rudi wasn't on the bench for the start of the third. The Germans were barely holding on. Then, during a stoppage of play, Rudi emerged on the bench, with his left shoulder drooping and forehead still bloody, and hit the ice to thunderous applause. As the puck hit*

the ice for the next faceoff, Rudi took the puck and dashed down the ice almost like a blur on the ice. He skated past the Hungarians towards their net. Two defensemen stood between him and the goalie. One defenseman crunched Rudi into the boards and Rudi heard another pop in his shoulder as he was lifted up and somersaulted. He got right back up, amazingly still in stride and the other defenseman stuck his stick between Rudi's legs as he forced all his weight into Rudi's chest and rose his stick into the back of Rudi's thigh, cutting him. Rudi, amazingly got the shot off and beat the Hungarians' net minder glove side to score the game winning goal. This even brought Hitler to his feet as he cheered on his team, and Jewish captain. One Hungarian came over and commended Rudi on his brilliant move. His teammates. came over to congratulate him then help him off the ice. As the last seconds ticked away in the third, Rudi stood up to bask in a moment he would remember forever."

Ball had been badly injured in the game, separating his shoulder, and suffering bad lacerations on his forehead and thigh. Motivated to continue to play well for their fallen teammate, the Germans tied the eventual goal medal winners, the Canadian supplemented Great Britain team 1-1. The actual Canadian side brought the German run to an end with a 6-2 victory, leaving the Germans to finish 5th overall, third in Europe. After the Olympics Ball would return to Germany, leading Berliner SC to a German championship in 1937, scoring both goals in the final game. He would be forced to stay in Germany throughout World War II, playing for Berliner, **but always fearing for his life**. Finally with the fall of the Reich, Rudi Ball was able to join his family in South Africa in 1948, where he would start several hockey programs and live until 1975. Later in life, in an interview, Rudi summed up his courage of himself and his teammates at the 1936 Winter Olympics,

"Hockey owes me nothing. I am the one that owes hockey. It saved me and my family from the Holocaust".

While the Germans had their own roster issues before and during the tournament. Canada had originally planned to send the 1935 Allen Cup Champions the **Halifax Wolverines**, who had defeated a team from Port Arthur in a hard-fought close final. Due to internal politics in Nova Scotia, the team had suddenly disbanded as players signed with other senior clubs. Halifax offered several suggestions on how they could put a team together to go to Germany, but all were rejected by the CAHA. Finally, the **Port Arthur Bear Cats** were asked to replace Halifax, but they would have to take on at least four Wolverine players. Halifax felt it should be a joint "all-star" team with mostly Halifax players, but CAHA head E. J. Gilroy stated firmly that Port Arthur would represent Canada and the four Wolverine players were now optional if those players didn't want to go. At this time, there was also unhappiness in Montreal and the Quebec province because the Montreal Royals were the top ranked senior team. Canada at this stage had different associations all bickering and the Olympic Games were only months away. Finally, by December 1935, a roster was set. Much like Team Canada in 1972, the roster would be built from multiple clubs. Canada would start with only 13 players, 7 from Port Arthur, 4 from Halifax and 2 from Montreal.

After a series of exhibition games in Manitoba and Thunder Bay, another Montreal player joined the roster. In January, the team was preparing for an exhibition game at Maple Leaf Gardens when word got out that the four Halifax players had been let go. Lou Marsh of the Toronto Star had reported that they each wanted $150 for three months for travel expenses, **a clear violation of CAHA rules**. This led to protests in Nova Scotia and further disarray among the team. The protests fell on deaf ears, so the Bearcats added more players from Montreal and set sail for Europe to win the Olympic hockey tournament. A long-term result of the Halifax player decision was that the CAHA formed a committee to study the definition of an amateur hockey player with relation to eligibility for international competition. This led to the amateur reforms which allowed for future travel expenses and compensation of lost wages.

On Feb 5th, 1936, the day before the games started, CAHA Executives Gilroy and W.A. Hewitt met with LIHG president Paul Loicq to discuss the issue of the eligibility of two of the 'British' players, **Canadians Jimmy Foster and two-time Manitoba All-star winger Alex Archer, who were under CAHA suspension for going to England to play professionally, without CAHA permission**. They also rightly felt that the entire British team was professional, as they were playing in the professional British League. However, the Olympic committee voted to suspend the two British-Canadian ringers, leaving a confident Canada ready to start the tournament against Poland. Canada won that first game an 8-1 rout outdoors in a snowstorm. However, a threatened **British tournament pull-out by Bunny Ahearne** led to an emergency meeting of the IOC on the evening of Feb 6th. At the meeting Bunny Ahearne was at his finest boisterous self-proclaiming:

> *"It was "preposterous' that the CAHA claimed jurisdiction over players transferring in the off-season, and that Canada received support at the IHF meeting on the 5th because the other delegations were "apprehensive over Great Britain's chance of winning the Olympic title."*

The IOC, probably fearful of a British pull-out, or against another Canadian victory, **retracted the original decision** and let Foster and Archer play for Britain. Canada accepted the decision; with a smug feeling they were being sportsmanlike and confident in victory no matter who played for the British team. As the tournament continued, Canada trounced Latvia by the one-sided score of 11-0, while Britain began its campaign by grinding out a 1-0 win over Sweden. Canada concluded its pool games by building up a 4-0 first period lead and cruising to a 5-2 victory over Austria. Britain with the stellar Foster in goal, kept up its defensive style of play, and shutout Japan 3-0, thus winning its group. Britain and Canada moved into a semi-final group which also included Germany and Hungary. The other semi-final group was composed of the United States, Czechoslovakia, Sweden, and Austria.

The first match featured the Britain Canadians facing off against Canada. The game itself became the talk of the tournament as fans clamoured to see the showdown. The British team was in great shape due to their strict regimen and Soviet style off ice training. Coach Percy Nicklin had thoroughly drilled a defence first philosophy into his team. Foster had been fantastic so far in goal, as Britain had not yet had a goal against in the tournament. In contrast, the Canadians had so far led the tournament in scoring but had a somewhat suspect defence that had allowed three goals to pool minnows Austria and Poland.

Played before a crowd of 10,000, the game got off to a fast start, as British winger Gerry Davey scored off a long shot 40 seconds into the game. Davey was well known to the Bearcats players, as he had played all his minor hockey in Port Arthur. Canada came roaring back and late in the first period Montreal Royals centre Ralph St. Germain scored from close in to even the game. Foster was strong throughout, as Canada spent most of the rest of the game on attack, but with two minutes to play, British winger Ed 'Chirp' Brenchley, who learned his hockey in Niagara Falls, Canada, scored and Britain led again, 2-1. Foster deftly turned away five more shots in the final minute, **leaving Canada with its' first ever loss in Olympic competition, and Bunny Ahearne smirking in glee.**

Much like the Sports headlines 36 years later after the Soviets shocked Canada in game one of the Summit Series, the newspapers in Canada were similarly outraged, despite the fact that it was Canadians defeating Canadians. The Globe lamented that,

"the fond thought about Canada being unbeatable in

Olympic hockey has become an exploded myth!"

Canada however felt that since the match had been in a preliminary round, and they could still qualify for the medal round with wins over Germany and Hungary. **Winning those games would put Canada into the final round, with a shot at the title.** Despite the loss, the reports that the Canadian team had carried the play against the Brits left commentators with an air of confidence that the medal round rematch would re-affirm Canadian hockey supremacy. Lou Marsh in the Star reported *"Canada must win from England in the next round unless some other team unexpectedly defeats England."*. That feeling of hope for Canada was to last no more than a day. On the night of February 12th, a new storm of controversy blew up, as **Canada discovered that somehow the tournament would not include a medal round rematch with Britain**. In the final round, the results of semi-final round matches between qualifying teams would carry over, and not be replayed. Had Ahearn gone to the IOC and convinced them to change the rules? The change meant that Canada would not play Britain again and would be burdened with a loss in the now "final" round. The story was front page news in The Globe again:

> *"The most exciting, dispute-torn hockey tournament in Olympic history developed a fresh sensation tonight when the Canadian team threatened to withdraw from the competition at once unless more equitable final round arrangements were made.*

In Canada's next game they overwhelmed Hungary by 15-0 while Britain struggled to a 1-1 overtime tie with Rudi Ball's German squad. Associated Press reported that "an indignation meeting" would be held by Canadian management, and a final decision made about withdrawal. In Garmisch Germany, both meetings and hockey matches continued. **Ahearne convinced even the Americans to side with Britain and at an emergency meeting, the tournament format was re-affirmed by a vote of 6-2, with only Germany**

supporting Canada's stand for a medal round rematch. Also, on that day and in front of a partisan crowd of 10,000 in the Olympic arena including Nazi officials, Canada defeated Germany 6-2 in a very physical game.

The result put Canada into the final round, along with Britain, the United States and Czechoslovakia. Canada's first match of the final round was against the Czechs. There was one glimmer of hope. In a game largely "devoid of anything resembling hockey brilliance" Britain had defeated the Czechs 5-0 on Friday night. However, it became known that if the United States beat Britain, and then Canada beat the U.S., the tournament would be decided on goal difference, a measure that favoured the relatively high-scoring Canadian team. It was not to be. While Canada thumped the Czech team 7-0, Jimmy Foster was again brilliant as Britain and the U.S. played to a scoreless overtime tie, ending Canada's last chance at the gold medal. A dejected, angry Canada finished the tournament by grounding out a 1 -0 win over the Americans, **clinching the gold for Britain**, winning the silver medal. Bunny Ahearne had won the day with Canada; it wouldn't be the last time.

Canada would get revenge on Bunny Ahearne and Britain at the following year's World Championships, ironically held in London, England. **The Kimberly Dynamiters** had beaten the Sudbury Falcons in two straight games to win the Allen Cup. Based out of Kimberly British Columbia, a small mining town in the Kootenay Rockies, the Dynamiters were actually a semi-pro team that was financed by the Cominco Mining Corporation. Cominco wanted badly to beat its corporate rival in Trail BC, where the Trail Smoke Eaters had dominated Senior Hockey for many years. As a result, Cominco recruited top talent, and paid them more to play hockey and work for Cominco than even the average NHLers of the day were making. The Dynamiters went on a **long draining 64 game exhibition tour of Europe** before playing the World Championship. This tour certainly helped grow hockey in Europe and showcase the game being played at a high level.

Canada would win its pool easily with one sided victories over Poland, France and Sweden who had seemingly sent a weak team. Britain who was icing their championship Olympic team of star-studded Canadians, as well as playing at home, also went undefeated in the preliminary pool. Jimmy Foster was riding an incredible eight game shutout streak when Britain and Canada clashed on Feb 27th, 1937 in the rematch of the Olympic games, of course Canada was using a completely different team. In a hard-fought game, with fights breaking out, the Canadians revenged their Olympic loss with a tough 3-0 victory. Canadas biggest challenge in this tournament was the vastly improved Swiss who took Canada to overtime in front of 10,000 pro Swiss fans at London's Harringay Arena. Canada prevailed with Red Goble scoring quickly in overtime.

After the tournament, at the annual IIHF general meeting, **the Swiss put in a motion to declare all professionals playing in Britain to be declared ineligible for amateur status**. The IIHF would comprise, allowing professionals and amateurs to play in the same league, but **only amateurs being eligible for the Olympics and World Championships**. Ideally this would prevent Ahearne from using his British Canadian pros moving forward, but the spirit of the ruling would come into great debate into the 1960s when Canada could no longer compete with Senior A club teams or an amateur National Team.

The final two World Championships before the breakout of World War II were won by a stacked Sudbury Wolves squad in 1938 and the Trail Smoke Eaters in 1939. Despite Sudbury really being an all-star team of the top Senior A players in Ontario, they struggled to beat Sweden 3-2, Nazi Germany 3-2 in overtime and tied Hungary 1-1. They would again barely beat Germany 1-0 in the semi-finals before facing the same augmented British team in the final. The Wolves would beat Britain 3-1 claiming the championship. Trail would have an easier time in 1939, except when facing Canadian Mike Buckna coached Czech team, who took the Smoke Eaters to the limit in a tight 2-1 Canadian victory.

With the war looming, and Germany already annexing Austria, World Championship hockey and international hockey would go on hiatus. The hockey world would start to look completely different after the War, with a new hockey superpower being arriving on the scene. The Russian Bear, the soon to be dominant nation in international hockey, the Soviet Union. The Canadian mindset wouldn't change though, they would hang on to the history of Canadian supremacy, which was now in question after the game one loss.

PART 4: GAME TWO -TORONTO

ALL YOU NEED IS CASH! (AND TWO ALL TIME GOALS)

CHAPTER 14:
TORONTO. SOVIET
PURGATORY

If Montreal is considered the birthplace of Hockey, Toronto would be considered, at least nowadays, as **the centre of the hockey universe**. Toronto is Canada's largest city, the Hockey Hall of Fame presides in the downtown core, and the major media outlets in Canada are either based in Toronto or focus on the Toronto sports scene. Modern day Toronto has a crowded professional sports scene with the Maple Leafs, baseball's Blue Jays and the NBA Raptors, plus the CFL Argonauts and professional soccer team the Toronto FC. In 1972, the Toronto Maple Leafs only had the CFL Argonauts to compete with, and they played different seasons. Hockey was the main sport and the only sport of note throughout the long winter season. With the Maple Leafs not yet started training camp, Team Canada had the full attention of the local hockey media. The shock of losing game one was felt as a major tragedy throughout the nation. With the day after being a Sunday on a long Labour Day weekend, Team Canada was given a momentary respite since Sunday papers were not present in 1972 Toronto. Losing Team Canada goalie would reflect on the quietness after the loss,

"On a regular team, everyone has a roommate. But with this team, the non-goalies had roommates and the goalies

didn't. The day after the game was Sunday. This was Toronto, 1972, on a Sunday. And in Toronto, 1972, on a Sunday, there were no newspapers, there were no sports channels, there were just a few mainstream TV stations. Awakening that Sunday morning, there was no evidence anywhere that Saturday night had happened. There was no roommate to remind me. There was no newspaper. There was no television or radio. It was literally one of those awful moments that is so awful you are saying to yourself, "Maybe it didn't happen. And there is nothing to confirm to me that it happened until I leave this room. So as long as I stay in this room, it didn't happen. So I stayed in that room as long as I could". Globe and Mail 1972.

When the newspapers did go to print, one prominent picture was that of Globe and Mail Columnist Dick Beddoes eating his column. Beddoes had promised that if Canada didn't win all eight games.

"Make it Canada eight games to zero. If the Russians win one game, I will eat this column shredded at high noon in a bowl of borscht on the front steps of the Russian embassy."

The NHL's Toronto Maple Leafs were used to media pressure. The city had been a hockey hotbed since the turn of the century. While arch-rival Montreal was the first to establish organized hockey in 1875, it didn't take the city of Toronto long to develop the game locally. There were several prominent amateur teams and leagues throughout the early 1900's. Those teams, however, were soon overshadowed by the launch of professional hockey in Toronto with the Toronto Hockey Club in 1906. The Team would also be come to be known as the **Toronto's**, then the **Blue Shirts**, winning a Stanley Cup in 1914. After an ownership change, which led to the end of the National Hockey Association, the team entered the newly formed National Hockey League. Soon after, the Blueshirts became the **Toronto Arenas**, the Arenas became the **Toronto St Patricks** and finally **the Maple Leafs** in 1927. Those teams would play out of the old Mutual Street

Arena, but on November 12th, 1931, the much larger, more glamourous Maple Leaf Gardens opened. It was considered the new standard in modern arenas at the time, becoming one of the true shrines of hockey.

In the summer of 1972, the Leafs were second only to the Montreal Canadiens for success, having won 11 Stanley Cups including four in the 1960's. They were a successful thriving hockey team with a passionate fan base and a famous arena. The Maple Leafs would play there until 1999, before moving to the Air Canada Centre. The Gardens were not only the home of the Maple Leafs. The landmark arena on Carlton St would host junior, senior, even international contests, including several games with the Soviet Union.

Unfortunately for Soviet teams, the games at Maple Leaf Gardens rarely ended well. In 1954, when the local Toronto East York Lyndhurst's area team lost to the Soviets 7-2 at the World Championships, Maple Leafs owner Conn Smythe offered to send the Maple Leafs to Europe to retake Canadian superiority. That of course never came to pass, but several Toronto teams did go overseas to represent Canada before 1972. The Toronto Granites with star Harry Watson were the first team to represent the city internationally at the 1924 Winter Olympics. They were followed by the University of Toronto Grads in 1928, the industrial league level Toronto CCMs in 1930, and the oddly named Toronto National Sea Fleas (go Fleas!) in 1933. The ill-fated Toronto area East York Lyndhursts were the first ever team to face the Soviets in 1954. The Toronto suburb of Whitby sent a young defenceman named Harry Sinden and his Whitby Dunlops squad to the World Championships in 1958. In fact, it was the same Whitby Dunlops who were the hosts of the **inaugural international game** at Toronto Maple Leaf Gardens, when the Soviets first came to Canada in 1957.

On a cold November 22nd evening, the Moscow Selects with a majority of players from the Soviet National Team, faced the Allan Cup Champions Dunlop's before a standing room only crowd of 14,327 fans in the Gardens. There were millions more watching across Canada. The game had sold out almost immediately. CBC had decided the game was of such importance they would televise it nationally on Hockey Night in Canada. The game was significant on several points, the first being this was **the first game on Canadian soil by a Soviet or Russian team.**

Canadians were extremely curious to see these upstarts from a closed communist country play. This was the country that was involved in the Cold War with the USA. During that time period, there was always the prevalent fear of war or even a nuclear attack. Yet here were representatives of the mysterious USSR. Actually, on Canadian soil to play some top amateur teams. The other curiosity was how could they have become so good at hockey so quickly? How were they able to win the World Championships and Olympics? They were considered an exotic novelty with their **V style sweaters and funny helmets**. The Canadian public wanted to see them play. The hockey establishment, media etc. was even more intrigued to the point that the Soviet practice had over 200 attendees!

From the Soviet side, this was the first opportunity for the Soviets to not only play in Canada, the home of hockey, but to face an actual bona fide NHL star, recently reinstated amateur former Toronto Maple Leaf, **Sid Smith**. While the Soviets had faced the Warwick brothers at the World Championships in 1955, Sid Smith was a whole different level. Smith was a dynamic player, a solidly built left wing who would score 55 goals in 68 games in the very strong AHL in 1948-49. This got Sid a job on the Leafs line-up, where he flourished, scoring six straight seasons of 20+ goals, peaking at 33 goals in 1954-55. This was at a time when the six team NHL was extremely competitive, star studded, thus scoring 30 goals was considered a significant accomplishment. Sid would be a two-time end of season second team all-star, and in his career 1954-55 season, he would be a first team all-star, sharing the limelight with legends such as Maurice Richard, Jean Beliveau and Doug Harvey. In 1957, Smith had become an amateur, but he was only a couple of years removed from being one of the best players in the NHL.

The final significance, unknown at the time, was that the Dunlops were led by 25-year-old Toronto defenceman named **Harry Sinden**. A fast-skating offensive defenceman, Sinden was the vocal leader and team captain. He would face the Soviets several times as a player with the Dunlops, and that experience would be a factor in his selection as coach for the 1972 Summit Series.

The game itself would have some odd similarities to the opening game of the Summit Series. The Soviets would jump out for two quick goals, shocking the Garden crowd. Just like the Soviets in game one, Whitby didn't fold, maintained their composure, and started skating, forechecking and playing a clean but physical game against the visitors. By the end of the first period the score was 5-2 for Whitby, outshooting Moscow 16-5. Whitby kept up the pace, ending the game with a resounding 7-2 win, outshooting the Selects 35-17. It was a clean game, played with sportsmanship. In one incident a Whitby player fell, and a Soviet player helped him up, to the appreciation of the Garden crowd. After the game Soviet Coach Anatoli Tarasov said the Whitby team played very well but that his team made a lot of mistakes and can play a lot better overall. His team did, going on to a 5-2-1 record on this tour, albeit not playing another team the level of the Dunlops.

On an interesting side note, there was some research compiled from this game by **Floyd Percival**, the Canadian who wrote the Hockey Handbook that Tarasov often used as a helpful guideline in building his hockey program. The studies revealed another aspect of the Soviet game that Team Canada would struggle with in the Summit. **They were very fast**. According to time checks during the game, at least four members of the Russian team flew over the Gardens' ice faster than any hockey player had before. Forward Nikolai Khlystov was clocked at 29.5 mph in one burst in the 3rd period. Percival said it was the fastest he had ever clocked a hockey player in the years he has been conducting his research. Fastest Whitby player timed was playing coach Sid Smith at 26.9. The Fastest previous time Percival recorded was by former Leaf Max Bentley, who was clocked at 28.4 mph. While the accuracy of his findings in 1957 might be debatable. there was no denying that the Soviet players could skate.

There would be something of a rematch at Maple Leaf Gardens in 1960, where Whitby would again hammer the Moscow Selects, this time 9-1. This version of the Moscow Selects was considered **the Soviet B team** though, behind the actual National Team. In 1962, the Soviet National Team would be back to beat a combined University of British Columbia Thunderbirds and a group of local Junior players 6-0. Future Canadian National Team coach **Father David Bauer** was the coach of the combined team. The Soviets would be back to defeat the newly formed Canadian National Team 4-0 at the Gardens on December 13th, 1964. Summit Series player **Vyacheslav Starshinov** was in his prime and it showed with two goals and an assist. This performance at the Gardens may have been a reason he was dressed for game two.

In 1965, the Soviet National Team played the OHA Junior All Stars in front of another sold out Maple Leaf Gardens. The Junior All-stars were stacked. They had several players who would either play in the Summit Series or have very solid NHL careers. **Serge Savard, Brian Glennie** from the 1972 Team Canada were on defence, with future Maple Leaf **Jim McKenny**. On forward, Summit 1974 WHA legend **Andre Lacroix** was joined by **Jean Pronovost.** who would go on to score 52 goals in a season for the Pittsburgh Penguins. **Danny Grant** was another future NHL 50 goal scorer on the team as were future Boston Bruins defensive stalwarts **Derek Sanderson** and **Don Marcotte**. The star of the team though, was a 17-year-old **Bobby Orr**. A Bobby Orr was already the talk of the hockey world, Orr had started playing Junior A hockey at the incredible age of 14. He was the most heralded young player in hockey history at that time, still a young boy. How would he do against the older more experienced Soviets? The Junior players jumped out to a 3-1 lead, before the Soviets stormed back to win 4-3. Anatoli Firsov, Ragulin, Vikulov and Starshinov all scored for the Soviets. 1972 National Team Captain Viktor Kuzkin also played in the game. **The player of the game? Bobby Orr who showcased his future Hockey dominance with dazzling skating and game control.**

Toronto didn't have any other international games until the late 1960's when the Canadian National Team would take **two out three against the Soviets** at the Gardens. This would include a 3-2 win on December 26th, 1969, against a young Vladislav Tretiak. The Gardens were a tough place for the Soviets. Including the three losses in 1972, 1974 and 1976 Canada Cup, the Soviets had a less than stellar record of 4 wins and 7 losses playing at Maple Leaf Gardens. Considering two of the four wins were against Junior squads, the **record is even more dubious**. There doesn't appear to be a solid reason for their consistently poor performance at the Toronto arena, other than the fact that the Canadian teams were extremely motivated to play those games. They were often must win games, just as the second one in the Summit Series would be for Team Canada.

CHAPTER 15:
GAME 2. THE NHL
STRIKES BACK

With the game one disaster for Team Canada and subsequent shock throughout Canada resonating, Coach Harry Sinden and Assistant John Ferguson felt the need to make significant changes to the Canadian line-up. Canada was now much more aware of their opponent's ability, style, and highly skilled players. **It was absolutely crucial that Team Canada make changes, the right changes in order to not fall behind 2-0 in the series at home.** Sinden and Ferguson reviewed the game one tape and decided on a structural change for Canada's defensive zone coverage. Rather than have the wingers high covering the Soviet defensemen, with the centre back helping the defence, they wanted the centre being the only player high, while the wingers came back deep to help the defence. This was based on the thought that the Soviet fore-checking was leaving the Canadian defence outnumbered deep in the Canadian zone, and that the Soviets didn't use their point men for offense very much. While the first aspect was true, the Soviet forechecking scheme had pinned the Canadian team in their own zone for long periods in game one, some of that could be attributed to the poor bench management in game one, and the resulting defensive fatigue. It should be noted that the Soviets also used all five players in a spread-out format to move the puck and fire shots on goal by the defencemen, so the strategy of Canada's wingers playing deep in their own end could **easily have backfired**.

For Canada, eight players from the first game were dropped. This included Rod Seiling, Don Awrey, Red Berenson, Mickey Redmond, goalie Ken Dryden, and the Ranger trio of Hadfield, Gilbert and Ratelle. In an uncomfortable twist of fate, this was the night that Jean Ratelle was presented the Lester B Pearson Trophy for the **best player in the NHL**, voted on by the players. He gracefully received the trophy despite not being dressed for the game. Added to the Canadian line-up on defence was the All-star Chicago Black Hawk pairing of Pat Stapleton and Bill White on defence, Montreal's Serge Savard was added and paired with teammate Guy Lapointe. Gary Bergman and Brad Park remained for a group of six. Upfront, legendary centre Stan Mikita was added to the line-up, as were three aggressive forwards in Minnesota's duo of Bill Goldsworthy and JP Parise, as well as Phil Esposito's regular left wing in Boston, the belligerent and skilled Wayne Cashman. Chisako's athletic goalie Tony Esposito was the starting goaltender with Boston's Eddie Johnson backing him up.

The Soviets countered up front by dropping talented Yuri Blinov, who had played well in game 1 and sniper Vladimir Vikulov, who was injured in the first game. They added long time Soviet legend Vyacheslav Starshinov at centre and one of their young up and coming players Vyacheslav Anisin, a 21-year-old. The Soviet group of Seven on defence remained the same, this included team captain Kuzkin, veteran Ragulin, Gusev, Tsygankov, Lyapkin, Paladiev and Luchenko.

Vyacheslav Starshinov had to be considered a surprise choice by the Soviet Coaching staff. The veteran was described this game by Brian Conacher as "the Soviet Jean Beliveau" but a better comparison might have been Stan Mikita. Both were small, skilled, feisty players who respectfully were past their primes in 1972. Starshinov himself, was a rarity on the Soviet National Team as he played for Moscow Spartak, rather than Central Red Army. His long career started with Spartak in 1957 and finished his career with Spartak in 1979 after being allowed to play in Japan for three years. He was a small player, standing only 5'8 and not a fleet skater by Soviet standards. What Starshinov could do was score goals. **A lot of goals**. His numbers are impressive in any league. He scored 405 goals in 540 Soviet league games, and led the league in goals in 1966-67, 1967–68, and 1968–69. Starshinov scored 149 goals in 182 international games and was named top forward at the World Championships in 1965. His trademark "look" was a chin strap that he wore around his mouth area, a perplexing look that he felt was more comfortable. He was a very intelligent man, eventually becoming a professor of Physics at the Moscow Engineering Institute. Hockey wise, he was a highly respected leader of his clubs and went into coaching and management after his playing career.

Whether Starshinov was selected to play in this game as a reward for his long and successful career, or whether it was because of the injury to Vikulov is unknown, but it was more than likely a reward for the legendary player. In fact, it was a fulfilling a personal wish Starshinov had since the beginning of his career, to test his skills against the best professionals in Canada.

"He had dreamed of playing the professionals all his career. Now in the twilight, he had his dream come true. It doesn't matter if he only played one game" Lev Lebedev Pravda."

Starshinov would have a tough time of it in this game, he appeared at times overmatched against a young, fierce, skilled Canadian centre named Bobby Clarke and unfortunately as a result this would be his only game of the Series. However, it was Phil Esposito and not Clarke who impressed Starshinov:

"I had never seen Phil Esposito play. Many journalists had

told me that we had a similar style. But in this series he taught me some new tricks!" Richard Bendall

The Soviets would be about to learn that it wasn't only Phil Esposito who had new tricks, the professionals would bring a different attitude to game two. One that was battle hardened from years of playoff wars in the NHL.

Game 2: Period 1. Who is Home Team?

The opening ceremonies include the presentation of the Lester Pearson award for the most valuable player in the NHL to Jean Ratelle, who comes out to accept the award in a sharp shirt and tie, after not being selected to play for the game. **The Soviets come out to a very loud applause, a classy tribute to their fine play in game one**. When Valeri Kharlamov gets introduced, he gets a huge applause, a new experience for a foreign player in Canada. The Canadian players with the largest ovation were the Toronto Maple Leafs Paul Henderson and Ron Ellis as well as Boston superstar Phil Esposito.

As the puck is about to be dropped for the second game of this series, both teams put out their starting line-ups for the faceoff. The crowd is chattering with nervous anticipation. For the Soviets, Starshinov is centring the top line with Maltsev moving to right wing and Kharlamov on the left side. Mishakov has been promoted to play on the second line with Petrov and Boris Mikhailov, while the deadly Shadrin Yakushev Zimin line stays intact. Young 21-year-old Anisin is slotted as the extra forward.

Canada counters with the Clarke line, Esposito centring Cashman and Jean Paul (JP) Parise, and Stan Mikita moving to centre the Big M and Cournoyer, a line that played together in training camp. Pete Mahovlich and Bill Goldsworthy are the extra forwards, allowing Canada to rotate three centres if necessary. Canadian defence pairs are set with Park/Bergman, Stapleton/White and Savard/Lapointe. Soviets remain with their seven defencemen strategy from game one.

The game begins with Clarke winning the draw and the puck goes deep in the Soviet end. Ron Ellis absolutely flies in on the puck with great speed, showing no sign of the neck injury he sustained in game one. As he was known to do, Bobby Clarke shows he has come to play by giving Tsygankov a nasty cross check from behind, right in front of the Soviet goal. No call on the play. At the first whistle, a coaching game of "who has last change?" starts. The Soviets start changing lines and Canada responds, both teams trying to match lines and get the upper hand. Chaos ensues, and finally Petrov's line is out against the Esposito line. Americans **Frank Larson** and **Steve Dowling** are the officials for this game, and they would struggle to deal with the line changing gamesmanship. They would also feel the wrath of the Soviets senior management after the game.

This moment is notable for the international debut of **Wayne Cashman**, a throwback style Canadian player that would have been prevalent in the NHL's original six. Cashman was a big, aggressive, mean, talented winger for the Boston Bruins. "Cash" had a long, distinguished career with the Boston Bruins, winning two Stanley Cups in 1970 and 1972. He played 17 years, served as the captain of Boston for seven years, and ended his career as the last player to have played in the NHL's original six era. The 6'1 200-pound winger was a tenacious forechecker, superb fighter and played a well-rounded, intense yet cerebral game. He was an excellent passer and would score over 20 goals in a season eight times. He was part of the best line in hockey for a few years with Phil Esposito and Ken Hodge. Hodge though would not be invited to camp, both due to being a notoriously streaky player but also not getting along with coach Harry Sinden when he had coached the Bruins. **Cashman was not the style of player the Soviets would have ever encountered before this game.** He was Gordie Howe light, a successful mixture of size, talent, and nastiness. He went into the corners to win, and ensured the other team paid a price in the process. Teammate Derek Sanderson said this about big Cash:

> *"You could see a guy go into a corner after the puck, and just before he got to it, he stopped and flinched a bit when he saw Cash. That's when he knew he had him on the ropes,"* Sanderson said. *Joe Pelitter Bruins Legend Blogspot.com*

Wayne would only play two games in the Series, the second and third ones. Harry Sinden felt he was a marked man by the referees and didn't dress him in game four. Cashman would get injured by an Ulf Sterner careless stick infraction in Sweden, causing a nasty cut on his tongue that put Cashman out of the games in Moscow. He did make a significant impression, and Canada was undefeated when he was in the line-up. He gave a little speech in the locker room during one of the games he played:

> *"Tonight you guys just concentrate on playing your own games,"* he said, *"and I'll play the Big, Bad Bruin."*
>
> *"When someone clobbered Clarke, I clobbered him right back,"* Cash said. *"When someone speared Henderson, I speared him right back - even though I didn't like the idea of spearing. I didn't know if these people understood English or not, but I'm sure they got the message. I just let them know if they were going to play that way, I was going to dish it back." Joe Peliteer Bruins Legend Blogspot.*

The majority of the Soviet players may not have spoken English, but they certainly noticed Wayne Cashman very quickly. "Cash" immediately makes an impact, taking it from his own end at full speed, dumping it into the Soviet corner, forechecking Viktor Kuzkin who subsequently gives the puck up. JP Parise is there, firing the puck out front. The puck springs over Petrov's foot right to Esposito who has an early chance on Tretiak. At the end of this early Canadian pressure, Cashman hammers Petrov in the corner for good measure. **Soviets, meet the Big Bad Bruin.**

The Soviets are again trying to match lines, and the

referees try and shut down their constant changes. The action goes back and forth as lines switch on the fly, and one thing has become instantly clear, this is a more focused, determined Team Canada. The Team Canada defence already looks much better with Pat Stapleton showing some speed and manoeuvrability and his playing partner Bill White adding size, composure, and experience. The Soviets are having some trouble cycling the puck in the Canadian zone as Canada seems determined to take the man on every single play. **The goal is to disrupt the Soviet flow and wear the strong Soviet players down.**

The Clarke line comes back out for an excellent shift, starting with a nice full ice rush by Clarke leading to a shot off the wing by Ellis. Clarke easily wins the faceoff from Starshinov, gets the puck back to Serge Savard who blasts a low hard slap shot from the point that Tretiak barely kicks out. The Montreal duo on the point are aggressively pinching in, and combined with the swarming Canadian forwards, Canada gets some real sustained pressure on the Soviets who are panicking a bit, penned in their own end, probably wondering what happened to the Canadian team they faced in Montreal.

Stan Mikita wins another faceoff, but Frank Mahovlich and Serge Savard both stumble for the puck at the Soviet blueline allowing Yakushev and Zimin to take off on a two on one break with only Guy Lapointe back. The Big Yak takes a page from the Canadian playbook by blasting a big slap shot wide. It should be noted that the break is caused by Shadrin cleverly giving Frank Mahovlich a sharp elbow, taking him out of the play. Yakushev's size and speed are noticeable every time he is on the ice.

Phil Esposito's line is out again and Espo gets a great chance right in front of Tretiak. While the play started with Brad Park skilfully slowing the game down and making a nice pass up the middle to Cashman, it's the ferocity of JP Parise that gives Esposito the opportunity. Parise annoys

Viktor Kuzkin so much that the Soviet veteran focuses solely on their battle leading Esposito unmarked in front. The puck comes out to Esposito who is the beneficiary of a wayward puck off Petrov's skate. Esposito gets control, reaches between the two Soviet players before attempting a backhand on Tretiak. A goal mouth scrum results, and Wayne Cashman is deeply involved, chirping, and pushing at the Soviet players. Canada continues the pressure as Esposito wins another draw clearly, Gary Bergman fires it deep behind the Soviet goal where Cashman and Parise outwork the Soviets, cycling the puck and attempting to get it out front to Esposito. The Soviets recover quickly with Boris Mikhailov flying up ice, but Brad Park takes control again, slowing the game down and sending a sweet pass to JP Parise at centre ice, breaking up any counterattack. Parise responds by making a nifty cross ice pass to a streaking Ron Ellis on the right side, who fires a hard shot against Tretiak in full flight. The Soviet goalie comes out enough to block the shot and **wisely covers up**, giving his team a breather from a few moments of intense Canadian pressure.

Before the faceoff, the Soviets are still playing games changing lines, an obvious attempt to slow any Canadian momentum down. On the next draw, Clarke outmuscles Starshinov, getting a quick dangerous shot away. **Bobrov has obviously seen enough**. He quickly changes the line to get his top line away from the Clarke group, but Sinden counteracts by changing Clarke's wingers to Goldsworthy and Pete Mahovlich. This coaching battle seems to slow the game down and the crowd continues booing the constant line changes for both sides.

Once this calms down, the deadly Shadrin/Yakushev/ Zimin lines produce a couple of excellent chances, with Zimin cleverly shooting a quick shot between the Stapleton/ White pair and then Yakushev showing brute strength tossing Stapleton out of the way and sustaining good pressure in the Canadian zone.

Zimin is everywhere on the ice, making a dazzling rush up ice and drilling a low hard shot through the backing up Canadian defence. Canada comes right back, and the Soviets seem to be realizing they are facing a different version of Team Canada tonight and respond by ramping up their physical intensity. After a few more fast paced back and forth exchanges, Maltsev goes offside and Cashman comes menacingly close to him, giving him a gap tooth intimidating smile and waving his stick high near Maltsev's face. The message seems to be **I'm here and you better be aware, or it's going to be a long game.**

Canada continues to change lines constantly and the crowd boos. Even Vladimir Petrov looks frustrated. The Esposito line starts cycling in the Soviet zone again, with Cashman getting a quick chance on goal. Canada stays too long on the ice; the Soviets change players and fresh players Yakushev and Shadrin apply pressure in the Canadian end. Now it's the Canada turn for a moment of panic, resulting in a Brad Park hooking penalty on Zimin, that gets called at cross checking. On the play where Park gets his penalty Zimin makes a clever behind his back pass to Shadrin, **a play an NHL player would never attempt.**

On the power play now, Alexander Maltsev sets up in the Canadian zone and tries to hit Kharlamov with the deadly Soviet back door play. Tony Esposito quickly shows he is much more aware of their tricks than Dryden was in game one. Esposito's nick name was Tony O, relating to his NHL record 15 shutouts in a season. The Chicago Black Hawk netminder reads the pass and makes **the first spectacular save of the night.** He shows his superb athleticism, coming right across the crease to rob Kharlamov of an easy goal. This had to have been a real confidence boost to the Canadian team moving forward.

Peter Mahovlich then does some stellar stick handling in the neutral and Soviet zone, ragging the puck for several seconds before passing back to Bill White who dumps it deep.

The Toronto crowd is ecstatic at both the spectacular Tony Esposito save combined with the Little M's (Pete's nickname) penalty killing and give a loud ovation. Clarke comes out and does a great job forechecking in the Soviet end, stealing the puck from Starshinov and then Gusev. The Soviet Power play was a dud this time, with only the one shot on goal by Kharlamov. To top that off, there was an embarrassing fan (or whiff) on a slap shot by Gennady Tsygankov at the Canadian blue line, in which the Soviet blueliner completely missed the shot and fell down awkwardly.

The Puck goes quickly back into the Soviet zone as Gusev shows again that he is vulnerable to forechecking. He loses the puck after being dogged by Phil Esposito and Cashman which leads to Serge Savard taking a blast on goal. Serge Savard regroups in the Canadian zone, passes to Cashman, who passes to Parise. This is a lightening quick sequence of passing that catches the Soviets on their heels. The Esposito line continues to dominate the play, with Savard and Lapointe playing effectively by keeping the puck in the Soviet end with timely pinches. Finally, the exhausted Soviet defenseman Kuzkin ices the puck to the chorus of boss resonating throughout the building.

Clarke's line is back out again against the Shadrin line. Quickly, Zimin tries to stickhandle around Bergman but is taking out of the play easily. Brad Park spins and makes a lovely, backhanded headman pass to a streaking Ron Ellis. Ellis' pass across the ice misses its target, but Gary Bergman jumps into a rush and hits Clarke on the wing with a nice recover. Clarke is now halfway into the Soviet zone, and off the left wing blasts a shot at Tretiak who has to make a great leg save to stop. The Soviets recover and try a long breakaway pass to Alexander Yakushev, Brad Park reads it, intercepts the pass, weaves in the Canadian end, before hitting Paul Henderson on the tap with a pass. Canada is playing wonderfully right now, skating, crisp passing and forechecking. **A completely different team than game one.**

In a strange reversal of game one, it's the Soviet players who are not playing as a team, stick handling ineffectively through the neutral zone. On that note, Zimin tries an individual foray into the Canadian zone but is easily taken out by Brad Park who is having a great first period. As Paladiev pinches in to try and create some pressure on Canada, Paul Henderson takes an unnecessary elbowing penalty (that was also a trip and called as such) as the Soviet defenceman gets dumped unceremoniously. During the same sequence the much smaller Stan Mikita drives big Yakushev to the ice with **a vicious, uncalled cross check**. The Soviets pull Tretiak during the delayed call and keep the puck for several seconds before Maltsev takes a weak shot that deflects into the corner. While Canada certainly was trying to make a statement with physical play, these two incidents stopped some real momentum for Team Canada.

Stan Mikita and Peter Mahovlich are out on the penalty kill, going against the Starshinov line with Kharlamov and Maltsev. With the faceoff deep in the Canadian end, the referee Frank Larsen keeps kicking Mikita out of the faceoff circle, so Sinden changes him at the last minute to Bobby Clarke. Starshinov wins the draw back to Tsygankov but loses the puck to big Peter Mahovlich. Mahovlich carries it through the neutral zone, but gets slashed, hooked, and grabbed by Tsygankov without a call. The Toronto fans boo the dual referees mercilessly both for the faceoff drama and lack of call against the Little M, obviously ignoring Mikita's crosscheck moments before. Kharlamov makes a rush, with a couple of nice moves before being hammered cleanly by the veteran Bill White. The puck however bounces out to Starshinov who makes a quick opportunistic pass to Yakushev who is now all alone on Tony Esposito. Yakushev attempts the same move he made across the crease on Dryden in game one, but Tony O has none of it, reading the Big Yak easily. **The Soviets are realizing there will be no easy plays today against**

this revamped Canadian defence, and no easy goals against Tony Esposito. Alexander Maltsev tries a rush, gets stopped by White and flops to ice in an obvious dive attempt. Esposito and Cashman come on to kill the remainder of the penalty, and both are skating well, troubling the Soviet puck carriers. Petrov takes a bad angle shot that gives Tony Esposito a bit of trouble as the penalty winds down, successfully killed by Canada. This was another ineffective Soviet powerplay, with really the only dangerous scoring chance being Yakushev's. **Bill White was outstanding killing this penalty as he stopped several Soviet rushes himself.**

Boris Mikhailov continues his high energy play from game one, harassing Serge Savard in the Canadian zone, causing a turnover, but little comes out of it as Canada is giving very little space out there. Guy Lapointe makes an energetic rush up ice but loses the puck before he was able to get a shot. The young Montreal blueliner shows some real speed on the rush. With a minute left in the period, Yakushev gets revenge from being cross checked earlier by Mikita and dumps him unceremoniously. Mikita appears hurt on the play and heads to the bench. The crowd screams from the lack of a call on what was an obvious **revenge-based tripping penalty**. A moment later Frank Mahovlich gets dumped by Paladiev and the normally quiet Maple Leaf Gardens erupts in a chorus of boos that could be heard across Canada. The period ends scoreless to the deafening noise of the Toronto crowd.

Game 2: Period 1 Review

If the Soviets thought that every game of this series was going to be like Game 1, they quickly learned that was not going to be the case. Canada was a completely different team than in the first game. They came out serious, physical, with a mobile defence that was taking the man at the blue line, rather than backing up or giving the Soviets speedsters too much space to operate. The Soviets proved they could dish it out as well in this period, getting involved physically sometimes to their detriment. Players such as Cashman, Parise and even Mikita were playing aggressively, with a bit of menace, and this seemed to periodically throw the Soviets off their game. Players such as Kuzkin, Tsygankov and Yakushev responded to the Canadian physicality by dealing out some aggressive plays of their own and were fortunate not to get called for penalties.

Canada had stopped the one man stick handling through the neutral zone and were now either dumping it past the Soviet defence and fore checking or making some solid passing plays to enter the zone. This allowed Canada to have the better of the play for most of the period but were left empty handed goal wise. While neither team had a lot of chances due to the tightness and physicality of the period, both Tretiak and Esposito made saves when they needed to. **Esposito especially made two key saves** that would have given the Soviets a lead that they probably didn't deserve at that stage.

The Soviet defence made some careless giveaways, not seeming to be able to sync with their forwards transition wise as they did in the first game. Much of that was due to the Canadian defensive changes. Where Seiling and Awrey had backed up or were often stationary in game one, Serge Savard, Guy Lapointe and the Chicago tandem of White/ Stapleton pinched and pressured the Soviets. This happened both at the offensive blue line with well-timed pinches and defensively where the Soviets felt the physical punishment of trying to get around mobile behemoths Savard and White and the smaller but mobile veteran, Gary Bergman.

The two American amateur Referees Dowling and Larsen seemed to be a bit in over their heads. They allowed both teams to constantly change lines and players, sometimes right before a faceoff, and this ruined the flow of the game for much of the first 10 minutes. They also missed several obvious penalties for both teams, either through incompetence or purposefully ignoring the infractions.

Notable players in this period for Canada besides Tony Esposito were Bill White and his partner Pat Stapleton who provided a great balance of offensive threat and mobility, combined with old school Canadian defence. Serge Savard and his partner Guy Lapointe were also notable in controlling the play while Brad Park was also superb in controlling the play and made some great first passes out of his zone. He seemed to have stopped his individual futile rushes that plagued him in game one. Bobby Clarke was again Canada's top forward, causing trouble, forechecking, being a pest and winning draw after draw. The Esposito line with his new physical linemates also showed the Soviets they would be a force to be reckoned with.

On the Soviet side, Yakushev was always dangerous, Zimin was flying, and Boris Mikhailov was skating very well and forechecking his heart out. The Soviet defence struggled a bit, especially Gusev who continued his pattern of giving the puck up. Kharlamov was always a threat but found his left side of the ice now patrolled by Bill White and Serge Savard. No easy rushes were to be had by the talented #17 (so far) as a result. Tretiak was steady and ready for the shots when they came.

Overall, this was a well-played, intense period. The first goal of the game should help set the tone for how things play out in the final two periods. One question that Foster Hewitt asks before the start of period two is whether the Canadian Team has the stamina to continue the hard hitting.

CHAPTER 16:
GAME 2. PERIOD 2.
YOU CAN'T LEAVE
ESPOSITO ALONE
IN THE SLOT!

As a nervous Toronto crowd settles into their seats, the Soviets start the Petrov line with Mishakov and Mikhailov, and Kuzkin/Gusev on defence instead of the starting Kharlamov line. The Soviets seem very intent on-line matchups this game. Canada goes with the Esposito line and Park/Bergman. Canada wins the draw, Wayne Cashman gets control and carries the puck, but gets stopped by Kuzkin at the blueline. The Boston forward responds with a little crosscheck to the back of the Soviet captain, a gentle reminder that he was on the ice. Bergman dumps it in, where Parise dogs Gusev into another turnover, this time right to the NHL's leading scorer Phil Esposito. Espo is still showing rust as he fires it wide. The puck goes into the Canadian zone where Brad Park does a poor drop pass to Gary Bergman who wisely fires it out of the Canadian end, down the ice. The Soviets quickly counterattack with quick transition passing. This leads to Boris Mikhailov showing some real speed outside on Bergman, then firing an off angle shot on

Esposito who stops it without issue. This play was similar to the Kharlamov goal in game one, but where Dryden let in a bad angle, weak goal, Tony O handles it easily. Park misses the rebound and it goes out to Gusev who makes a quick shot which Esposito is again ready for. Foster Hewitt now remarks that *"Canada is getting outstanding goaltending by Esposito in the Canadian net"*. One has to wonder if game one would have had a different result if Sinden had started Tony Esposito instead of the inconsistent Dryden.

Cashman and JP Parise do some crisp back and forth passing as they get it deep in the Soviet zone, yet a solid pass to Parise bounces off his stick. The Soviets recover the puck, quickly counterattack as Boris Mikhailov makes a quick move on Pat Stapleton and then fires a hard shot as Stapleton turns. A clever play, but Tony Esposito is great form, and kicks out another superb save. Gusev pinches in fires a quick shot on the rebound that is again stopped by Esposito. While Gusev is struggling defensively, he has two now shown good offensive instincts with timely pinches in from the blueline.

Phil Esposito flies back up the ice, gets a great pass from Brad Park, dekes Gusev out easily who trips him before he can get fully around him. The referee signals a penalty and then Gusev does a very strange thing for a player of his level: He gives up on the play, (possibly expecting the whistle to be called). It isn't, and this leads to a close chance in front of the Soviet net. Canada continues controlling the play for several seconds as they get a sixth attacker out. They work the puck around until Park gets a great chance for a big point shot which Tretiak kicks out. Finally, the Soviets get the puck, ending a few moments of intense action. On this sequence, Stan Mikita came out for the extra attacker, as Canada controlled the puck in the Soviet zone for an incredible 22 seconds. The lack of effort by the Soviets to recover the puck is shocking. They look like a lazy unmotivated bunch, certainly not the regular energetic dynamos they had been so far in the series. In this short sequence of events, Team

Canada look like the dominant all-star team they were proclaimed to be.

Esposito starts the powerplay at centre with Cournoyer and Frank Mahovlich, Brad Park and Stan Mikita on the points. The Soviets send out Starshinov and Kharlamov, Tsygankov and Ragulin. Its noteworthy that Evgeni Mishakov who has shown excellent penalty killing ability so far, has not yet been used. Alexander Ragulin attempts to clear the puck but throws it to Park at the point. The puck goes to Stan Mikita at the other point. The veteran makes a bad pass on the point straight to Kharlamov, who flies down the ice deking Mikita, pulling the puck to his forehand, where he gets a shot off on Tony Esposito. Brad Park recovers the puck, calmly takes his time making a pass up to Cournoyer. Cournoyer flies up ice, breaking into the Soviet zone before making a very Soviet like drop pass to the pinching Mikita, who gets a hard high point-blank shot at Tretiak. Tretiak makes his best save of the night on the laser shot.

Guy Lapointe is out for Canada. He jumps into a rush with Cournoyer that is whistled offside, but after the faceoff Lapointe makes his venture into the Soviet zone, quickly gaining the blue line and firing a hard slap shot at Tretiak who covers up. Tretiak was a master at covering the puck to get a whistle in an attempt to slow any opposition momentum down. The Soviets recover, and ice the puck. Tony Esposito comes way out of his net to pass the puck, much like a modern goalie, something that was rarely seen in 1972. A few moments later a Soviet giveaway by Ragulin leads to a 2 on 1 break for Henderson and Esposito. Henderson head mans it to Phil who gets a good shot off on Tretiak. The Soviet goalie is matching his Canadian counterpart save for save at this stage in the game.

As Canada sets up in their own end, Yvan Cournoyer makes a terrible, terrible pass in front of Canada's goal that gets intercepted by Shadrin. Shadrin is now all alone on the

Canadian goal and attempts to deke out Tony Esposito. Guy Lapointe dives for the puck and trips Shadrin just before he could shoot. Shockingly, even though Lapointe's stick swings and takes Shadrin's feet out, no call was made on the play. The penalty was obvious, with the no call being a potential turning point in this game. The powerplay ends with very few chances for Canada and a couple of excellent shorthanded chances for the always dangerous Soviets.

As soon as the Canadian powerplay ends, the Soviets are furious with the non-call, yelling at the officials. Instead of getting a powerplay on the Lapointe trip, they now get a bench penalty for arguing with the referees. They seem confused by this, rightfully so, eventually sending Zimin to serve the two minutes. Starshinov and Mishakov are back out to penalty kill and Canada counters with Clarke centring Henderson and Bill Goldsworthy, with a hybrid defence team of Stapleton and Savard. Stapleton carries the puck up ice before dumping the puck in, but Goldsworthy is called offside. Goldsworthy is like a freight train, not slowing down before semi-colliding with Tretiak. They both get in each other's face for a moment, as Tretiak gives Goldsworthy a jab with his stick. Despite his youth, Tretiak is far from passive as he shows he won't tolerate any incursions into his crease area.

Goldsworthy continues the aggressive playing hammering Petrov twice, the first time with a clean bodycheck the second time with a nasty knee to his midsection as Petrov is semi prone on the ice. This is a terrible, unwarranted dangerous play; yet again, no call on the play. Mishakov is out killing the penalty, clearing the puck into Canada's zone. Serge Savard recovers, looking very smooth as he makes a full-length rush, ending with a clever short, sided shot on Tretiak. Phil Esposito comes back out with Frank Mahovlich and Cournoyer. Mishakov continues his strong penalty kill, doing a nice job stick handling the puck for a time-wasting rush, showing he certainly deserves more ice time than he received in game one. Canada struggles again on the power play, as Frank Mahovlich is starting to look out of sorts, with some bad passes and puck struggles. He and Cournoyer really do not seem to mesh with Phil Esposito. With that line being so disjointed, the Soviets are having little issues handling the Canadian power play.

Esposito, Parise and Cashman are now out against Petrov, Mikhailov and Zimin. Park and Bergman are on defence for Canada, against Kuzkin/Luchenko for the Soviets. Canada quickly takes control during this shift as the Soviets seem a bit out of sorts, and as a result make a couple of early giveaways. Zimin attempts a drop pass in the Canadian end that Park reads, and Canada recovers the puck bringing it through the neutral zone. The puck goes to Cashman, who attempts to go by Luchenko on the right side but gets stopped just over the blueline and seems to tackle the Russian rear-guard bringing them both to the ice. Another official may have called Cashman for holding, but since both players were entangled, it was ignored. This non call would have a definite effect. Luchenko has lost his stick (or broke it) just before the Cashman pileup. This would be unfortunate for the Soviets as Canada was about to open the scoring.

Goal 1: Phil Esposito. Canada 1 Soviet Union 0 (the goal that shouldn't have counted)

The play comes back into the Soviet zone and Luchenko attempts to kick the puck at the blueline but misses it. As a result, Luchenko gets trapped behind Esposito and Cashman as they attempt to bring the puck towards the Soviet goal, on Tretiak's left side. Petrov has been hanging all over Esposito for the past few seconds to the crowd's consternation. Espo gets a pass from Cashman but gets tripped by Petrov. The referee signals a penalty. This is where a significant officiating mistake is made. Instead of blowing the whistle when Petrov touches the puck, the action continues. **In hindsight, this goal shouldn't have counted as the play should have been stopped once Petrov had control of the puck;** a fortunate break for Canada, especially considering their woeful powerplay to that point.

Since Petrov's touching the puck isn't whistled, the usually reliable Soviet centre, now being chased by Cashman behind the Soviet goal, apparently panics, and makes a careless, blind, backhand of the puck. The puck goes around the boards, but instead of chasing it, Luchenko abandons his side of the ice, and goes in front of his own goal. Kuzkin reads this and begins skating hard to get to the puck on Luchenko's side, no doubt cursing his defensive partner's name. He is a half second too late, as Park pinches in front the point, intercepts the puck and pokes it up to Cashman. Cashman looks up, sees Esposito in the Soviet goal area, and takes a quick half pass, half shot on goal. This hits Tretiak's pad and Esposito collects the rebound. Luchenko is now beside Esposito but instead of taking the big Boston Bruin centre out of the crease area physically, he oddly and ineffectually tries to kick the puck again, **misses and then decides to go for a skate behind the Soviet goal!** He obviously was not aware that the top goal scorer in the NHL was crease bound, in his favourite position and that was a recipe for disaster for any team. As expected, Espo uses some deadly hand eye coordination to pull the puck quickly to his forehand and tucks it under Tretiak for the first goal of the game.

This goal was a sequence of events rather than one single play. It could be best be described as a total group breakdown. The Soviets were having a seemingly rare "off shift" and were not really skating hard or checking with any real sense of urgency. Zimin gives the puck away three times in a period of about 10 seconds, the last with the failed drop pass. He then goes for a large circling skate away from the action as it builds in the Soviet end. Petrov seemed to be the only Soviet forward involved in back checking, as Boris Mikhailov also turns away from the play in his own end, perhaps hoping for a quick Soviet transition pass that doesn't happen. This was an ongoing issue with Soviet forwards during the series, who would circle looking for that transition game that didn't always come. This would leave the defence outmanned in their zone.

Petrov is the only forward back now and after taking the tripping penalty, he makes another bad play deep in his own end, throwing the puck away blindly. He then makes things worse when he fails to cover Phil Esposito, who has gotten up and is right in the goal area and instead goes for a big swooping circle behind his own net. Petrov comes back out in front, sees Espo now with the puck and attempts a desperate poke check but he is a moment too late to make a difference.

The defence team of Luchenko and Kuzkin get their wires crossed. Luchenko has lost his stick, and then stands virtually watching the action in front of Tretiak, forcing his partner Kuzkin to chase the puck on Luchenko's side. As he does this, Luchenko reacts too slowly to seeing Esposito near Tretiak, finally going towards him when Cashman shoots the puck off Tretiak's pad. He makes the crucial key error of not taking Esposito out physically, instead attempting a failed kicked at the puck. Tretiak tries to poke check the puck away as Esposito pulls it across his crease, but like his teammates he is a half second too late.

While it would be easy to point out Luchenko's lack of a stick as the cause of the goal, it was really all five Soviet skaters who played a part through indifference, lack of physicality or simple bad decision making. Kuzkin maybe gets a pass as he tried to cover for his defensive partners mistakes. Tretiak attempted to play Esposito's move but was beaten by the hockey's best goal scorer. Not really his fault. **The Soviets have now shown they are just as capable of defensive zone breakdowns as Canada**. They will have to adjust their game to be more physical in coverage, especially against the big strong Canadian forwards like Esposito and Cashman.

After the first goal of the game, Mikita's line and then Clarke's line maintain the pressure on the Soviets, who still seem a bit listless and continue giving the puck away. Frank Mahovlich is skating well but is starting to make some poor passes, not taking his time. After Maltsev tries an errant drop pass that Paul Henderson easily intercepts, Bobby Clarkes skates up the ice using the angled dump in play in Ron Ellis's corner. This play confuses the Soviets, again, as Ragulin fails to anticipate the play. The big defenceman looks ponderously slow as Ron Ellis outskates Ragulin to the puck and throws it quickly out front. With Clarke on the doorstep, Tretiak has to make a quick save.

On the next whistle the Soviet weakness at the faceoff circle leads to the surprise choice of defenseman Tsygankov taking the draw against Clarke. As expected, Clarke wins easily. The puck goes to Ron Ellis who gets a point-blank shot from the slot area that Tretiak stops. Tretiak is certainly keeping his team from going down 2-0 with a solid save after save. Canada is completely dominating play now, with the Clarke line taking the Starshinov, Kharlamov, Maltsev line to task. The Soviets are not only being outskated, outhit, and out hustled; they barely touch the puck for a period of time. When they finally do get control, Ragulin gives it away to Clarke. A scrum ensues with Ellis, Lapointe and then Clarke jousting with the veteran Starshinov. As expected, the small but feisty Starshinov doesn't back down.

The scrum fades away without penalties or further incident.
The Mikita line goes up against Shadrin's trio, off the draw Lyapkin drops to his knees to block a Frank Mahovlich drive. Blocking shots was something the Soviet players rarely did. Strangely, the officials hold the faceoff in the slot area where Lyapkin blocked the puck rather than at the faceoff circle. Very odd. The puck goes back into the Soviet end.

Lyapkin suddenly gives it away to the forechecking Mikita. Stan Mikita is having an excellent game, controlling the play as Canada cycles the puck. Frank Mahovlich continues his game one strategy of blasting the puck from bad angles at Tretiak, but he does give a nice drop pass to Cournoyer after getting a lovely cross ice pass from Bill White. White has a shot from the point but it's blocked. This frees Yakushev and Zimin for on a 2 on 1 against Pat Stapleton. Stapleton plays the two on one with precision positioning, taking the pass away and forcing Yakushev to shoot. Stapleton half blocks the Yakushev shot, forcing it to go wide, ending the first real Soviet chance in several minutes. In another odd sequence, Frank Mahovlich tries to get a whistle by holding the puck against the net behind Tony O, but brother Phil comes and tries to get the puck, pulling the feet out from Mahovlich who gives him a shocked, somewhat angry look.

Brad Park makes two lovely moves as he brings the puck up ice but makes one move too many and loses the puck just inside the Soviet zone. The puck goes back into the Canadian zone as Bergman easily strips Petrov of the puck. Phil Esposito carries the puck himself this time, showing great stickhandling ability as he beats three soviet forecheckers with deft moves. Cashman and Espo show their Boston synergy with some excellent puck cycling that momentarily has the Soviets back on their heels in their own zone. This line has been superb on the forecheck.

Serge Savard has been a very strong addition to team Canada. He uses his sublime puck control to slow the game down. The Soviets soon encounter the move that Savard was known for, his **Savardian spin-o-rama**. Kharlamov goes after the Montreal defenseman, but Savard smoothly spins away from the puck and hits Clarke with a beautiful long pass into the Soviet zone. Clarke fires a slap shot to the side of the net, finishing off a Canadian version of the Soviet fast break play. Maltsev comes flying back down the ice, at full speed, turns into the Canadian zone and then makes a horrible blind drop pass that Clarke intercepts. Bobby Clarke was everywhere this shift, singlehandedly controlling the pace of the game.

After a few moments of scrambly play and good puck control by Zimin and Yakushev, Canada comes close to making to 2-0 when Cournoyer gets a clear breakaway against Tretiak. Cournoyer speeds in, makes a move to his left, but fails to deke Tretiak out. The play had developed from a heavy Yakushev slap shot that went around the boards to Frank Mahovlich who makes a wonderful long pass to his streaking Montreal Canadians line mate. The play gets called offside, but the Soviets would do well to remember just how fast Yvan Cournoyer can skate.

After some more pressure from the Esposito/Cashman/Parise line, which included a Wayne Cashman uncalled elbow to Mishakov, Gary Bergman takes a tripping penalty giving the Soviets a chance to tie the game before the end of the period. Bergman seems a little upset at Boris Mikhailov for what he perceives as a dive and lets him know it. With a language barrier the two make gestures at each other before Bergman accepts his fate and heads to the box. Replays show Bergman certainly hooked him as Boris had beat him to the outside, but Brian Conacher also calls it a dive on the review. **It wasn't.**

The Soviets put out Starshinov, Kharlamov and Maltsev with Luchenko and Tsygankov on the points. The Canadians have Clarke and Peter Mahovlich with Lapointe and Park for the penalty kill. Clarke switches with Frank Mahovlich as he and his brother Peter have made a good team killing penalties together. After another terrible blind drop pass by Alexander Maltsev, Peter Mahovlich intercepts makes a beautiful long pass to Frank for a nice shorthanded blast at Tretiak. Peter M is fantastic on the penalty kill, showing some world class stick handling in centre ice and using his very large frame to shield the puck. The Soviets continue to be out of sorts, and simply cannot get anything going against the penalty kill. They finish the Power Play without a single shot on goal. As Bergman rushes back on the ice, the Soviets finally set up in the Canadian zone, but a poor pass by Yakushev out of the Canadian zone stops any momentum.

With a minute left, Mikhailov tries a long rush but as the Soviet forwards have encountered all game, **Bill White is superb on one-on-one encounters** and strips the crafty player easily. The puck ends up deep in the Canadian corner, where Mikhailov, Mishakov, Parise and Stapleton battle intensely. Tempers ensue and Parise jousts with the very game Mishakov who then challenges Parise to a fight. As Rod Gilbert would find out later in the Series, Mishakov was built like a tank and not someone to mess with. Parise wisely declines.

With 30 seconds left, Canada changes to the Clarke line, to match up against the Starshinov group and probably for the only time in his career, **the Toronto crowd cheers Clarke as he steps on the ice**. Park keeps the puck deftly in the Soviet end, makes a nice pass to Clarke who one times it to Ellis for a clear chance on Tretiak. Ellis fires a quick hard shot, but Tretiak makes a pad save. Again, the young Soviet goaltender is up to the task, preventing his team from falling further behind before the end of the period. Clarke and Tsygankov battle in the corner. Tsygankov falls with Clarke to the ice, and while his glove hits Clarke in the face somehow the Soviet player gets a slashing penalty. **It's a terrible call**. In a moment of undisciplined behaviour Valeri Kharlamov becomes enraged by this iffy call and pushes the referee in protest. As the second period ends, he gets dinged with a 10-minute misconduct, a real blow to the Soviets for the third period.

Game 2: Second Period Review

The second period of this game started out poorly for Canada with Boris Mikhailov having an excellent scoring opportunity on a nice rush, with Gusev having a point-blank shot on the rebound. Tony Esposito had to make two clutch saves. Shockingly, that was the only offense the Soviets showed until much later in the period. For the majority of the second frame Canada rolled three lines and kept the Soviets on their heels in their own end. The Soviet defence became somewhat exposed and unsure of themselves, perhaps **unused to the heavy forecheck, speed and aggressiveness of the Canadian forwards.**

Except for the short time when Canada dominated part of the third period of game one, the Soviet team had been composed and fluid with their passes. That composure ended for much of the second period, as players such as Maltsev, Gusev, Zimin and Ragulin all had notable giveaways, often resulting in solid chances for Canada. Tretiak kept his team close in coming up with several key saves. Canada, however, was not completely innocent in the giveaway department, as they had a couple of bad gaffes of their own, the worst being Cournoyer's shocking handoff to Shadrin right in front of Tony Esposito.

The two American referees, Dowling and Larsen, continued their struggles with **borderline calls or absolute missed calls.** The worst of the missed calls was Lapointe's hook/trip on Shadrin after Cournoyer's giveaway. Shadrin was alone on Esposito, with a legit scoring opportunity. The fact that Shadrin was interfered with while shooting mandates a call on the play. While the Canadians were not playing overly rough compared to an NHL playoff game per say, the Soviets seemed enraged by the non-calls, getting a bench penalty, and then having star of game one, Valeri Kharlamov, receiving a 10 minute misconduct. In reality, there were missed calls on both sides, but certainly enough for the Soviets to be upset. **Where the Soviets should have protested was on the Esposito goal.** Petrov had not only touched the puck while the referee had his arm up, but he played it around the boards. That should have ended the action, and a resulting Canadian power play would have taken place, instead of a goal against. **This was a game changing non call**.

Strong players for the Soviets in the second period were few: Boris Mikhailov had a couple of strong rushes, but at other times was invisible and lacked his usual dogged forechecking. Kharlamov was very quiet. Alexander Yakushev continued to be dangerous on several rushes, but as a whole, the Soviet forwards were not skating or engaged. On defence, Viktor Kuzkin was the only Soviet defender who was somewhat physical and involved. Tretiak had to be the player of the period for the Soviets, keeping his team in the game with several stellar saves. **They easily could have been behind 3 or 4 to 0**.

On the Canadian side, it was a good period for Team Canada. Phil Esposito was starting to take control of the game, perhaps much happier with his linemates than in game one. As a result, the Soviet backend was having trouble corralling the big Boston centre. It wouldn't be the last time. Wayne Cashman and JP Parise were excellent on the forecheck and seemed to be getting into the Soviets collective heads. Bobby Clarke was still playing strong, as was Stan Mikita, winning seemingly every faceoff and showing diligent work at both ends of the ice. Peter Mahovlich was excellent, **even mesmerizing**, on the penalty kill using his elite stick handling ability to waste time. Serge Savard and Bill White were significant additions to the Canada defence, as the Soviet forwards were having trouble getting space on the two big mobile defenders. Tony O, while not tested often, kept his shutout going with a couple of early key saves. Overall, a well-played, often dominant period by Team Canada and a somewhat lax, unorganized one by the Soviets.

CHAPTER 17: GAME 2. PERIOD 3. THE GREATEST GOAL OF ALL TIME

Entering the third period, people watching are on pins and needles. Canada has a nervous 1-0 lead. Despite dominating the play for the majority of the second period, the Soviets are still very much in the game. Team Canada cannot afford to go down two games in this series. This is a key period for them. Soviets might be happy to sneak out a tie or even get a couple of quick goals and steal the game, totally deflating a country's pride. This is something in which the Soviets excel.

The third period starts with Canada on the power play. Esposito starts with Cournoyer and Frank Mahovlich up front and the offensive tandem of Park/Lapointe on defence. The Soviets counter with Starshinov and Mishakov as the penalty killing forwards and Luchenko/Ragulin on the back end.

Almost immediately Yvan Cournoyer shows some great speed, blowing past the penalty killing forwards but giving the puck up with a weak drop pass once he entered the Soviet zone. **His speed was the prelude of things to come, moments later**.

Goal 2: Cournoyer Canada 2 Soviets 0

There were several memorable goals in the Summit Series of 1972. In game one, Valeri Kharlamov used his speed and high skill level to beat Don Awrey wide, shocking Canada with his first of two goals that evening. In game two, Yvan Cournoyer and Brad Park combine to top that performance with **a fantastic pass and a breathtakingly fast strike**.

The play starts with a whistle break, where the penalty killing Mishakov can be seen speaking to Coach Bobrov at the bench. He was assumedly getting direction on how to best kill the remaining 42 seconds of the Canadian Powerplay. The faceoff takes place on the Soviet blue line, where the pucks goes over to Luchenko, who dumps it deep behind the Canadian net. Tony Esposito plays the puck over to Brad Park who corrals the puck behind the Canadian net. Park picks up speed through the Canadian zone, unencumbered, as Yvan Cournoyer flies down the right wing, despite being a left-hand shot. With perfect precision, Park makes a brilliant, hard pass **right on the tape** of the streaking "roadrunner". The pass is so well timed it is on Cournoyer's stick virtually a step before the Soviet blue line, preventing an offside. Ragulin is positioned at the blue line, but Cournoyer **blows by him easily** to the outside, and cuts in on Tretiak. He drives in with the puck on his forehand, giving himself a better angle to release a perfect wrist shot between Tretiak's pads or "five hole". **The goal itself takes less than 7 seconds from end to end.**

While this goal was a work of beautiful timing and skill on Team Canada's side, it was also the result of the Soviets team continued apathetic play in this game. Park was allowed to come up the ice completely unfettered as the two penalty killers backed off in mid ice. The Soviets penalty killers had spread out in a mid-ice "box" format rather than a more effective "I "formation. The "I" formation would have allowed Mishakov to wait in the Canadian end for the puck carrier and then try and both harass him and move him to one side of the ice. The other penalty killer would move to that side as well, following the lead of his teammate, and preventing any cross-ice pass capability.

The passive penalty kill of Starshinov and Mishakov allowed Park the time to make that pass and opened up the neutral zone for the fleet Cournoyer. Mishakov isn't even watching Park, while Starshinov was only focused on the puck carrying Canadian defenceman and doesn't notice Cournoyer picking up speed behind him. Ragulin had positioned himself in a semi stationary pose right on the Soviet blue line. He would have had to be moving backwards to have any chance of stopping the Roadrunner. The play seemingly happens so quickly that Ragulin doesn't even attempt a poke check, and instead turns towards Cournoyer, but he is far too slow in reacting and is soon a couple of steps behind him. Tretiak has come out to the top of his crease to cut the angle off but leaves too much room in his five hole, similar to Dryden on the Kharlamov first goal in game one, and like Ragulin reacts too slowly to stop the goal. **To be fair to Ragulin and Tretiak, there was probably not a defenseman or goalie in the world in 1972 that could have stopped the Roadrunner on this wonderfully executed Canadian goal.**

A very big man, standing 6'1 and weighing 225 pounds of muscle, Alexander "Rags" Ragulin was nick named the "Bear". Like his teammate on this night Vyacheslav Starshinov, Ragulin was a long-time veteran of the dominant Soviet National Team that won 9 straight World Championships from 1963-1972, winning the best defenseman award in 1966. In the Soviet Elite league, he started with Khimik Voskresensk for his first five seasons before transferring to the fabled Central Red Army team, where he played 11 seasons before retiring in 1973. Comparable in mannerisms to the legendary NHL strongman Tim Horton, Ragulin was a gentle giant. He rarely used his size and strength unless needed and instead played a controlled cerebral game. He was a weak skater by Soviet standards and would have to change his game during the Summit Series to become more effective, ideally preventing a recurrence of the Cournoyer goal. He played in 6 of 8 games and battled hard with another large man, Phil Esposito. There is a famous picture of the two combatants' nose to nose in Moscow. Ragulin himself said this about his battles with Espo:

"The coaches gave me the unenviable task of covering Phil Esposito. He was a different kind of centre for me, very big, very strong, always in the slot. Ours was a battle of two huge bears!" Richard Bendall

The Soviets would drop the big bear for game 3, more than likely because Cournoyer's goal had exposed his skating weakness. However, he was put back into the line-up and played better as the series went on, adapting to the different yet also higher level of play of the matches. Soviet sportswriter Igor Kuperman had this to say about Ragulin's performance:

"Alexander Ragulin always felt uncomfortable when writers asked him if he could play against the NHL professionals. Now we know without any doubt that Ragulin could have played in the NHL. He proved it in the whole series". Igor Kuperman

Unfortunately for the well revered veteran, he will forever be remembered for being a step too slow to stop the amazing goal by Yvan Cournoyer.

With Canada up 2-0, Coach Bobrov gets the matchup that he has been trying to get with the Shadrin line out against the Clarke line. The puck goes deep into the Soviet zone with Henderson using his speed to pester Lyapkin. Lyapkin gives it away behind his own goal, straight to Henderson who uses to feed Bergman for a heavy shot on goal. Clarke digs for the rebound at the side of the goal, which seems to annoy Tretiak. Peter Mahovlich takes Phil Esposito's place between Cashman and Parise, but the line gets in trouble in Canada's end. Sinden's strategy of having the wingers come back and help the defence has been working well so far, but in this case the lack of coverage allows the Soviet defence to keep the puck in the Canadian zone, eventually leading to a scoring chance for Zimin. Tony Esposito comes up big with the save, Parise gets hauled down roughly by Shadrin during this shift, but no call is made on the play.

The game picks up pace significantly as the Soviet team roars to life. Yakushev gets a point-blank shot, and Canada switches back to the Clarke line. Ron Ellis displays his significant speed and backchecking focus as he angles Mishakov off the puck and jets back down the ice, giving Henderson a cross ice pass. Kuzkin reads the play, bodies Henderson off the puck as the Soviets shift it into a higher gear.

Mikhailov and Petrov both have solid shots on goal. Tony O reads the play and makes another key stop. Boris Mikhailov had a very "heads up" way of carrying the puck. He skated less bent over than a North American player. The puck would be ahead of him with his hands higher up on the stick than most players. This allowed for quick puck movement, but also quick body movement, which lets him to jump out of the way of a Henderson body check, right after he passes to Petrov. He maintains his balance enough to get the rebound from Petrov's backhand.

The game gets a bit scrambled with Kuzkin giving it up to the forechecking Mikita and then Frank Mahovlich circling in his own end before giving it up back to Kuzkin. Mikhailov decides it's his turn to do the full circle back into the Soviet zone, but Mishakov gives him a terrible "suicide" pass as Boris jumps into the neutral zone. Bergman reads the play and Boris can't get out of the way this time as Bergman flips Mikhailov head over heels with an old school hip check. Mikita picks it up, attempts to penetrate the Soviet zone but is bodychecked to the ice by an awaiting Kuzkin. Mishakov who has been skating well all game, rushes it up to Starshinov, who gets slashed by Bobby Clarke as he tries to get it deep into the Canadian zone. The soviet veteran cleverly gets the puck back to his defence who pass amongst themselves, giving the Soviet bench time to get an extra attacker out. One thing to note on this sequence of events, Brad Park can be seen slashing, then hooking Starshinov, then finally hitting him with a two-handed slash as he attempted to strip the puck from him. **Canada easily could have been two men short on the play**.

Pete Mahovlich has been the go-to guy so far for Canadian penalty kills. He comes out again with Ron Ellis for Canada. Bergman and Park stay on the points. The Shadrin line with the dangerous Yakushev/Zimin connection start the Powerplay with Lyapkin and Paladiev. The Soviets do not seem to have set powerplay units, as **Bobrov seems to be more of an instinctual coach than a regimented one**. His instincts in the Canadian end of the series turn out to be more successful than his counterpart Harry Sinden as proven by the Soviets first goal of the game.

Goal 3: Alexander Yakushev. Canada 2 Soviet Union 1.

Canada starts out strongly on the penalty kill, with Peter Mahovlich landing a solid mid ice hit on Yakushev in a collision of giants. Ron Ellis is darting everywhere, keeping the Soviets a bit bottled up in their own zone. Of course, being in their own zone is when the Soviets were often deadliest. They had the incredible ability to counterstrike with the long breakout pass, and this is exactly what happens here.

The goal starts from the Soviet end. Peter Mahovlich makes a poor decision to pick up Shadrin who is exiting the Soviet zone on the right wing. This opened the middle of the ice for the deadly Soviet long pass play. Paladiev hits Zimin with the long transition pass and the speedy winger splits the defensive pair of Park and Bergman and finds himself alone on Esposito. Zimin aims for the top glove side corner on Esposito and fires a hard wrist shot high and wide. The puck goes into the Canadian corner where Lyapkin has pinched in. Soviet defender Lyapkin beats the trailing Gary Bergman to the puck. Lyapkin carries the puck to the right of Tony O, close to the goal line and then hits Yakushev with a nice backhand pass. The Big Yak is wide open and drills a quick wrist shot into the bottom left corner of the Canadian goal.

Canada's second goal seemed to wake the Soviets up. If Canada was complacent with the 2-0 lead, they certainly showed it here with some defensive sloppiness. While the Soviets were guilty of passive penalty killing in the neutral zone leading to the second Canadian goal, Canada was guilty on this goal of **not being cohesive in their ice coverage**. Ellis and Peter Mahovlich are caught deep in the Soviet zone, with Ellis watching the puck carrier. Zimin and Paladiev do a quick back and forth passing which seems to freeze Ellis, while at the same time Zimin picks up speed behind the Soviet goal and breaks into the centre ice zone. Mahovlich ignores Zimin and makes a fateful choice of picking up Shadrin instead who has also circled and speeds along the boards. Gary Bergman and his partner Brad Park are both positioned too deep in the Soviet zone, and too far apart from each other. Bergman was at the Soviet blue line near the boards area, and Park was almost at the other side of the ice, perhaps fooled by Shadrin coming up the far boards. **This gives Zimin wide open space to receive the long pass from Paladiev.**

The two Canadian defensemen are now in pure panic to catch the speedy Zimin and hopefully get back to stop his breakaway or get into some semblance of positioning if Esposito makes a save. Brad Park is first back. He dives for the puck. **This was a crucial error as he took himself out of the play, sliding on his stomach past Tony Esposito.** This left the front of the net wide open. Bergman goes after the rebound but as previously noted he is a step behind Lyapkin who has jumped into the play. Yakushev is all alone as he fires it past Tony O. Esposito had little chance on the play as the Soviet star fired it quickly and accurately before Tony could get set, much like his sniper brother Phil would do in the same situation. While Brad Park has been very composed offensively, he will need to improve his positional play, and not take himself out of plays like this as it will lead to further goals.

Full kudos to the five Soviet players out on the powerplay. They didn't panic under the Canadian forecheck and used a nice decoy with Shadrin to get the Canadian defenders out of position. Paladiev makes a beautiful pass. Zimin shows his world class speed as he pulls away from the chasing Canadian defenders, and Lyapkin jumps into the play at the opportune time. Yakushev was in the right place at the right time to finish the sequence and now, the USSR were back in the game.

Canada gets in penalty trouble almost right away after the Soviet goal. Boris Mikhailov goes into the Canadian end on a one on one with Bill White. Pat Stapleton skates over to Whites side of the ice to help out. This of course leaves the front of the Canadian goal wide open, so as Mikhailov dances by White, Stapleton has no option but to hook him to the ice. This was a bad positional decision leading to a poorly timed penalty.

At this stage in a crucial must win game for Canada, a penalty that potentially could allow the vaunted Soviet powerplay to tie this game up. Canada starts the penalty kill with Peter Mahovlich with Phil Esposito. The Summit Series had many memorable, fantastic moments. No one on the ice or in the stands could have anticipated what was about to take place as Canada looked to kill off a penalty in a very tight 2-1 contest.

What happens next is one of the greatest goals in hockey history.

Goal 4: Peter Mahovlich. Canada 3 Soviet Union 1

The "Zone" is a term often heard in athletics. An athlete was "in the Zone" when they accomplished that feat or performed beyond the norm.

In the book Flow: The Psychology of Optimal Experience, Mihaly Csikszentmihalyi describes the zone as:

"a state in which an athlete performs to the best of his or her ability. It is a is a magical and special place where performance is exceptional and consistent, automatic, and flowing. An athlete is able to ignore all the pressures and let his or her body deliver the performance that has been learned so well. Competition is fun and exciting.' (Murphy, 1996, p. 4)".[2]

Maurice "Rocket" Richard was once asked what he thought of when he scored some of his magical goals, his reply? Nothing. He was focused totally on the task. His drive to score goals allowed him to ignore all distractions, to have that single focus of being in the now. The ability to tap into this zone is often what separates the great athletes, the Tiger Woods, Tom Bradys, Michael Jordans and Wayne Gretzkys from the rest. They could perform feats that were beyond the norm, even for the top players in their respective sports.

For one short, magical sequence, Peter Mahovlich from Timmins Ontario was in the "Zone". **The result was one of the greatest goals in the history of hockey.**

Peter Mahovlich was often referred to as the "Little M" in deference to his more famous brother Frank's nick name "the Big M". Pete at 6'5 was bigger than his older brother but played in his shadow most of his career. Peter wasn't a Junior Star who racked up big numbers, but Detroit saw bloodlines and selected him as their first pick in the 1963 Amateur draft. He struggled for several years to make an impact with Detroit and bounced between the minor leagues and the NHL until finally being traded to Montreal in 1969. Once united with big brother Frank, Pete blossomed scoring 35 goals in

1971 and 35 again in 1972, earning him an invite to Team Canada.

Peter would go on to have two 100 plus seasons in the mid-70's and earned a place on the powerful 1976 Canadian Canada Cup team. Unfortunately, he was traded from the 1977-78 mid dynasty Canadians squad to the Pittsburgh Penguins. He would again be traded to the Detroit Red Wings, where he finished his NHL career in 1981. He made a brief comeback in 1986 with the IHL's Toledo Goaldiggers (actual name) before moving into coaching and scouting which he still does for the Florida Panthers to this day. While Peter had a very solid, Stanley cup winning career, **he is probably best remembered for the spectacular short-handed goal he scored on September 4th, 1972, in Toronto.**

The goal itself begins as Phil Esposito comes out to help Peter Mahovlich kill the Stapleton penalty. Guy Lapointe and Bill White are on defence. The Soviets remain with the Shadrin Zimin Yakushev line, and Paladiev/Lyapkin on the back end. Right off the faceoff, the Soviets work the puck around the perimeter as the Canadians set up the standard "Box" formation, where 2 players are high, 2 players are low, forming a flexible square. Bill White strips Yakushev of the puck in a bit of a scramble and Guy Lapointe takes it and attempts to throw it up the boards. Lyapkin pinches in from the point and keeps it in the Canadian zone near the hash mark area on the boards (the wall for modern readers). Shadrin gets involved but for some reason makes a blind pass to the boards that Phil Esposito recovers.

During this time, big Pete Mahovlich anticipates Esposito getting possession and skates quickly outside the Canadian zone behind Lyapkin, **an aggressive move for a penalty killer**. Esposito sees this and fires a hard backhand pass off the boards and past the pinching Lyapkin (who for a second time tried to keep the puck in the Canadian end). The puck comes directly to Mahovlich who is now just before the centre red line, gathering speed. The other Soviet defenseman, Eugevny Paladiev reads that Mahovlich was leaving the defensive zone and hangs back. **It's now a one-on-one situation between Mahovlich and Paladiev**.

Pete is in full flight now. As he heads just over the blue line, he fakes a slap shot which absolutely freezes Paladiev. The 24-year-old Soviet defender tries a poke check but is a second too late as Mahovlich uses his large reach to walk around Paladiev's left side. Paladiev tries a desperate hook, but big Pete is already around him and moving in on Tretiak. Mahovlich, who was a left-hand shot pulls the puck to his left, causing Tretiak to react and drop, stacking his pads towards Pete's right side. Pete then pulls the puck back across the sprawling goalie, onto his backhand and tucks the puck behind Tretiak, (as he crashes into the crossbar). Poor Tretiak even takes an accidental giant knee to the head as Mahovlich falls over him. Big Pete gets up out of the crease and does a short joyous happy dance with his arms outstretched to the **deafening noise** of the delirious Toronto crowd. Half the Canadian bench empties to jump into Peters arms to celebrate **the pure artistry and skill of the goal**. The announcers join into the spirit as Brian Conacher remarks,

"The Russian is still wondering where the puck is!"

Tretiak to this day still doesn't know how the goal got by him.

"I played that shot perfectly," said the Soviet goalie.

Pete would remark both on the goal and his surprising selection to Team Canada.

"Nothing compared to the goal I scored in the second game of the series. In retrospect, I didn't deserve to be there in the series, but I went with thirty-five other guys ready to play and work hard. It all paid off." Pete Mahovlich

Yevgeny Paladiev for his part, was not looked on favourably by the Soviet Coaches or writers for the rest of the Series. He would only play in one more game for the series and admits he may have been in over his head against the Canadian pro's. Although he had played decently up to that point, with no real glaring errors and some solid offensive instincts. He was quoted after the series:

"I thought I was prepared for the series, but that was a mistake. I had no idea professionals like Peter Mahovlich and Dennis Hull were so strong."

Soviet sportswriter Oleg Spassky from Smena had this to say about Paladiev's series performance:

"Some of our players looked out of place with the Canadian Professionals. Paladiev was one of them and that is why he didn't see much action in the series".

Yevgeny Paladiev himself was not Russian. He was from Ust Kamenogorsk in what is now **Kazakhstan**. He would start his career in 1965-66 with Torpedo Gorky and then move on to Moscow to play for the Spartak club. He would play 10 years in the Soviet Elite league, making the all-star team in 1970. Despite his fine season in 1970, but the mid-1970's, Paladiev would be out of the Soviet Elite league, finishing his career in the Soviet 2nd division in 1976. Overall, he played 65 National Team games winning three World Championships and was a solid serviceable defender. In 2020 he was named by the IIHF to the all-time Kazakhstan team.

Tragically, Paladiev passed away in 2010, due to heart disease, at 61. **He was living in a Moscow tenement** when Gary Mason of the Globe and Mail interviewed him before his death:

"Mr Paladiev spends his days indoors, drinking and watching a 10-inch black and white TV with rabbit ears. His fridge was full of vodka. He insisted I drink with him, straight up in wine glasses filled to the rim. Once movie-star handsome, Paladiev's skin was now red and blotchy, his knees were wrecked, and he walked with a cane". Gary Mason Globe and Mail 2012

This is a dark side to the Summit Series. Alcoholism and poverty were the unfortunate end result of some of the Soviet players. Sadly, Paladiev explained how the non-stars on the Soviet team had been discarded and neglected,

"That's just the way it is, the guys who weren't stars have been totally forgotten". Gary Mason Globe and Mail 2012

The goal itself was not a result of a team wide breakdown or even a glaring individual mistake. Paladiev had played in both game 1 and 2 and had experienced the constant slap shots the Canadian players made, usually from far out and different angles. There would be no reason for him to not expect this giant Canadian forward to rifle a shot at the goal instead of attempting to deke past him. Yes, he froze, but big Pete was a fantastic stick handler and he certainly made both Paladiev and Tretiak look foolish. Phil Esposito also needs to be recognized for the heads up play he made off the boards to Mahovlich. Lyapkin's pinch was not a terrible play for a team behind a goal and on the power play and his partner Paladiev had covered for him. **They were simply the victims of a once in a life goal by Mahovlich.**

If Maple Leaf Gardens had been considered a quiet arena, it was deafening after the Mahovlich goal. With the crowd still humming, Canada needed to refocus. While they had a two-goal lead, there was still 13 minutes left in the game and the Soviets could score goals quickly, considering they were still on the power play. After the goal, Coach Sinden can be seen giving instruction to Peter Mahovlich, possibly telling him to focus on killing the penalty as the Soviets would be pressing hard. Canada changes Espo with Frank M while the Soviets do a full-scale change. Petrov, Mikhailov and Mishakov come out with Kuzkin and Gusev. The Soviets pick up the pace on the powerplay, showing some desperation after falling two goals behind. Soviet Captain Victor Kuzkin makes a good attempt to get the puck to a wide-open Boris Mikhailov, but it hits Brad Park's skate. The Soviets are frantic, trying to score. Brad Park is held and somewhat mugged by first Mikhailov and then dumped by Mishakov. The boisterous crowd howls with boos for the non-call. Stapleton comes out of the penalty box with renewed energy, grabs the puck in the Canadian zone and using his running like skating style, flies up the ice into the Soviet zone.

With the penalty killed off successfully Canada goes back on the Offensive. Cournoyer fires a long slap shot from centre ice that Tretiak dumps into Luchenko's corner. The Soviet defence has been guilty of several giveaways in their own end this game, and Luchenko does it again this time, **meekly letting Cournoyer take it off of him**. Cournoyer makes a lovely saucer pass over Kuzkin's stick which lands right on Mikita's tape, now alone on Tretiak. Mikita takes a quick shot, but Tretiak makes another stupendous save, almost falling over to stop the Chicago chance. Canada has control now in the Soviet end, pressuring hard. The fourth goal would be forthcoming with a couple of legendary veterans combining for Canada's final tally.

Goal 5: Frank Mahovlich Canada 4 Soviet Union 1

The Soviets in 1972 were ahead of North American hockey in both conditioning and game strategy. They tended to rotate players much quicker than was practiced in the NHL, where players would often be on the ice for two minutes plus, or five minutes plus if your name was Phil Esposito. After the Peter Mahovlich goal, Bobrov changed all five players, with Luchenko and Kuzkin being the defenders. That was at the 6:47 mark of the third period. The fourth Canadian goal was scored at the 8:59 mark which meant that the mistake prone Luchenko and the 32-year-old Kuzkin had been out **for well over two minutes**. With the pressure of trying to score on the powerplay, and the overall intensity of this game, Kuzkin and Luchenko had to be hitting the exhaustion wall by the time Frank Mahovlich scored. **This was a rare bench management mistake for the Soviets, and it sealed the game for Canada.**

The Soviets had changed their forward line and

Starshinov was out with Maltsev and a young university games star making his debut in the Series, **Vyacheslav Anisin**. Anisin was the youngest person dressed on team in game 2. He had just turned 21 in June, and this was his first shift in the Summit Series. While he would play in 7 games and be impactful in games 3 and 5, his debut in this game was unfortunately when Frank Mahovlich scored his only goal in the series. Frank on the other hand would struggle badly after game 2, eventually losing his place in the line-up.

The goal really starts with the prementioned Luchenko giveaway to Yvan Cournoyer that leads to a point-blank chance for Mikita. After Tretiak's save, Mikita gets the puck back behind the Soviet net, but the puck deflects around the boards on Tretiak's left. **The Soviets then become guilty of over passing, back passing to each other instead of simply getting it out of their end relieving the pressure.** This would haunt them later in the series as well. Vladimir Luchenko throws it back behind him to Starshinov who circles behind his goal, but decides to drop the puck back behind him, spotting Stan Mikita on the hunt for the puck in front of him. Viktor Kuzkin picks it up and seems to be saying "enough playing around" as he fires it hard around the left side boards. This went to young Anisin, who continued the circling pattern curling towards the centre of his zone and then making a terrible pass that is intercepted by Mikita. Stan gets control and circles behind the Soviet goal, and then makes a nice pass to Frank Mahovlich who is open in the slot. Frank drills a shot into the bottom left corner for Canada's fourth goal of the game.

Whether it was the fact that Luchenko and Kuzkin were at the end of a very long shift, or the Soviets had a young rookie on the ice (Anisin) combined with an older veteran who had struggled in this game (Starshinov), **this was poor defensive play by the Soviets**. Certain players on the Soviet team were seemingly intimidated by the aggressive hard hitting of the Canadian team in this game.

Luchenko starts the series of turnovers when he loses the puck to Cournoyer despite at 6'1 and 205 pounds he was significantly bigger than the 5'7 170 pound Cournoyer. As a National Team level player, it's surprising to see Luchenko's weakness on the puck in the third period, in the highest stakes series of his career, especially when his team was down two goals.

Luchenko gave the puck away a second time when he passed back in his zone to Starshinov instead of getting it clear of the forechecking Canadians. Starshinov then repeats the mistake as he throws the puck back behind him once he sees Mikita about to hit him with a bodycheck. Starshinov should have held onto the puck, **taken the hit or fired it out of his end.** Kuzkin attempts to make up for his teammates mistakes by firing it hard up the boards, but Anisin decides to go for another circling skate, losing the puck to Mikita who is everywhere in this sequence. Luchenko chases Mikita ineffectively, never getting close to him, or stopping the pass to Mahovlich. As Luchenko was doing his ineffective chase of Mikita, it left Kuzkin alone in front of Tretiak, to deal with Cournoyer. Maltsev stands stationary near the blue line watching the play, probably anticipating a quick transition breakout. When the puck does get to Frank Mahovlich, Anisin is near him, but just does a weak poke check attempt, and skates right by the big Canadian. Tretiak may have been screened as Kuzkin was battling hard with Cournoyer. However, Frank's shot was hard and quick, and he really did not have much of a chance to stop it.

The Mikita, Cournoyer, Frank Mahovlich line put this goal together by skating hard, forechecking and being physical. This seemed to expose a flaw in the Soviet quick transition game, **as the Soviet players continued the back passing and circling, trying to re-set so they can hit the long pass,** but it ends up backfiring on them. This inability to change style and on ice strategy would sometimes hurt the Soviets, (despite their success) as some well coached teams (like the Philadelphia Flyers in 1976) adjusted to counter their style.

Overall, while it was a complete Soviet breakdown, all three Canadian forwards can take some credit on this goal, as both Mikita and Cournoyer caused the turnovers, Mikita made a sweet pass to Mahovlich who wasted no time drilling it home and giving Canada a much deserved three goal cushion.

The teams go back and forth with a few line changes, with Parise and Cashman still causing the Soviets fits in their own end. They really do not seem to have an answer to the forechecking and corner work by the two NHL pluggers. Alexander Maltsev makes a nice rush down the ice as Guy Lapointe backs up almost onto Tony Esposito's lap, showing they haven't quite learned from game one that backing up on the Soviets is very dangerous. As a result, the clever Maltsev does a quick shift to his forehand and drills a hard shot that Esposito stops.

The buzzer goes for the 10-minute mark of the third period and the teams change ends and lines. The Mikita line goes back out for Canada, with Coach Sinden probably expecting their momentum to continue. They are up against the Shadrin line for the Soviets. Paladiev is back out with Lyapkin, his first shift since the Peter Mahovlich humiliating goal. Yvan Cournoyer is absolutely flying this shift as he back checks hard, taking the puck from Yakushev in the Canadian zone, and then making a full ice rush where he dekes out the Big Yak again at mid-ice and fires a long slap shot at Tretiak.

The next couple of shifts are anticlimactic as the Soviets seem to have given up on the game. They are not forechecking at all and seem content letting Canada pass the puck around and dump it deep into the Soviet end, wasting time. Kharlamov comes back out for the first time in this period after serving his 10-minute misconduct, but besides one long range shot, he is ineffective. **The Clarke line seems to have bottled up the Soviet starting line of Starshinov, Kharlamov and Maltsev who have been unable to generate**

any offence. Tsygankov reminds Tony Esposito that the Soviets can take hard slap shots when he rushes the puck and lets a howitzer go from the blue line that Esposito struggles with. Mikita recovers the puck and he and Frank Mahovlich pass back and forth, finally setting Ron Ellis up in the slot for a great chance, but Ellis fans on the shot.

After some circling in the neutral zone, Cournoyer intercepts a sloppy Shadrin pass and gets it deep. Tretiak shows he can also play the puck like his Canadian counterpart, skating out halfway to the blue line and firing a pass back up the ice. Cournoyer isn't done as he retrieves the puck, bursts back into the Soviet zone, and switches hands to shoot a hard wrist shot right-handed. Esposito does the same thing on the next shift as he leads a solo rush down the ice, goes wide on Paladiev and fires the puck right-handed. This was something Gordie Howe did a lot, rather than switch his entire body to deliver a backhand as his rival Rocket Richard used to do. Gordie, and obviously Phil and Yvan, simply changed hand positioning and fired a shot ambidextrously from their opposite hand.

With four minutes left in the game, the Soviets suddenly spring to life, skating and pressing the Esposito line in their own end. Mikhailov gets a point-blank shot on Tony O, who makes another athletic save with his toe, kicking the puck into the corner. Kuzkin shows some real speed as he rushes the puck the length of the ice, something he hasn't done in the two games and probably should have done more of. His shot just misses the far post. Canada comes roaring back with Henderson getting a heavy shot away on Tretiak from the slot. Tretiak gloves the high shot, and Henderson is so impressed he goes over and gives the goalie a tap on his pads. That good will gesture doesn't last as Ellis high checks Ragulin shortly after and when the lines change, **Starshinov can be seen taking a nasty flying elbow at Stan Mikita,** and just missing the Czech Canadian legend. Starshinov seems to have a real issue with Mikita, perhaps going back to Mikita's bodycheck on the Frank Mahovlich goal, as the two chirp at each other before Starshinov heads to the Soviet bench.

Canada keeps the pressure on, controlling the play and constantly dumping the puck deep into the Soviet zone before clogging the centre ice area, preventing that transition. In these last two minutes, Canada was playing an early version of the neutral zone trap. The trap was a strategy Sweden would come up with to counter the Soviet transition game in the early 1980's and later perfected by the New Jersey Devils and coach Jacques Lemaire. It involves clogging the neutral zone instead of aggressive forechecking. As a result, the Soviets are completely bottled up in the last minute with Yakushev getting knocked off the puck by a clean hit from Peter Mahovlich and Paladiev giving the puck away to the always swarming Cournoyer and several other uncharacteristic giveaways.

The game ends anticlimactically with the jubilant Canadian players congratulating Tony Esposito and then **remembering to shake hands this time**. The handshakes are full of smiles on both sides as the Soviet players seem to recognize the strong game Canada played. The Soviet coaches and authorities would be another story.

Game 2: Period 3 Review

Team Canada put together a very strong, quite memorable period. They outscored the Soviets 3-1; two of those goals **were remarkable, once in a lifetime, individual efforts.** Canada had control of the tempo and play for most of the period, with some periodic bursts of energy by the Soviets. When those periodic counter attacks happened, the Canadian defence had help from the backchecking forwards and Tony Esposito in goal. After the final fourth Canadian goal, the Soviets seemed to deflate and failed to mount any sustained comeback. This is atypical of the Soviets as Canada would find out in this series and in future matches. They were certainly a comeback team, who could strike quickly and score goals in bunches. In this game, the expected comeback never materialized. The Soviets seemed to be penned in their own end for much of the last half of period three, but also seemed to lack energy. As a group the Soviets seemed to hit a conditioning wall in the period, similar to Canada in game 1. **While the Soviets were by far the better conditioned team, the travel, crowds, and foreign life combined with an aggressive motivated team Canada was simply too much and they appeared to run out of gas.**

Strong players in period three for Canada were Cournoyer, Mikita, Parise, both Espositos and Paul Henderson was starting to really show his skating ability. For the Soviets, Tretiak was solid, and Kuzkin was very involved both defensively and offensively.

CHAPTER 18: GAME 2 SUMMARY: NEW SHOW- CANADA HAS TALENT

Vladislav Tretiak would get the player of the game for the Soviets, receiving a deserving ovation from the appreciative Canadian crowd. While a losing goalie who let in four goals might seem an odd choice, the Soviets really did not have another player who put in a stellar enough effort to earn the nomination. Tretiak kept the game close and made several stellar stops when his team's defence was lacking.

In Sault St. Marie, Ontario, Pat and Frances Esposito must have been beaming with pride as both their sons are named players of the game. Tony played very well, making some key saves when the Soviets pressed and a few spectacular saves that kept Canada from falling behind early. Phil put in a typical 1972 Phil Esposito game, scored a goal, got an assist on a short-handed goal and was a force throughout the game. The best player on Canada was Yvan Cournoyer who was flying all game, causing the Soviets fits with his speed, forechecking and of course scored a spectacular goal.

This was a must win game for Canada. After the shockwave of the first game, the Canadian players became very aware that their opponent was significantly stronger, more cohesive, and unique than they had been led to believe. While coaches Harry Sinden and John Ferguson could be taken to task for the poor decisions in game one, **they certainly redeemed themselves** with both the player personnel and game strategy invoked for game two. The six defensemen selected settled Canada down, especially Bill White and Serge Savard who made the Soviet forwards forays into the offensive zone difficult.

"All through training camp" Serge Savard mentioned after the game. "I don't think we really put enough emphasis on defense. All the time it was goals. How many goals we were going to beat them by. Score! Score! But tonight, we brought some defense back into the game" Serge Savard Montreal Gazette

Fatigue was not a factor, as 3 sets of defensemen could be rolled out consistently. Pat Stapleton added more speed from the back end.

The forwards that were brought in added a real edge to the team, something the Soviets were unaccustomed to. Boris Mikhailov remarked after Game 2:

"They were more respectful of us in the second game," said Soviet captain Boris Mikhailov. "They understood we could play good hockey. They played very well, a very physical game. We had not seen such a style of game."

The strategy of having the wingers come down low and help the defence paid dividends. While this was a dangerous strategy that could have backfired, the Soviets only had a few opportunities from the defensive points. Canada was able to get possession of the puck in the corners, out manning and outworking the Soviet forecheckers. This was also because the Soviets for whatever reason seemingly abandoned the game one strategy of aggressive weaving forechecking, often with two men on the puck.

Goaltending was a major difference for Team Canada in game two. While Ken Dryden made some solid saves in game one, he also let in goals that were potential saves, at the very least. Where Dryden played shakily and unsure of himself much of the game, Esposito was the opposite. Focused, composed, he was simply fantastic. He displayed a quick athletic style, completely focused on the task at hand. Brother Phil remarked in his autobiography that teammates didn't tend to speak to Tony before a game. He would be so focused on the upcoming challenge, he didn't want to be disturbed. Tony O kept Canada from falling behind early when the Soviets got a few good chances, with the best save on Kharlamov early in the game. Paul Henderson remarked on the difference between the two goaltenders in the first two games of the series:

> *"Tony Esposito had a great game that night," Team Canada forward Paul Henderson told NHL.com. "Ken Dryden had a tough night in Game 1. When he thought they were going to pass, they would shoot, and when he thought they were going to shoot, they passed. He had never seen anything like it before, and it unnerved him. Tony was better against that style."*

The insertion of Wayne Cashman, JP Parise and Stan Mikita changed the Canadian game style. They added a sense of menace and agitation. The Soviets started "hearing footsteps" when they went after the puck and that hesitation consistently led to turnovers. Cashman especially seemed to have the Soviets off their game.

> *"He had them looking," said Stan Mikita. Because with Cashman playing the way he was, a lot of our other guys simply picked it up from there". Mikita continued*
> *"There was one time when Bobby Clarke went after a puck in the corner. A little guy see? There's this big Soviet defenseman who has eight strides on Bobby and he stops and looks. When somebody as big as that stops to look for Bobby, it means they are thinking. They're looking". Montreal Gazette 1972.*

Harry Sinden remarked about Team Canada's aggressive playoff style hockey.

"I think they knew we weren't the same team they had run into in the first game. They knew we were playing aggressive hockey and some of them were looking at it and maybe doing a little thinking. "

The Soviets appeared off their game. Their defence seemed hesitant to engage the Canadians at times, especially Luchenko and Gusev; those hesitations led to turnovers. The forwards seemed to lack the skating and consistent effort they had in game one, possibly because of the upgraded Canadian defence. The players also seemed to be focused on playing the Canadian game, and easily could have been called on several penalties. The worst incident being Starshinov's MMA style flying elbow at supreme agitator Stan Mikita towards the end of the game. **While as Boris Mikhailov said this was a foreign style to them, they would have to adapt, settle down and go back to their game of speed, teamwork and transition play moving forward.**

To continue the thought that this game took the Soviets out of their comfort zone, even the Soviet executives and coaches also seemed out of sorts. There was an incident between the 2nd and 3rd period. Andre Starovoytov, a former Soviet player, referee in the Soviet Elite league, and General Secretary of the Soviet Ice Hockey Federation from 1969 to 1986, was instrumental in helping the Summit Series get organized. He believed the Soviets would be able to defeat the professionals. On this day however, Andre Starovoytov was livid with perceived biased officiating by American amateur IIHF officials Steve Dowling and Frank Larsen. He grabbed an interpreter and in a bizarre moment went into the Referee dressing room between the 2nd period intermission, kicked over chairs and exclaimed:

"You American referees let the Canadian players perform like a bunch of barbarians!"

Coach Bobrov jumped into the fray, picking out Wayne Cashman as the main culprit on Canada. In an interview in Winnipeg before game 3 he stated:

"If that game had been played in Europe, he would have spent the entire game in the penalty box. He must be prepared to spend some time in the penalty box in Europe".

Bobrov continued his complaint by saying,

"The game was a mess of mistakes; the first game was officiated pretty well but we couldn't understand the reasons for some penalties in Toronto."

Soviet player Eugeny Mishakov chimed in with more and somewhat exaggerated Wayne Cashman complaints

"Cashman cut me in the face and I got two minutes. If he had given me a black eye I would have got five minutes".

One interesting note was the Soviets, and seemingly everyone else in the arena, missed the fact that Petrov had played the puck during the delayed call on Canada's first goal. **Of all the missed calls the two referees were responsible for, this may have been the most damaging, but it was never mentioned**. Certainly, they missed some Canadian penalties, the Lapointe trip on Shadrin was a terrible miss while Cashman taking down Luchenko before the first goal was a potential penalty that led to a goal by Phil Esposito to start the game. Bill Goldsworthy's knee to Petrov's head was another, so **in some ways the Soviets did have a legitimate dispute.**

Cashman would make some amusing comments about his role in Game 2's victory. In an interview with Ian MacLaine of the Canadian Press he gave the following responses. When asked what if his role was as a "policeman" for team Canada, he responded with a *"my job is to play right wing."* When asked about the chirping between himself and the Soviet players he remarked.

"I don't understand what language they were talking in, but they seem to understand what was being said".

When asked about his aggressive play from the Soviet News Agency TASS, Cashman responded ominously,

"I enjoy both giving and receiving pain".

Canada had not played an overly "beyond the

rules" aggressive game. It could be summed up as controlled aggression. Cashman, Parise, and Mikita added a bit of hustle, intimidation, and corner work to a game one pedestrian Team Canada, but **that was nothing that was out of the ordinary for a high stakes NHL game.** Did the Soviets expect another free-wheeling, open game where they could play their transition game to a T? Of course not. Canada had to change, play a more Canadian style of game, **forcing the Soviets to adapt to that**. This is what happened. Both teams had now given their opponents a taste of what the other could do.

The Soviet management showed poor sportsmanship by complaining about the referee's work instead of acknowledging Canada's strong game, and the great individual efforts of Cournoyer and Peter Mahovlich. While there were numerous calls on both teams that could have been made, Canada was the culprit more often. Why? Canada responded to their humiliating 7-3 loss in game one with an expected, raised up, NHL playoff game mentality. This style was nothing out of the ordinary in North America. In intense close games, North American referees often just let the players play, only calling the blatant infractions or those taken during scoring chances. The reason for this was simple, the belief was that the Officials should strive to no effect the outcome of a game. Calling borderline penalties in close intense game situations would lead to power plays and this would of course have the potential to change the outcome.

In hindsight, the Soviet coaches, executives, even the players should have spent less time complaining about the officiating and take notice that when Team Canada's backs were against the wall, they would respond with controlled aggression, increased focus, skill, intensity, and drive. **That would have been a very valuable lesson for them to learn**.

PART 5: THE WORLD VERSUS AMATEUR CANADA 1948-1970

CHAPTER 19:
A CANADIAN
DEVELOPS THE
CZECHS. CZECH
TRAGEDY

After Team Canada successfully rebounded from the game one opening defeat, a new realization was slowly settling in. The Soviets were very good. Yes, they had lost game two, but it never felt like a romp or a one-sided affair. In fact, it might have been starting to feel like this would be a long difficult series for both teams. While this realization was a huge turnaround from the eight straight gang, the media and experts who had predicted total Canadian domination, it was also a testament to just how good European hockey had become. Team Canada wouldn't know it yet, but the Swedes had become very good players, great skaters with high skill levels. Even better than the Swedes were the Czechoslovakians, who played a hybrid European-Canadian style, a style with which the Soviets had issues. This was because the Czechoslovakian's game had been developed not internally, but by a transplanted Canadian.

Mike Buckna was born in 1913 in Trail, British Columbia to Slovakian parents. He was an excellent hockey player who joined the Trail Smoke Eaters in the 1931-32 season and played for them for four years. Mike went to Czechoslovakia in 1935 to see his parents' home country, and despite being just 22, accepted an offer to join the Czech club team LTC Praha as a player coach. Mirroring the opportunity Soviet coach Anatoli Tarasov took in 1967 with Toronto Maple Leafs Carl Brewer, this was the first time a European hockey country could watch, learn from, and be coached by, a young good Canadian hockey player.

Buckna taught the defensive game, Canadian forechecking and physical play, all strong aspects of future Czechoslovakian hockey that were integrated into the grass roots of Czechoslovakian hockey by Buckna. In a short time period, he had reorganized the country's hockey system, pioneering hockey clinics, coaching junior and senior teams, and introducing minor hockey. The results were immediate on the world stage. By 1938 Buckna was the head coach of the Czechoslovakian hockey team. World War II interrupted his coaching. Mike was back in Czechoslovakia coaching the National Team in 1946, leading them to a surprise victory in the 1947 World Championships and a silver in the 1948 Olympics.

After the Czech National Team won a third European title in 1948, Buckna predicted the NHL would be coming to Europe for players; at the time people laughed. **Decades later, he would be proved correct.**

Since the 1948 Olympics, the Communist Party of Czechoslovakia, with Soviet backing, assumed undisputed control over the government of Czechoslovakia, marking the onset of four decades of communist rule in the country. Buckna left to come back to Canada where he played and coached for several years. His legacy and impact on Czech/Slovak and European hockey was significant. He was inducted into the IIHF Hall of Fame in 2004. Sarah Benson-Lord, manager of the Trail Smoke Eaters Museum said this about Buckna at his induction ceremony:

"Mike is considered the father of Czechoslovak hockey and

we are certainly proud of his achievements," IIHF.com

It could probably be safely said that without Buckna's influence Hockey in the modern countries of the Czech Republic and Slovakia, hockey success would have been limited and possibly not be as prevalent as it is today.

The hockey world looked entirely different after the war. With Germany divided and devastated they would no longer be a strong European hockey nation. The damage from the war was severe to most European nations, so that many would look at sports as a way to rebuild moral and restore or enhance their reputations globally. This would be especially true in the heavily damaged Soviet Union. The USSR, reeling after losing millions of lives in the war, had strategically placed themselves as the world's major communist power. Sport was a way to showcase their strength. The Russian Bear, with all its might, would pick up a hockey stick.

If Canada had a pre-World War II international rival it would have been Czechoslovakia. Hockey was ingrained in the small nation. After a horrible war of Nazi occupation, with the USSR controlling most of Eastern Europe by 1947 with the Czechoslovakian government in its' sights, the country was looking for anything to bring positivity to its' beleaguered populace. **One way was to re-establish their hockey programs**.

This started with the 1947 World Championships held in Prague. Canada did not send an entry that year, while the host Czechoslovakians would win their first World Championship title. Canada had missed the 1947 worlds due to an ongoing debate regarding amateur status, internally with the CAHA and externally with the international hockey powers such as Avery Brundage who ran the Olympics and Bunny Ahearn. Canada would get its amateur status issues at home resolved in time to send the Ottawa RAF Flyers to the 1948 Winter Olympics. The issue of amateurism was hotly debated for these Olympics as the IIHF, the United

States Olympic Committee and the International Olympic Committee were all at odds. The Ottawa RAF Flyers would win all their games except one. They were unable to defeat the strong Czechoslovakian side as the two teams would battle to a 0-0 draw. This meant the gold was decided by goal differential, with Canada holding a slight advantage.

Despite Buckna's building the program to the level that they could match the top Canadian Senior A teams, **the early success was not to last**. The Czechoslovakian hockey program suffered two terrible setbacks after the 1948 Olympics. **One, a result of internal politics, the second, a plane tragedy that shook up hockey nation.**

In November 1948 the Czechoslovakian National Team arranged to fly to London, England for exhibition games against the British league. As was common at that time, smaller planes were used, and the team was split up. The first plane took eight players, the second to leave Paris the next day. On the morning of November 8th, London was covered in a heavy mist. The players were very concerned because their teammates had not shown up. The Czechoslovakians had a game to play at Wembley Arena later that day, so the eight players departed for the game hoping their six teammates were going directly to the arena. In the second period the English players showed great sportsmanship and also played the game with only eight players. The Czechs won the game 5-3, but the players were more worried about their teammates. **Later that evening the news arrived that the plane carrying the players had disappeared over the English Channel**. The remains were never found. The National Team program had lost half of their players, this would take several years to recover from, and rebuild.

A month later, in December 1948, several members of the LTC Prague hockey club **defected** at the Spengler cup in Davos, Switzerland. In 1949, former hockey player and Wimbledon tennis champion Jaroslav Drobny also defected.

These defections were very troublesome to the Communist government, which was under the heavy-handed influence of the Soviet Union. When the rebuilt Czechoslovakian National Team was preparing to leave for London England for the 1950 World Championships, two journalists from Czechoslovakia were told they were not allowed to go, their flight cancelled. The hockey players were escorted from the plane and told they were not going to England. The players got together that evening in a pub and started complaining about the news on the radio that that hockey team had been involved in anti-communist behaviour with the journalists.

The players were furious and started making anti-communist comments, complaints about the government, admonishing Soviet control. This was overheard in the pub. **Shortly after, military police showed up and arrested all the players.** It would come out later that the real focus was goalie Bohumil Modry who had been in contact with the US embassy as a potential flight risk. Twelve players were put on trial. Twelve players were convicted. Their sentences ranged from 15 years for Modry, the goalie, to eight months for a player deemed to be less involved in the plot. **Stanislav Konopásek**, one of the convicted players, feels it the Soviet Union who had them arrested.

> *"And the reason was, that it was at this time in the late 1940s, in the early 1950s, that the Soviet Union was developing their own hockey program. So, by getting the world champion Czechoslovak hockey team out of the way, this would open up the path for the rise of the Soviet hockey team."*

The players were sent to work in horrible conditions at the uranium mines in the western part of Czechoslovakia, close to the German border. The last player would be released in 1955. Whether it was a Soviet plot or a Czechoslovakian collaboration government showing that hockey players were not above the law, the damage was done. The very successful Czechoslovakian team would have to be rebuilt post World

War II.

CHAPTER 20: HERE COME THE SOVIETS! WHAT'S A LYNDHURST?

Despite the loss of their strongest opponent, Czechoslovakia, Canada would send the Edmonton Mercurys to the 1950 World Championships. With the European countries still recovering after the war, the competition was not strong. The Mercurys would have a very easy time, even defeating Belgium 33-0. The only close game for the Edmonton squad was a 3-1 victory over Sweden. Without the Czechoslovakians, the gap between Canada and the rest of the world was back to pre-World War II levels.

In 1951 the Lethbridge Hurricanes would have an easier time winning, with the closest game a 5-1 dismissal of Sweden. The Canadian team would defeat Great Britain 17-1, Finland 11-1 and the USA 16-3. **These scores had to resonate in the minds of the older media in 1972 who still hung onto the notion that the best Canadians should easily defeat all challengers.**

Much like the 1948 games, the 1952 Oslo Norway Winter Olympics were not without political turmoil and drama. Due to the ongoing debate over amateurism, hockey was dropped from the Olympic Games in 1951. The absurdity of the decision caused immense protests from all participating countries; hockey was considered the showcase event of the winter games. The financial cost in excluding hockey would be significant.

The Games committee reinstated hockey soon afterwards. Once re-established, Canadian and former IIHF resident W.G. Hardy advocated for the inclusion of the Soviet Union to the list of participating hockey countries, but the Soviets did not apply in time. Czechoslovakia and Germany did and re-joined the list of participating countries.

Canada was represented by the 1950 World Champion Edmonton Mercurys. They would win all their games leading to the final round robin game against the USA. If Canada won the game, the newly rebuilt Czechoslovakian team would win a surprise silver medal. Canada played a strong US squad to a 0-0 tie, which forced the Czechoslovakian squad to play a tie breaker for bronze against Sweden, won by Sweden 5-3 eliminating the Czechoslovaks from the podium. A newspaper in Moscow cried out that it was a fix or collusion between Canada and the Americans, to deny the Czechoslovakians silver. Swiss newspapers followed suit and **complained about the violent nature of the Canadian team**, also supporting a hockey ban at the Olympics. Infuriated, Doug Grimson, CAHA president responded that Canada may drop out of international hockey altogether.

> *"There is no point carrying on any further. European nations in particular will not agree with uniform rules. As a result, every game is a confusion of shinny, with the odd sprinkle of hockey. I also told the Russians they were cry-babies!" Fairbanks Daily News Miner, Fairbanks, Alaska Thursday, Mar 6, 1952*

An angry, frustrated Canada would pull out of the 1953 world hockey championships in Switzerland. CAHA president W.B. George explained the reasoning to the Associated Press:

> *"Every year we spend $10,000 to send a Canadian hockey team to Europe to play 40 exhibition games. All these games*

are played to packed houses that only enrich European hockey coffers. In return we are subjected to constant, unnecessary abuse over our Canadian style of play."

The Soviets, who had decided not to participate in the championships, sent observers, including Anatoli Tarasov. Czechoslovakia originally participated. They were sent home by General František Janda, the Chairman of the State Committee for the Physical Education and Sport, when communist Czechoslovakian president Clement Gottwald became gravely ill. With the Czechoslovakian results annulled, Sweden would win their first World Championship.

The 1954 World Hockey Championships was a watershed moment for hockey. Canada had enjoyed a long, unrivalled period as the alpha dog in international hockey. Senior A clubs, usually the Allan Cup champions, had enough firepower to handle any European nation that challenged them. The Mike Buckna trained Czechoslovakians, and on a really good day the Swedes, could often give Canada a challenge, but overall, even ties were rare, let alone losses. Foreshadowing the arrogance of Canadian hockey experts and media before the Summit Series, a European country being able to compete with, or even defeat, a team from Canada in 1954 seemed **outrageous**. That would change. The 1954 World Championships started the greatest rivalry in hockey history. **Canada versus the Soviet Union, or Canada-Russia as it was commonly known.**

After dropping out of the 1953 World Championships, George Dudley and the CAHA struggled to find a Senior A club to represent Canada at the 1954 World Championships in Stockholm, Sweden. Teams saw little upside in going to Europe with the costs involved, complaints about Canadian rough play, and assumptions that the Canadian rough style would lead to significant time in the penalty box. When the Allan Cup winners the Kitchener Waterloo Dutchmen declined, it led to a steamroll effect with other clubs declining. Not a single Senior A club was willing to go, with even the Senior B Champions for Kingston and the finalists from Woodstock Ontario declined. When a promise that some Senior A reinforcements would be added to their line-up, a local Toronto Senior B squad, **the East York Lyndhurts**, a Senior B semi-finalist, agreed to represent Canada.

The Lyndhursts were so named as they were sponsored by local Toronto auto dealer Lyndhurst's Motors. They had one former professional player on the team, the captain Tommy Campbell, who had played one season with the AHL Pittsburgh Hornets. They were led by diminutive **Moe Galand**, a former professional baseball player who was the team's leading scorer. The team was sent to Europe to begin an uninspiring exhibition tour. The Lyndhurts looked like a Senior B squad, getting pounded by Canadians playing in the British professional league in their first game by a humiliating 11-2 score. They would win some easy victories against lower-level European club teams but struggle to defeat Switzerland 6-5 and lose to the Swedish B team 5-4 in Stockholm. **The Swedish press called them "the worst team ever sent abroad by Canada."**

The CAHA would panic after a tough 4-1 win against Germany and send the East York team the originally promised reinforcements. Senior A players Don Lockhart, Eric Unger, Tom Jamieson, Doug Chapman and Bill Shill were flown over to join the Lyndhurts. Four of those players would go on to play minor pro after the championships, with **Bill Shill** playing 79 games for the Boston Bruins. The Lyndhurts were an offensively focused squad, **the highest scoring team in Canadian senior hockey that season.** With the reinforcements there was even more offensive strength.

East York opened the World Championships with high scoring victories over Switzerland, Norway, West Germany and Finland by a combined score of 52-3. They continued the high-octane scoring output with a surprising 8-0 victory over Sweden and a 5-2 defeat over the rebuilding

Czechoslovakians. All seemed right with the hockey world, as the Canadian team was seemingly back to historical form over European challengers.

The new entrant in the tournament, the Soviet Union, was also defeating all challengers, by closer scores. A 5-2 Soviet victory over the Czechoslovakians was the same winning score as the Canadians, but when the Soviets tied the Swedes 1-1, Canadian confidence soared. East York manager said the,

> *"Soviets would not show us anything new. The only similarity between their game and the Canadian game is the equipment"* Epic confrontation Greg Franke

While trying to disparage the Soviet level of play, Preston was prophetic. There would be no similarity between the teams in the final match. None.

The Canadian team had never faced an athlete like **Vsevolod Bobrov**, a world class soccer player, the dominant player in Soviet hockey. They had never faced a team that was as fit or could skate as well as the Soviets. The Senior B team from Canada was tight, nervous and on a stage, they had never imagined when they accepted the role as Canada's representatives. Moe Galand remarked on the tension the Canadians felt before the game.

> *"A lot of our guys had never been in this position before. You were fighting for your country. There was unbelievable tension."*

The Soviets were prepared for the aggressive offensive style of the Lyndhurts, who would send two men deep on the forecheck. This had worked against inferior opponents who the Canadians could outskate. **Similar to 1972, the Soviets caught the Canadians deep in their own zone and used long passes to counter strike**.

With smooth transition hockey and a five-man offensive style, the Russians would score the first goal in the sixth minute of play. Lockhart would play his worst game of the tournament giving up two soft goals. The Canadian

GRANT DOUGLAS PENNELL

team could never get on track resulting in a 4-0 Russian first period advantage and **a 7-2 victory for the Soviet squad**. Bobrov would win the tournament top forward honours, despite Moe Galand being the tournament's top scorer at 15 goals to Bobrov's 8. Goalie **Don Lockhart** attributed his poor play to bad nerves, caused by the pressures placed on the team before the game. He would remark:

"The Russians are wonderful hockey players. Their skating, passing and stick handling are excellent. They deserve the victory they got."

The nearly 17,000 fans who gathered in the Stockholm outdoor Royal Stadium were shocked. The unbeatable Canadians had lost to the unknown Soviets. As Soviet officials jumped onto the ice to congratulate the winners, Bunny Ahearne presented them with their championship. The Canadians would suffer the indignity of hearing the Soviet anthem being played to honour the victors.

In 1954 Lyndhurst reinforcement Eric Unger would state *"Their slowest skater was faster than our fastest skater"*. Eighteen years later in 1972, coach Harry Sinden would ice for game one a line-up of offensive players. After the game Sinden would remark that this was what he what he thought might be his fastest line-up, but the Soviets were faster.

In both cases the end result would be a one-sided loss. The Canada-Soviet hockey rivalry had begun.

Outrage over the result was quick and ruthless in Canada. The Montreal Herald wrote that it was *"A national calamity, a national humiliation, and a mortifying experience"*. The CAHA quickly used the Lyndhurst's as scapegoats stating that the East York team lacked the experience. Former NHL star player and athlete Lionel Conacher suggested sending over the top pros to re-establish Canadian dominance, a sentiment echoed by the Toronto Maple Leafs owner Conn Smythe who suggested sending his team overseas.

Considering the lack of respect shown the Soviet hockey standards by the Canadian media before the Summit

Series, it's not surprising that in 1954 there was **little credit given to the Soviet players ability, team game or shocking rise to that level in eight years**.

While the 1954 East York Lyndhursts were not the level of the top Senior A teams, they had been reinforced by some top players making them competitive enough to beat Sweden and Czechoslovakia fairly easily. They were not as bad as the press made them out to be. For the rest of the 1950's the Soviets would show that if not the equal to the top Senior A clubs in Canada, they were close and constantly improving. Canada could never again send a team the level of the Lyndhurts and believe they could win overseas.

CHAPTER 21: THE UNBEATABLE PEACHES AND CANADA'S FADING GLORY

There have been numerous teams in sports that were at their best coming back from insurmountable odds. Perhaps the best-known comeback team was baseball's 1969 Miracle Mets. The traditional also ran Mets were 9.5 games behind the division leading Chicago Cubs in mid-August. They mounted an unprecedented charge until the end of the regular season, catching the Cubs, winning the National League championship before defeating the best team of the era, the Baltimore Orioles in the World Series. **Despite this amazing achievement, even the Miracle Mets had nothing on the 1954-1955 Penticton Vees.**

That season the Vees were the greatest comeback squad in the history of sports. Located in a small town in British Columbia with a population of 14,000, named after a variety of peaches grown locally, the Vees had been able to entice former professionals **Grant, Bill and brother Dick Warwick** to join their squad. Grant had been a very good NHL player. He won the Calder Memorial Trophy as the NHL's top rookie in 1942, played in the 1947 NHL All Star Game and scored over 20 goals 4 times in an era where 20 goals was a significant achievement. Bill had less success but made it to the NHL with the New York Rangers. centre iceman Dick Warwick was the youngest of the three yet possessed his brother's skating ability and talent. The Warwicks were talented, but small, players. They were skilled, very fast, gritty as sandpaper and **ideally suited for the wide open, less physical, international game.**

Despite possessing the talented trio, the Vees would fall behind Vernon in their local league playoffs, forcing them to win successive games to win the league. In the British Columbia Senior A final, the Vees again fell behind. This time it was 3-0 in games to the Nelson Maple Leafs, who needed a tie to advance. The Vees clawed back in the Series, winning 4 consecutive game to clinch the provincial championship. In the Western Canadian finals, the Vees fell behind the Winnipeg Maroons who only needed a tie to advance. Backs against the wall, the Vees would dig down, winning consecutive games to earn the right to face the Eastern Champion Sudbury Wolves.

In the Allan Cup finals, the Wolves would go ahead 3 games to 1, a seemingly insurmountable lead. Despite the Wolves being ahead 5-2 with ten minutes left in game 5, with the Allan Cup ready to be presented, the gritty Vees would tie the game and win in overtime. In game six the Wolves would start the third period up 4-2 but the Vees would, again, come back with four third period goals. The Vees would finish the incredible series of comebacks with a 3-2 victory in game 7, winning the Allan Cup. With **four straight series comebacks,** the Vees were a worthy, incredibly stubborn, representatives for Canada to send to the 1955 World Championships and reclaim Canada's presumed rightful place as World Champions.

The hockey establishment was not sold on sending the Vees overseas. Canada needed to ensure victory. Montreal

Canadians coach Dick Irvin suggested direct NHL help when he said,

> *"Let each NHL team put in two players and Penticton can fill the hole". It's Our Game: Michael McKinley*

Soon after the Montreal Canadians and Toronto Maple Leafs offered players to supplement the line-up, talk was made of Leafs goalie Harry Lumley replacing Vees netminder Ivan McLelland. The Vees would decline any offers of help.

The Vees went to Germany with one intention, to win the World Championship. European media and onlookers were shocked when Bill Warwick and defenceman George McAvoy got into a spirited fight in practice. The Vees meant business. Those intentions carried over into one sided victories over the Americans, 12-1, a game in which they had 96 shots on goal, Finland 12-0, the Swiss 11-1 and Poland 8-0. These easy wins gave playing coach Grant Warwick enough confidence to retort his earlier concern about replacing two sick players with calls ups from their British Columbian senior loop. This confidence must have been on the coaches' mind as the Vees again fell behind in a crucial must win game.

The Czechoslovakians had been rebuilding their program since the player arrests and plane crash tragedy and were a tough opponent for Canada. Mirroring their playoff comebacks in the Allan Cup, the Vees were now behind the Czechoslovakians 3-2 with ten minutes left. Czech star **Vladimir Zabrodsky** had been all over them, scoring two goals to give his team the lead. The Warwicks dug deep, again, as Bill and Grant both scored goals to give the Vees the lead with under five minutes remaining. A final goal by Doug Kilburn sealed another comeback for the Vees.

This victory changed the Vees mindset. Two players from the BC senior league joined the Vees. The Soviets had shown up to the tournament with the full intention of repeating as champions. They had used the 1954 victory for internal propaganda in the USSR, and had just won a hard fought, 4-0, fight filled game against the Czechoslovakians in which even star player Vsevolod Bobrov had been punching Czech player Jan Lidral in a skirmish. The Vees had to grind out a tough 3-0 victory over the much-improved Swedes. The stage was set. **Canada -Soviets round two would take place on March 6, 1955 in Krefield, Germany with the World Championship on the line.**

In game one of the 1972 Summit Series, the Soviets were able to outskate, out hustle, and out play a Team Canada that tried a strategy of an offensive international game. The result was a hot, out of shape, exhausted team Canada overwhelmed by the speedy skilled Soviets. In game two, Canada went back to play an NHL style playoff game, intense, gritty, skilled, with enough physical menace to upset the Soviet rhythm.

This was the style of team that star Vsevolod Bobrov and his Soviet mates would face March 5th. **The Vees were gritty, physical, skilled, and intense**. They ground out victory after victory against overwhelming odds, time and again. They would not be denied. Not by the Vernon Maple Leafs, the Winnipeg Maroons, the Sudbury Wolves, or the Czechoslovakian National Team. The Vees never gave up, always fighting to the end, pulling out some unknown effort to gain a comeback win. Over and over. They were Team Canada 1972 in Moscow 17 years earlier. They exemplified Canadian hockey. Canadian spirit.

The Soviets had never faced a team like that before. It showed.

Foreshadowing 1972, Foster Hewitt would broadcast the game, CBC would show the contest across Canada, and TV crews from both the western and communist world would film the game, replaying it to millions worldwide. The Soviets come out skating and press the Canadians early, forcing goalie Ivan McLelland to make some key saves. The Vees ramped up the intensity in return, pressing the Soviet defence deep and winning battle after battle for the puck.

Mike Shabaga opened the scoring for the Vees at 4:25 of the first period.

The game would continue at fervent pace, both teams having chances to score.

As the game continued, one team took control. Slowly but surely the Vees forechecking intensity wore the Soviets down. The Soviet defence started making poor passes and attempts to make the long pass to centre was broken up by the Vees defence. This pressure resulted in a fluke goal midway through the second period that gave the Vees a 2-0 lead. The Vees would never look back. They focused on Bobrov, eliminating his chances shift after shift, standing him up at the blue line as he made his solo incursions into the Canadian zone. **Eventually Vee defenceman Hal Tarala would catch Bobrov with a devastating body check, sending him crashing to the ice**. The Soviet star, too much to handle for the East York Lyndhursts the year before, would finish the game without a single point.

The Vees would not have to make a comeback in this game, finishing their miracle season with a well-earned 5-0 victory. Goalie Ivan McLelland, who hockey "experts" wanted replaced with an NHL goalie, became the first goalie to shut out the Soviet Union. The Vees had played a tough, smart, hard, but clean game.

> *"We outsmarted them, outskated them, out passed them and outplayed them."* said top forward award winner Bill Warwick.

Grant Warwick emphasized the shutting down of Bobrov as being a key to the victory,

> *"That Bobrov never got a shot on goal, we got on him in the first period"*.

Soviet Goalie Nikoli Putchkov agreed that the Vees played a smarter, more complete game than the Lyndhurts.

> *"They learned a lot from the previous year, they weren't just taking long shots that were easy to stop, or dumping the puck and letting us counterattack. They kept possession*

of the puck and got much better shots". Epic Confrontation Greg Franke

The Vees had re-established Canadian supremacy. The presumed Canadian order of things had been restored. Canada was back on top. Across Canada the Vees would celebrate with a combination of pride and silent relief.

There was a political feeling seeping into these Canada versus USSR clashes. Vees Clem Bird manager would call it "A good win for democracy". It would be a glorious yet short lived victory. The Soviets were not going anywhere.

CHAPTER 22: 1956-1961 WE ARE STILL THE BEST, RIGHT? RIGHT?

The next international tournament in which the Canadians participated was the 1956 Winter Olympics, sending the 1955 Allan Cup champion **Kitchener Waterloo Dutchmen**. The Dutchmen would finish a shocking, disappointing third in the tournament, losing to the Americans 4-1 and the Soviets 2-0. Denis Brodeur, father of one of the best goalies in hockey history, Martin Brodeur, was in goal, was outduelled by the Soviet goalie Nicoli Puchkov in the **tight 2-0 loss**. Observers were shocked at how much the Soviets had improved in just over a year. No longer could Canadian hockey minds assume the Allan Cup champion would win easily.

Canada and the USA would skip the 1957 World Championships held in Moscow to protest the Soviet invasion of Hungary. That wouldn't stop Canadian officials from welcoming a Moscow Selects team to Canada for a tour against assorted Senior A clubs and junior teams. The opening game to the series was highly anticipated across Canada. As a result, it was shown across Canada on TV, as Canadians revelled in an easy 7-2 victory for Harry Sinden and the Whitby Dunlops. The Kitchener Waterloo Dutchmen had their revenge on some of the Soviet national players who were on the touring Moscow team by defeating the Selects 4-2. Those would be the only Canadian victories as the Soviets went undefeated the rest of the tour, leaving Canada with a 5-2-1 record and thumping a combined Ottawa/ Toronto junior club 10-1 the last game.

Canada responded to the Soviet 1956 Olympic victory by sending those very same Whitby Dunlops to the 1958 World Championships in Oslo, Norway. Coached by Wren Blair, who found success in scouting and signing a 14-year-old Bobby Orr, the Dunlops were a powerful squad. **Former Toronto Maple Leaf star Sid Smith** had become a reinstated amateur and joined the team, but the Dunlops also had several other former professionals or players who would turn professional later in their careers. Goalie Roy Edwards was one, along with top scorer **Connie Broden** who finished the season on the Stanley Cup winning Montreal Canadians. The Dunlops would prove their 7-2 victory over the Moscow Selects was not a fluke by running through the World Championships uncontested. The Dunlop's would rout the Swedes 10-2 and the Czechoslovakians 6-0. It had been many years since a Canadian team had made such easy work of the traditional European powers. A 12-1 spanking of the USA led to a gold medal tilt with the Soviets. The Soviets and Czechoslovaks had tied 4-4 in a previous game, in which the Czechoslovakian team had physically dominated the Soviets. As a result, the only way for the Soviets to win gold was to defeat the Dunlop's. A tie wouldn't get it done.

The Dunlops were nervous before the game. Perhaps not to the same extent that Team Canada would experience in 1972, but they felt the pressure of representing Canada and the expectations of gold or nothing that came with it. Their nerves were enhanced when they learned Boston Bruins General Manager Lynn Patrick had mentioned that the **Soviets had at least five players who could play on the Bruins**, and he would offer $2500 to anyone who could land

Ivan Tregubov or Nikolai Solugubov for Boston. Top scorer Connie Broden was quoted as saying:

"We were expected to win and if you lose, you're a bum. We all felt the weight of Canada on our backs. "

The nervousness showed as the Soviets scored the first goal in the game. A two-man Soviet advantage from two quick Canadian penalties ensued, but the Dunlop's dug deep and killed off the penalties. Both teams traded chances, and goals, leaving the game tied at 2-2 deep into the third period. The Soviets had a great chance as their star **Veniaman Alexandrov** broke in on a breakaway but hit the crossbar. The Dunlop's recovered from near disaster by scoring two quick goals to finish the Soviets off 4-2. **Harry Sinden would have his first great international victory**. That experience would help land him the job as coach of Team Canada fourteen years later.

1958 saw Canada sending its first team to ever play in the Soviet Union, the Allan Cup finalist **Kelowna Packers**. The Packers started off the trip by playing three games against a team called the Swedish All-stars. After losing the first game 5-2, the Packers would rebound with two straight victories in Sweden, strangely by the same score, 5-2. When they landed in the Soviet Union, two players with **Ukrainian heritage** had their **passports confiscated** as part of a Soviet law that could reclaim even the offspring of former Soviet nationals. While the players were allowed to leave after the series, they played the entire time fearing detention.

In 1972, the players felt their rooms in Moscow were bugged, that they were always being watched by the KGB. The Packers were told outright that this was the case, they should be very careful about what they said. The Soviet public on the other hand, was excited to see a Canadian team play and all the games were sold out. The first two would take place at the 15,000 seat brand new Lenin Palace with the last three played outdoors in the **60,000-seat soccer stadium**. While the Packers practiced, Anatoli Tarasov was everywhere, taking notes, talking to the Canadian coaches, even filming the practices.

In 1958, the Central Red Army team was not yet the best club team in the world as they would come to be called in the 1970's and 1980's. The Soviets were still at the Senior A level of hockey, so the first game against the Red Army was a very competitive 4-3 win for the Red Army. In the second game, the Packers goalie Dave Gatherum was the star, holding the Moscow Wings squad to a 1-1 tie. The Soviet hockey authorities would be duplicitous by adding some of the previous CSKA top players to the Moscow Dynamo for game 3 which ended in a 2-2 tie. The Soviets would reinforce the Soviet youth or junior National Team for the fourth game a 4-2 victory for the Packers. The fifth, deciding game was against a Moscow Select squad, a similar team to the one that had toured Canada in 1957. The Packers would have little issue defeating the Selects 5-1, **winning the Series 2-1-2**.

The Globe and Mail reported the love for the Canadian team and players.

"They cheered and applauded wildly. The Canadians tossed their sticks to the fans".

Anatoli Tarasov was reported to have wanted regular Canadian tours, a wish that, *"Canada would make the USSR a regular destination, traditional games will be welcomed, the Canadian masters of hockey".*

The grand master of Soviet hockey would change his tune by 1968 proclaiming his team the best in the world; in 1958, they had a long way to go.

With this being a period of rapid development for the Soviets, as well as the Swedes and Czechoslovakians, Canada would send another very strong Senior A club, **the Belleville McFarlands,** to defend the world title. Belleville would ice 13 reinstated or future professionals for the tournament.

Despite the influx of professionals, the McFarlands lost to the Czechoslovakians 5-3. They rebounded to defeat the Soviets 3-1 and win another championship for Canada, but it was becoming obvious that even the most powerful Senior A clubs were going to struggle to defeat the ever-improving European National Teams.

As the decade closed, Canada had encountered the Soviet challenge in either the Olympics or World Championships five times. After the East York Lyndhurts lost, Canadian teams won in 1955, lost in 1956, but won again in 1958 and 1959. **The Soviet teams learned and improved year after year, forcing Canada to send stronger and stronger teams to have any hope of success.** That problem would increase significantly in the 1960's until finally it would be Canada's best or nothing.

The 1960 Winter Olympics is sometimes referred to as "the other miracle on ice". The USA squad riding the great play of goaltender **Jack McCartan** defeated the Kitchener Waterloo Dutchmen 2-1 on route to winning a surprise gold medal. The Dutchmen added future Montreal Canadian star **Bobby Rousseau** to their squad. They had been offered a young **Dave Keon** from St Michaels College in Toronto but decided to use Rousseau who was playing in the minors that season. The Dutchmen did revenge their 1956 Olympic loss to the Soviets by defeating them 8-5 to win the silver medal. That of course was never going to be good enough back in Canada, where the expectation was Gold or nothing. This attitude was exemplified by Kingston Ontario's Alderman George Webb sending a telegram to Kitchener Coach former NHL star Bobby Bauer stating:

"From the birthplace of hockey, I am going to call for an official day of mourning and ask that our flag be hung at half-mast. Thanks for nothing!" It's Our Game Michael McKinley

It didn't matter how well the rest of the world was playing or how strong those countries were becoming.

Canada was expected to win. Without exception.

The 1960-61 season saw the 1960 Allan Cup champion Chatham Maroons tour Europe. While it was only three years since the Kelowna Packers had toured the USSR, the Maroons found vastly improved competition. The Maroons would go 1-5-1 against the best Soviet clubs, including an 11-3 pounding by the Soviet selects. Interestingly enough, the Winnipeg Maroons had an easy time in Czechoslovakia, winning 8 games and losing 1. The Maroons would return in 1963 and find the competition far harder.

CHAPTER 23:
THE GREAT SETH MARTIN & THE END OF AN ERA

Any discussion about Canadian international hockey history has to include goaltending great **Seth Martin**. If you asked European hockey fans in the 1960's who the best goalie in the world was, one would be shocked at how often the name Seth Martin would be mentioned. Throughout the early 1960's, Martin was often considered the best goalie not in the NHL. While he did have a brief foray into the NHL, he became the face of international hockey for Canada, becoming an overseas superstar, loved, and respected by the European hockey world.

Martin was from Rossland, British Columbia, a village just outside Trail. A late bloomer, Martin didn't have any solid professional offers after his junior career in Lethbridge, so he went home to join the Trail Smoke Eaters of the Western International Hockey League. Martin would dominate the league, named top goaltender nine times. In a twenty-year career, he would win the Allan Cup twice with the Smoke Eaters.

Seth would receive multiple offers to play in the NHL but like most Trail players, Martin had a very good job with Cominco Mining. He preferred the security of Cominco, instead of the high-risk low pay of the NHL. In 1967, aged 34, Seth accepted an offer from the NHL's **St. Louis Blues**. One reason was a chance to share duties with one of history's great goalies, **Glenn Hall**. Martin did well with the Blues, posting a 2.59 goals average in 30 games. **After his one season he didn't want to lose his pension at Cominco and returned to Trail and the Smokies**.

Despite his great career in senior hockey, it was international hockey where Martin left his true legacy. Seth would backstop the Trail Smoke Eaters to the World Championship title in 1961. This would be the final time a Senior A team would win the Worlds. He would represent the Smokies in 1963 at the same championship and afterwards join the Canadian National Team for the 1964 Olympics. He was named the outstanding goalkeeper at four World Championship tournaments between 1961 and 1966. He was also selected to the All-World All-Star team three times including the 1964 Olympics. As an Olympian, Martin recorded a 4-1-0 record with 1.21 goals against average, earning his place as the 1964 Games All-Star goalkeeper.

"Martin's heroics are recalled with particulars reverence by European fans who watched him," writes Murray Greig in his book Trail on Ice. *"For years afterwards the Soviets regarded him as something of a goaltending wizard. Coach Father Bauer recalled that the Europeans thought he was invincible. His very presence was enough to psych out the opposition."*

Martin would be inducted into the IIHF Hall of Fame in 1997. During the induction, Soviet legend Vladislav Tretiak put his arm around Seth, telling him in broken English that **Seth had been his goaltending idol**. When the Summit Series began, the Soviets asked if Team Canada's goaltenders Dryden and Esposito were as good as Seth Martin, he was that revered by Tarasov, Chernyshev, and the Soviet hockey authorities.

How good was Martin? It's impossible to say how

effective Martin might have been in a long-term NHL career, but with his record internationally, especially as the Europeans advanced to NHL level and beyond by the mid-60s, there can be little doubt he would have been an excellent NHL netminder. It's possible that he was perhaps one of the best of the later 1950's and into the - mid 1960's. After all, he was Tretiak's idol.

The Trail Smoker Eaters of 1961 were the end of an era. They were the last Senior A Canadian club to win the World Championships. Trail was the Allan Cup runner up in 1960 to the Chatham Maroons. Chatham turned down the offer to represent Canada at the 1961 World Championships, deciding to tour the USSR instead. The tour turned out badly for the Maroons, who came home suggesting Trail reinforce their team to have any hope of success. Coach **Bobby Kromm** added five of the best senior players across Canada, including **Jackie McLeod**, a skilled veteran who had played five seasons for the New York Rangers.

In today's time period there have been major issues with Hockey Canada. Sadly, Hockey Canada has become an elitist organization that has been unaccountable, using millions of dollars (of parent's money for minor hockey payments) to pay off sexually based lawsuits. Knowing the millions of dollars in Hockey Canada's coffers nowadays, it's inconceivable that teams once representing Canada **had to pay for their own way** to the World Championships and even the Olympics. Trail was no exception. The city and surrounding cities in British Columbia banded together to raise enough funds for the Smokies to tour Europe, culminating in the 1961 World Championships in Switzerland.

Trail would have an easy time on their European tour, starting off losing to the Swedes but winning three out of four games in Sweden. In Moscow they would defeat the Soviet Junior team, tie the Soviet Selects, and lose a tightly contested 3-2 game to Moscow Dynamo. Travelling next to

Czechoslovakia, they would win five straight games there, including two against the national squad. They would finish their European tour with a robust 19-1 humiliation of the Canadian army team in Germany. They would arrive in Switzerland ready to defeat the world.

Trail reinforced their earlier dominance over Sweden in the opening game, a 6-1 rout. They had little trouble defeating West Germany 9-1, then held off the unpredictable Americans 7-4. The Smoke Eaters struggled against East Germany, defeating them 5-2, but the game was much closer than the score, as the teams were 0-0 going into the third period. In the other tournament games, a slight upset happened. The Czechs defeated Russia 6-4. Suddenly, the Czechoslovakian game became a must win for the Canadians.

The game ended in a 1-1 tie, with the Czechs going ahead in the first period. Hugh "Pinoke" McIntyre played the hero role for Canada by taking a pass from Jackie McLeod to score the equalizer late in the second period. Seth Martin was a standout in the net for Canada, with the Smoke Eaters playing short-handed most of the game. The Czechs almost won the game when a fluke dump in bounced on the ice and hit the post, shocking Martin in goal. **Even more shocking was the revelation afterwards from Czech coach Zdenek Andrscht that his team had played for the tie, knowing their advantage in goal differential**.

Trail recovered for an easy win over Finland 12-1 but had to face the Soviets in their final game. With the tie against the Czechs, the Smoke Eaters had to win, and they weren't sure by how much. They knew the gold would be decided on goals for an against and they needed to beat the Soviets by at least two goals. A loss and the Canadians would be relegated to the bronze medal.

The game was a sell-out with over 12,500 fans eager to see the already entrenched Canada-Russia Soviet hockey rivalry. When the game started, the Soviets came out flying, putting pressure on the Smokies. Much like Tony

Esposito in game two of the Summit Series, Seth Martin withheld the barrage, keeping the score 0-0. As Canadian teams tended to do when being pressed by the Soviets, Trail took a couple of penalties. Martin again kept the Soviets off the scoreboard, until Jackie McLeod made a great pass to pinching defenceman Harry Smith, giving Canada a 1-0 lead. McLeod then scored to make it 2-0 before the Smokies added one more to end the second period up 3-0. Seth Martin had been a virtual brick wall in goal, stoning every Soviet opportunity, including a couple from their new young star Vyacheslav Starshinov.

Trail playing coach Bobby Kromm, the eventual coach of the European styled, WHA Winnipeg Jets and NHL coach of the year with Detroit in 1978, had focused on intense physical conditioning all season with his team, ensuring they would be able to fight fatigue when it counted. His strategy paid off when the Smokies, instead of fading as Canada did in the opening game of the Summit Series, Trail kept pressing the Soviets to start the third period. Jackie McLeod would soon score his second goal of the game, giving Trail a seemingly insurmountable 4-0 lead. The Soviets would finally get a goal past Martin halfway through the period. This motivated the Smokies to press harder, as they were still worried about the goal differential with the Czechoslovakians. This resulted in a final goal for the Canadians, ending a one sided 5-1 rout. **The Trail Smoke Eaters had won gold**.

In a rare instance of good sportsmanship after a loss, Soviet coach Arkady Chernyshev would note that Trail was a great team, that their win was absolutely deserved. Jackie McLeod was the Smoke Eaters' leading point getter in the series, with 12 points, including 10 goals in 7 games. Seth Martin was picked the outstanding netminder in the tournament. While this was the beginning of Seth Martin's international hockey legacy, it was the end of an era for Canada, as **the last senior club team to win gold for Canada**.

European nations had improved to the point where a senior club from Canada would be hard pressed to win again, even with reinforcements like Jackie McLeod. No one in Canada or in Canadian hockey knew it at the time, but **this would be the last gold medal for Canada until 1994, a period of 33 years.**

The reinforced Allan Cup Champions Galt Terriers would head to Colorado for the 1962 World Championships. It was portrayed as an easier tournament for Canada as the Soviets and Czechs would not attend due to cold war politics after the East Germans were denied visas. Despite this, the Galt team would **lose to the rapidly improving Swedes 5-3**. Penalties would hurt the Galt team, as the Swedes would capitalize on Canadian aggressive play and jump out to a 4-0 lead. Canada would settle for silver. Swedish star Sven Tumba **(Tumba Johannson)** would win the top forward award. Canadian Jackie McLeod, added to the Galt line-up, would again make the all-star team.

Canada would send the Trail Smoke Eaters in 1963 hoping that lightning would strike twice in three years. However, a change in admission requirements for reformed professionals by the IIHF would hurt Canada. Previously, professionals could convert to amateur status before the World Championships, augmenting Canadian Senior clubs. With this new role, amateur status had to be claimed by September 1. **This rule appears to have been designed to limit Canadian strength**. Canada had won three of the last four World Championships and with the Soviets not having won the World Championships since they surprised the hockey world in 1954 – the Soviets other win was the 1956 Olympics - the focus was seemingly on weakening the Canadian entries.

Without their former professional reinforcements like Jackie McLeod, the Smokies would tie Czechoslovakia 4-4, lose to the Swedes 4-1 and lose to the Soviets 4-2. They would finish fourth in the tournament. This was the beginning of the Soviet international hockey dynasty. The Soviets would not lose another World Championship **for nine years**.

On the Canadian side, a major shift in strategy for international hockey was about to

take place. **The birth of Father David Bauer National Team program was at hand.**

In the 1963 Allan Cup finals, **the Windsor Bulldogs** defeated the **Winnipeg Maroons** 4 games to 1 to win the Allan Cup. In one of the last Senior A ventures into international hockey, both teams would go on European trips against some of the top club teams and National Teams of Europe. **These trips would be disastrous for both teams**. In hindsight, the **signs of rapid European improvement** had been there. In December 1962 the Saskatoon Quakers would travel to Europe but would get destroyed by the Swedish National Team 7-0 and 13-3 in successive games. Things wouldn't get much better for the Saskatoon Senior A squad losing to the Czechoslovakians 9-4 and 4-1. The previous year another senior club the Port Arthur Bearcats had lost 10-1 to the Czechs.

The Allan Cup champion Windsor Bulldogs **would lose eight straight games** in both the USSR and Czechoslovakia, finishing their tour of those countries with one win in nine games. Adding to the humiliation were two straight blowouts by the Soviet National Team, 8-0 and 9-1 over the Bulldogs. The Winnipeg Maroons only won one game out of eight against Czech clubs, the National Team and a final 2-1 loss in Switzerland to the Soviet club Chimik Voskresensk. In two short years since the Winnipeg Maroons won the majority of their games in Europe, they struggled. To add further clarity to the sudden, shocking disparity between Canadian Senior A clubs and the European teams, the two Allan Cup finalists would have a record against Swedish, Czech and Soviet teams of 2 wins, 13 losses and 2 ties. Could NHL teams have beaten these good Senior clubs that badly? It was a fair question, few people in Canada seemed to ask that or realize what was happening overseas. Father David Bauer was one.

A new approach was needed.

CHAPTER 24: NATIONAL DREAM TEAM, FLYING STICKS AND BUNNY'S TRICKS

David William Bauer was part of a famous hockey family, not the skate manufacturers, in Waterloo, Ontario. His brother **Bobby Bauer** was a top player for the Boston Bruins, and a member of the famous Kraut line with Milt Schmidt and Woody Dumar. David was a very good junior player with St. Michael's College in Toronto. He would turn down an offer with the Bruins when he was 16 years old, but captain St Michael's to the Memorial Cup. While his team was not successful in winning the trophy, the next season Oshawa added Bauer along with Ted Lindsay and Gus Morton to their team for the playoffs winning the Memorial Cup. Heavily influenced by his father's preference for education, coupled with his devotion to the church, **David decided to forgo any professional desires and instead become a Catholic priest.** He would go on to coach St Michaels, as a priest, to a Memorial Cup win in 1961.

In 1962, **Gordon Juckes** was the Secretary Manager of the CAHA, the Canadian Amateur Hockey Association.

Juckes was a bold thinker, especially for that time period. He had written an article stating that he believed Canada needed more coherence and continuity in its international representatives. He felt a change was needed from the pattern of sending Senior A squads overseas. Father Bauer had a concrete vision of how that would look. He would call Juckes, as well as CAHA President Art Potter to ask for a meeting, **explaining he had a new vision for Canadian international hockey**. They knew Father Bauer as both the former coach of St Michaels and current coach of the University of British Columbia Thunderbirds and agreed to meet. Father Bauer had been reassigned by the Basilian fathers to St Marks College at UBC.

During the meeting, Bauer suggested a revolutionary concept that would help attract top junior players across Canada. Stressing the importance of education, the players would become scholar-athletes, living, and playing at the University of British Columbia, coached by Father David, preparing to represent Canada as a unified squad for the 1964 Olympics. He asked for money for room, board, expenses, and tuition. Juckes and Potter agreed. **The Canadian National Team was born.**

The players would go to school in the mornings, with daily practices up to two hours in the afternoon. **The goal was to mimic the Soviet team concept**, so that the players would be in excellent condition and play as a unified club. The National Team put together their roster for the 1964 Olympics, and despite little, if any, support from the NHL they were able to put together a competitive team. The team would have some good bloodlines, with Hall of Famers King Clancy's son Terry and Lionel Conacher's son Brian. They would be led upfront by **Roger Bourbonnais**, a dynamic forward and future IIHF Hall of Famer. The National Team was strong on defence with standouts **Terry O'Malley** and **Barry McKenzie** and Summit Series defenceman Rod Seiling. The National Team's biggest strength was in goal with Seth

Martin, the oldest player at 31. His backup, **Ken Broderick**, was a very solid netminder who would go on to play in the NHL and WHA.

After a year of exhibition games against senior, junior and minor professional teams, the National Team went on a European tour to prepare for the 1964 Olympics. **The Nats**, as they were often called, though still the UBC Thunderbirds in Canada, did very well against the local Canadian competition including splitting a game versus two teams from the very competitive Western professional league. They would find the National Teams of Europe much more difficult foes. The young team would start by splitting a game against the always tough Czechoslovakians, and then splitting two games against the always improving Swedes. They would lose four in a row, including two in Moscow against the Soviets. Their first game against their soon to be nemesis was a humiliating 8-1 loss to the Anatoli Firsov led Soviets. The next game in Moscow was lost by a closer margin, a 2-1 loss, but they returned to Prague to get spanked by the Czechs 6-0. They would split a series with the Czechoslovakian B squad, beat hockey minnows Yugoslavia and Switzerland before losing another to the Swedes. The losses taught them lessons. After a long trip, the players could say they were suitably battle hardened, ready for the Olympics.

Father Bauer had implemented a clear directive for his young troops. **They would play clean, dignified, energetic hockey. Penalties would be rare, and there would be zero retaliation if they received stickwork or a foul against them.** The boys would keep anything they were formerly taught such as violent hockey or poor positional hockey, in the past where it belonged. Through repetition, discipline, enforcing a strong work ethic and, more importantly, a code of ethics, Bauer felt he could and would mould his team into a unified team that would properly represent their country. And win.

Arriving at Innsbruck, Austria, the Nats were ready

to win gold, and play hockey the way their coach expected. The Canadians would easily defeat the Swiss 8-0 with Martin and Broderick sharing the shutout. Next up was a close win over the West Germans 4-2, the Finns 6-2 and a tense come from behind win over the USA 8-6. The Nats were playing well, but certainly not dominating the B level teams they encountered. Next up was Sweden, a country that had become a real challenge both on the ice and mentally. Sweden had already produced stars in Sven Tumba and Ulf Sterner and had a reputation of complaining about Canadian rough play. The games between the two countries often led to numerous uproars in the Swedish press and hockey authorities regarding Canadian rough play, referring to them as goons and hooligans. It would be worse in 1972 after Team Canada played two penalty filled exhibitions against Sweden en route to Moscow. **There was no love lost between the opposing hockey cultures.**

This time, the Canadian National Team was ready for the Swedes and put on a clinic of clean, intense, creative, disciplined hockey. They shut the Swedish offence right down in a one sided 3-1 win. An incident occurred late in the game when Swedish forward **Carl Oberg** broke his stick. Oberg was frustrated at how the game had gone and threw a piece of the broken stick at the Canadian bench. The stick hit Father Bauer, opening a small cut on his forehead. The Canadian players rose up on the bench in anger. Terry O'Malley recounts the moment in Greg Frankes book Epic Confrontation:

> *"We were livid and ready to go after him. Father Bauer yelled at us to sit back. He literally started throwing us back."*

There would be no retaliation for the Canadians that day. In fact, Father Bauer accepted the Swedish players' apology after the game, and invited Oberg to watch the Soviet -Czechoslovakia match with him afterwards. Oberg accepted the offer. Long-time Canadian antagonist IIHF

President Bunny Ahearne would give Canada a back handed compliment regarding the incident,

"We hate to think what might have happened if the Canadians had left the bench".

While he obviously took the high road and led by example with his team, Father Bauer couldn't resist a last dig at the Swedes.

"The Swedes would have made a federal case out of it if it had been the Canadians".

A final note about the incident. The IIHF would present its gratitude for Father Bauer's restraint by presenting him with an honorary gold medal. It would be the only medal Canada would get.

With Canada undefeated after five games, they only had to defeat the Czechoslovaks and the Soviets to win gold. A big ask, but the players felt they were up to it. The young, inexperienced university students had two very solid efforts that came up short.

First up, the Czechs, with disastrous results. Seth Martin, the backbone of Canada, got hurt in the game. The injury happened early in the third period. It was 1-1 in a heated battle at the time, when Jaroslav Jirlik accidently slid into Martin. Ken Broderick was forced to enter the game cold, and subsequently gave up two late goals to seal the 3-1 win for the Czechs. Martin was injured and was iffy for the game against the USSR. That game was crucial. The Soviets had beaten the Czechs earlier 7-5, and if the Swedes beat the Czechs in the final game, **Canada could still win gold by defeating the world champion Soviets.**

The Soviets had added a group of world class young players to their squad in the last couple of years, with names like Davydov, Firsov, Starshinov, Ragulin, Kuzkin now mixed with top veterans like Lokev, Alemtov and Alexandrov. They had quickly gone from being the same level as a top Senior A or minor pro team to an NHL level team in a few short years. The young Canadian Nationals were in deep. 1972

Team Canada defenceman Rod Seiling summed up his team's chances before the game:

> "It was really boys against men. We were young players going against much stronger, talented and more experienced opponents, some who definitely were of NHL calibre. We had to play our absolute best to even have a chance!"

Six months of Father Bauer's intense training led the Nationals to this moment. They were ready and proved it by grabbing a first period lead. Ken Broderick was playing great in goal and the energetic young Canadians were matching the Soviets stride for stride. Yevgenii Mayarov tied the game for the Soviets in the second, followed by Bob Forhand for the Nats, reclaiming the lead shortly after. The Soviets had their own young stars as prolific goal scorer Vyacheslav Starshinov scored to tie the game before the end of the second period. Brian Conacher had done the one thing Father David Bauer stressed, don't take retaliatory penalties. Conacher did and the Soviets had scored to tie the game.

At the start of the third period, the Canadian coach tried an interesting ploy. Knowing the reputation of Seth Martin, especially the reverence of the Soviets towards the goalie, Bauer started Martin for the third period. Broderick had played well for Canada, but Bauer felt this might throw the Soviets off their game. Seth Martin explained the difficulty his injury gave him as he entered the game:

> "I was a butterfly-style goalie, with my knee taped, I couldn't get all the way done. It didn't feel too bad. I'm not sure if I would have done the same thing if I was coaching, but I thought it was worth a try!"

Arkady Chernyshev was the Soviet head coach, but his assistant coach Anatoly Tararosv was the strategic outside the box thinker. **Tarasov told the Soviet players to not take many shots at Martin**. He explains the strategy in his book Road to Olympus:

> "I immediately ordered our boys not to get Martin involved

in the game. Shoot only to score. Let Martin be without a job, but any attack must be finished with a goal. It is most important not to let Martin get warmed up, to get into the rhythm and tempo of the game!"

The ploy worked for the Soviets as Alexandrov scored early in the period. Martin was superb for the rest of the game, but the lack of offensive power on the Nationals caught up to them; they couldn't get the equalizer. The Soviets won 3-2, ensuring their second straight World Championship. While disappointed at coming up short, the Canadians took solace in the knowledge that they had won the bronze medal on goal differential. Or had they?

With the Canadians tied with the Swedes and Czechoslovakians, and each team had taken turns defeating the other, the only way to determine standings was goal differential. Controversy ensued. Canada believed the standings would only count for the final medal round games, which would give them the bronze. The Swedes who had convincingly beaten the Czechs 8-3 in their final game would get the silver. The Canadians were on their way to the awards ceremony when they were told the formula being used **was actually for all the games**. Not just the medal round. This would put Canada in fourth.

In a moment of rare sportsmanship from the Communist authorities, the Czechs and Soviets backed Canada's understanding of the tie breaking rules, even though it would have eliminated the Czechs from a medal. The controversy heated up, so Bunny Ahearne got the IIHF directors together for a vote that went 6-3 against the Canadian version of the rules. The Soviets and Czechs cast the other two votes in favour. When pressured for explanation, Ahearne dug in. He stated that those were the rules right from the start and he had told members of the press that two days earlier. **However, no set tie breaking rules were ever found that were written prior to the results.** The World Championships the year before only counted results from the top five teams. Why would it have changed? Another interesting aspect to the controversy; in 1965 the World Championship rules were **formally changed** to include a tie breaking formula: for the top four teams, exactly what Canada felt in 1964 was the correct ruling.

Ahearne always claimed he stated the rules beforehand, but again there is no proof in writing. Was it collusion to prevent Canada getting a bronze? Possibly. While the members of the press backed up Ahearn's claim to have stated the rules two days earlier, as he would have no way of knowing at the time that it would hurt the Canadians, it was suspicious knowing Ahearne's anti Canadian stance. The other reality is that the Canadian hockey code was against running up the score against weaker opponents. Would that mindset have changed if the Canadians thought the goal differential for all the games counted? Impossible to say. In 2005, a motion was tabled to award Canada a retroactive bronze. The motion was declined. One thing is guaranteed: Ahearne had nothing to do with the 2005 decision, he had died in 1985.

CHAPTER 25: A RINGER, A VICTORY, A WITHDRAWAL 1965-1970

In May 1964, the CAHA held a general meeting with Father Bauer explaining some of challenges with the National Team program. The players were often more focused on hockey and representing Canada than school, many players had dropped out of courses or didn't finish them. Bauer also mentioned his personal time restraints, travel issues, and funding issues. The CAHA agreed to continue the program, but **Father Bauer would stop coaching the team and focus on management and advisory duties.** Changes were needed.

Former international hockey star **Frank Fredrickson** was an alderman in Vancouver in the 1960's and had helped approve the building of a new rink for the University of British Columbia Thunderbirds/National Team. Despite this, a decision was reached that a more central location was required for the program, so **the National Team was shifted to Winnipeg, Manitoba.** The players would continue courses at the University of Manitoba.

The team would merge with the local, successful Senior A club, the Winnipeg Maroons. The Maroons had been Allan Cup runner ups in 1961 and 1963 before winning it in

1964. They had plenty of international hockey experience, having travelled to Europe twice, most recently in 1964 for a series of games versus Czechoslovakian clubs. The current Maroons coach, **Gordon Simpson**, would take over the reins of the national squad.

The merging of the two teams was less successful. The 1965 World Championships in Finland resulted in a second straight fourth place finish for the Canadian team, but this time there was never a real challenge for a medal. The Canadians would give the Swedes a decent game in a 6-4 loss but would lose 8-0 to the Czechoslovakians and 4-1 to the world champion Soviets. The 8-0 loss would be the worst in Canadian international hockey history at that time. Brian Conacher explained the lack of chemistry:

"It was never a good fit, the senior players were quite a bit older than the Olympians, most of whom were students, so there wasn't good chemistry. In fact, there was a lot of resentment among the senior players towards the National Team players."

Canada bid for the 1967 World Championships to be held in Winnipeg for the Canadian 100th Centennial. The IIHF wanted Canadian teams to go to Europe to fatten the pockets of the European hockey nations, while treating Canada as a second-class citizen, **denying the bid**. Despite this, the Canadian National Team carried on, hiring former NHLer and World Championship star **Jackie McLeod as the new coach**. The Nats would win 17 straight exhibition games against minor pro, junior and university teams before meeting the Soviets for a six-game series in December 1965. The National Team would only win one of those six games. They would do better against the Swedes and Czechs in local exhibition games, going 3-1-2, although they would lose two more in Prague as they prepared for the 1966 World Championships.

The extensive training and exhibition schedule paid off for the National Team as Canada would win a bronze medal at the 1966 World Championships. It was not without incidents. In the 2-1 loss to Czechoslovakia, the Canadians were beyond frustrated with the Polish referee. After the game the players had a meeting. With two disallowed goals plus numerous penalties against the clean playing Canadians, the players voted to forfeit the remainder of the games, leave the World Championships, and go home. Father Bauer spoke to the players, and explained to them that they were representing Canada, they had obligations and they should play against Sweden and the Soviets with pride and class. Roger Bourbonnais who had established himself as one of the top Nats players, explained the players' reversal:

"We were afraid the withdrawal might just look like sour grapes. And it could have hurt the CAHA and Father Bauer."

However, with his years of playing in Europe, playing-coach Jackie McLeod had a different opinion:

"As far as I'm concerned, we should have just pulled out. You have to make a stand some time, protests do no good. But we're staying for one reason: Father Dave."

While the Nats stayed, defeating the Swedes 4-2 and losing 3-0 to the eventual champion, the Soviets, a pattern had formed. The Nats could play well against the Swedes and even the Czechs but would always struggle to beat the Soviet team. They had become a completely different level of team. **With their fitness, skill sets and star players, the Soviets would be a challenge the Nats would rarely be able to overcome**.

This tournament was another great international performance for Seth Martin, as he left with best goaltender donors. On a final note, about the 1966 World Championships, the vote to leave and go home foreshadowed events to come in 1970. It also foretold the issues with European and seemingly biased officials that Team Canada would encounter in 1972.

Carl Brewer was a unique person in the 1960's hockey world. He had a strong-willed persona combined with a bright, questioning mind. This led Brewer to be consistently at odds with the authoritarian status quo of professional hockey. He had constant clashes with dictatorial Toronto Maple Leaf boss Punch Imlach. Despite the Leafs years of success, Brewer had enough. During the 1965-66 Leafs training camp, Brewer walked out and quit hockey. This was no small loss for the three-time defending cup champion Toronto team. **Brewer was one of the world's best defencemen**. He was a first team all-star in the 1962-63 season, a second team all-star in 1961-62 and again in 1964-65.

The next season, Brewer went to university, fought with the powers that be at the NHL as he applied to become a reinstated amateur player, succeeded, and joined the Canadian National Team. This was a godsend for the young Nats, who now had a bona fide world class superstar on defence. As a player, Brewer had it all. He was an excellent skater, good offensive instincts, very cerebral and superb defensively. He also had an edge, much like his off-ice persona, he didn't take nonsense from anyone who challenged him.

With Brewer on the squad combined with goalie Seth Martin, the Nats had become a much stronger team. The chemistry after two years of playing together had become more coherent, and the players were now used to the schedule and intense training. The results showed. **They would beat the New York Rangers two out of three games in September**. That result alone should have woken up the NHL to the reality that international hockey teams, especially the Soviets, had become NHL level quality. The Nats would sweep the US National Team in a four-game series in December 1966, winning three and tying one. They would also sweep the Moscow Selects in three straight games at the end of December. Closing out the first part of that season, the Nats played 25 games, losing only once. They were seemingly ready for the next level. The Soviets and the Czechs.

The 1967 Canadian Centennial tournament was part of the Centennial birthday celebrations of Canada, hosted in Winnipeg from December 31st to January 6th. As described in greater detail in the Winnipeg chapter, the tournament was a successful one for the Canadian team, as they defeated the Czechoslovakian National Team 5-3 on New Year's Eve, then the Americans 7-1 a few days later. This set up a final game showdown vs the four-time defending world champions Soviets. In a great game, telecast across the country, the Canadians took down the Soviets 5-4, winning the tournament. Father David Bauer's original vision was coming to fruition. His National Team was now competitive enough against the best teams in the world and would be a **viable candidate to win the World Championships** that spring.

The 1967 World Championships were held in Vienna, Austria. Canada had bid on the games, with plans to showcase the tournament during the Canadian Centennial. One caveat was that Canada only wanted the A pool teams to play, similar to the 1976 Canada Cup. That was all the IIHF needed to decide against Canada, despite the Centennial celebrations. When the IIHF led by Bunny Ahearn awarded the games to Austria, a traditional non hockey nation, it was a slap in the face to Canada. **Canada was outraged**. There were several statements echoing Canadian withdrawal from international competition, highlighted by CAHA second vice-president Lloyd Pollock saying,

"Possibly we should consider now whether or not it's worth going to future championships."

This would become a prophetic comment in a few short years.

Despite the Canadian snub, the National Team was prepared to win Canada's first World Championship since 1961. The Canadians would open the tournament with four straight wins over Finland, East Germany, West Germany, and the United States. The 2-1 victory over the USA was a surprisingly hard game for the Nats, considering the ease in which they had defeated their continental rival all winter. The next challenge was the team that had almost caused the Nationals to withdraw from the previous year's championships, the always tough Czechoslovakians. The two teams would battle to a 1-1 tie. With the tie, the road to the championship had become harder for the Canadians. The Soviets were undefeated at that point, having beaten Sweden easily, so Canada would need to defeat them to have a chance at winning the World title. In fact, the Soviet win was so one sided that the **Swedish coach Arne Stromberg had said the Soviet team** *was "the greatest team in the history of hockey, amateur or professional."*

The Nationals had not faced the Soviets since January, where they played them three more times after the Centennial Tournament. They would tie them in Montreal 3-3, defeat them in Toronto 4-3 before losing the last game 5-3 in Kitchener. Canada had only lost to them once in those four games, and defeated an NHL team two out of three games. If the Soviets did not view them as worthy opponents before this, they were certainly aware of the threat they now posed, especially with Carl Brewer on defence.

Tarasov had not yet invited Brewer to practice with his squad - that would take place a year later - but **the Soviets devised a plan to limit Brewer's effectiveness against them**. They would throw the puck in his corner repeatedly, allowing him to skate it out of the Canadian zone. The goal would be to exhaust Brewer, so that by the third period, he would be less effective. In the 1974 Stanley Cup final, Philadelphia Flyer coach Fred Shero had a similar strategy, except the goal was physical contact on Bobby Orr, wearing him down. For the Soviets in 1967, the strategy was never really used to full effect as Brewer was high sticked earlier in the game in a small altercation with the feisty Starshinov, leaving in the second to get stitched up and returning for the third period.

The Nationals would take a first period lead on a goal by Fran Huck, but a long fluke shot by Anatoli Firsov would fool Seth Martin in the second period tying the game. Starshinov would score on a rebound for the winning goal, on a play that coach Jackie Mcleod would protest was offside. Replays show that the goal appears to be onside.

The Canadians gave the Soviets a great battle, but as the 1960's Soviets were prone to do, they would win when it counted. This time it was **a tough 2-1 victory over the Nats**. The Soviet players would heap praise upon the National squad. Veteran Viktor Kuzkin had this to say about the National Team:

"Father Bauer said when he started that in five years he would have a team that could beat us. He almost did it! The 1967 team was great, and they very easily could have won. In fact, that experience of playing them helped a lot when it became time to play the NHL." Greg Franke Epic Confrontation

Summit Series stalwart Alexander Ragulin agreed:

"When we played successfully against Carl Brewer, it made us believe we could definitely play against the best NHL players. Even show them what we could do!"

Much like Team Canada in 1998 after a heart-breaking shoot out loss to the Czechs, resulting in a lack of motivation for the bronze medal game against Finland, the Canadian Nationals in 1967 played terribly in their final game against Sweden. The 6-0 loss relegated the Nats to the bronze where a win would have garnered the silver.

The Canadian National Team would never again be able to challenge the Soviets to the level they did in 1967. They would lose their two superstars. Seth Martin would join the St Louis Blues for a season. Carl Brewer would go back to professional hockey as a coach and GM in the minors for a season, then go to Finland to play. Brewer would be very impactful in Finland, finishing his university degree and leading his Finnish team to the championship. **He is often**

as revered in Finland for helping develop their hockey program as Mike Buckna did for the Czechs. Brewer would eventually return to the NHL, as an all-star, in 1970, spend some time in the WHA, make an impressive comeback with Maple Leafs in 1979, ironically for Punch Imlach, and be a catalyst in the take down of Alan Eagleson regarding the NHL players pension misuse. He was a unique man and a great player.

The Canadian team would play the Detroit Red Wings twice in September, losing both games. They would travel to France for three games, beating the Czechslovakian B team before losing to the Americans and club team Moscow Dynamo. To kick off the new year in 1968, a second "Centennial" tournament was hosted in Winnipeg, with less successful results for the Canadians. While they would beat Sweden twice, they would lose twice to the Soviets.

The next major tournament for Canada in international hockey was the 1968 Olympics in Grenoble, France. The National Team had added **Wayne Stephenson** in goal to replace Seth Martin. Stephenson was an excellent goalie who would go on to have a good career in the NHL beating the Central red Army 4-1 for the Philadelphia Flyers in 1976. The National Team would play well at the Olympics except for one blip. They would have a shocking loss to Finland 5-2. Finland was improving as a hockey nation but was not yet at the level of the top countries. This was a huge upset. The loss was the perfect example of overlooking a team which cost the Canadians dearly.

The Canadians would go on to defeat a very strong Czechoslovakian team 3-2. This would be many of the same players that Team Canada would face in a 3-3 tie in Prague. The Canadians would also beat the Swedes 3-0. When the Czechs defeated their arch-rivals the Soviets 5-4, the door was opened for Canada to still win gold. Again, they just had to defeat the Soviets in a must win game. This time, without Seth Martin or Carl Brewer.

Playing in a rink that had see-through glass boards, the Soviets would prove to be too much for the Nationals, winning 5-0. Superstar **Anatoli Firsov** would dazzle Canada scoring two goals. Despite the loss, it was still a good Olympic tournament, better than expected. Canada would win bronze, but without the loss to the Finns, they would have won silver. After the Olympic victory, Anatoli Tarasov would boast after the victory that his team could defeat any team in the world. Including the NHL.

The gauntlet had been laid.

The 1968-69 hockey season would be the last full season for the Canadian National Team. **They added a second team to the program, a Canadian B team for development,** a practice European nation had been doing for many years. For the next season and a half, the Nationals A team would possess a solid group of players that would eventually be joined by two future Hall of Famers in goalie Ken Dryden and defenseman **Guy Lapointe**. They also had **Chuck Lefley**, a future 43 goal scorer with the St Louis Blues.

The Nats would play a series of games against two NHL expansion teams in September, the St Louis Blues and the Los Angeles Kings. **They would beat the Blues twice in a row**, and then lost both games to the Kings, showing they were certainly competitive at that level. The Soviets on the other hand had simply become too much for this version of the Nats. Attending the Izvestia tournament in Moscow, the Canadians would tie Finland 2-2, then get easily defeated in four straight games in Moscow, including an ugly 8-1 loss to the Soviet B squad. As per the usual pattern however, the Canadians would play better against the Czechs, splitting four games in Canada with two wins apiece and then finishing off 1968 with an 11-4 pounding over the Swedish B team in Winnipeg.

The Soviet domination continued on Canadian soil as the USSR travelled to Canada for a series of nine exhibition games. The Soviets would win eight of those games, with

Canada's only victory a 4-0 one in Ottawa on a rare off day for the World Champions.

These results show the absurdity of the NHL and hockey media mindset before the Summit Series as they believed the NHL would have an easy time with the Soviets. **The results were telling a completely different story.** The Canadian National Team had played eight exhibition games against NHL opponents in those years, **winning four and losing four**, including half those games against original six clubs. In a short two-month period, the Soviets would beat the National Team **twelve times in thirteen games**. It is highly unlikely even the Stanley Cup Winning Montreal Canadians could have beaten the Nats 12 out of 13 times, especially adding that nine of those games were in Canada.

The 1969 World Hockey Championships would be dramatic. **Firstly, it was the first championship to have hitting allowed in all three zones**. Secondly it was full of political drama between the Czechs who had been suffered through Soviet occupation in 1968, and the Soviets. This resulted in two hotly contested games between the countries, both won by the Czechs with celebrations and rioting in the streets of Prague. **Thirdly it would be the last time Canada would participate in the World Championships until 1977**. The National Team would struggle in the tournament, starting off by getting badly beaten by the Czechs 6-1, then by the Soviets 7-1. They would lose all their games except the ones against Finland and the USA, finishing fourth in the tournament. Unlike other years, **the Nats were simply no longer competitive**. Forward Fran Huck would admit this openly,

"We do the best we can but we are no match for them."

The Europeans had become too strong for a group of amateurs to defeat. The best players in Canada were playing professional. A change was needed.

In running for election in 1968, Pierre Trudeau commented:

"Hockey is considered our national sport. Yet, in World Championships we have been able as amateurs to perform as well as we know we can. "

He promised that, if elected, he would create a task force that would give the power to change Canadian amateur sporting culture to an open pursuit of excellence. This task force led to the creation of Hockey Canada. The mandate would be to develop the national hockey teams of Canada and restore Canada's rightful place as the best hockey playing nation in the world. That would require the use of the best Canadians. The professionals.

Hockey Canada would attend the IIHF's annual meeting in July 1969. They demanded that Canada be allowed to be represented by professional players. **The Canadians viewed the Soviets and Czechoslovakians as professional in anything but name**, as they were full time hockey players, and had government sponsored housing and expenses looked after. The vote for open inclusion didn't go Canadas way, so Canada counter proposed that they be allowed to use 6 professionals on a roster. Bunny Ahearne, still the IIHF president, led the IIHFs own counter proposal which allowed 9 professionals, but with a clever caveat, none would be an active player in the NHL. This would be a one-year trial period while the IIHF sought clarification on how this would affect Olympic eligibility.

After the 1969 World Hockey Championships Alan Eagleson delivered the news to Father David Bauer that Canada had won the right to use professionals in the 1970 World Championships, to be held in Winnipeg and Montreal. **His National Team would be reinforced with up to nine pro players, and they would test out the strategy in late August 1969 with a nine-game series in Europe.** If successful, they would use the same strategy at the World Championships.

The Montreal Canadians offered three players from their minor league team, and included two more players in the Montreal organization, Guy Lapointe and Bob Berry. The

Maple Leafs offered five players including top prospects Jim McKenny and Wayne Carlton. Thus augmented, the National Team would start the European tour by beating Soviet club team Voskresensk Khimik 6-5. This was a squad that was a middle of the pack team in the Soviet elite league. Certainly, a good start.

The Canadian team would have little trouble with two third division squads in Leningrad (St. Petersburg), beating the Leningrad Army 6-1 and the Leningrad Dynamo 7-2. These games were supposed to be part of the Soviet Sportsky tournament, a tournament that happened every fall that often-invited foreign teams. On September 1^{st,} 1969, the reinforced Canadians would meet another good Soviet club the Soviet wings. They would lose 4-1 in a fight filled game. Coach Jackie McLeod was livid at the two-man officiating set up and realized that with the new adaptation of body checking in all three zones, combined with a flawed 2-man official system, the Canadian pro game would become a penalized one in Europe. The National Team would have four easy victories against Jokerit, a top Finnish club team and four successive victories over the Swiss and Finnish National Teams. The hockey officials in Canada had seen enough, professionals were the way to go, they could compete with the Soviets and defeat anyone else. **The professionals were the way to go for the 1970 World Championships.**

This success by the combined pro-Nats squad opened some eyes at the IIHF. It would get worse after the same team would go to Moscow for the 1969 Izvestia tournament. Using only five professionals, the Canadians would beat the East Germans 5-4, the Swedes 5-2, and the Finns 10-1. That would be impressive enough. Then they tied the mighty Soviets 2-2 in Moscow, with only five pros! This was enough for the bureaucrats at the European hockey nations. Adding professionals to the Canadian squad would upset the status quo. **Why allow an opponent they could generally beat to get stronger? Maybe too strong?**

After the Izvestia tournament, IOC (Olympic) Head **Avery Brundage** made a statement regarding the inclusion of professionals at the upcoming World Championships in Winnipeg. The head of the International Olympic Committee wrote,

"For the IIHF to open its World Championship in such a manner would jeopardize Olympic eligibility, not only for Canada, but for all the players and nations that competed against Canada. "

Brundage, known today as an anti-Semitic, racist, sexist man, in 1970 he had this elitist view on amateurism. His was a view from the turn of the century that anyone who was paid for playing a sport, no longer did it for enjoyment but for income. It was against the "spirit of amateurism" and the Olympic code. **This was nonsense and hypocritical**. Firstly, the European nations had been playing games against the professional British hockey league for many years while the Soviets played the Philadelphia team from the Eastern Hockey league in 1959. A professional team and league. Secondly, if playing against professionals tainted a player's status, it had already happened. The Soviets, Finns and Swedes had already played professionals at the Canadian tour in August and the December Izvestia tournament. **They could not be tainted twice**. Using Brundage's logic, those countries were already not eligible for the Olympics. The USSR soccer team had also played against professional players, which didn't affect their eligibility. It was hypocritical at the very least, and possibly geared towards maintaining the hockey power balance status quo. This was all from the bureaucrats who ran the hockey organizations. Anatoli Tarasov had long wanted to play the professionals, even the best in the NHL.

Ahearne would quickly call another meeting in Switzerland to discuss the issue. The Canadian contingent led by CAHA president Earl Dawson, Nats team organizer CAHA Gordon Juckes and Hockey Canada's Charles Hay would counter with an exhibition tournament, a prequel to the 1976 Canada Cup in which the top four or six countries would play against the Canadian professionals. This idea was warmly received, the Canadian delegation left the Saturday meeting relieved, not wanting to pull out of international hockey completely. An agreement was made to reconvene the next morning.

The next morning as the Canadian delegate entered the room, **they were told by Ahearne that the meeting had started ninety minutes earlier.** They were also informed that all former agreements had changed, and professionals would no longer be eligible to play at the World Championships. **The Canadians angrily countered that unless professionals were allowed, Canada would pull out of international hockey.** The IIHF said that's fine. The furious Canadians would call Ahearn,

"An errand boy for the Swedes and Russians".

Ahearne would counter by calling the Canadians *"cry-babies"*.

The tournament would be moved to Sweden, who had joined the Soviets in voting against Canada. Winnipeg alone would stand to lose hundreds of thousands of dollars in ticket sales, but hockey would lose more. Canada was firm. **After nearly 50 years of international hockey, after hundreds of games, after multi country tours, after years of invested development of European hockey, rarely asking for anything in return, Canada would no longer participate.**

The last international game by the Canadian National Team was an anticlimactic 2-1 victory over the Czechoslovaks. The National Team program was all finished. Canada would only return to the international arena if they could use professionals. Their best players.

In two short years, that would happen.

The hockey world would never be the same.

PART 6: GAME 3. WINNIPEG:

PAGING BOBBY HULL TO THE DRESSING ROOM

CHAPTER 26: WINNIPEG, A PLACE FOR VICTORIAS, FALCONS, MAROONS AND NATS

Hockey and the Canadian prairies are a natural pairing. Long, windy yet bright and sunny winters that have temperatures dropping as low as minus 50 combined with flat landscapes to create **perfect outdoor hockey conditions**. It's little wonder that the city of Winnipeg has a long hockey history going back to the 1800's. Winnipeg was a booming town in the late 1800's, a major source of agriculture, and with its' geographical positioning at the centre of Canada, it was a major transportation hub. Word of this new sport of Hockey, a game on ice, developed in Montreal, quickly spread to Winnipeg, where the hearty prairie folk took to it immediately.

The first organized game in Western Canada took place in 1890 in Winnipeg between the **Winnipeg Victorias** and the **Winnipeg Hockey Club**. By 1896, the city had **a Stanley Cup championship** as the Winnipeg Victorias defeated the Montreal Victorias (team names were not overly creative it seems in those days). In the early 1900's, the Winnipeg powerhouse Victorias would win **three straight Stanley Cups** in 1901, 1902, and 1903. The Victorias were led by **Dan Bains**, a fantastic athlete who immediately excelled at the new sport. Bains would be inducted into the Hockey Hall of Fame in the second class of inductees in 1947. Four other Hall of Fame players hit the ice for the Victorias over the years including Herb Gardiner, Jack Marshall, Fred Scanlan and Bullet Joe Simpson. They were truly one of the great amateur teams of all time also winning two Allen Cups in 1911 and 1912.

Winnipeg's next great team, the first Winnipeg team to represent Canada internationally, were the Icelandic players who formed **the Winnipeg Falcons.** When the Falcons won Gold at the 1920 Olympics, they were three-time Allen Cup champions in 1912, 1919 and 1920. Like Dan Bains with the Victorias, one of the games finest players in Frank Fredrickson was the star of the Falcons. The 1930-31 University of Manitoba Grads (Bisons) represented Canada at the 1931 World Hockey Championships in Poland, but despite winning the championship, the Grads were also the first Canadian team to not win every game, tying Sweden 0-0. Next up was the Winnipeg hockey club who won gold in Lake Placid, New York in 1932. During this time period Winnipeg and Toronto seemingly rotated sending top teams abroad. The 1935 World Championships were won by the Winnipeg Monarchs in Davos, Switzerland, ending an era of dominance by the city of Winnipeg in amateur hockey.

The first international game played at the Winnipeg Arena was on January 31, 1960, between the Manitoba Junior A All Stars (called the Junior Warriors for the game) and the Moscow "Selects". It was the third time a Soviet team toured North America. In November and December 1957, the Soviet National Team had toured Ontario and Montreal. In 1959 they had been in the USA playing university squads, the US Olympic team and a 3-3 tie against the professional Philadelphia Ramblers of the Eastern Hockey League.

The **Moscow Selects** were seen as a **development team** for the Soviet National Team. The squad was a mix consisting of fringe National Team players and promising prospects in need of competitive seasoning and international experience. They were supplemented with veterans who had just lost their spot on the National Team, and or players in their prime who were career B national level players that never reached the A level. The team was coached by former (and future) National Team coach **Arkady Chernyshev**. The team also two of the most dominant Soviet players of the 1960's, sniper **Vyacheslav Starshinov** and a small, offensive defenceman named **Vitayl Davydov**. These two future stars were still junior age players, just 19 years old, but the rest of the squad were Soviet League veterans, all the way up to 30-year-old Boris Sedov. The Manitoba Junior All Stars were just that, a select group of under 20 players who toiled in the Manitoba Junior Hockey League. The result was the expect men versus boys setup with the Selects jumping out to a first period 5-0 lead before thrashing the Manitoba Juniors 8-1 before a packed Winnipeg Arena.

In the 1960's, **Winnipeg was Canada's home for international hockey**. While games were being played sporadically in other cities, including Toronto and Montreal, Winnipeg would host a great many games throughout the decade. This would start with the **Winnipeg Maroons**, a Senior A Hockey club, that used only local Winnipeg players. The Maroons were one of the top Senior Clubs in Canada in the early 1960's, losing the Allen Cup final in 1962 and 1963 before winning it handily in 1964. The Maroons would play three international exhibitions at the Winnipeg Arena, beating an overmatched Japan 11-4 in 1960, followed by a 5-5 tie against the Czechoslovakian National Team in 1963 and a 7-4 loss to the Swedish National Team in 1964. That same year the Maroons would head to Europe and play several exhibition games. Those would include six games against the Czechoslovakian National Team who kept their dominance going over the Maroons with 4 wins and 2 ties in six games. The Maroons were also able to get in a game against the Soviet league club **Khimik Vosresenk** in Geneva Switzerland. A game in which the Soviet team won 2-1. To show how quickly the European teams were improving in the 1960's, the Maroons had gone on a Czechoslovakian tour in 1960, winning 7 out of 8 games. This time they were soon to be Allan Cup champs and winless. The Maroons represented as Team Canada on these tours.

The following season, **Father David Bauer's National Team**, which had been based out of the University of British Columbia, **was transferred to Winnipeg, where they merged with the Maroons**. From that point until the disbanding of the team in 1970, Winnipeg and the Winnipeg Arena would be their home base. At the Winnipeg Arena on January 4th, 1965, Canada would get some revenge on the Czechoslovakian National Team with a 4-2 victory. They would follow that up with a pasting of West Germany 9-1 in February. Later that year, the World Champion Soviet National Team would make its first ever appearance in Winnipeg, defeating the Canadian National Team 6-2 on December 17^{h} and then again 4-1 on December 20th. The Manitoba Junior All-Stars would face Finland on December 27th, 1965, and like in 1960, the Juniors would find themselves overmatched against a National Team, losing 7-1. In early 1966, the Winnipeg arena would host the Swedes, with Canada handling them easily 8-3. Five days later on January 7, 1966, Canada would tie the Czechoslovakians 3-3. They would beat the Moscow Selects 6-1 later that year and finish 1966 undefeated at the Winnipeg Arena, in international contests, with an easy 7-3 win over Poland. That success would carry over into what was the to become **the highlight of the Canadian National Team's legacy,** and the most important pre-Summit Series international hockey games in Winnipeg. **Winnipeg hosted the 1967 Centennial Tournament.**

CHAPTER 27: THE BEST TOURNAMENT IN 100 YEARS

The 1967 Centennial tournament in Winnipeg was a great success. Participating teams included Czechoslovakia, Canada, the Soviet Union, and the United States. Canada started out the tournament on a high note, defeating a team they historically had a lot of trouble with, the Czechoslovakian National Team, 5-3. In a precursor to another great international game ten years later, this game would be held on New Year's Eve. The Czechoslovakian team had renowned goalie **Juri Holecek** in goal, combining with a defence that included Czech legends **Frankisek Pospisil** and **Jan Suchy**. The forwards were several of the players that would tie Team Canada in the 1972 exhibition game, including Hall of Famer Vaclav Nedomansky, the **Holik brothers** and **Jan Klapac**. Three days later Canada would smoke the United States 7-1. The Czechoslovakian would upset the Soviets 5-2 on January 4th and then defeat the overmatched Americans 8-2 a day later. This would set up the final game as a chance for Canada to win the entire tournament. All they would have to do is defeat the mighty Soviets at the tournament's final game on January 6th, 1967.

1967 was Canada's Centennial with the tournament being one of the first planned events for the year. The game would be televised nationally by CTV, their first stab at televising a hockey game. Suddenly learning the Canadian boys had a chance to win the tournament, the buzz in the city was immense as people clamoured for tickets, the Arena sold out, with people lining up to get standing room only tickets. An estimated 10,400 people crammed into the building, which was the largest hockey audience ever, at the time, at the Winnipeg Arena. **Prime Minister Lester Pearson** was in attendance, as they sang O Canada in front of a new national flag,

While Canada was stocked with young amateur players, attending classes at the University of Manitoba, they had a new player in their midst. That player was one of the world's best defenceman, **former Toronto Maple Leaf Carl Brewer.** Brewer was the full package. He was a wonderful skater, a sublime passer who played a tough, hard game defensively. The Soviets had not faced a player of this level since Sid Smith at the 1958 World Championships. Anatoli Tarasov was fascinated by Brewer to the point that Tarasov invited him to train with the Soviet team. Brewer, an open minded, free thinker accepted the offer. Brewer would also play in the Finnish league, playing a season for HIFK Helsinki in the 1968-69 season, leading them to the Finnish league championship, losing only two games in the process.

"For the first time I could observe a Canadian professional, make him perform all our exercises, get to know his manner of playing and compare it to ours" Anatoli Tarasov Canadian Press 1968

Tarasov started Brewer at forward, playing him with **Anatoli Firsov,** both to make Brewer happy playing with the Soviets best player, but also to gauge his skills against Firsov's. When Tarasov put Brewer back on defence, he remarked how difficult and composed Brewer was defensively, especially once a scrimmage started. He also mentioned that Brewer could be flustered by speed and unexpected tactics.

"In the tactics exercise with three forwards attacking the

goal against two defencemen, Brewer on defence was quite at home. Each forward tried to get the upper hand over Brewer alone by skating around him, but he would be driven to the corner and done with. But then I changed the tactics. They danced around Brewer with different rhythms, rushed to him unexpectedly, tried to hit him before he hit them. Sometimes our guest was at a loss, but more than often he was brilliant! "Anatoli Tarasov Canadian Press 1968

Tarasov then asked Brewer how he felt the Soviets would do against the best Canadian professionals. Brewer's answer that the Soviets would win at first and then lose, was incredibly prophetic.

"The professionals won't consider you worthy opponents until you beat them. Your tactics and ways are going to be unfamiliar to them, so at first that would be to your advantage." Windsor Star December 21, 1968.

This was certainly **a pivotal learning experience** for the Soviet program as they moved towards playing the professionals. Unfortunately for the Soviet team about to face Brewer and the Canadian National boys in the Centennial Tournament final game, the learning experience was a year too late. **This would not be their night**.

Like the Czechoslovakian team, the Soviet team in the 1967 Centennial tournament was very strong. Although the young stars that were showcased in the 1972 Summit Series were not yet at the National Team level, this was a stacked Soviet squad. Up front, one of the world's top players in 1967, **Anatoli Firsov**, was at his peak. He was supported by top forwards **Starshinov,** and **Boris Mayorov**. This group also included a young **Vladimir Vikulov.** On defence, big **Alexander Ragulin** was a younger faster version than Team Canada 1972 would face, and the small, quick, and dynamic **Vitali Davydov** would lead the back end. The Soviets had won the last four World Championships, on route to winning five more (9 in a row) before finally losing to archival Czechoslovakia in 1972. Despite playing in their home arena, with 11,000 passionate Winnipeg fans and a national tv audience cheering them on, **the Canadians had their hands full**.

As would happen often in games between Canada and the USSR, one team jumped out to a quick 2-0 lead. This time it was the Soviets, on a power play goal by Ramishevsky, followed by a second goal at the 10-minute mark by Striganov. The Winnipeg crowd would quiet down in fear of a blowout, but Father Bauer's team would not be denied. Carl Brewer set up diminutive Regina product Fran Huck for Canada's first goal of the game. Huck was only 5'7 and had been a junior star with Regina, but instead of joining the NHL he wanted to follow the Ken Dryden route and become a lawyer. Huck became a successful lawyer after a short professional career with Montreal in the NHL, and other stops in St. Louis and the WHA. He was also a dynamite player internationally, being named a first team all-star at the 1966 and 1968 World Hockey Championships.

In the second period, Huck would get himself in trouble with a holding penalty that allowed the devastating Soviet power play to get to work. Paramoshkin would make it 3-1 for the visitors, but Carl Brewer would take charge again with a Canadian power play goal to make it 3-2. The Canadians started to really forecheck the Soviets, bottling them up in their own end, resulting in two straight Soviet penalties. With Romishevsky in the box for interference, Canada would tie the game on a goal by the little-known **Jean Cusson**. Then, with less than two minutes left in the period, Soviet star Anatoli Firsov would take a tripping penalty. Cusson would continue the game of his life by setting up Gary Dineen for another Canadian Power play goal. With the Canadians holding a tight 4-3 lead entering the third period, the sell-out Winnipeg crowd was on pins and needles.

In the third, Canadian Danny O'Shea would get penalized for an illegal body check as hitting was still not allowed in all three zones in international hockey.

Parmaoshkin would get his second goal of the game for the Soviets, tying it up at 4-4. Finally with thirteen minutes left in the game, Jean Cusson would set up future NHL player and coach Billy Macmillan for the go-ahead goal. Macmillan's brother Bob was a very good NHL player who once scored 108 points in a season for the Atlanta Flames and would be named to the NHL Challenge Cup team against the Soviets in 1979. Bill Macmillan would take a penalty a minute later, but the Canadian team would kill it off. The Soviets would pepper **goalie Wayne Stephenson** with 28 shots in the game, but he would hold the fort, refusing to let in the tying goal. Wayne Stephenson would have the Soviets number again in 1976, backstopping the Stanley Cup Champion Philadelphia Flyers to their memorable 4-1 win over the Central Red Army team.

With the crowd on their feet counting down the seconds, the Winnipeg Arena would burst into joyous, nationalistic celebration with the win. Team Captain Roger Bourbonnais would receive the tournament trophy, celebrating the Canadian National Team's finest moment. Winnipeg would host numerous other international games after that one, **but none would have the impact of pure nationalistic joy of the Centennial Tournament victory.**

Prime Minister Lester Pearson would remark of the incredible victory,

> *"... when they ran up that new flag, and the teams lined up opposite each other, we sang O Canada. Then I knew, what the definition of being Canadian was" T Hawthorn; 'The Year Canadians Lost Their Mind and Found Their Country, The Centennial of 1967 Madeira Park' 2107*

The Soviet National Team would come to Winnipeg to face the Canadian National Team six more times before the disbanding of the National Team program, winning 5 and losing only once, a 4-3 Canadian win on December 17th, 1969, the last game the Soviets would play in Winnipeg until the Summit Series. Canada would also face the Swedes, Finland, Japan, the Moscow Selects and the Czechoslovakian

National Team at the Winnipeg Arena in 1968, and 1969.
The very last game being a 3-2 Czechoslovakian victory
on December 30th, 1969, thus ending a **glorious era** of
international hockey at the old Winnipeg Arena on Maroons
Road.

CHAPTER 28: SOVIET CHANGES, CANADA STAYS THE SAME

Winnipeg, Manitoba was a city that was very "Russian like" in 1972. Similar in climate to Moscow, it had a large Ukrainian and Eastern European population, especially in the north end of the city. The Soviet players would have felt at home with the perogy shops and Orthodox churches. While it had a small and outdated rink, the Winnipeg Arena had one distinguishing aspect: the **absolutely huge portrait of Queen Elizabeth** hanging over the ice on the southern side of the building. Winnipeg had also installed new ice making equipment, in anticipation of hosting this game, and anticipating the Winnipeg Jets franchise in the new league the World Hockey Association. This would cause the ice to be slow and sticky with a piece coming out late in the 3rd period.

Before Game 3 began, it came to light that the Soviet officials spoke to Canadian officials, including Harry Sinden and requested that Game 2 referees Dowling and Larsen no longer officiate in the Series (they were scheduled for game 4). They asked in the spirit of "**friendship**". Coach **Sinden agreed**, hoping this would make the relationship smoother moving forward, and that if something happened in Moscow, he now had a favour he could call in. That of course would not be the case, and the Soviets would have a very selective memory of this "friendship favour" when Sinden called up the refereeing situation before game eight. Perhaps if Team Canada officials had read former Canadian National Team member Herb Pinder's warnings against the quality and potential bias of the officials in Europe, they would have been less willing to compromise.

"I'm not saying it's gonna happen, but it could. You could see that the officiating becomes so bad in Europe that the Canadians pull out and head home. People don't know how bad it can get. You have to see it to believe it!"
Canadian Press Edmonton 1972

Team Canada only made one change in this game. They brought back Lester Pearson trophy winning centre **Jean Ratelle** and omitted seldom used physical right-wing Bill Goldsworthy. This would give Canada Hall of Fame depth down the middle with Esposito, Clarke, Mikita and Ratelle, three set lines from game two with the extra forwards Ratelle and Peter Mahovlich. It would mean that Ratelle's wingers, the already unhappy Vic Hadfield and more supportive Rod Gilbert, two thirds of the NHL's best line in 1971-72, would be watching for a second straight game. After playing very well in game two, Team Canada's defence remained the same. As the star of game two, Canada stayed with Tony Esposito, who will start for the second game in a row. Unfortunately, Team Canada could only look longingly into the Winnipeg Arena crowd where one of the world's best forwards, if not the best, **Robert Marvin Hull** (known as Bobby) sat and watched, **banned from playing by the NHL**.

The Soviets, on the other hand, were smarting from the game two loss, made several significant line-up changes. **Youth would be served with several of their young stars inserted into the Series**. Starshinov was taken out of the line-up, moving Alexander Maltsev to centre a potential "power line" with Kharlamov and Mikhailov. Twenty-two-year-old **Vyacheslav Solodukhin** would take Zimin's place on the highly effective Shadrin line. The question of whether Zimin had been hurt in game two or penalized for either attempting to defect or being a potential defector would remain a mystery. Zimin was a dynamite player in the first game, and while he struggled a bit more in game two, with some careless giveaways, he was still a factor on the Soviet's most effective and consistent line. **His absence was certainly shocking**.

Solodukhin himself was a bit of an odd choice to make the Soviet National Team for this series. He wasn't a high scorer with only 12 goals in the 1971-72 season and he played for SKA Leningrad, a lesser-known Soviet Elite League team. Despite this he was considered a top prospect for the Soviets at that time. Noted Soviet hockey historian Artur Chivlodski had this to say about Solodukhin,

> *"As a promising center of the second Army club in the Soviet League in Leningrad, he showed high ranking scoring, good technical skills and steady defensive performance in several championships."* Chivlodski.net

Solodukhin would only play in this one game, but it was impactful for the young Leningrad forward: *"I was a reserve for most of the series, but even from the bench it was a great experience to watch the play. It's something I can tell my grandchildren."*

Tragically, Vyacheslav Solodukhin became another sad story for many of the lesser-known players who played for the USSR in the Summit Series. **Vyacheslav Solodukhin would commit suicide in 1979, from carbon dioxide poisoning, alone, in his car**.

The other two forwards added to the Soviet line-up were both 21-year-olds, fresh from the World University Games. **Alexander Bodunov** and **Yuri Lebedev** would be centred by Slava Anisin to form the Soviet "kid line" or the more familiar "headache line" (after the headache medicine of the same name). This line would start slow but end up having a **significant impact** in the game.

On the Soviet defence, both Ragulin and Paladiev were not dressed, assumedly because of the way that

Canadians Cournoyer and Pete Mahovlich exploited them in the previous game. Little used Yuri Lyapkin was the third defender dropped. Replacing that threesome was **Valeri Vasiliev**, a young, inexperienced, rough, and tough defender who would go on to have a Hall of Fame level career, eventually captaining the Soviet National Team. **Yuri Shatalov**, a 27-year-old Soviet veteran from the Soviet Wings was the other addition on defence. Shatalov would only play in two games in this series but would play in the 1974 Series against the WHA, and have a long 20-year career in Soviet hockey. The Soviets would only be going with six defensemen instead of the seven they had used in the first two games. Tretiak would remain in goal.

As the players enter the ice, the Winnipeg crowd gives an appreciative cheer for both squads. For the opening ceremonies, Hockey Canada's Al Scott comes out to honour Father David Bauer's Winnipeg based Canadian National Team. Gold medals are presented to the Soviet and Canadian coaches, and silver medals to the players. Why the players would get silver and the coaches gold is another oddity in a series of oddities. A moment of silence is observed for the seven Israeli athletes who tragically died the day before at the Munich Summer Olympic Games.

The Soviet players are introduced, with polite cheers for Tretiak and Kharlamov, much more subdued that the rousing cheers the two players received in Toronto. When it is Team Canada's turn, the loudest noise is for **local Manitoba boy Bobby Clark**e who gets a rousing ovation, one of the few times outside Philadelphia. The players exchange crests, with the Soviet players getting a provincial crest of Manitoba.

CHAPTER 29: GAME 3 PERIOD 1: DIVES, NO CALLS, PETROV AND RATELLE

Canada would start the Clarke line to match up with the new Soviet power line of Kharlamov, Maltsev and Mikhailov. Brad Park and Gary Bergman would be on the points while the Soviets go with the defensive pair of Vladimir Luchenko and Gennady Tsygankov.

Clarke wins the draw cleanly, but it's too clean and it goes deep into Canada's end. The Soviets immediately go to **their effective two man weaving forecheck** and bottle first Park and then Bergman into the corner. The quick pace seems to catch Canada unprepared, and it shows. The puck bounces out to Boris Mikhailov who then makes a quick pass to Maltsev. Maltsev takes his time going around **a sliding Brad Park** before firing a point-blank shot at Tony Esposito. Esposito is forced to make an early, sudden save. **After two full games, Park has still not realized that he simply cannot drop to the ice against the Soviets**. They are too patient and will just walk around the prone player. Park would make another bad play on this shift when he is on a 3 on 1 break with Phil Esposito and Paul Henderson, he makes a horrible pass straight to Tsygankov, instead of his breaking teammates.

Esposito's linemates jump on the ice against the revised Shadrin line and quickly get the Soviets penned down in their own end. A bad pass by Yakushev gets intercepted at the Soviet blue line, leading to a sequence of events that (despite the energetic Soviet start), lead to Team Canada drawing first blood.

Goal 1: Jean Paul Parise. Canada 1 Soviet Union 0

At 31, Minnesota North Stars left wing Jean Paul Parise (JP) was possibly the biggest surprise choice of the 35 players named to Team Canada. A self-professed journeyman, he was a Boston farmhand who had spent six years in the minor leagues before finding a home on the expansion North Stars. He was a small, stocky, **absolute bundle of energy**. A Tasmanian Devil on skates, he battled passionately in the corners, he was rugged, defensively sound and could score the odd goal. Like Gary Bergman and Bill White on Canada's defence, Parise was a throwback player who would have fit in during the original six days in a Bert Olmstead type way.

As Parise had been part of the Bruins farm system in the 1960's, he had played with and was coached by Harry Sinden in the 1965 season on the Oklahoma Blazers in the Central Hockey League. Sinden knew what kind of person and player Parise was, so when Canada needed energy, tenacity, and someone to work with Esposito and Cashman, he chose Parise. JP rewarded his coach with spirited play and some offense, scoring 2 goals and 2 assists in 6 games in the Summit Series.

After being traded to the New York Islanders in the 1974-75 season, he put in four solid seasons, one more in Cleveland with the Barons, and a final season as the North Stars captain when they merged with the Barons. Parise, of course, would be remembered for his threatening stick swinging gesture towards West German official Joseph Kompalla in game 8. Despite that out of character moment, **Parise was a valued member of Team Canada, who**

contributed at both ends of the ice, starting with the first goal of the match and his first goal of the series in Game 3.

The goal begins with Alexander Yakushev circling back with the puck in his own zone. Canadian forwards Phil Esposito and Wayne Cashman take a page out of the Soviet 2-man forechecking scheme and pressure Yakushev. Yakushev loses control of the puck and then fires it blindly up the boards on the right side of the Soviet zone. The puck goes to Parise who trailing his linemates, at the Soviet blue line. The Minnesota forward carries the puck back into the Soviet zone, taking a weak backhand shot that is deflected into the left corner. Yakushev goes after it, but Parise hits him with a clean, hard bodycheck, **causing the much bigger Soviet to make a weak clearing attempt up the boards.** This is easily intercepted by Phil Esposito who passes it back to a wide-open Bill White on the point. White lets a hard high slap shot go that Tretiak has trouble with. The rebound comes right out in front to Parise who does a golf swing at the puck knocking it underneath the Soviet netminder.

This goal was a perfect example of how forechecking pressure can lead to bad defensive decisions and turnovers. Cashman starts the sequence off with dogged pursuit of Yakushev. Esposito joins in, until Yakushev loses control of the puck and makes a bad decision with a weak flip up the boards. Parise gets full credit for reading the play and causing a second Yakushev mistake with his bodycheck in the corner, where the Big Yak again throws the puck weakly up the boards. Esposito goes for the puck, but the key error from the Soviet side happens when Vladimir Luchenko chases Esposito onto the side hash marks, **leaving the front of the net open.** Yakushev then collects a hat trick of defensive errors when he simply lets Parise go to the front of the net, and doesn't pick him up, his third mistake of the sequence.

When Bill White was taking his shot from the point, Shadrin had time to skate towards him for an attempted shot block but instead was **interfered with for a moment**

by the clever Cashman. Tretiak had trouble with the shot, and should have cleared the rebound, instead it went directly in front to Parise. Defenseman Gennady Tsygankov was also within reach of Parise, but instead of covering him up, he simply gives a weak whack of his stick from behind. **This sequence was a complete Soviet breakdown on the ice**, all started by the Canadian forecheck. Ironically, the Soviets were victims of Canada using the same swarming forecheck they themselves used so effectively.

After the goal, Canada puts out the Mikita/Frank Mahovlich/Cournoyer line. The Soviets counter with the first shift of the "Kid Line", Anisin, Bodunov and Lebedev. Defenseman Yuri Shatalov gets his first shift in the series as well and is completely flattened by Cournoyer in the Soviet corner. Shatalov seems both shocked and annoyed by the hit and gives Cournoyer a shove. Stan Mikita shows some smooth stickhandling, deking out several Soviets before dumping it in. The young Soviet line seem completely overwhelmed by the veteran Canadians, as their only puck touches ended in two long shots from beyond the blue line that Tony Esposito handles easily.

Both teams change on the fly. Defenceman Valeri Vasiliev gets his first shift of the series. Vasiliev is a tough, great open ice hitter, a real rugged, skilled player, something Canada has yet to encounter from their opponent. After making a nice long transition pass to Bodunuv, Vasiliev introduces himself to Team Canada by introducing his elbow to Jean Ratelle's face. This gets him a well well-deserved two minutes in the box. Ratelle gets short shifted as Sinden puts out Esposito, Frank Mahovlich and Yvan Cournoyer on the powerplay with Park/Lapointe on defense. Ratelle was on the ice for 15 seconds before Vasiliev elbowed him. The Soviets counter with Petrov and Mishakov up front, Luchenko and Tsygankov on the back end. Unfortunately for Canada, **the decline of Frank Mahovlich** was about to begin.

Goal 2: Vladimir Petrov. Soviet Union 1 Team Canada 1

Vladimir Petrov must be considered an **underrated legend of hockey**. While his teammates Kharlamov, Yakushev and Tretiak have all been inducted into the Hockey Hall of Fame, Petrov's name has rarely come up as a potential inductee, if ever. His career in the USSR was certainly legendary. Born in a suburb of Moscow in 1947, Petrov was 25 in 1972 and had already turned in one of the greatest seasons in Soviet Elite League history. In the 1969-70 season, Vladimir scored an incredible 51 goals in 43 games playing for the CSKA or Central Red Army team. He was the last player in the Soviet league to score 50 goals in a season, and that season was his first of **five league scoring titles**, comparable to the Art Ross Trophy in the NHL. He was a model of consistency, winning his first scoring title at 21 and his last at 32.

Petrov debuted with the Krylya Sovetov (the Soviet Wings) team based in Moscow in 1965. A couple of years later, in 1967, when Petrov was 20, prominent Soviet coach Anatoly Tarasov invited him to play for the CSKA squad. While playing for that club, he won 11 Soviet League championships, matching Henri Richard who won 11 Stanley Cups for Montreal, although CSKA was not an equal member of the Soviet League as players were diverted to join the Army club in Moscow, forming a virtual all-star team.

As a member of the Soviet National Team, Petrov won gold medals at the 1972 Olympic Games in Sapporo and the 1976 Olympics in Innsbruck. In addition, he won silver at the 1980 Olympics in Lake Placid, losing in the famous "Miracle on Ice" game to the USA. Petrov also won four World Championship's scoring titles and was a four-time World Championship All Star. Locally, he was **a two-time Soviet Player of the Year** in 1972 and 1973, and he was a four-time Soviet Elite League All-Star. He was a member of one of the greatest lines in hockey history, centring Valeri Kharlamov and Boris Mikhailov. While this line was not together full time in 1972, they dominated international and local hockey scoring 1086 goals in the Soviet league and 539 goals on the National Team. In the World Championships All-time scoring lists, they are 1st, 2nd and 4th overall. Petrov who eventually became President of the Russian Ice Hockey Federation in the 1990s remembers the line with personal humility:

> "We complemented each other very well. We always gave it our best and we had a very good chemistry both on and off the ice, and I believe that was a big part of our success Petrov said. " We played together for a long time. I always knew where they would be on the ice. It was easy to play with Boris and Valeri because they were always in the right place. And we had a lot of fun The only reason why I had such a good career was because I played with two such great players." 72Summitseries.com

A fairly big man at 6'1 and 190 pounds, Petrov was by appearance more Canadian than Soviet in style. He wasn't a great skater by Soviet standards, and despite his significant offensive statistics, he was a more defensive minded player. Much of that was because of the Soviet system of using the centre position more as a soccer midfielder, the player who tends to hang back and focus on the oppositions counter attacking. He was strong, a cerebral player, possessing a very good slap shot. All of those attributes would be on display as he scores the first Soviet goal of the game, his second shorthanded goal of the Series.

Frank Mahovlich would have a very difficult Summit Series. While he was skating well in game one, he made some poor, even selfish offensive decisions. He settled down in game two, on a line with Stan Mikita and his Montreal line mate Yvan Cournoyer, resulting in his only goal of the series. Game three was the start of his truly puzzling disappointing play that would eventually cause him to lose his roster spot in Moscow. For Mahovlich, this begins with **a terrible**

giveaway in his own zone to Vladimir Petrov.

With the baby-faced Valeri Vasiliev in the penalty box, Phil Esposito lines up against Petrov in the centre of the ice, just outside the Canadian blue line. Esposito wins the draw cleanly, and it goes to Cournoyer who is standing near the far boards. The Roadrunner skates towards Lapointe in the Canadian zone and gives him a pass, ideally to set up a rush. The Big M is standing still on the boards with Mishakov watching him. Petrov is just off the Canadian blue line, limiting Mahovlich passing options. As a result, Mahovlich aimlessly throws the puck back into the Canadian zone where it's picked up by a circling Brad Park. Park gives it back to Mahovlich who still hasn't moved from the boards. Mishakov is now right in front of Frank who inexplicably decides to fire a pass through the two Soviet forwards who were directly in front of him. The puck deflects off Mishakov's skate to Petrov who kicks it up to his stick and skates to just inside the faceoff circle to the left of Tony Esposito. Esposito comes far out of his net, so far, he is actually in the faceoff circle himself as Petrov blasts a hard slap shot through the goalie's legs. Esposito had gone into a butterfly pose which opened the five-hole area between his pads.

This goal was a result of the **aggressive penalty killing scheme** the Soviets often used, which was constant skating, pressure on the puck and reducing the passing lanes. Mahovlich folds under the pressure twice, the first time in his missed pass to Lapointe which Brad Park intercepts and then the terrible giveaway at the Canadian blue line seconds later. Park himself should not have passed to the stationary Mahovlich, who was not skating or in a position to make a head manning pass, however the Big M showed terrible decision making which led to an unnecessary and embarrassing shorthanded tally against Canada. **Two legendary Canadian players, two terrible passes.**

Petrov himself showed he possessed a powerful slap

shot, scoring from a position off the right wing that Guy Lafleur would often score from in his prime. Despite this goal, Petrov's overall play in the Series was not without criticism. Lev Lebedev a writer for the Soviet Newspaper Pravda had this to say about Petrov's effectiveness:

"Our best center Vladimir Petrov was not very effective on offense. He took so much time firing his powerful slap shots that Canadians had time to block them. Our best players have to learn to release their shots more quickly. That's one of the important lessons in the series". Leb Lebedev Prada

Petrov himself added how the Summit Series made him a more complete hockey player:

"By Soviet standards I had always been considered an offensive centreman. Phil Esposito and Bobby Clarke forced me to play a more defensive style. The experience made me a better all-around player." Richard Bendall Summit

On the morning of 28th February 2017, the hockey world heard the sad news that Vladimir Petrov, one of the greatest Soviet forwards in the history of the game, had died, four months short of his seventieth birthday. Vladislav Tretiak had this to say about his long-time teammate:

"He was a legendary hockey player, a very elegant centre, and we will always remember him for his strength of character. In the Summit Series, he excelled against the Canadian professionals, playing in that line with Kharlamov and Mikhailov, which at that time was the first offensive troika for CSKA as well as the USSR National Team. Petrov's contribution was huge, as he had to lead the offense and track back to help out in defence. He was an interesting character and very determined, which no doubt helped him become such a great hockey player. After retiring from full-time hockey, he was still working with the Golden Puck children's tournament. He devoted his whole life to hockey and was helping our youngest players. My deepest sympathies to his nearest and dearest." https:// www.championat.com/hockey/ 2017

Canada keeps the same five out on the power play, and once the puck gets into the Soviet zone, Brad Park gets a good shot away at Tretiak after he dekes around Petrov and moves in from the point. The Big M gets another quick attempt, but Tretiak stones him. Petrov continues his great shift, working incredibly hard at both ends of the ice. He forechecks Brad Park in the Canadian zone, then shows great hustle in backchecking as Guy Lapointe carries the puck deep into the Soviet zone. Lapointe's pass out front gets deflected, but Brad Park makes a nice pinch at the blue line to keep the puck in. Park passes it to Frank Mahovlich who crosses into the slot and gets a decent shot away off Tretiak's pad. The puck goes to Phil Esposito who passes it back to Guy Lapointe, but Petrov is there again, intercepting the pass, lugging the puck deep and finally taking a hit from Phil Esposito in the Canadian end. **A fantastic penalty kill by Petrov.**

Canada has a strange, ineffectual habit of taking long range shots at Tretiak rather than dumping it around the boards. Tretiak easily handles these shots from outside the zone, and it seems to just be handing over possession to the Soviets. Cournoyer and Bill White are both guilty of this on the power play, ending with Team Canada failing to orchestrate any sort of chances.

With the penalty successfully killed, both teams switch lines as the game gets into a bit of a frantic back and forth pace. Clarkes line comes out, starts forechecking, and after a Gusev give away, the Soviets ice the puck to relieve any pressure.

The Soviet Kid Line comes back out. Anasin tries stickhandling through centre ice but is stopped easily by Bill White. The Chicago Black Hawk defensive specialist makes a lumbering rush through three Soviet players that has to be making Harry Sinden wish Bobby Orr was playing. Valeri Vasiliev skates the puck out of the Soviet zone and Bobby Clarke blatantly dumps the young defender with a trip. Vasiliev recovers, flies behind his own net before making a nice headman pace to Anasin on the wing. The diminutive young Soviet star continues into the Canadian zone, where he gets hit by Wayne Cashman. Cashman hit on Anisin was a low hip check, that was also a borderline trip. Kuzkin then rocks Cashman at the Soviet blue line with a clean check and finally JP Parise absolutely crushes the 21-year-old Vyacheslav Anisin cleanly into the boards, knocking his helmet off and ending a very physical few moments, especially for Anasin.

Serge Savard carries the puck out of his zone after a rare Soviet dump in, making a lovely cross ice pass to a streaking Parise. Parise's long slap shot is easily handled by Tretiak. Alexander Maltsev uses his great speed to counterattack, but **his poor drop pass,** he did this several times in game two, **gets intercepted** and the puck goes back into the Soviet zone. The Esposito line is cycling the puck deep when Cashman takes a needless slashing penalty against Vladislav Tretiak, ending the pressure.

The Soviets put out their power line of Maltsev, Kharlamov and Mikhailov, with Luchenko and Tsygankov on defence. Canada has the Mahovlich brothers with Park and Bergman. Kharlamov gets hit hard by Brad Park in the Canadian zone, but the incredibly tough little forward shrugs it off. A second later Frank Mahovlich hits Kharlamov from behind in the slot area, knocking him to the ice. **No call on the play**. Canada should be two men short after that blatant hit.

The Soviets get control and start their deadly tick-tac-toe passing. Canada uses a very tight 4-man box that keeps the Soviets on the perimeter, but the Soviets get a couple of close shots after some slick one touch passing. Tony Esposito makes a superb save on Boris Mikhailov as some slick one touch passing. This is a more composed Soviet squad than in game two. Canada on the other hand is continuing the edgy play from game two. **Gary Bergman gives Boris Mikhailov a nasty slash**

behind the net, again not called, and when a whistle is blown the usual clean playing Peter Mahovlich comes into the scrum and high sticks Kharlamov. This was probably due to the embarrassment of the 6'5 210-pound Mahovlich **being knocked on his keester by a clean hit** from the 5'8 165-pound Kharlamov a few moments earlier. The Soviets are passing and moving, passing, and moving, almost like a basketball team, and it mesmerizes the Canadians who are being forced to aggressiveness to slow their opponents down.

The puck gets dumped deep into the Soviet zone and Gusev hesitates seeing Bobby Clarke coming at him, a sign that he is still a little intimidated by the Canadian aggressive play. Gusev proceeds to cough the puck up to Clarke without a struggle. Gusev has given the puck up several times already in the series, and the Soviet coaches seem to have noticed and limited his ice time. The Shadrin line finishes the powerplay against Clarke and Ellis, Stapleton and White. An interesting note was that Bill White had Yakushev tied up neatly at the side of the net, nullifying the clever Soviet back door play that Shadrin was trying to make. As the penalty ends with a successful kill by Canada, Alexander Maltsev can be seen on the bench getting his wrist looked at and taped.

Since Canada is using four centres this game, Ratelle, Peter M, and Cournoyer are put together as a makeshift line against the Soviet "Kid Line". Canada gets a turnover at centre ice from Alexander Bodunov and Serge Savard makes a nice pass to Peter Mahovlich, who springs Ratelle for a wide-open shot on Tretiak. Tretiak makes a solid skate save after the nice Canadian passing play. The line comes roaring again as Ratelle makes a nice little flip pass to Cournoyer streaking down the right side. The Roadrunner cuts in on Tretiak who is forced to make another solid save. Cournoyer looked like Kharlamov in game one cutting in on Tretiak, but the Soviet netminder kept his pads tightly closed unlike Dryden who allowed a shot to trickle between them. Despite the Soviets not dressing Ragulin or Paladiev, their defence is still having trouble with Yvan Cournoyer's speed.

Phil Esposito takes the draw in the Soviet end against Maltsev. He cleverly pushes the puck past Maltsev, then powers himself and the puck straight to Tretiak for a dangerous chance. Esposito is skating everywhere for a few moments, backchecking hard and then leading a rush with Cashman that has the Soviets on their heels. This is a really effective line for Canada. Quickly, the Soviets counterattack as the speedy Kharlamov roars down the right side and makes a nice pass across to Mikhailov whose wrist shot goes wide, just missing the low bottom corner.

Both teams are changing players rapidly as the play goes back and forth, end to end, at a frantic pace. Against the Clarke line, who are forechecking vigorously the Soviets do their own version of the angled dump in. The ploy works as Shadrin diligently forechecks a turning, swirling Brad Park. Canada ices the puck to relieve the Soviet pressure. One of the interesting things about the Soviets is **how quickly they can change tactics**, the dump in being a perfect example. They saw Canadian success and tried their own version of it.

Stan Mikita, back centring Frank Mahovlich and Cournoyer, gets hauled down by Anisin at centre ice with no call. The referees seem to be just letting both teams play at this stage. Frank Mahovlich does a nice Wayne Gretzky impression going back and forth behind the Soviet net before getting it out front to Cournoyer who jams it into Tretiak's pads.

The Soviet Kid Line has their first real chance on a nice three-way passing play ending with a Bodunov shot on Esposito. The 21-year-olds seemed quite overwhelmed in their first few shifts, but **Coach Bobrov keeps putting them back out and they appear to be getting more confidence with each play**. Anasin does another Canadian like dump in, and suddenly, the Soviet kid line springs to life. They apply pressure off the faceoff as Lebedev fore checks hard on

White, and then causes Stapleton to surprisingly freeze up as Lebedev looks to hit him. This causes a turnover behind the Canadian net as Lebedev pushes Stapleton off the puck and gets it out front to Anisin for a clean chance. Weak defending by Stapleton who showed little inclination to take the hit from Lebedev or win the battle.

Bobrov, sensing his troops are ramping up their game, sends out his top line of Kharlamov, Maltsev and Mikhailov. They are flying as Kharlamov has a one on one with White. He knows that the NHL veteran is extremely hard to get around, so he fires a quick surprise shot off the wing. This surprises Esposito, and as Tony O tries to clear the rebound, it hits Pat Stapleton and almost bounces into the Canadian net. Canada again comes storming back as Parise hits Cashman with a nice bank pass off the boards and the rangy Boston winger blows by Luchenko but then fans on the shot attempt as Tretiak makes a flopping pad save. Kharlamov is really skating, and he hits Maltsev with a nice pass at centre. Maltsev then does an **Academy Award winning dive** over the Canadian blue line that the referee believes and calls a tripping penalty on Parise. **The knowledgeable Winnipeg hockey fans rain down angry boos of displeasure loudly.**

Phil Esposito stays out to kill the penalty and Peter Mahovlich joins him with the Montreal pairing of Serge Savard and Guy Lapointe. The Soviets again put out the Kharlamov, Maltsev, Mikhailov trio with Luchenko and Tsygankov. Serge Savard gets the puck deep in his own zone and the Soviets for whatever reason allow him to come out of his zone unencumbered. He picks up speed, shrugs off Kharlamov and then goes by Luchenko on the boards. Savard is now on a 2 on1 with Peter Mahovlich against the remaining Soviet defender, Gennady Tsygankov. Savard makes a nice pass over to the Little M who drives a hard shot wide of Tretiak. Savard then intercepts a Mikhailov pass at the Canadian blueline, makes a wonderful spin away from two Soviet forwards and then clears the puck deep into the

Soviet end. **Great penalty killing by Savard**.

The Soviets are completely out of sorts on this powerplay, as the Canadian players pressure the puck carriers, forcing the Soviets back into their zone consistently. Canada seems to have taken another page out of the Soviet playbook with aggressive penalty killing, and it's very effective. Bobrov changes the entire five-man unit, as Shadrin's line comes out with Gusev and Kuzkin. Canada counters with Clarke. Ellis, Park, and Bergman. Gary Bergman hits Gusev at the Canadian blue line, the Soviet defender appears to embellish the hit, but this time the referees fail to bite on the theatrics. As the penalty ends, Clarke hits big Yakushev with a clean hip check which causes the crowd to give the Manitoban player a loud ovation. The Soviets really struggled on the power play, with only one shot on goal.

In the 2014-2015 NHL season, a new rule was adopted on "Diving". *64.1 Diving / Embellishment – Any player who blatantly dives, embellishes a fall or a reaction, or who feigns an injury shall be penalized with a minor penalty under this rule.*

This rule was brought in to help punish those who seemingly regularly acted on this practice, obviously with the intent to draw a penalty. While this was not unknown in North American hockey in 1972, diving was considered **"against the hockey code"**. It was something a player did not or should not do. The North American hockey code was based on an unwritten set of expectations of players, much of it based on honour and a sense of macho pride. The expectations were numerous. Players got stitched up and finished the games, you defended your teammates, injuries were fought through with minimal time taken off, players did not back down from a fight, etc. Diving was considered against this code; it was theatrics and unmanly.

In Europe, where soccer reigned as the top sport in every country, diving was generally less frowned upon, and used consistently by soccer players to draw penalties. Crowds would whistle in derision, but quite often a referee would buy the act and award a yellow (or even red) card to the offender or worse, a game changing penalty kick. This practiced seeped into European hockey.

While the Soviet players weren't not the only players to embellish plays hoping to draw penalties (throughout his career Philadelphia Flyer Bill Barber was a notorious diver), they quickly seemed to acquire a reputation in this game. In fact, the earlier Maltsev diving play (leading to a Parise penalty) seemed to hurt the Soviets moving forward. There **were several border line non- calls** in the preceding end to end action on Canadian hits that could have been easily called for penalties. The officials in this game, American amateurs Gordon lee and Len Gagnon ignored them, possibly unsure if the Soviets were embellishing. One of those non calls would lead directly to Canada's second goal of this game and his only goal of the series by the elegant New York Ranger, Jean Ratelle.

In 1972 Jean Ratelle was one of the top forwards in the world. He had just completed the greatest season of his career, scoring 46 goals and 109 points in 63 games. The Rangers made the Stanley Cup final that season, but Ratelle had broken his ankle taking him out of the last 15 games of the season and while he returned for the final, the Bruins took the series in six games. Often compared to Jean Beliveau, Ratelle had the same graceful statesmanship about him, a quality that garnered enough respect to be named one of the Team Canada co-captains. He was a graceful, fluid skater, a good passer and faceoff man. Despite all these qualities, **the Canadian coaching staff struggled to find a place for Jean**.

The GAG New York Ranger line would only play one Summit game as a full line. This was the first game, and Sinden seemed to believe they were not the right "type" of line to play against the Soviets. As a result, Ratelle missed game two in Toronto, was used sparingly in game three and not dressed again in game four. He did play in all four games in Moscow on a revamped line. Vic Hadfield would head back to the New York Ranger training camp leaving a gap on left wing. Chicago's Dennis Hull replaced him and fit in seamlessly with Ratelle and Rod Gilbert. In game three however, Ratelle seemed to have immediate chemistry with speedy Yvan Cournoyer and the two would combine for a well set up breakaway goal, **with a non-call assist from the referees.**

After successfully killing Parise's penalty, Team Canada is ramped up with renewed energy, and the Soviets continue to appear unsure. The puck goes deep into the Soviet end, and Ron Ellis delivers a clean bodycheck on the solid Viktor Kuzkin who stands his ground. The Winnipeg crowd, known for its loudness, is becoming frantic as they sense something is about to happen. The puck goes to Gusev who fires a cross ice pass to Lebedev, but the pass is behind him and Lebedev weakly gets rid of it in mid ice. Brad Park recovers the puck, and headman's it to a streaking Paul Henderson. Henderson uses his speed to carry it deep, stops and makes a pass back to Park, who fires a long shot wide. Gusev recovers, turns behind his own goal and fires a second long pass that misses Lebedev, hitting his skate and going straight to Shadrin. Shadrin circles in his own end and passes up to Lebedev again who carries it gingerly towards the centre red line. Paul Henderson is waiting and hits the young Soviet with a half hip check, **half trip** that easily could have been called. **This was the third borderline tripping hit Canada had done in last minute, and none of these were called.** The one delivered by Gary Bergman was probably the most blatant trip. Whether officials Lee and Gagnon felt these were clean checks or whether they felt they were embellished dives by the Soviet players is unknown, but the non-call on Henderson led to a Canadian goal.

Goal 3: Jean Ratelle Canada 2 USSR 1

After the Henderson/Lebedev collision, Gary Bergman gets the puck at the Canadian blue line, strides past the red line and hits Jean Ratelle with a pass. This was Ratelle's second shift of the game, but he shows no sign of rust. Team Canada now had four players pressing at the Soviet blue line. Yvan Cournoyer is streaking down the right side, and Ratelle tips it to Cournoyer. The New York Ranger centre shows a great burst of speed, streaking past Yuri Shatalov. The Roadrunner completes the give and go with a nice pass back to Ratelle who is now alone on Tretiak. Ratelle shows why he scored 46 goals the season before by snapping a nice shot on the right side past a flopping Tretiak.

From the Soviet standpoint, Tretiak played this goal somewhat poorly, as he stayed back in his net, and gave Ratelle an opening at which to shoot. The play happened quickly, but if Tretiak had come out of his crease, it would have limited Ratelle's shooting options and perhaps led to a different outcome. On defence, Yuri Shatalov had just come onto the ice, as **Gusev had committed a bit of a cardinal sin in hockey by changing with the puck still in the Soviet end of the ice**. Yuri Shatalov had to rush into the play and was stationary at the Soviet blue line allowing the smooth Ratelle to easily get past him. Kuzkin was on the other side of the ice and unable to get back to the front in time to cover for his teammate. Yuri Lebedev gave the puck away twice, the second time while getting dumped by Henderson. However, to be fair, he was the victim of two straight poor cross ice passes by Alexander Gusev.

The Soviets on this goal were again exposed as a bit inflexible in their approach, as they kept constantly circling and regrouping, despite the Canadian pressure, until finally a tired group made the expected bad passes and poorly timed player changes.

The goal itself was a beautiful give and go by Ratelle/Cournoyer, ending with a solid shot by Ratelle. Good goal for Canada, but this goal would never have happened if the officials called Henderson or Bergman on their mid-ice hits.

Ratelle, Cournoyer and Frank Mahovlich keep the Soviet Kid Line bottled in their end with a couple of prime scoring chances by Ratelle and the Big M. Mahovlich drills a backhand from the slot that Tretiak has trouble with. The period comes to a halt soon after, but before that, Yuri Lebedev does a viscous two hand slash on Jean Ratelle in mid-ice that doesn't get called. The crowd is so loud the players on the ice seem unsure as to whether the siren had gone off. As the players leave the ice, Wayne Cashman can be seen chirping with the Soviet players, who are giving it right back.

Game 3: Period 1 Review

This was a well-played intense period of hockey. Both teams had opportunities to score, but it was tightly played. The period had the feel of a boxing match where both fighters have been hurt, and they are aware of how dangerous their opponent was. Canada despite a slow start the first shift, was overall skating very well, continuing to gel as a team. As a result, Canada was the stronger team overall as they continued the aggressive play from game two. **This strategy appeared to be effective in taking the Soviets off their game**. The Soviets while more composed than game two, still seemed to be a bit out of sorts with their passes and teamwork. While the Soviet transition game was still dangerous, Canadian defenders such as Serge Savard and Bill White seemed to be able to read the play and limited the puck receiver's ice in the neutral zone. Canada's defence was playing effectively, with the notable exception of Brad Park, who while making his usual offensive contribution, was continuing to sometimes struggle defensively. The Soviet defence was having more trouble, as they made bad outlet passes under the Canadian pressure. Canadian bench management seemed problematic again, as the decision to go with four excellent centres seemed to cause a lack of rhythm with the forward lines.

Strong players in period one for the Soviets were Kharlamov who was skating again and causing Canada trouble every time he was out there, although the Soviet "Super Line" with Mikhailov and Maltsev failed to generate any real offense. The star of the period for either team had to be **Vladimir Petrov**. The two-way player had a super period, especially on the penalty kill. Tretiak continued his strong play, despite giving up two goals. On the Canadian side, Serge Savard was a rock on the defence, controlling the play and making excellent outlet passes. Phil Esposito was really skating well, as were his linemates Parise and Cashman. Bobby Clarke was still forechecking and causing problems and Jean Ratelle looked good with Cournoyer, but with the limited ice time, the duo was only together twice. Tony Esposito was solid, making saves when needed. The question would be whether Canada would and could continue the physical game in periods two and three and would the officials let them? How would the Soviets adjust? Canadian TV personality, and former National Team player, Brian Conacher notes this trend in between periods where he states, "the game tonight will be won in the corners".

CHAPTER 30: GAME 3 PERIOD 2. WHO ARE THESE GUYS?

The Soviets, noticing the lack of effectiveness of the Maltsev line, match up Shadrin, Yakushev and Soludukin against the Esposito line. Gusev and Kuzkin are on defence as are Park and Bergman for Canada. The Soviets win the draw and do another dump in, deep into the Canadian zone. These dump in plays seem to be a bit of a new Soviet strategy for this game. Gary Bergman gets the puck to the side of his own goal with Shadrin gingerly pressuring him. Bergman then shockingly throws it blindly back behind the Canadian goal right onto Yakushev's stick. Park does a half-hearted attempt to stop the pass, but the big Yak hits the pinching Alexander Gusev with a quick pass into the slot. Tony Esposito is forced to make an excellent save on the first shot. JP Parise blocks the rebound with a bit of desperate defensive awareness. **This was sloppy play by Canada to start the period, especially by the usually reliable Bergman**. The puck gets out of the Canadian zone, and Gusev gives the puck away, again, with a blind backhand pass that Phil Esposito intercepts.

Esposito flies up the right side with tons of open space, until he is just off the faceoff circle in the Soviet zone. This was an area where Phil would score in the 1976 Canada Cup playoff game vs the Czechoslovakians, which a quick snapshot off the wing. Kuzkin catches up to him, but Espo fires a similar low hard shot that Tretiak gingerly stops. Phil gets the rebound which trickles through Tretiak's pads. The Esposito line presses, with some excellent cycling of the puck by Parise and Cashman. The Soviets seem unable to contain this line when Cashman and Parise are forechecking. After the whistle, Canada fails to continue the momentum, as the Soviet Anasin, Bodunov, Lebedev or kid line has their first good shift. All three are flying and using their bodies. They are out against the Mikita, Cournoyer and Frank Mahovlich trio, a group they were outplayed by in the first period. Mikita trips Shalatov in mid ice, with no call and then Lebedev high sticks Pat Stapleton while forechecking.

The top Soviet line comes on, where a dancing, weaving, turning Boris Mikhailov sets up Maltsev for a solid chance on a clever pass through the Canadian defensive pair of Savard and Lapointe. Tony O reads the play, and makes a quick, athletic save. On the next play, Serge Savard shows off his legendary **Savardian spin'o'rama move**, fooling Mikhailov before making a rush through the neutral zone. Savard does the angled dump in play for the first time this game, and it works to perfection as Henderson is all alone in front of Tretiak. Tsygankov pulls him down with a blatant penalty, but no call is made. The puck comes back to Ellis who hammers a hard slap shot at Tretiak from just inside the blue line. Tretiak wisely covers up, getting a break in the play. **A livid Paul Henderson can be seen protesting about the non-call at the whistle**.

In 1969, one of the most important changes in international hockey took place. Aligning the game with the NHL, the IIHF voted to allow bodychecking in all areas of the ice. Previously, hitting was allowed only in the defensive zone. A defenseman, inside his blue line, could hit an attacker, but the opposing forward was not allowed to bodycheck a defenseman in his defensive zone. The neutral zone was a "demilitarized zone", no hitting allowed.

For Europeans, the rule also meant making a permanent adjustment. **They would have to be prepared for physical contact all over the ice.** This meant not only taking hits but delivering hits as well, learning when and how to hit in the offensive end, learning how it can be used as a strategy and an effective style.

As a result of this rule change, Soviet hockey had only **three years of full ice body contact** in contrast to close to 100 years of Canadian full contact hockey. Whether this gap in body checking experience concerned the Soviet players as they went into the Summit Series is unknown. The Soviet system of play as designed by Anatoli Tarasov was one of movement and team play and focused on avoiding body contact or using it to the Soviet advantage as mentioned earlier.

Teams, of course, are made of individual players, personalities, styles, and preferences. On the Soviet team in 1972, players such as Kharlamov, Mishakov, Vasiliev and Kuzkin seemed to have little issue with the Canadian aggressive style, and often dealt out more contact than they received. A smaller player like Kharlamov was incredibly strong on his skates, and in the first few games in Canada knocked over giants such as Vic Hadfield, Guy Lapointe and Peter Mahovlich.

Alexander Gusev, a large man in that era at 6'1 and 190 pounds, had a reputation of being a physical player in the Soviet Elite league. By 1972, he had been a regular on the Soviet National Team since 1969, often partnered with Viktor Kuzkin on defence. Born in Moscow in 1947, he had been a political inclusion on the famed Central Red Army development program, as his mother was an accountant for the organization. She persuaded coach Boris Afanasyev, a former player, to take her son in the school. Alexander proved to be much more than a token appointment to the program as he developed into a true prospect, moving up the ranks in the CSKA program. Anatoli Tarasov felt Gusev, and future star Valeri Kharlamov needed more development in 1966 and sent the two teenage prospects to the Ural minor league team (lower 3rd division) Zvezda Chebarkul. The two future stars would lead this team to their league championship and promotion to the second division. Both players would be back on the main club the next season, with Gusev securing his spot permanently by 1968. He would play ten years on the Red Army club and eight on the Soviet National Team before being replaced by new National Team coach Victor Tikanov in 1977. He played six games in the Summit Series, played in the 1974 WHA Summit Series and 1976 Canada Cup. Gusev died in July 2020 at 73.

Alexander Gusev was known for his well-rounded game with a heavy shot, calm intelligent play, and willingness to be physical. Boris Mikhailov described his former teammate:

"Gusev was a key figure on the blue line. We played together on the same line-up for more than one season. He could pick out a killer pass, finish off a play with his shot, he had great vision on the ice, superb technique, and he wasn't afraid to play hard when he needed to."

"He was always a calming presence; the opposition respected him because he didn't let anybody take liberties; he would always come to the aid of his comrades. Off the ice, he was a modest guy, he never pushed himself forward, but he was always ready to help out his friends." Soviet TASS . https://www.iihf.com/en/news/20013/olympic-champion-gusev-passes

Knowing that Gusev was a player who adapted to the IIHF rule change, and had a reputation for physical engagement, makes his play in the first three games in Canada perplexing. He seemed hesitant to engage with the Canadian players, and gave the puck away on multiple occasions. His passes seemed off, and he lacked the tenacity needed to be effective in these hard-fought games.

His primary partner in the Series and back in the USSR was Soviet Captain Victor Kuzkin who at times had to overcompensate for Gusev's mistakes.

Gusev himself seemed to hint at a lack of confidence when he spoke of his first introduction to the top Canadian professionals:

"I thought I had one of the hardest slapshots in the world. When I arrived in Montreal, I discovered that almost every Canadians shot was at least as hard as mine!"

Vyacheslav Gavrilin writer for the Soviet newspaper The Red Star summarized Gusev's struggles:

"Gusev couldn't intimidate the Canadians with bodychecks like he does Soviet players in league play. He came to lose confidence in himself. The aggressiveness and never –quit attitude of the Canadians forwards shocked him".

Unfortunately for the USSR, Gusev would have another ineffective shift in period two of game three, showing a real lack of tenacity on the puck. This certainly was a main contributor to Canada's 3rd goal of the game and Phil Esposito's 3rd goal of the Series.

Goal 4: Phil Esposito. Team Canada 3 USSR 1

Phil Esposito once said *"Scoring is easy. You simply stand in the slot, take your beating, and shoot the puck into the net"*. While this was true of Esposito who made the slot area his 'office", it was just as often in the "high slot" where his one-time shot was deadly. This goal was a perfect example of that, a quick deadly shot, in the high slot, after a perfect pass from long-time line mate Wayne Cashman.

The goal begins with a faceoff deep in the Soviet end, to the left of Tretiak. Esposito, Cashman, and Parise are out with Park and Bergman, while the Soviets counter with the trio of Petrov, Mishakov and Yakushev up front, Gusev with Kuzkin on defence. Esposito wins the draw cleanly back to Brad Park who fires a slap shot from the point. The shot goes wide, where **Gusev plays it leisurely up the left boards, right**

back to Park. The puck bounces around a bit, finally ending up behind the Soviet goal where Cashman muscles Petrov into the boards, leaving the puck unattended. Gusev picks it up but loses control and it goes into the right corner. Gusev sees JP Parise going after the puck and the Soviet defender **hesitates** before pushing Parise against the boards. Parise is able to still poke the puck to Cashman, who has been left alone by Petrov. Cashman does what he did on a regular basis in Boston, feeding a quick pass out to Phil Esposito who one times the Cashman pass into the net. Tretiak had no chance on the shot, a hard snapshot which was rifled into the top corner. **A true goal scorers' goal, one that resembles a modern-day Alex Ovechkin strike**.

While it would be easy to dismiss the goal as simply one of the greatest pure goal scorers in hockey history scoring a trademark goal, this was a goal that could have easily been prevented by the Soviets. Alexander Gusev had a great opportunity to get the puck out of the Soviet end after the Park slap shot, but seemed lackadaisical in firing it up the boards. He also could have taken the puck back behind his net and set the play up but didn't. When the puck came loose, Gusev lost the puck when he attempted to carry it behind his net, saw that it went to Parise, but then failed to take Parise out of the play. **The smaller Parise was able to outmuscle Gusev** and get the puck over to Cashman. Petrov had let Cashman go, anticipating Gusev getting the puck to him up the boards, **a gamble that failed**. Esposito was high enough in the slot that Kuzkin going after him would have left the front wide open, but Mishakov was standing just watching the play and should have seen the NHLs top goal scorer wide open.

Poor Soviet defensive decision-making and a lack of effort on the puck allowed for Canada to outmuscle the Soviets and set Espo up for the goal. Parise and Cashman were excellent on the play, forechecking hard and cleanly, working in tandem to hit the wide-open Esposito with the puck. Since the end of game one, Canada has outscored the Soviets 7-2 and appear to be the stronger team. The USSR will need to improve their defensive coverage and win more physical one on one battles to stop Team Canada's momentum.

The same ten players remain on the ice after the goal. Canada quickly dumps it back into the Soviet zone. Cashman easily out muscles a pedestrian Gusev, the puck goes to Parise, and the Canadian cycling success seems to be repeating itself. With Kuzkin and Cashman battling hard in the corner, and JP Parise making Gusev's life miserable behind the net, the Soviets look vulnerable again. One difference however, this time **Vladislav Petrov is all over Phil Esposito**, obviously trying to cover him in the slot to prevent a repeat of the previous goal. Petrov is soon called for an interference penalty, however since behind the net Gusev had tripped Parise, another penalty could have been called against the Soviets.

For the power play, Jean Ratelle comes out to centre Frank Mahovlich and Cournoyer with Park remaining out there with Guy Lapointe. The Soviets send out Mishakov, who seems to be getting a regular duty as a shorthanded specialist, with Shadrin up front and Vasiliev with Luchenko on defence. Coach Bobrov seems quite comfortable sending the inexperienced players like Vasiliev and the Soviet Kid Lineout against Canada's top players. At the faceoff Frank Mahovlich seems very upset at the official, as the Soviets seem to be unsure as to whom to put on the ice. This appears to be a strategy used occasionally when Canada has momentum.

Canada tries to set up in the Soviet zone, but Brad Park makes a poor pass, and the Soviets clear the puck down the ice. Tony Esposito comes out of his net, skating with the puck to play it around the boards. Frank Mahovlich makes one of his big swooping rushes, attempts a give and go with Ratelle, then **inexplicably gives the puck away in the Soviet zone.**

The puck heads back into the Canadian zone. Guy Lapointe makes a terrible pass out of the Canadian end, and the Soviets press the advantage. Vasiliev gets time from the point to unleash a slap shot that just misses. Lapointe recovers the puck, makes a full ice rush that has him hooked and pestered by Mishakov through the neutral zone. Lapointe recovers from his earlier bad pass by feeding Yvan Cournoyer in the slot for a close chance on Tretiak. Whether it's rust, a lack of coherence or Soviet checking, Team Canada isn't in sync.

The Soviets do an excellent job killing the penalty, pressuring Canada as they attempt to carry the puck into the Soviet zone. Brad Park struggles to bring the puck up, as Mishakov pesters him incessantly. Mishakov is out for the entire two minutes. He ends an excellent shift by blocking a rushed Guy Lapointe shot, elbowing Brad Park behind the Canadian net, and then being dumped himself by Guy Lapointe with an aggressive hit from behind. Despite Canada changing personnel on the powerplay, they barely get a shot on goal the entire time and seem unable to set the puck up in the Soviet zone.

The successful penalty seems to energize the Soviet team who start to really skate and move the puck quickly. Canada matches the intensity as the Clarke line applies pressure deep in the Soviet zone, forcing Tretiak to make a couple of difficult saves to keep his team within two goals. Ron Ellis mugs Luchenko near the goal crease, his arms and gloves in the defenseman's face, yet no call came from the quiet officials.

As the Soviets were prone to do, they suddenly counterattack. The power line of Maltsev, Kharlamov and Mikhailov, recover the puck near the Canadian blue line and spread out in the Canadian zone. **Once again**, **Valeri Kharlamov shows why he is the most dangerous forward on the Soviet team**. After a weak clearing attempt by Pat Stapleton, the puck comes around the boards in the Canadian end. Kharlamov reads this, intercepts the puck, spins back gaining some momentum. He then walks around Bobby Clarke with ease, makes a shift on Bill White and then fires a fantastic pass right across the ice to a waiting Maltsev at the side of the Canadian goal. **Tony Esposito makes the stop of the night** as he flies across the crease and kicks his left pad out to make an incredible save. Canada switches to the Esposito line, where Boris Mikhailov picks JP Parise off the ice, dumping him unceremoniously near the Soviet blue line. No call.

The Kharlamov show continues. He makes such a slick move on JP Parise at the Soviet blue line, putting it through his legs and dancing past him, that Parise gets spun around and almost falls. The speedy winger flies up the ice, dances around Wayne Cashman easily, before letting go a long shot on Esposito that is blocked.

The game is now at a frantic pace, and Canada gets a good chance with Cashman doing a slow, yet successful rush up ice. He gets into the corner with Tsygankov, falls clumsily yet gets the puck back and makes a great pass (again) to Phil Esposito in the high slot. Unfortunately for Canada, Espo misses the net this time on his one timer. **This play was almost an exact mirror of the earlier goal.**

Stan Mikita comes out for a rare shift. When carrying the puck, he gets dumped by Lebedev for a tripping penalty. Stan goes flying on the play, and while it's an obvious trip, **it also certainly appears that he embellishes the trip significantly.** Canada gets two excellent chances on the delayed penalty call, one with Mikita right on Tretiak's doorstep, and a second excellent save on a blast by Serge Savard. One note on this sequence, just before the tripping penalty, Lebedev gets hit into the boards headfirst by Serge Savard on what could have been a very scary incident. Luckily, he seemed unaffected, except probably being angry enough to take a tripping penalty a moment later.

Jean Ratelle replaces Mikita at centre between Cournoyer and Peter Mahovlich. Canada uses Park and

Lapointe on defence. The Soviets send out what Bobrov seems to have determined is their best, go-to, penalty killing players, Mishakov and Petrov. On defence is Valeri Vasiliev who is having an excellent game, and Luchenko. The Soviet forwards are hanging back into the neutral zone, clogging it up as Park or Lapointe carry the puck. This is effective, neither defenseman seeming to want to dump it deep. When Petrov decides to chase Park deep in his own end, Canada does some quick transition passing, catching both Petrov and Mishakov behind the play and feeding the pinching Guy Lapointe for a clear shot on goal. Lapointe fires a high hard shot that causes causing Tretiak to make a spectacular glove save. The appreciative Winnipeg crowd applaud both players. The Big M has replaced his brother, as Phil Esposito replaces Ratelle. Frank drives to the net before doing a clever dish to Esposito. Phil misses the net for a second consecutive solid chance. **These missed chances for Canada to put this game away come back to haunt them**.

So far in the series, Bobrov and Kulagin have been outcoaching their Canadian counterparts. He seems to read the game better, adapting accordingly. At the whistle Bobrov changes Petrov and Mishakov with the dangerous offensive players Kharlamov and Mikhailov. Canada seemingly didn't notice this change but should have. **This was a strategic decision that would pay off with another fast break shorthanded strike for the USSR.**

One of the greatest coaches and innovators in the game of Basketball was Boston Celtic coach Red Auerbach. When Auerbach took over the Boston Celtics in 1950, basketball was a slow plodding game that was focused around getting the team's biggest player the ball under the basket. The first real dominant big man in basketball, George Mikan and his Minneapolis Lakers ruled the basketball world in that time period, by building their offence around the strategy of getting Mikan the ball under the hoop.

Auerbach didn't subscribe to that mentality, not all

the way. From his earliest days in college, he had always recognized the potential of the fast break — **a technique that involves passing the ball ahead to a streaking guard, who can attack the basket before the defence has time to get set.** He implemented this strategy after drafting Bill Russell, a 6'11, extremely athletic player and matching him with Bob Cousy and later KC Jones, a fast, skilled passer. When a rebound was grabbed by Celtics on defence, primarily by Russell, he would quickly pass it to Cousy who by then was either moving quickly down court or who would then fire a long court length pass to a breaking Celtic player. Sometimes the pass would be directly down the court to Cousy himself, and sometimes it would be Cousy firing it down court to Russell. Either way, defences were not prepared for the speed of execution by the Celtics. The greatest dynasty in sports history was born. Between 1959 and 1966 that Celtics team won 8 straight NBA titles.

Anatoli Tarasov was a great innovator in hockey. As he was developing Soviet hockey, Tarasov believed in learning from other sports. Two of the sports he studied were soccer and basketball. Basketball had the Boston Celtic fast break tactic, and soccer had **the long ball**. This was a strategy where the ball is sent down the field quickly, usually with one long pass, hopefully on the foot of a fast or perhaps tall striker, catching the defensive team off guard for a quick shot or header. The Soviet hockey team used this strategy in hockey to launch lighting quick counter attacks that would catch their opponents unawares. They used this play whenever the opportunity presented itself and to great effect in the Summit Series.

Why was Canada unaware of this tactic? It goes back to Canadian arrogance before the Series. The information was out there for Team Canada to learn from, even locally in Canada. In the Globe and Mail an article was published by Hockey Canada's training consultant Canadian Lloyd Percival that broke down what he felt would be the Soviet Summit

Series strategies. Percival was also the author of the Hockey Handbook, a book Tarasov revered for its' forward-thinking hockey training strategies. In the Globe and Mail article, Percival remarked that:

"The Soviets would use their excellent passing to counter Canada's heavy forechecking by launching quick counter attacks from within their defensive zone, once puck possession is granted".

If Percival was not established enough in the Canadian hockey establishment to be taken seriously, Toronto Maple Leafs scouts John McLellan and Bob Davidson should have been. One of the takeaways from their pre-Summit Series scouting trip to the USSR was a warning about what they called "the surprise fast-break play."

"They make good use of the international rule that allows a player to take a pass from behind his blueline, across the redline as long as the puck precedes him. On one play Zimin stays out near the red line when the opposition is pressing and the puck goes to him very quickly. It's not a move they use all the time, but they pop it on you suddenly".

Team Canada should have been aware of the Soviet usage of this play before the Series but seemed oblivious of it. Coach Sinden should have also suspected the possibility of this play happening once the Soviets put Kharlamov and Mikhailov on the ice to penalty kill, but that didn't happen, and the Soviet Union were back in the hockey game with **another memorable Valeri Kharlamov goal.**

Goal 5: Valeri Kharlamov. Canada 3 USSR 2

The sequence begins as Valeri Kharlamov and Boris Mikhailov come out to replace Mishakov and Petrov as penalty killers. Canada moves the puck around the Soviet 4-man box formation. As they do this, the puck gets to the right point where Brad Park has it precariously, with Kharlamov attempting to strip it from him. Kharlamov knocks it off Park's stick from behind, as the Ranger defenseman attempted to pinch in with the puck. The puck goes behind the Soviet net, where Park makes a bold decision in chasing it. Yvan Cournoyer picks it up, and circles in front. Park follows him and is tied up by Luchenko. The puck scampers over to the right corner where Frank Mahovlich chases it but gets neatly tied up by Tysygankov against the boards. Boris Mikhailov comes in to help his teammate out and is able to get control of the puck. As all great players, Mikhailov had the ability to read opportunity and react. **He looks to his left and sets the fast break play into motion with a quick hard pass off the boards into the neutral zone.** Park has finally gone back to the blue line but is out of position allowing Kharlamov to pick the puck off the boards and race in on Tony Esposito.

Kharlamov is too fast for Park to catch. Brad does a desperate dive on his stomach reminiscent of Don Awrey's desperate ineffective dive on Kharlamov's first goal of the series. Kharlamov ignores the sliding Park and controls the puck on his forehand. Tony O comes out of his goal but gets surprised as Kharlamov does a fantastic quick deke pulling the puck to his backhand and sliding it past Esposito. If there were any doubters left about how good Valeri Kharlamov was and if his game one performance was a one hit wonder, they would now be silenced. **This was a beautifully orchestrated, textbook Soviet fast break goal**, showcasing the speed and athleticism of Valeri Kharlamov, as well as the flexible, aggressive penalty killing strategy the Soviets used.

From a Team Canada perspective this was a tough goal to give up. They were on the power play, looking to stretch their lead to three goals. That might be why Brad Park was overly ambitious in chasing the puck deep and then coming out front. Parks decision to chase the puck wasn't the main defensive lapse for Canada. It was his teammates who failed to cover up for Parks foray that allowed Kharlamov to break free. For example, once Park pinched deep why didn't

Cournoyer cover the point? The answer is that he too had been caught up in trying to score at the goalmouth scramble. On defence, seeing his defensive partner leaving the blue line to go deep into the Soviet end, **should have forced Pat Stapleton to move to the centre of the blue line area, closer to Kharlamov, as he was now the only defensive person left on the point.** Since Stapleton stayed in his standard spot near the boards on the blue line, he was too far from Kharlamov when Mikhailov made the fast break pass. On the chase, Stapleton also seemed to give up a bit on the play, perhaps not seeing Kharlamov's break down the wing as a real threat. Those glaring omissions led to this goal. Canada was dominating the game, but the Soviets were now only a goal behind.

With both sides at full strength, Clarke's line is out against Petrov, Yakushev and Mishakov, seemingly replacing Solodukhin. Stapleton remained out with his regular partner Bill White, while the Soviets have Gusev back out with his usual partner Team Captain Viktor Kuzkin. The play is a little sloppy for both teams. When Pat Stapleton tries to stickhandle through two Soviets at the Canadian blue line, the Winnipeg crowd starts to grumble in displeasure. They would soon have something to cheer about again as Manitoba product Bobby Clarke, with help from Bill White, sets up Paul Henderson for his second goal of the Series.

Goal 6: Paul Henderson. Team Canada 4 USSR 2

Bobby Clarke has always been one of hockey's most polarizing figures. Fans, historians, even other players have chastised Clarke for his on-ice actions and for being the leader of the notorious mid-70's Philadelphia Flyers, known as the Broad Street Bullies. Clarke's insensitive comments when he was in management alienated him from many in the hockey community. His slash in game six on Valeri Kharlamov has been seen as a terrible, unsportsmanlike moment in hockey history. Yet, despite all that, Bobby Clarke has garnered immense respect as one of hockey's greatest leaders. He was considered so valuable to those Flyers championship teams that he garnered three Hart Memorial trophies as the player deemed most valuable to his team in the NHL. As a player who suffered with Type 1 diabetes, he showed incredible perseverance in grinding out a Hall of Fame career.

What is undeniable about Clarke was that he was an excellent hockey player. One of the reasons for that was his playmaking ability. As a junior player with the Flin Flon Bombers, Clarke had an incredible 117 assists in 59 games. As captain of the two-time Stanley Cup champion Philadelphia Flyers, Clarke had three seasons with over 100 points and led the league in assists twice. He twice had his career high seasons of 89 assists which in 1974 was the NHL record for a centre. His linemates benefited from his exceptional ice vision, with Reggie Leach scoring 61 goals in the 1975-76 season and an incredible 19 goals in the Stanley Cup playoffs that same season, a record that stands today. Clarke's left-wing Bill Barber had 50 goals that year, a career high for him. While Barber and Leach were excellent hockey players, Bobby Clarke showed throughout his career that he simply made his linemates better. His linemates in 1972 on Team Canada, Paul Henderson and Ron Ellis were no exception. Clarke remembers the line chemistry in an interview with the Globe and Mail in 2012:

> "I was a good puck-chaser, a good passer. If you play that style of game, you've got to have somebody with you to finish and Henderson could do that.
> "Henderson could do that real good with his speed. It opened up the ice a lot more. The defencemen couldn't be standing [still] when he came down." Dave Shoalts Globe and Mail

Henderson had speed to burn, while Clarke had the vision to exploit that speed to Canada's benefit.

In International hockey in 1972, the neutral zone (between the blue lines) had three faceoff areas. These were the traditional centre ice faceoff dot, then two more dots in the middle of the ice, one near each blueline. The NHL had, and still does have, five neutral zone faceoff dots, two on the left, both close to the opposite blue line and the same on the right side. The centre ice dot was the same in both versions. When there was an offside, the faceoff would take place **in the middle of the ice, near the Soviet blueline**, which is where Clarke wins the draw over Petrov.

The puck goes back to Bill White who stickhandles while skating backwards in the Canadian zone. White makes a nice pass underneath Vladimir Petrov's stick to Bobby Clarke who is halfway between the Canadian blue line and the centre ice red line. Clarke gets control of the puck and skates a couple of strides towards the right boards and then unleashes a long backhand pass. Paul Henderson is in full flight on the left side of the ice, streaking just past the red line. In front of Clarke are the defensive pairing of Alexander Gusev and Viktor Kuzkin, both have turned around heading towards the Soviet zone with their backs to Clarke. Clarke's pass doesn't get all the way to Henderson, as it hits the turning Kuzkin in the skate, deflecting into the Soviet zone. Henderson is too fast for the Soviet veteran, beating him to the puck. Henderson is now all alone on Tretiak, and he fires a perfect wrist shot into the right bottom corner of the net.

The goal happens so fast, after a seeming lull in the play that Kuzkin, Gusev and Tretiak seem to be caught flat footed. Kuzkin doesn't recognize that the puck is behind him until it's too late. Henderson was one of the world's fastest skaters in 1972 so there was no chance Kuzkin was going to catch him once he had a step on the Soviet veteran. Tretiak comes out, but Henderson is on a slight angle and rifles the puck into the low bottom corner. He picks the low bottom corner so perfectly that Tretiak really couldn't be faulted. A heads up play by Bill White, then Bobby Clarke, a fortuitous bounce and great speed and execution by Paul Henderson all led to Canada's fourth and final goal in this game.

With the Soviets now down two goals halfway through the game, Bobrov changes his line-up strategy, instead of going back to his top line, **he goes in a different direction**. On the faceoff after the Henderson goal, the Soviets have the Anisin "Kid Line" out with Vasiliev and Shatalov, four players who didn't make the 1972 Soviet Olympic team, with Vasiliev the only one who participated in two games. **Whether this was a moment of inspired genius by the Soviet coaching staff, or a case where they wanted the younger players to get more experience, is unknown.** The Kid Line had several shifts so far in the game but have been ineffective. Whatever Bobrov's strategy had been putting them out again, certainly paid off.

Goal 7: Yuri Lebedev Canada 4 Soviet Union 3

Canada has a strong line-up on the ice with the Esposito line upfront and the Montreal Canadians duo of Savard and Lapointe on defence. Despite this, **the younger and smaller Soviet group outworks and outmuscles the Canadians,** leading to Lebedev's deflection goal.

The puck is deep in the Soviet end, but Shatalov gamely holds off big Phil Esposito, allowing the Soviets to break out quickly. Yuri Lebedev makes an outlet pass to his line mate Alexander Bodunov. This pass catches Wayne Cashman and Phil Esposito deep in the Soviet end as Bodunov races down the ice towards Savard and Lapointe. He bulls his way through the two Montreal defensemen, before falling near the Canadian goal. The puck goes into the corner, to the right of Tony Esposito, where Vyacheslav Anisin goes after the puck. He is pursued by both Serge Savard and Phil Esposito who has just skated the entire length of the ice to catch up to the play. Anisin's linemate Lebedev comes in to help. Esposito bumps Anisin into the boards **who does a twist to avoid the hit, similar to Maltsev on the first Soviet goal in game one**. Cashman gets involved but the Soviet youngsters out work the Canadian veterans and Anisin comes up with the puck kicking it to his stick. Anasin throws it to a wide-open Valeri Vasiliev on the point who takes a couple of strides towards the Canadian net and fires a long wrist shot. The front of the Canadian net is congested as both Lebedev and Bodunov are now battling with Canadian defensemen Savard and Lapointe. Lebedev gets his stick on the low shot from Vasiliev and deflects it into the bottom left corner of the Canadian net. The lack of visibility of the puck due to the scrum in front of him, combined with the direction change after the tip, totally handcuffs Tony Esposito.

This goal is a testament to the Soviet buzzing two-man forecheck. When they decide to attack the puck in the corners, their tenacity, balance and focus on puck retrieval rather than body contact, cause the Canadian players all sorts of issues. Phil Esposito and Wayne Cashman were significantly larger and more experienced than the young Soviet duo of Anisin and Lebedev, but they lose the puck battle. Were the Canadian veterans guilty of not taking the Soviet Kid Line seriously enough?

A moment earlier both Savard and Lapointe had difficulty stopping a determined Bodunov as he raced down the ice. Before the series began, Canada felt smug that **their size, aggression, and experience would be too much for the Soviets**, especially in hockey's dirty areas: the corners, the front of the nets. **That would prove to be another falsehood**, as the Soviets had prepared for this style of game, were very strong on their skates, and in better physical condition. The Esposito line was a combined 28 years older than the Anisin Kid Line who were all 21. They were caught off guard by the younger, hungrier line and learned two valuable lessons. The first lesson should have been **every single battle for the puck in this series needed to be taken very seriously**. The second lesson? **Every player on this Soviet team needed to be taken seriously**, even a line of 21-year-olds.

After the goal, both teams do a full-scale change. Ratelle is out centring Frank Mahovlich and Cournoyer against the Soviet stacked line of Maltsev, Kharlamov and Mikhailov. Right off the draw, Ratelle pulls down Kharlamov as he carries the puck. The official seems to not see a penalty, or perhaps sees embellishment, and the play continues. Ratelle gets possession and makes a beautiful flutter pass over Tsygankov's stick right onto the tap of a streaking Frank Mahovlich. The big M is all alone on Tretiak and attempts to pull him across his crease, but Tretiak reads the move and stops Mahovlich cold. The usually very clean Ratelle is certainly having a fiery shift, he hooks Tsygankov in the corner, the two tangle up with Ratelle getting a facewash from a stinky red Soviet glove for his troubles.   From the first moment of the series. the Canadians were shocked at the foul smell of the Soviet equipment.

Whether or not Harry Sinden senses that Team Canada is tiring is unknown, but he is changing lines quickly. The Clarke line comes out, still against the Maltsev trio. Brad Park is starting to show some decline in his game. He fails to clear the zone, resulting in the Soviets getting a good chance with Luchenko blasting a shot at Esposito after some quick Soviet passing. Of all the Canadian players who are struggling to adapt to the different game the Soviets play, Brad Park seems to have the most issues. **He is continually falling back onto his NHL style of stick handling the puck in his own zone,** with the result often being dangerous turnovers or sustained Soviet pressure.

An interesting note on the next sequence as Bill White does a textbook angled dump in, yet Kuzkin plays its quickly off the boards to Mishakov who hits Yakushev at centre ice in full flight. This was a play that flustered the Soviets in the first two games, and they seemed to have solved it with quick positional passing. The Soviet ability to adapt to Canadian strategies is another lesson Canada needs to learn quickly.

The Esposito line has a couple of chances after a bit of a Parise mugging on Kuzkin in the soviet end. Parise is everywhere and makes a nice dish to Esposito in the slot.

Viktor Kuzkin has recovered from being thrown to the ice by the tenacious Parise and gets his stick on a point-blank shot by Esposito. Parise is relentless every time he is on the ice, always moving, winning battles, making plays. Parise and Cashman are also backchecking hard, matching Henderson and Ellis as strong two-way wingers for Canada.

Canada changes again quickly as Ratelle Frank Mahovlich and Cournoyer are matched against the Soviet "Kid Line". The Soviets use Shatalov and Vasiliev on the points the same group that scored before. This was the first time in the series that Coach Bobrov created and went with a very effective 5-man unit, at least for this game.

Almost immediately the puck gets into the Canadian zone, where the Soviets have their own version of Parise's relentless style. **The Kid Line is weaving and skating and dropping passes to their awaiting linemates nonstop and everywhere**. They quickly have the Montreal Canadians duo of Lapointe and Savard on their heels, a very déjà-vu experience for team Canada and one that results in a second straight goal for the "Kid Line".

Goal 8: Alexander Bodunov Canada 4 Soviet Union 4

The World University Games, known as Universiade, were first held in conjunction with the Congress of the International Students' Federation (CIE) in Warsaw, Poland, in 1924. The Games have been held bi-annually since. The host sites have varied around the world, and the Games are seen an opportunity for students to compete and interchange ideas and experiences. Ice Hockey was added to the list of sports in 1962. The Soviet Union won the gold in 1966, 1968 and in 1972 in Lake Placid (no miracle to be had in 1972) but lost to Czechoslovakia in 1962 and 1970. Canada sent either their top University team or as was the case in 1972, a Canadian University All Star team.

The University games tournament in 1972 was not an overly competitive one as only three countries took part, Canada, the Soviet Union, and the host United States. American college hockey was not as competitive in 1972 as it would become in later years, and they lost all four games by fairly large margins. The Soviets won the tournament by going undefeated, with the only blemish a 4-4 tie with Canada. The victory was notable for the Soviets for one reason: **the play of Alexander Bodunov, Vyacheslav Anisin and Yuri Lebedev, who dominated the tournament**. The line had great synergy probably resulting from the fact that Lebedev had been on the same line with Anisin since they were 10 years old. The University games success earned them a place on the Soviet National Team for the upcoming Summit Series against the top Canadian professionals.

The line was unique in that all three had brief stints with CSKA as junior players but failed to stick with the famous Red Army Sports Club, and instead worked together as a line for Krylja Sovetov or the Soviet Wings as they were known in North America. Lebedev especially seemed to benefit from being a part of this trio, as in the 1971-72 season he only scored 5 goals in 32 Soviet Elite league games. His linemates were more productive however, with Anisin scoring 19 goals and Bodunov 18. Their selections onto the National Team for the Summit Series shouldn't be considered a surprise though, **as it was commonplace to slowly introduce younger players to high level competition, grooming them for future National Team success**. The trio also played domestically for the Wings of the Soviet in the Soviet Elite league for assistant coach Boris Kulagin.

The lines sudden emergence in game three certainly took Team Canada by surprise. Harry Sinden describes his recollection of the kid line, in which he gets the periods incorrect, but the shock is evident:

"The game was going well in Winnipeg until the third period. We were up 4-2 or something and they still hadn't played their fourth line. Well, they put out this fourth line

in the third – it was a bunch of kids – and they were all over us. It was like that last scene in Butch Cassidy and the Sundance Kid. And the Soviets ended up tying the game."
Patrick White Globe and Mail 2012

After the two quick goals, Harry Sinden admitted that it was the first time in the Series that he was concerned Canada wouldn't win.

"Who are these guys? They all seem to look the same, skate the same, shoot the same, and they keep coming at you the whole game with the same unchanging expression. The only thing difference was the number on their backs. It was like nothing we had ever seen before". Harry Sinden

While it would appear after these two goals that the "Kid Line" would be impactful in the Summit Series and these three 21-year-olds would be the future of the Soviet National Team, that wasn't the case. Yuri Lebedev would only play 3 games in the 1972 Summit and his goal in game 3 was his only one. He would have a long career in the Soviet Elite league playing 13 seasons for the Wings but never a star. His highest scoring season would be 22 goals in the 1973-74 season. He would be a semi-fixture on the National Team playing in the 1974 WHA Summit Series, the 1976 Canada Cup, the 1976 Super Series, six World Championships and the ill-fated 1980 Olympics. Lebedev was known as a solid technical player with a physical side. While he only played the three games, he felt the impact of going up against the physical defence of Team Canada:

"...the Series taught me an important lesson. Canadians like Gary Bergman and Bill White played a very tough game. As a result, they created a lot of free space around them. After the series, I tried to play tough all my career". Yuri Lebedev

Alexander Bodunov was known as a talented yet inconsistent player. Like his line mate Lebedev, Bodunov would only see action in three games in the Summit Series scoring the one goal. Bodunov was known for his booming slapshot, and for his lack of focus on the defensive side of the game. That inconsistency led to his limited time on the Soviet National Team. He did play in the 1973 and 1974 World Championships as well as the 1974 WHA Summit Series. Bodunov had trouble against the top professionals, scoring only one goal in the WHA series in 7 games. Bodunov reflected on his struggles in the 1972 Summit Series:

> "I was completely overwhelmed. I was too young to understand my role in a series that involved the greatest hockey players in the world. Still today, I find it hard to believe that I faced players like Brad Park and Guy Lapointe".

Bodunov did have a long career in the Soviet Elite League, playing 9 seasons for the Soviet Wings and another two for Moscow Spartak. He had a long coaching career in Russia, dying in 2017 at 66.

Vyacheslav Anisin is probably the best-known member of the "Kid Line". His last name reminded fans in North America of Anacin aspirin tablets, so the line was also given the dual meaning name **"The Headache Line".** A small, fast, talented centre, he played seven games in the Summit Series scoring 1 goal and 3 assists. Vyacheslav would go on to have the strongest career of the Kid line, **winning the Soviet scoring title** in the 1973-74 season with 48 points in 31 games. He would play on the National Team until the 1977 season where Victor Tikhonov took over and started making wholescale changes. This included the 1974 WHA Summit Series, and the 1976 NHL Super Series for the Wings. Anisin would continue to have a long and productive hockey career, with 5 seasons on Central Red Army after leaving the Wings, and two more for both Spartak and SKA Leningrad before finishing his 20-year hockey career in Italy. Anisin's children also grew up to be world class athletes as his daughter won Olympic gold in figure skating in 2002 and his son a hockey player in the Russian KHL league.

One of Anisin's fondest memories are of the Summit Series in 1972 and his comment shows his superior confidence in comparison to his linemates:

"It was my rookie season with the National Team. I was amazed by Phil Esposito, Ron Ellis and Pat Stapleton. I was proud that my size and speed could compete with them" Vyacheslav Anisin

The Soviet press of the time would agree with Anisin's effectiveness in the Series:

"This was Anisin's first test at the high level. He proved that small players could play with the big players". Dmitri Ryzhkov, The Soviet Sport

The Kid Line would have a short, memorable run in Soviet hockey. They heavily impacted game three in the 1972 Summit, but domestically **they took the Soviet Wings under coach Boris Kulagin to a surprise league title in 1974**. The line was awarded the top line in the league that season, aided by Anisin's career year. The line broke up for the 1976-77 season when Anisin transferred to the Central Red Army team.

The fourth goal of game three for the Soviet Union begins on a faceoff just outside the Canadian blueline, in the middle of the ice. Anasin wins the draw against Ratelle and fires the puck midway into the Canadian end to the left of Tony Esposito. Guy Lapointe gets the puck but lazily attempts to flip it out of the Canadian zone. The puck goes along the boards where Frank Mahovlich fails to obtain possession and loses the puck to the pinching defenseman Vasiliev, who throws it into the Canadian corner. Anasin out hustles Lapointe to the puck but rather than playing it, he leans into Lapointe and angles him away. This is a very clever play that Lebedev reads, probably from the years of familiarity playing together.

Lebedev picks up the loose puck and attempts to throw it to his linemate Bodunov who is in the slot area. Cournoyer intercepts the pass and clears it back towards the left side of the ice. Team Canada is now in a bit of panic mode. The usually composed Serge Savard (who plays the opposite side of Lapointe) is now turned around, as he goes after the puck on Lapointe's side. Frank Mahovlich also skates towards the puck, but both are beaten to it by the speedy energetic Anisin. The small Soviet centre has shrugged off the bigger Guy Lapointe and is now able to fire a quick pass to the wide open Bodunov. Bodunov, is in the high slot on Serge Savard's now vacant side of the ice. **Bodunov gets the puck and fires a quick wrist shot that beats Esposito.**

Team Canada is a mess on this goal. **They had breakdowns all over the defensive end.** It begins with the weak clearing out by Lapointe, the weak play along the boards by Mahovlich and continues deep into the Canadian corner. Here, Lapointe gets outmuscles by the much smaller Anisin, and Ratelle fails to cover Lebedev who has the opportunity to attempt a pass to his linemate in the slot. Yvan Cournoyer makes a good play in intercepting the Lebedev pass, but then either in panic or a moment of poor decision making, he bats it back over to the other side of the ice, possibly trying to get it to Frank Mahovlich. Yvan then goes for a big circling skate leaving Bodunov wide open. The Roadrunner needed to pick up the Soviet winger until Canada had control of the puck. The usually reliable Serge Savard also becomes guilty of leaving Bodunov open as he turns his back to the Soviet winger. By deciding to go after Cournoyer's odd clearing he attempt, Savard does the cardinal sin of defence, **he leaves the front of the net open.** Tony Esposito has little chance on the goal, Bodunov was known for his heavy shot and gets it away with a speed and accuracy that should have reminded Tony of all those years playing goaltender against his brother Phil, while growing up in Sault St. Marie, Ontario.

The Kid Line is playing the high tempo "pass and move" Soviet style in this sequence, again catching veteran, experienced, Canadian players seemingly unawares. Anisin especially needs to get full credit for his winning of the faceoff, putting it deep into Canada's end, outmuscling and outhustling Lapointe and finally making a solid pass to Bodunov for the fourth goal of this game. The kid line has now scored two lightening quick goals, overwhelming two different groups of experienced NHL stars.

Team Canada, your opponent has a plethora of weapons, strategies, and players.

Almost immediately after the goal, Canada's Bobby Clarke line gets the puck deep into the Soviet zone. The pressure effects the Soviet defence who start to panic. Luchenko makes a long clearing attempt that gets intercepted by Bergman at the Soviet blue line. The cagey Detroit Red Wing veteran then makes a beautiful backhand pass right onto Paul Henderson's stick who fires a great shot on Tretiak who makes an even greater save, keeping the score tied. Luchenko's partner this ship, Tsygankov spins, turns around behind the net and then carelessly throws the puck away directly to Ron Ellis. Tsygankov then does it again, a second bad clearance intercepted by Ellis.

Phil Esposito drives to the net off the faceoff, a clever play that fooled Alexander Maltsev in game two. Wayne Cashman is doing a great job cycling the puck, keeping the Soviets penned in their own end but is unable to get the puck to Esposito. As Gary Bergman accidentally falls with no one around him, to a chuckle from the Winnipeg crowd, the buzzer to end the second period goes off.

Game 3 Period 2 Summary

This was great hockey. An eventful, well played period. As the siren went to end the 2nd period in game 3, Foster Hewitt is heard accurately describing this period as a *"terrifically hard-fought period"*. This was a bang on description of one of the best periods of hockey in the 1972 Summit Series. Canada dominated play for much of the period, but Tretiak was able to prevent the game from getting away from the Soviets. He made saves on Frank Mahovlich and Phil Esposito when the score was 4-2 that would have broken the game open and possibly prevented the Soviet comeback in the period.

Canada was at its most successful when players such as Parise, Cashman, Ellis, and Clarke were forechecking aggressively. The Soviet defence had trouble with this; a good example the last 30 seconds of the period where Tsygankov threw the puck away twice under pressure. Canada spent a lot of energy but failed to put the pesky Soviets away.

On the other side, the Soviets continued the ability to counter strike from the Canadian pressure. While several of the long passes failed as Canada read them, **any momentary Canadian defensive sloppiness was punished by the opportunistic Soviets**. Kharlamov's shorthanded goal was a perfect example of this.

Overall, this was the period that would forever belong to Anisin, Lebedev and Bodunov, the Soviet Kid Line. Despite struggling in the first period against the Canadian professionals, Bobrov stuck with them, and together with sterling efforts from the new defence team of Vasiliev and Shatalov, the group of five struck for two key goals. This success from a previously unknown group rattled Team Canada, as they began realizing this would be a very long, hard series.

CHAPTER 31:
GAME 3 PERIOD 3:
EVENLY MATCHED

With the game tied, the teams must have felt the third period could decide the direction the series may take. A Canadian victory would give them momentum going into Vancouver and a Soviet victory, would be demoralizing for the Canadian team and country.

The Soviets start the powerful, so far underachieving, Maltsev line against the dogged Clarke line. Soviets also have their top pairing of Luchenko and Tsygankov out. The Canadians counter with their top pairing of Park and Bergman. Canada gets an early opportunity as Luchenko attempts to hit Ellis with a hip check at centre ice. The Leafs forward successfully avoids the hit, which takes Luchenko out of position, creating a 3 on 1 against Tsygankov. Showing their line chemistry, Ellis gives it to Clarke, who makes a delayed pass to Henderson, who fires a quick shot from the wing on Tretiak. Henderson could have passed to Ellis at the far post for an easy tap in, but as **Canada prone to do, they shot first instead of that final pass.** Ellis gets a second chance for Canada with a backhand in the slot, but Tretiak comes up strong on both chances. Kharlamov makes a nice rush, quickly changing direction on Brad Park, but fails to get a decent shot away on Esposito. Both teams change on the fly as Esposito's line comes out against Shadrin's, and the action speeds up with some good end to end play.

The sudden rise in intensity leads to the fiery Mishakov, who has replaced Solodukhin on the Shadrin line, tangling with Bill White. As they both get penalties, the game becomes 4 on 4. Soviets put out Petrov and Yakushev against Phil Esposito and big **Peter Mahovlich who despite his fine play so far in the series, has been sitting on the bench.** Yakushev does some good work using his large size to hold off Savard and Stapleton as he and Petrov cycle the puck deep. Canada seems to have lost some energy, with some bad habits from previous games start to re-emerge. Peter Mahovlich is the first to do so by firing a long-blocked slap shot from the Soviet blue line that is completely ineffective.

Mikhailov and Kharlamov are out against Mikita and Cournoyer. The Soviets put on a clinic getting the Canadians trapped in a four-man box with the Soviets moving the puck around quickly. The Canadians seem unfamiliar with 4 on 4 hockey, playing like they're shorthanded. This leads to Luchenko pinching in to make a nice pass to Boris Mikhailov who drills a shot wide on Esposito. Mikita gets control, does the angled dump in play which works this time as Canada recovers the puck and Guy Lapointe gets a point-blank shot at Tretiak. Whether Stan Mikita was injured in the earlier trip, his back was acting up or there was a fitness issue, he's not skating this shift. He coasts around looking disinterested. The coincidental penalties end without any further real chances for either side.

The game has become cautious, with both teams doing a lot of circling and slowing the play down, obviously afraid of giving up the go-ahead goal. Part of this might be because of the poor Winnipeg Arena ice which was getting slow and bumpy.

Valerie Vasiliev is having a good game on defence for the Soviets, but he makes a dangerous pass to Lebedev at the Soviet blueline that results in Paul Henderson delivering a solid, clean bodycheck on the Soviet youngster, knocking him down hard. The resulting turnover leads to some pressure by the Clarke line, and a great chance for Canada. Vasiliev tries to throw a hit at the blue line but misses and is caught out of position. The young Soviet blueliner is panicking now, retrieves the puck in the corner but blindly throws it behind the Soviet goal to a waiting Bobby Clarke. To create a hat trick of mistakes by Vasiliev, he doesn't bother to hustle to cover the slot area in front of Tretiak. As a result, **Clarke passes to a wide-open Paul Henderson who snaps a quick shot that he thinks has beaten Tretiak.** Henderson puts his arms up in celebration, but the Soviet goaltender has grabbed the puck with his catcher, to the disappointment of the Canadian crowd. **With the score tied. this was the most crucial save of the game so far.**

Canada dumps it back in, but Luchenko carries the puck quickly behind his own goal and headmans it to a streaking Maltsev. The Soviets are discovering that quick skating and puck movement can counter the dump in forecheck. Maltsev shows some blazing speed as he carries the puck into the Canadian zone and then unleashes a Canadian like long slap shot at Esposito that misses the net.

Luchenko makes a bad outlet pass to his partner Tysygankov at the Soviet blueline. Paul Henderson races in to steal the puck but is hooked by Tysygankov and unable to get a shot away. No call on the play. The pace of the game changes again with the Soviets picking up speed with their circling and passing but fail to penetrate the Canadian zone for any prolonged time. They just don't have any space in the neutral zone. Clogging up the neutral zone to minimize the Soviet passing schemes would be a very useful strategy over the years against the Soviets.

The Soviets finally penetrate the Canadian zone, but an errant pass is intercepted by Wayne Cashman. He makes a nice pass to Parise who is streaking up the left side. Cashman follows up, receives a drop pass from Parise in the high slot yet fires a high shot that misses the net. The Soviet Kid Line come out for their first shift of the third period matched up against Ratelle, Cournoyer and Frank Mahovlich. The game is still being bottled up in the neutral zone and despite both sides moving the puck quickly, neither team gets any sustained pressure. Guy Lapointe tries to rush the puck into the Soviet end but is jolted by Vasiliev with a clean hit at the Soviet blue line.

Maltsev gets a close in opportunity, the best Soviet chance in several minutes after two Canadian players collide at the blue line chasing the crafty Kharlamov. Kharlamov dances past them and lays a pass to an open Maltsev on the left side of Tony Esposito. Maltsev attempts to slide the puck through Esposito's stacked pads, and almost succeeds as the puck was trickling into the net before Brad Park is able to get to the puck in time and clear it. **This was a great chance for the Soviets that could have been the game winner.**

The game becomes more intense as the Soviets play more aggressive, forcing the play, perhaps sensing Canadian fitness is still lacking. Vasiliev knocks Parise down, recovering the puck, as the pair of Parise and Cashman have a rare ineffective forechecking shift. Boris Mikhailov gets hit by a Brad Park half hip check in the Canadian zone that knocks the feisty winger to the ice. With only a few seconds left in the first half of the third period, Jean Ratelle comes out with Cournoyer and Frank Mahovlich for a faceoff in the Canadian end. Coach Sinden obviously has little faith that Ratelle can win the draw, replacing him with Bobby Clarke. For whatever reason Sinden seems to have very little respect for the classy Ranger centre or his regular Ranger wingers who are watching in the stands. Clarke proves the Canadian coach right, winning the draw as Canada gets possession before the buzzer sounds for the ten-minute mark.

Ratelle is back out to start the second half. The puck goes into the Canadian zone, but Canada recovers. Pat Stapleton rushes the puck to mid-ice where he makes a quick no look pass to Yvan Cournoyer who gets called on the offside. Cournoyer would have more offsides than any other player in the series. Despite this line only being on the ice for twenty seconds, Sinden puts the very effective Esposito, Parise, Cashman line back out.

Yuri Shatalov gets the most impactful hit of the period in, when he decks Wayne Cashman at the Soviet blueline with a clean body check. Cashman retaliates with a two hander on Shatalov and then a few choice words for the referee. This lands him a 10 minute misconduct and a two-minute penalty for slashing. Canada would have no idea that this would be Cashman's last shift of the series. Stan Mikita, who has had very little ice time in this game, is called to serve the penalty.

Peter Mahovlich comes out with Phil Esposito as the penalty killers. Sinden seems to like these two as a Penalty killing duo. **Phil Esposito was never known as a defensive centre in the NHL but seems both comfortable and adapt at the role so far in the Series**. The Soviets, hoping to get a late goal that can steal this game, counter with their top line of Maltsev, Kharlamov and Mikhailov. Maltsev gets a good chance in front of Tony O, but his shot is deflected. In another odd faceoff spot, the official drops the puck between the two faceoff circles, ominously in the slot area in front of the Canadian goal. The only assumption that can be made from this is that the official decided the faceoff should take place where the presumed deflection of Maltsev's shot took place.

The Soviets mount some pressure. Boris Mikhailov easily goes around Brad Park who is a step too slow and flops to the ice as Mikhailov flies by. This allows the Soviets to set up the powerplay, and they go to work passing it around. Gary Bergman goes to slash Maltsev, a vicious strike that misses the Soviet player completely. As the puck goes to Tony Esposito, he makes two quick saves, then covers the puck up, getting a whistle. Brad Park continues his poor play by failing to get the puck out of the Canadian zone when he had the chance. This results in Tsygankov keeping the puck in at the Canadian blueline. The puck goes quickly over to Mikhailov on the right side who fires a quick, beautiful pass across the slot to Maltsev. **Maltsev goes wide on Esposito and slides it just across the Canadian goal mouth for the second close call for Canada.** With his partner flopping on the ice again, Gary Bergman is able to clear the puck out of the Canadian zone for a moment of relief. Serge Savard and Guy Lapointe come on to relieve the beleaguered duo of Park and Bergman.

The relief is short lived as the Soviets keep up the pressure. Kharlamov flies back into the Canadian zone with his dancing skating style, puts on the breaks and sets up the power play again. The Soviets continue to move the puck around Canada's box setup without any further chances, until Stan Mikita comes out of the box, energetically dives for the puck, and is able to poke it of his zone to Phil Esposito. Esposito has a clear angle to the net and gets a good shot away on Tretiak, who seems to have some trouble with the wrist shot from the wing. The Soviets roar back. Alexander Maltsev spins at the Canadian blue line but seems nervous about being hit and gives the puck away. Maltsev's apparent fear of being hit come to fruition as Guy Lapointe knocks him down. The puck goes the lighting fast Yvan Cournoyer who flies down the ice to a panicky, backpedalling Shatalov. Cournoyer speeds past him but Shatalov's partner Valeri Vasiliev is there to cover, preventing Cournoyer from getting a good shot away. The Soviets ice the puck relieving the sudden Canadian pressure.

On the ensuing faceoff, Jean Ratelle steals a trick from Phil Esposito by driving to the net off the draw. He is nearly successful, getting a good shot off on Tretiak. The Soviet Kid Line continues their high pace they set on previous shifts, rocketing down the ice with Bodunov showing his famed slap shot from just outside the Canadian blue line, its power rivalling any shot the Canadians had shown so far. Tony

Esposito cannot corral the shot, it goes to the dangerous Vyacheslav Anisin, but any further pressure is stifled as the Kid Line go offside. **At the end of this shift, Guy Lapointe is reported to be hurt. He would not play in game four.**

The ice has become almost unplayable, with a bad area behind the Canadian goal. The game takes a break while it gets repaired. Brian Conacher astutely mentions that the Canadian players probably need the break more than the Soviets.

The game returns to action, with both teams skating hard to try and break the tie. Another strange faceoff takes place above the Canadian Faceoff circle, perhaps because that was where Bill White froze the puck. Phil Esposito attempts a rush, but the dogged, defensive minded, Vladimir Petrov chases Espo, harassing him until the centre ice zone, causing a turnover. Mishakov is all over the ice on this shift as well, causing a turnover off big Peter Mahovlich who was out replacing Wayne Cashman in the Soviet corner, spinning and easily outskating Mahovlich up the ice, intercepting an Esposito pass and carrying it into the Canadian zone.

The Soviets have awakened, raising the pace of the game. Team captain Viktor Kuzkin spins and circles in centre ice, gaining speed before dishing it over to their star Valeri Kharlamov who continues his strong game with another foray into the Canadian zone. He speeds over the Canadian blueline, puts on the brakes, and makes a nice cross zone pass to Luchenko who drills a long hard slap shot at Tony O.

The Soviets seem to have much more energy in these final minutes of the game. Boris Mikhailov is skating well, and the Canadian defence seems to be tiring. Coach Sinden sends out Bobby Clarkes line against the top Soviet line, hoping to slow the Soviet pace down or perhaps match it with his fittest players. The strategy almost pays off as a fortuitous bounce through the neutral zone gets speedy Paul Henderson free on Tretiak. He roars into the Soviet zone ripping a high shot off Tretiak's shoulder. The Winnipeg crowd moans at a potential game winning opportunity lost.

Pat Stapleton has been one of Canada's better skaters all game. He is aggressively pinching on the play but has the speed and wherewithal to get back into position. He tries a single man foray into the Soviet zone. The Soviets are well aware that it's a tie game and are backchecking feverishly; as a result, Stapleton runs into **four Soviet players**.

As the final minute of the game ticks away, Canada has a spurt of energy with Esposito and Ellis leading a rush and Ron Ellis getting a dangerous shot from the wing on Tretiak. Parise almost gets the rebound in the crease but is unable to convert. The Soviets come roaring back, carrying the puck into the Canadian end, and Maltsev getting a decent backhand away on Tony O. Like his counterpart at the other end a moment earlier, **Tony Esposito makes a clutch save preserving the tie.** The game finishes with Bergman being taken down hard by Petrov, a penalty most likely would have been called if there weren't only a few seconds left in the game. The game ends in a 4-4 tie. Foster Hewitt sums it up as *"A fair appraisal of a tremendous game"*.

Game 3: Period 3 Analysis

This was the 9th period between these two teams. Familiarity was showing. **This was two evenly matched boxers, in the late rounds, cautious, weary, still wanting to win**. While the period had several good chances on both sides, it was a period that was played somewhat cautiously as neither team seemed willing to forecheck consistently or deeply and risk getting caught on a turnover. The Soviets rarely went to their two-man buzzing forecheck, instead patiently waiting for Canadian mistakes. Tony Esposito and Vladislav Tretiak both came up big when needed, although Canada was fortunate that two of the Soviet chances dribbled through the crease and a Canadian player was able to get it clear.

Canada did seem to tire a bit and almost took the

role of a counter puncher, a role in which the Soviets were masters. They broke quickly off some sustained Soviet pressure but lacked the finish to secure the game. The Soviets had some excellent passing plays around the stationary Canadian defensive zone coverage in this period but were unable to break through besides the two Maltsev chances.

Strong players in this period were Kharlamov and Mikhailov who were constant threats. Alexander Maltsev had chances to convert on those threats, while Valeri Vasiliev made his case for being in the Soviet line-up. He added a lacking physical element yet was mobile enough to help counter any Canadian rushes. For Canada, Phil Esposito continued his stellar play, **showing a work ethic unseen in his NHL career**. Bobby Clarke and JP Parise added the energy and forecheck, while Bill White, Gary Bergman and Pat Stapleton all helped keep the Soviets from scoring in the period.

Unknown at the time but the most impactful event may have been triggered by little regarded defenseman Yuri Shatalov. Shatalov played a very solid period, but his hit on Wayne Cashman led to Wayne Cashman's 10-minute misconduct. In a domino effect, this bodycheck would be a catalyst for some of Harry Sinden's poor line-up decisions in Game 4, **especially his decision to not play the extremely effective duo of Cashman and JP Parise.**

Game 3 Summary: A Forgotten Classic.

In many minds this was the game in the Series that was the most forgetful. The game lacked a pivotal moment, a standout player, a definitive winner. It was contested in a non-NHL city, at the time, in a small arena that lacked the NHL history of the Montreal Forum or Toronto's Maple Leaf Gardens. The main drama of this game was the great Bobby Hull sitting in the audience watching the game, denied the chance to play because he had signed a contract with the new World Hockey Association's Winnipeg Jets.

Yet, despite that, the game itself may have been the best played game of the Series. It was playoff hockey in September. Team Canada started out skating well, aggressive on the puck and at times overwhelming the Soviet defence. The Soviets played in spurts, at times skating hard, using their weaving two-man forecheck, but lacking the consistency to reverse Canadian momentum. As a result, Canada had the lead for most of the first two periods, twice with two goal leads. Tretiak was solid in goal when it counted, making several clutch saves, when Canada had the lead, that kept his team within striking range. **This was what Tretiak would do in the Canadian games, keep his team in the game when needed**. The game's turning point was the two quick goals the Soviet Kid Line scored that rattled Team Canada. The third period was a back-and-forth affair as both teams had chances to go ahead, but also played intense defensive hockey, fearful of a late game clinching strike.

Coach Bobrov's changes for this game paid off significantly. The Anisin/Lebedev/ Bodunov line added energy, hunger and synergy that seemed a bit lacking in game two. While intimidated at first by the level of play, they dominated the last two periods every time they were out. Much of that has to do with Vasiliev and Shatalov on defence, forming a young, aggressive 5-man unit. Despite the reputation, five-man units were not common in 1972 Soviet hockey. Shatalov had a significant hit on Wayne Cashman and Vasiliev was the best defenseman on either team throughout the game. He added a physical presence combined with excellent first passes out of his zone. This was a significant improvement over players like Gusev, Paladiev and Ragulin who were inconsistent in the first two game of the series. The other new player Solodukhin was less effective and as a result did not receive much ice time. **Without Zimin, the Shadrin/Yakushev line went quiet and were not the force there were in the first two games**. They finished a combined minus 2 in the game, obviously missing

Zimin, barely seeing any ice time in the third period. That continued into game four.

Soviet notables in the game were Yevgeni Mishakov who did a fantastic job penalty killing and playing dogged defensive hockey that would make Bob Gainey proud. Boris Mikhailov also stood out. Boris was starting to impact the series with his unique combination of skill and irritability. **Canada would have done well to note this before game four**. The star of the game for the Soviets was again Valeri Kharlamov. The uber fast, shifty Spanish Russian was flying all over the ice causing issues for Team Canada throughout the game. With every shift, Kharlamov was proving he was the real deal for the Soviets. Vladimir Petrov scored an important shorthanded goal off the brutal Frank Mahovlich giveaway. He also played very strong defensively, backchecking hard and helping his defence time and time again. Despite the large task of going against Phil Esposito, **Petrov was proving to be a very solid contributor for the Soviets.**

Harry Sinden seemed satisfied with the result, although he obviously would have preferred a win. His adding Jean Ratelle certainly paid off as the smooth New York Ranger forward wasn't played that much. yet scored a goal and combined well with Yvan Cournoyer. Phil Esposito was starting to emerge as **the dominant player in the Series**, and his linemates Parise and Cashman continued the strong game two play. The Soviets struggled to find an answer to the relentless forceful forechecking of Parise and Cashman.

After a very strong game two, and a hard-fought game three, there were some signs that **the Canadian team was beginning to wear down.** Serge Savard and Guy Lapointe struggled a bit on defence as they were on for both goals against in the second period. Frank Mahovlich was starting to look completely lost, skating hard, but without focus, his game all over the place. **His powerplay give away to Petrov was as shocking to see as it was devastating to Team**

Canada's momentum. The slow game-by-game decline of the Big M was both surprising and sad to see for the well revered Canadian legend. It would get worse in game four. Brad Park also continued to struggle. Whether he was affected from the probable training camp concussion, or the stress of his wife just given birth, he was having some significant issues with the Soviet speed on the outside. His flopping to the ice during those moments left his team vulnerable. While he would make some strong contributions to the offence, he also continued to over stickhandle the puck, leading to turnovers, often in the neutral zone. Like Mahovlich, it was a bit disconcerting to see one of the NHL's best defensemen play poor defence and appear out of sorts.

What was the impact of this third game of the Series? On the Soviet side, it was a solid comeback after game two, a game where they were outmuscled and outplayed. This game also demonstrated to Team Canada that the Soviet team had more weapons than Kharlamov. **They had youth, depth, and surprises in store**. That alone was probably the biggest awakening for Team Canada, who must have felt that the tie was like a loss.

After game two, the Canadian public had to be relieved, as many were probably convinced game one was a bit of a fluke and Canada would still go on to dominate the series. Game three proved that was obviously not going to be the case after the Soviets came back twice from two goal deficits. They were able to match Team Canada across the board, in talent, in speed, in goaltending, and with unexpected depth. **Canada was in a dogfight.**

Canada's Ron Ellis sums up Game 3 in Winnipeg,

"For me, the most crucial game for maybe the whole series was the Winnipeg game. We had a 4-2 lead with two minutes left in the second period and the Russians scored a couple of quick goals to tie it. If we'd won that game, I think we'd have gone into Vancouver with a whole different mindset. Because it ended in a tie, the Russians felt strongly

they could beat us in Vancouver, and they'd have the Series won" Ron Ellis; The Hockey News August 29, 2012

Three games had been played in Canada, and the public's emotions had been on a roller coaster. Game one while seemingly a rout, had actually been very even until the last seven minutes of the third period where terrible Canadian bench management, weak goaltending and superior Soviet skill and fitness, in a hot stifling arena all contributed to the Canadian collapse. While Canada turned in a playoff like performance in game two, they met their match in game three. **The one thing the game in Winnipeg showed fans and media in both countries, was that these two teams were very evenly matched.**

Who would blink first? That would be determined in Vancouver.

PART 7: A BEAR WITH A STICK:

HOCKEY IN THE USSR

CHAPTER 32:
POLITICS, PLANE CRASHES AND DICTATORS

As Harry Sinden would say after the game three's tie in Winnipeg, "Who were these guys?"

It was a fair question. Canada had a long history against countries like Sweden and the Czechs, but the Soviets were somewhat of a mystery. Why? As far as embracing the sport of hockey, the Soviet Union was late to the party. By the time Canadian style hockey was introduced into the USSR, Canada had been playing the sport at high levels since the 1800's. By the 1930's into the late 1940's, other countries such as Sweden, Germany and the Czechs had also built semi-solid hockey programs. The Russians were late to the game, but they would certainly catch up and surpass their European counterparts quickly.

During that time period when Europe was developing the game of hockey, the former country of Russia had gone through two world wars, civil wars, before ushering in a new form of government, Communism. The adaption of Communism led to the formation of the USSR (Union of Soviet Socialist Republics); as a result, the country of Russia no longer existed at this time, nor did it exist in 1972. **Canada was not actually versus Russia; it was Canada versus the**

USSR or the Soviets, an amalgamation of countries where the former Russia was the major one.

Due to the turmoil of revolution and world wars, adoption of the game of hockey didn't take place until after the end of World War II. The Second World War was devastating on the USSR; the government was looking at several ways to rebuild both the country and the moral of the people. The Soviet government also had long term goals, wanting to show the world the superiority of their communist system. **Sports would be one of those avenues to showcase that superiority**. As a result, the USSR and their satellite nations such as East Germany would quickly grow to become one of the world's strongest athletic powers, excelling in many sports, dominating both the Summer and Winter Olympics.

In 1945, **Nikolai Romanov** became chairman of the All-Union Committee for Physical Culture and Sports, the governmental body overseeing sports in the Soviet Union. His vision was the Soviet Union should demonstrate its strength, unity, and success of its athletes and systems by taking part in the Olympic Games. His belief was that the international appeal of the Olympic Games would be the ideal stage for Soviet athletes. Their anticipated success would demonstrate that their system of government led to athletic superiority, **bringing glory to their home country**, an argument that tied in with how the Soviet leadership under Stalin had come to view international sports during the 1930's.

It didn't come to pass: the traditional Communist stance after the effectives of the long, hard World War II was to reaffirm Communist ideals. **That led to a surprising rejection of the Olympic games plan.** This rejection from ideologically motived opposition against Romanov's plan would delay the Soviet entry to the Olympics until 1952. However, one of the steps taken in 1945 couldn't be undone: the introduction of Canadian hockey to Russia. In fact, hockey had been shown to several Soviet sports officials during a tour of England by the soccer club FC Dynamo Moscow. 1972 Summit Series coach Vsevolod Bobrov was the star of the touring Soviet Soccer team, and after watching the British hockey exhibition, he began his lifelong love affair with the game of hockey.

Despite the internal opposition, Romanov continued to press. He gave **Sergei Savin**, the head of the soccer and hockey department of the All-Union Committee for Physical Culture, the task of studying the Olympic Winter Games. When Savin handed in his report, he emphasized that a game called Canadian hockey was "in the centre of the public attention" at the Winter Games. Having studied the report, Romanov gave out the directive: *"This Canadian hockey must be put on Russian tracks immediately."*

The sport of bandy had been played for years in the USSR. Played on a frozen soccer field, with a ball, the sport required great skating abilities and team play. The game itself had been imported from England into Russia in 1898. It was as an easy transition as many Russians had enjoyed skating outdoors and using a stick and a ball to play games including the Tsar, Alexander I, since the mid-1860's. By 1908, there were already more than a dozen bandy teams in Moscow. Regular tournaments were contested between the teams in Moscow and St. Petersburg, later Petrograd and Leningrad) which continued intermittently until 1941; the last game was played January 22, 1941. In February 1914, the Russian Bandy Union, which united 34 clubs from 6 cities, was established. By this time there were leagues in place in Riga and Revel (Tallinn). Tournaments were held in Novgorod and Vladivostok ("AI Egon Cup"). In 1915, the first women's tournament was held in Russia. It was also decided to hold the first All-Russian Championship in the 1914-15 season, plans interrupted by World War I.

While bandy was very popular, Russian bandy players were soon introduced into the Canadian game of ice hockey.

In 1932, a German trade union team had visited Moscow and demonstrated how the game with the puck was played. They played three exhibition games against Soviet bandy players. The Soviet athletes took to the game easily, using their skating abilities to surprise the Germans. The games had been well received and popular. The State Central Institute of Physical Culture in Moscow then started lectures on the strange, exciting sport of Canadian hockey. Among those who had attended those lectures was **Anatoli Tarasov.** While the theory and descriptions of Canadian hockey were available, what was missing in Moscow in 1945 was an updated list of rules and strategies.

The Soviets turned again to Sergei Savin, who found a resource in Latvian hockey player **Edgars Klāvs**. In Latvia, hockey had been played since the early 1930's. While they weren't a world power, they did understand the game, competing at the highest amateur levels. Klāvs, who had been a member of the Latvian National Team at the 1937 and 1938 World Championships, invited Savin to the Latvian capital, Riga.

The meeting in Riga was crucial, as Savin recalls:

"Once I was accommodated in my hotel, Klāvs brought me a hockey stick, gloves, skates and several pucks. The next day I was shown footage of a pre-war newsreel where some moments of the Latvian championship and several international matches were captured. And two days before my departure, Edgars gave me the dearest present – he brought the rules of Canadian hockey, translated from Latvian to Russian. Believe me, there is nothing I have ever treated as carefully as those few sheets, written in the neat handwriting of Klāvs."

Savin took everything to Moscow and called a meeting to present his findings to the sports clubs and governing bodies. Leading coaches and bandy players, including Pavel Korotkov of the Army club (CDKA) and future National Team coach **Arkady Chernyshev** of Dynamo Moscow, learned about the potential of this new game, including potential strengthening of Soviet international relationships with other hockey playing nations. **They would have no way to envision the 1972 Summit Series would be a result of those broad international ties.**

Among the students at the State Central Institute of Physical Culture, two teams were formed to prepare them for a public demonstration game: The students trained for five months, learning the new game, adapting the bandy skillset to hockey. The public demonstration game took place outside on February 17, 1946, at Moscow's Petrovsky Park. It would take place following a bandy match between CDKA (later CSKA) and Dynamo Moscow. Videos of the game show players wearing long baggy dress pants with tight winter hats, playing in heavy work shirts with workers gloves. They had not yet acquired any hockey equipment or padding.

"Sovietsky Sport", the main sports newspaper, reported in descriptive shock at the odd spectacle:

''The match between Dinamo and CDKA has ended, but thousands of spectators remain. Their attention is attracted by a small goal, like in water polo. The small field is surrounded by boards. On the field there is a referee with a 'police whistle' and there are two teams – one red and one white – with six players per side. On the back of the players there are numbers and, in their hands, unusual sticks – long, light, with a long hook at an almost right angle. On the ice there is a solid black rubber 'disc', heavy and gliding over the ice with lightning speed. This is a demonstration match held by students of the Institute of Physical Culture. In Europe and North America, Canadian hockey is very popular. Without a doubt, it can be developed in the Soviet Union as well. ''

The Central Army group was also learning hockey. Led by **Pavel Korotkov,** guided by **Anatoli Tarasov**, they visited Sverdlovsk in February 1946, where they staged another public demonstration of "Canadian hockey" for the local audience. Much like the first exhibition, this one took place after the scheduled bandy game.

The Soviet Armed Forces went one step further: in March 1946, the northern city of Archangelsk hosted their first tournament in Canadian hockey. CSKA prevailed over two other teams from Army divisions that had picked up the game. **Mirroring what took place in major hockey cities such as Montreal, Winnipeg, and Toronto in the later 1880's, the sport of hockey became quickly popular in Moscow and beyond.** After the experiments and exhibitions during the 1945-46 season, the first Soviet championship in Canadian hockey was announced for the 1946-47 season. The All-Union Committee for Physical Culture and Sports called for the bandy clubs to enter teams for the new sport.

Nikolai Romanov's goal was becoming fulfilled. **Canadian hockey was quickly embraced by the USSR on its way to usurping bandy as the winter ice game of choice.** The game reached the highest level of authority as **Soviet leader Joseph Stalin's** son **Visily Stalin** developed the Air Force team, known as VVS Moscow, using Anatoli Tarasov as the player coach. The Air Force team would be very successful in the first few years of the Soviet league, winning the Soviet championships in 1951,1952 and 1953. While Tarasov was the star the first year, leading the league in goals, he would clash with Visily Stalin. This resulted in his only playing one season for VVS and instead joining CSDA (CSKA), the Red Army club. Stalin was very passionate about his team, however, and soon after was able to get the top line from Moscow Dynamo to join his squad. While the Dynamo line certainly strengthened the VVS club, it was the emergence of the two stars of early Soviet hockey, **Viktor Shuvalov** and **Vsevolod Bobrov** that turned VVS into a dynasty. While those players would lead the team to three championships, **VVS would suffer one of the worst tragedies in all sport.**

On January 7, 1950, as the VVS team was on the way

to Chelyabinsk, the airplane crashed in Yekaterinburg, then Sverdlovsk. The entire team died as explained by historian Pawel Pomroski:

> "The weather made landing impossible, and plane was redirected to near Sverdlovsk. Visibility was so unclear that pilots made five unsuccessful landing attempts before they smashed into the ground during the sixth one."

After the crash, Visily Stalin was terrified to tell his volatile father. He ensured the team completed the game but with additional players using the deceased players sweaters. The crash was somewhat covered up and the players were put into a mass grave. Pomroski describes the terrible deception:

> "Vasily was afraid of his father's possible wrath and decided to keep tragic news in secret, so there was no sign of it in newspapers. Also families had no information what happened that day. Corpses were as mutilated as hard to identify, so gov't service buried them in a mass grave near crash site. It was known that Joseph Stalin had no knowledge about the crash and further Vasily's roster moves. And it was some horror-like expansion draft. VVS had still two days to play game at Chelyabinsk, so to avoid people's or Stalin Sr.'s suspicions Vasily completed the team with... players who have the same last names as deceased ones. Also, he ordered the press to publish Moscow team line combinations or scorers only with last names, unless scorers are Bobrov, Vinogradov, Shuvalov. Yuriy Zhiburtovich was replaced by his brother Pavel, and in the press he was just Zhiburtovich with no first name. Alexander Moiseev was replaced by non-related player with the same last name. The other players were also replaced by new players, but each time when some of them scored, official press didn't mention his name and credited a goal to notable players. The Moscow team won 8:3 and returned to the capital city."

The surviving players, Viktor Shuvalov and Vsevolod Bobrov, survived because they never took the flight. Bobrov, the team's biggest star who often acted like it, overslept, and took the train instead. Shuvalov was injured. Shuvalov led the league with 31 goals, and Bobrov placed second with 29 that season, but the VVS team never recovered and finished fourth. The team rebounded, perhaps motivated by the loss of their teammates to become the first great Soviet Club team. However, after the death of Joseph Stalin in 1953, Vasily was arrested and judged an enemy of the state. He would live the rest of his life in seclusion and alcoholism before dying aged 40 in 1962. **His beloved VVS team merged with CSDA, forming one of the greatest club teams in any sport: The CSKA or Central Red Army club.**

CHAPTER 33:
TARASOV, PERCIVAL AND BOBROV: SOWING THE SEEDS

Anatoli Tarasov is often called the Father of Soviet hockey. He had the greatest impact on the Soviet style of play, training methodologies and strategies. The master was a player first. In the late 1940's he was still playing hockey at a high level. When Tarasov left the VSS club after clashing with Visily Stalin, Tarasov joined the Army hockey club as playing coach. This allowed for his being mentored by **Mikhail Tovarovsky**, a former soccer player who worked in the State Central Lenin Order Institute of Physical Culture as an instructor.

Tarasov attended classes at the institute, forming a relationship with Tovarovsky. When the two discussed the growing sport of hockey, Tovarovsky gave some guidance to Tarasov that was, unbeknownst to both, about to change the face of hockey forever. He instructed his disciple to not copy the Canadian style of hockey, but instead **create a new style of play. A unique style of play, a Soviet style**. When Tarasov wanted to attend the 1948 Winter Olympics, Tovarovsky talked him out of it, explaining that seeing other countries playing the game would only influence his coaching methodologies, potentially stifling improvisation.

1948 was the year where the Soviet hockey program would play its first real opponents. **It was also the first ever true international hockey series involving a team from the Soviet Union**. The Soviets invited the best club team in Europe, **LTC Prague**, to come to Moscow and play three exhibitions against the best players from the newly formed Soviet Hockey league. The LTC Prague team was coached by Canadian Mike Buckna, the Canadian who was instrumental in developing hockey in Czechoslovakia. With most of the National Team together on the club team, they possessed a very strong line up. **Vladimir Zabrodsky** was the leader of the LTC Prague team, and probably the best player in Europe. Zabrodsky was the captain of the World Champion Czechoslovakian National Team. Canada didn't participate in the 1947 Worlds, but the Czechoslovakians were certainly the best hockey playing country in Europe at that time and his defending Spengler Cup Champion LTC Prague club. He would light up the 1947 World Championships with 29 goals in 7 games. A year later at the 1948 Olympics, the Czech star would score 21 goals in 8 games. The Soviets had never faced a player of this calibre or a team of this calibre in their short hockey history. While the Soviets were gracious hosts, they were adamant about learning the nuances of the game from the Czech team, including measuring, and taking samples of all the equipment they wore. As reported by the International Ice Hockey Federation:

"The hosts welcomed the Czechoslovak team with Russian hospitality. And when the hockey players were at a banquet, several people entered their dressing room, copied and photographed protective equipment, which was not produced in the USSR at that time."

The Czech team was stunned by the calibre of their hosts. The Soviets were already great skaters and had used their bandy backgrounds to pick up the game of hockey almost instantly. The Soviets won the first game 6-3, lost the second 5-3 and played a 2-2 draw in the last game. This shocking result would be a precursor to the 1954 World Championships when the entire hockey world would be shocked at the sudden capability of the Soviet team. **The series of games would be the benchmark for the Soviet hockey level.** They now knew where they stood against the best in Europe. As a result, the next six years would be ones of organized development for Soviet hockey, improving rapidly. Ironically, while they were developing a new brand of hockey away from copying the Canadian style, part of their template was based on the teachings of an unknown, disrespected Canadian.

Lloyd Percival was a Canadian sportsman, a finalist in the 1929 Canadian junior tennis championship, a noted cricket player and coached junior hockey in the Toronto area. His focus on technique in tennis led him to research other sports, learning about diet, interval training and the benefits of multi-sport participation. He had a semi successful career teaching Canadian athletes' better ways to train and approach their sport. Some of the top athletes he helped were PGA Tour golfer George Knutson, boxer George Chuvalo and figure skater Sandra Bezic. In hockey, Percival worked with the Detroit Red Wings in 1950, with top players Gordie Howe and Terry Sawchuk feeling they benefitted from Percival's training programs. Concepts such as weight training, cross-training, massage, homeopathic medicine, and diet were decades ahead of its time. The NHL and Canadian hockey establishment **was less than supportive of Percival's ideas** and even borderline hostile at times. When Percival produced his booklet How to Train for Hockey, Hap Day, then coach of the Leafs, called it *"a lot of bunkum — the good parts are stuff he heard from NHL coaches."*

Percival spoke to McLeans Magazine in 1964 about the NHL mindset:

"NHL players are the most primitively coached and trained of all major athletes, and since 1932 I've been offering to

*show the Smythes and more recently Imlach how to improve
their players' performance by twenty percent or more. They
have always turned me down. When Imlach took over
as coach-manager we had a long talk about my training
and conditioning methods, and he seemed excited about
the idea of bringing the physiology of hockey out of the
nineteen- twenties and in to the nineteen-sixties. But I just
never heard from him again."*

Percival published "The Hockey Handbook " in 1951.
This book was largely ignored by the NHL. It wasn't the case
in Europe however, as the book made its way to Sweden.
Legend has it that Tarasov was given a copy of the book,
as he attended some exhibitions in Sweden or perhaps
received the book from someone in the Czechoslovakian
hockey establishment. While it appears to be a mystery how
Tarasov came into possession of the book, it was certainly
immediately impactful in shaping European hockey in
the 1950s. **Swedish coaches had looked at the book as
the first authoritative, analytical treatment of hockey
fundamentals.** They started to base some of their training
regimes on the principles Percival described. Tarasov loved
the book. He had hundreds of copies translated into Russian
and imported into the USSR. Tarasov, wrote to Percival
stating,

*"Your wonderful book which introduced us to the mysteries
of Canadian hockey, I have read like a schoolboy."*

Tarasov agreed with Percival's principles of fitness
and skill development; however, he brought his own beliefs
into his coaching and development that were not directly
lifted from the Hockey Handbook. Tarasov believed that the
future of ice hockey would be reliant upon firstly enhancing
skill development, starting with the youngest players. He
was a huge proponent of fitness, feeling that through fitness
and strength came success. Finally, he believed in importing
tactics from other sports, including chess. This would give
his teams a variety of skills, strength, and strategies to deal

with any opponent. To enhance the skill development of his athletes, Tarasov would shrink the area of the ice and create small area games for his athletes to perform. The aim of such games was to educate athletes how to play in tight spaces and how to protect the puck so they would be prepared for increased body and stick checking at higher levels of ice hockey. Much of these drills are used in some formation today, as coaches implement tight space 'battle "drills.

One of the unique, for that time, yet greatest attributes of Tarasov-coached ice hockey teams in the middle of the 20th century was the **focus on puck possession**, which was undoubtedly influenced by his background in soccer. Tarasov wanted his teams to gain the blueline or entrance to the offensive zone using creative puck handling techniques and passing. This was a very different from the "dump and chase" style of zone entry used by North American-coached teams. It was almost a throwback technique to the late 1920's NHL where forward passing was not allowed. As a result, players would pass laterally, or circle back into the neutral zone to regroup.

Tarasov incorporated "box-out" drills he borrowed from sports such as basketball and handball to teach his players how to prevent the opposition from penetrating the centre of the ice in the defensive zone. Tarasov also integrated exercises from different sports such as gymnastics, weightlifting, and track to improve the physical preparation of his athletes. This integrated athletic approached was directly lifted from the Hockey Handbook.
The results began to speak for themselves. The game became deeply ingrained in the culture and mindset of the military superpower. Hockey in the USSR had significant growth during the 1950's, especially at the grass roots level. That growth and the resulting development would increase significantly with the first major victory for the new Soviet National Team. The 1954 World Hockey Championships.

The Soviets had plans to enter the 1953 World

Championships, but an injury to star Vsevolod Bobrov and internal bickering prevented an entry. When they arrived in Stockholm on February 26th, 1954, the existing hockey nations were unsure what to expect. The Soviets were unknowns, without the historical track records of the Swedes, Czechs and especially the Canadians. Canada of course was the favourite, as they were every year, but that year's entry was not a team that was considered a topflight team in Canada. The East York Lyndhurst's were a Senior B team, not the usual Allan Cup winners or top Senior A squad. That didn't stop the Lyndhursts from being undefeated in the tournament leading up to the final game. The Soviets had an easy time in their first games, easily defeating Finland, Norway, and West Germany before a matchup with the Czechs. This led to a surprising 5-2 victory over the always strong Czechoslovakian squad. The Soviets had now given notice that they were for real. A 1-1 Soviet tie with Sweden set up a final match with Canada for the gold medal.

The Soviets would truly shock the hockey world with an easy 7-2 victory over the Canadian squad. This was a watershed moment for Soviet hockey: They now knew they could not only compete with the rest of the hockey playing world, **they could win.**

Despite a World Championships finals loss in 1955 to the physical Canadian representatives, the Penticton Vees, the Soviets learned from that game and came to the 1956 Olympics with one goal, to win the Gold. As a result, the 1956 Winter Olympics in Cortina D'Ampezzo Italy was an even more notable win for the developing Soviet hockey program. Canada had sent a strong Senior A representative in the 1955 Allen Cup winning Kitchener Waterloo Dutchman. **A victory against a top Canadian team and an Olympic gold would be a powerful testament to Soviet hockey development and the resulting Soviet sports propaganda both internally and externally.**

With Tarasov's preparation behind the scenes and

head coach Arkady Chernyshev motivation his players, the Soviets had a perfect tournament. The Soviets won every game including a hard fought 2-0 win over the Dutchman in the gold medal match. Star player Bobrov would lead those Olympics in goals with 9 in 7 games, showing his best forward award in the 1954 World Championships was not a one-time fluke.

Vsevolod Bobrov was much more than the Soviet coach in the 1972 Summit Series. **He was also one of the greatest athletes in Russian sports history**. A star soccer player with CSKA Moscow, VVS and Spartak. He scored 97 goals in 116 games with those clubs. He would also play internationally with the Soviet Union, leading the 1952 Olympics in scoring with 5 goals. He also joined Dynamo Moscow for a tour in 1945 against top English clubs, scoring six goals on the tour. This was also where Vsevolod first saw the game of hockey being played, and he was instantly drawn to the sport. With his natural athletic ability and bandy background, Bobrov quickly became a top player in the developing Soviet hockey program. He had good size, was extremely strong, and an expert at driving to the net to score. A soviet combination of Rocket Richard and Phil Esposito, he was known to be more of an individual player than the pass first team concept his former teammate Tarasov would implement. He was the go-to player on the first Soviet teams to play internationally to the point that the offence often depended solely on Bobrov scoring. As a result, one of the key turning points in the 1955 World Championship final Penticton Vee 5-0 victory was a devastating bodycheck by Vee defender Hal Tarala on Bobrov that somersaulted him across the ice, rendering him less effective afterwards.

Unfortunately, age combined with knee problems limited Bobrov's hockey and soccer careers. He would finish his hockey playing career in 1957, with an incredible 91 goals in 57 Soviet Elite league game. Retiring as a playing coach, he would focus on coaching and sport development, both hockey and soccer in the USSR for the next 20 years, culminating in his being chosen the coach for the 1972 Summit Series. **As a former great individual player, one of the first changes Bobrov instigated with the 1972 Soviet team, was more freedom for individual play. He wanted them to play more like he did.**

After winning the gold medal in 1956, the Soviets would go through the period from 1957-1962 of frustration, experimentation, and progress, culminating in the first of nine straight World Championship titles in 1963. Starting in 1957, the Soviet program had some developments, losses, and travel. This was a year in which the western countries boycotted the World Championships in Moscow, as a protest to the Soviet invasion of Hungary, The World Tournament went ahead, with Sweden winning the gold. What was significant about that tournament was the attendance. The final game was played outdoors at a soccer stadium with a record 55,000 people attending. **This was the largest audience for a hockey game until 2010, showcasing the popularity of the sport in the USSR.**

The Soviets would come to Canada later in 1957, playing seven games against Senior Teams and junior squads from Ontario and Quebec. They would have a 5-2-1 record, losing the first game at Maple Leaf Gardens against the Whitby Dunlops 7-2. While the Soviets were great skaters, they were still learning the other aspects of the game. They used these exhibition games against Canadian competition to test themselves, to see what needed to be worked on, to learn. The Soviet coaches also took in NHL games and remarked that while the calibre of hockey was high, their team already skated better than the NHL.

Having seen the NHL play, the Soviets continued the path of developing their own unique game, not a copy of the Canadian game. Anatoli Tarasov was leading that development, especially as he took over as head coach of the Soviet National Team in 1958. The success of the Soviet hockey program seemed to stagnate during this period as they would lose the next two World Championships to strong Canadian Senior A clubs, the Whitby Dunlops in 1958 and the Belleville McFarlands in 1959. While these Canadian clubs were loaded with ex professionals, the Soviets were able to give them close games losing 4-2 to Whitby and 3-1 for Belleville. They would also lose the 1960 Olympics in Squaw Valley California to the Americans and the 1961 World Championships to another Canadian Senior A representative, the Trail Smoke Eaters. The Soviets would skip the 1962 World Championship played in Colorado.

While this period would seem to not be very successful, the Soviet hockey program was improving steadily under Tarasov and Chernyshev. The players at the National Team level were training daily, but with a lack of indoor ice, much of the training became dryland or in a gym. Daily dryland exercises focusing on footwork, stickwork, strength conditioning and cardiovascular conditioning. On ice, teamwork became a huge focus combined with heavily regimented discipline. **This was the Tarasov way, discipline, fitness, and teamwork were essential to success.** On the ice the focus became on constant movement and passing. Repetition was key as players would do the same drills over and over. While skating, edging and balance were vital, the key element was passing. There were few stationary passes. Players learned to pass where the player was going to be, instead of where he was at that moment. **Over and over and over the players would learn this new unique system of hockey, until it became second nature**.

Still, despite all the new advances and training, the Soviets didn't win, not to the desired level. This period for the Soviet National Team could be seen as a similar period to the great NHL dynasties where the team went through a growth period, a period where losses in key matches while hurtful at the moment, ended up being the key to learning how to win. The New York Islanders of the late 1970's had a period of underachieving, with several years of being knocked out of the playoffs. This culminated in the 1979 semi-final upset loss to cross town rivals the New York Rangers. The Islanders would win the next 19 series en route to four straight Stanley Cups. The 1980's Edmonton Oilers dynasty also underachieved losing to the Los Angeles Kings in 1982 in the Miracle on Manchester, then losing in the final the next season to the battle-hardened New York Islanders. After that the Oilers would go to win five Stanley cups in seven years. Those teams were learning to win, learning what it took to be great, as were the Soviets of this era.

CHAPTER 34:
SEEING STARS, ITS
A RED WORLD

Domestically, the sport of hockey was growing exponentially in the Soviet Union with thousands of boys playing the game on outdoor rinks and ponds. A national youth tournament called **The Golden Puck** tournament was developed, allowing for competition throughout the nation. This tournament is still played today and run by Tarasov's grandson. Sports clubs across the nation would recruit the best young players from as young as age 11 and start them on the development path. This explosion in participants across the vast nation would lead to the recruitment and development of the great future star players that would help the Soviets completely dominate international hockey in the 1960's and beyond.

The Soviets, from 1957-1963, had several very good players who excelled on the world stage. **Konstatin Lokev** was a small fast forward who led the 1957 World Championships in scoring. He would become a fixture on the Soviet National Team until 1966, ending with 48 goals in 56 games at the World Championships and the Olympics. An earlier version of Valeri Kharlamov, he was 5'7, so relied on his speed and cleverness to succeed. Lokev was also part of one of the most dominant lines in Soviet hockey history, combining with **Veniamin Aleksandrov** and **Aleksandr Almetov** to form a formidable offensive trio.

Aleksandr Almetov was the centre on the line. He was unique, being born in Kiev Ukraine. His family moved to Moscow when he was young to an area of the city that allowed him to frequently watch the Moscow Dynamo team practice and play. The young boy became enamoured with Dynamo star player Vsevolod Bobrov. As a result, Aleksandr started playing youth hockey, imitating Bobrov, until he was noticed by the Central Red Army club, where he would play his entire career. He was solidly built at 5'10 and 190 pounds, a good skater and excellent goal scorer. He would lead the Soviet Elite league in goals in 1964 with 40 goals. He was a stalwart on the National Team, playing with them until 1967, scoring 75 goals in 107 games. Unfortunately, Almetov's story did not have a happy ending. In 1967 Almetov was dropped from the CSKA Army club because of his extensive drinking. They also felt he had a lack of discipline and would undermine the strict Tarasov authority. At the young age of 27, Almetov was finished as a player and retired from hockey. He tried his hand at coaching with the CSKA junior team, but his drinking problems continued. Hockey great Aleksandr Almetov **ended up working as a gravedigger** in the Vagankovsky Cemetery in Moscow, dying of pneumonia at 51.

The star of the line, the most noteworthy Soviet player of that era was **Veniamin Aleksandrov**. A slick, clean player, Aleksandrov was known for his elegant game and masterful stickhandling. He developed from an individualistic player early in his career to a strong proponent of Tarasov's team concept. Tarasov would advise young Red Army CSKA young players to try to play like Aleksandrov:

> *"Play Aleksandrovian hockey, which meant playing purely, with ease, without apparent constraint"*
> www.hockeyarchives.info/register/
> AleksandrovVeniamin

Veniamin was the first Soviet player that the NHL showed interest in. During the 1957 Canadian tour by the Moscow Selects, the Chicago Black Hawks put him on their negotiation list. After the 1959 World Championships the Toronto Maple Leafs also showed interest but neither team was able to make any headway with the Soviet authorities. Aleksandrov would play 400 games in the Soviet league, scoring 351 goals. In 1962-63 playing for CSKA, he would set the Soviet league record for goals in a season with 53. He also played on the Soviet national squad from 1956-1968, scoring 119 goals in 161 games. Despite his elegant on ice manner, Veniamin wasn't without controversy as he was arrested in 1961 for drunk driving after hitting a woman who was leaving a movie theatre. Aleksandrov was given some leniency as a star athlete and the father of a young boy, avoiding jail time, but was suspended from hockey for 8 months. **That same son would grow up to marry the daughter of Vsevolod Bobrov, forming a marriage of hockey royalty.**

Aleksandrov's long career gave him the flexibility to be allowed to coach in Bulgaria for three years before coming back to coach SKA Leningrad in 1974. He finished his coaching career as an assistant coach on the Central Red Army team in 1975 and 1976 including the eventful Super Series 1976 games against NHL teams.

Despite having these great players, the Soviet National Team struggled to consistently win the World Championships, nor could they defeat the top Canadian Senior A Clubs. While they were very good, they seemed stuck at a Senior A, lower North American minor pro level; they had tied the Eastern Hockey Leagues Philadelphia Ramblers 3-3 in a 1959 exhibition. Tarasov's training was still being developed during these years and they lacked the depth of world class players to take that training program to the next level. **That wouldn't last.** It would all change with the arrival of stalwarts Viktor Kuzkin, Alexander Ragulin,

Vitali Davydov, Vyacheslav Starshinov and one of the world's best players in the 1960's, **Anatoli Firsov.**

While much was made before the start of the 1972 Summit Series about Bobby Hull not being able to play for Team Canada, an even greater loss for Team Canada would be Bobby Orr not being fit to play in any of the games. Succeeding theories would be discussed by historians and hockey enthusiasts about whether Canada would have had an easier time defeating the Soviets with those two players in the line-up. One aspect of that discussion that rarely comes up is how would the Soviets have done if **Davydov and Firsov** had participated? **How good were these two veteran stars in 1972 and who were they?**

Vitali Davydov was one of those boys who got noticed by one of the Moscow Sports clubs while he played shinny hockey with friends. Vitali was a small boy whose father died during World War II. His family lived in Moscow near the rink where the Moscow Dynamo club played. Davydov was noticed one day during a shinny game by coach Ilya Bizykov. Young Vitali would be invited to skate with the youth team the next day. Vitali would progress through the Dynamo age groups, playing forward using his skating ability to make up for his small stature. His success led to him being noticed by Dynamo coach, long-time National Team coach Arkady Chernyshev who moved Davydov back to play defence to replace an injured player. He would excel in this role for the rest of his career.

Despite standing only 5'8, Davydov was a tough defender. He was nicknamed the "little tank" and often played through injuries after battling much bigger players. He once played against Canada with a broken jaw. Davydov had been knocked by Canadian Roger Bourbonnais, breaking his jaw. Despite this, Vitali jumped back into the play, stripping Bourbonnais of the puck. He would finish the game before collapsing and going the hospital afterwards. Coach Anatoli Tarsov described the incident,

"In our National Team, there have always been smart and fighting hockey players. But they were once amazed by the feat – I'm not afraid to use this word – of the defender Vitaly Davydov." Tarasov continued. "It was in the United States, in the state of Colorado, where we met with the Canadian team. In the second period, the Bourbonnais centre, seeing that he could not honestly win a one-on-one fight against Davydov, struck him with a stick. Like an axe, holding with two hands, struck. And there was a blow to Vitaliy's lower jaw. Our defender fell, but when he saw that the Canadian picked up the puck, one rushed to the gate of the USSR National Team, jumped up and, pressing his left hand to his bloody face, rushed after him.   Then the unexpected happened, even for us coaches who had seen a lot. Vitaly caught up with the Canadian, knocked the puck out of him and deflected the threat. Vitaly still had enough strength to rise from the ice. He was already being carried to the side by his comrades. And when they gave me a ride, Vitaly lost consciousness. The hospital diagnosed Vitaliy's lower jaw was broken in eight places. What willpower did you need to have to, despite the hellish pain, rush not to the doctors, but to help your goalkeeper. "

Davydov would play his entire career with Moscow Dynamo, captaining the team while winning numerous best defenceman awards, but never won a league championship. He made up for that on the Soviet National Team, winning three Olympic gold medals and nine World Championships. He would win the best defenceman award at the 1967 World Championships and was a six-time Soviet League all-star. After retirement, Vitali would go on to be a respected youth coach, before being allowed to coach in Hungary in the 1970's. He would return to Moscow to coach his beloved Moscow Dynamo squad.

Noted Soviet hockey historian Artur Chidlovski had this to say about Vitali Davydov

"In my opinion, Vitaly Davydov was one of the best

defenseman in the history of Soviet hockey. In the pre-1972 Summit Series era, he is in a top 3-10 blueliners list. Size wise, Davydov was a tiny defenseman. Paired with Alexander Ragulin, they looked almost comical but... Lack of size, Davydov compensated with his smart play - very precise, great read of the game and discipline. He was one of the first to use shot blocking with his body. One of the best captains of the teams to be found. Highly respected by teammates and coaches.

Despite his great career and being a major part of the National Team's success in the 1960's, Davydov was left off the Summit Series roster. The reported issue was a torn hip muscle. **It was more likely his long-time association with deposed coach Chernyshev that resulted in his roster omission**. At 33, it was unlikely Davydov would have had a major impact on the Summit Series; with his wonderful skating ability he may have provided a puck moving resource from the back end that could have helped the Soviets alleviate the strong forechecking issues the aggressive Canadian forwards caused.

While Vitaly Davydov was an important part of the Soviet dominance in the 1960's, it was Anatoli Firsov who was the key player. Like many Soviet players of that era, Anatoli's father was killed in World War II. His family was poor and, as a result, Anatoli couldn't afford to play hockey. He made a stick cut from a tree and tied blades onto his boots as skates so he could play bandy with his friends. Despite the primitive equipment, Anatoli was a gifted athlete who decided he wanted to commit full time to hockey in his teens. These humble beginnings allowed Firsov to show the tenacity and devotion required to catch up to the other boys who had been playing since they were little. This drive, coupled with his natural athleticism led to Anatoli becoming one of the best young talents in Moscow.

Firsov would become the prize pupil of Tarasov, joining the Red Army club as a young skinny boy, quickly embracing Tarasov's teachings and focus on physical fitness. Tarasov soon found his match in the fanatical Firsov, who dove into the extreme regimen with eager glee, often surpassing the exercises and changing them to make them even more difficult. On the ice Anatoli became a whirlwind of movement, jumping over defenders, quickly moving laterally, firing shots from all angles. He improved rapidly until he was promoted to the National Team. Soviet hockey had previously never seen anything like Firsov; he became an offensive weapon that intimidated opponents as the Soviet National Team became the dominant team internationally. Summit Series interpreter Igor Kuperman had this to say about Firsov:

> *"Three things made him better than everyone else. He invented the stick-to-skate-to-stick move and made it look like he lost control; he had a lethal slap shot that bent goalies' knees at a time when few goalies wore masks and he had amazing stickhandling skills. He was a fanatic about hockey and practiced without stopping."*
> **-- Igor Kuperman**

Firsov would hit his prime in the 1966 season where he led the Soviet League in both goals and points. He would go from there to be named the top scorer and goal scorer at the World Championships between 1967 and 1971. This would give him best forward honours at the championships in 1967, 1968 and 1971. Marshall Johnson who had a long career working in the NHL, was a player captain on the Canadian National Team that played in the 1964 and 1968 Olympics. In 1968, as Firsov would set an Olympic record with 12 goals, Johnson would proclaim years later that

> *"Firsov might have been the best player he ever saw"*.

Firsov's exploits became the stuff of legend throughout the 1960's. He once scored on a slap shot from the centre red line as he was changing shifts. He called it his goal from the cosmos. In 1964 Firsov scored six goals in a 10-1 rout against the Canadian National Team. Opponents found him impossible to stop, as the Soviet National Team racked up nine straight World Championships and three straight Olympic gold medals. He was extremely versatile, playing all three forward positions and being named to the World Championships tournament all-star team at both left and right wing. He became the face of Soviet hockey, stoic, incredibly driven and immensely talented. Future Soviet star Viacheslav Fetisov had this to say about Firsov.

"He was a legend. A couple of generations of kids grew up wanting to play hockey because of Firsov and what he did on the ice. He was electrifying. His shot was unstoppable. All the tricks he did on the ice are unrepeatable."

As the Soviets named their line-up for the 1972 Summit Series, observers were shocked to see that Firsov was not on the active roster. Said to be injured, it was much more likely **he was omitted for his unwavering support for his long-time coach and mentor Anatoli Tarasov**. Firsov and the long-time coach were forever linked together.

How would Firsov have done in the Summit Series? Probably extremely well. His game was very strong, he was the leading scorer at the 1971 World Championships where he was named the top forward. While he was at the end of his career, he was 31 and fanatical about his fitness. He would have given the Soviets another weapon at forward, especially on the smaller Canadian ice **where his quickness and athleticism would have been a factor.** While Soviet hockey fans were unable to see Bobby Hull or Bobby Orr perform, North American fans missed out on seeing one of the great Soviet players of all time. It's impossible to determine the outcome of the games had Firsov played. However, one thing is for certain; Anatoli Firsov's presence would have been a valuable addition to the Summit Series and another star for Canadian fans to celebrate.

The start of Soviet hockey dominance can be traced to the 1963 World Championships. The Soviets won the tournament with one loss to Sweden, but more impactfully they only had Alexander Ragulin as a tournament all-star, without another player winning an individual award, a testament to their developing focus on team play. At the 1964 Olympics, the Soviets continued to dominate, winning all seven games, with Konstatin Lokev beating out Swedish legends Sven Tumba (Tumba Johannson) and Ulf Sterner for the scoring title. Anatoli Tarasov was so confident of his National Team in 1964 **that he asked Muzz Patrick, the General Manager of the New York Rangers, for an exhibition game.** Patrick declined, thinking that maybe Tarasov was not serious. He felt that the Rangers, despite being one of the weaker teams in **the NHL, would win easily**.

The next two World Championships in 1965 and 1966 would continue the Soviet unbeaten streak as they would win both titles undefeated. Only a 3-3 tie with Sweden would blemish their record. Loktev, Alemtov, Starshinov, Ragulin and Alexandrov would be all stars in these tournaments. With three straight victories, the Soviets had cemented their status as the best in international hockey.

The 1967 season would be a memorable one for the Soviet Union as they found the Canadian National Team to be a much stronger challenger than in previous years. The National Team had excellent goaltending in 1961 World Championship winner former Trail Smoke-Eater Seth Martin. He was joined by one of the NHL's best defenceman Carl Brewer. Following a system similar to the Soviet collective, Father David Bauer had been training the young Canadian National Team as a group for several years, and with the addition of Brewer, they had become a much more difficult opponent for the Soviets.

The Soviets would lose the Centennial Cup in Winnipeg that winter and would have to face the Canadian team again in the 1967 World Championships in Austria. Both teams were undefeated heading into the quarterfinals. For the first time since 1963, the Soviets looked vulnerable as Canada took a 1-0 lead into the first intermission. Anatoli

Firsov would score from a long floating shot that goalie Seth Martin lost sight of in the second period to tie it up. Unfortunately for Canada, Carl Brewer was injured by a stick in the eye in the second, only returning late in the third period. Throughout his career Vyacheslav Starshinov was an excellent goal scorer. He did it again for the Soviets in this game, banging in a Boris Mayorov rebound for the winning goal. **The Soviet undefeated streak continued as they won their fifth straight world title.**

Carl Brewer would not be eligible for the 1968 Olympics for Canada. The Soviets had little trouble with the Canadian entry, defeating them 5-0 to win a second straight gold medal. The Soviets were seemingly unbeatable at this point. The Olympic top four scorers would all be Soviets, with Firsov dominating the tournament with 12 goals in only 7 games. **Tarasov would declare that his team could beat any team in the world, including the Stanley Cup Champion Montreal Canadians**. He boasted they were unbeatable.

They soon found that they were not unbeatable. An old adversary, the Czechoslovakian National Team, would beat the Soviets in the tournament, a hard fought 5-4 win. The Czechs would lose to Canada and tie Sweden though, giving the Soviets the gold. This would not be the last time the Czechs would cause the Soviet National Team issues.

By this point the Soviet team was a team in transition, with the old guard of Lokev, Aleksandrov and Almetov no longer on the team. With hundreds of thousands of youths taking up the sport since the 1950's meant there were a new generation of stars. **A generation that was about to change the face of Soviet hockey forever.** As that changing of the guard in Soviet hockey was happening, a greater political crisis was taking place in Czechoslovakia that would further paint the USSR as an aggressive and oppressive state. If the western hockey playing nations didn't see the Soviets as an evil empire pre-1968, they did after August 1968.

CHAPTER 35: CZECHOSLOVAKIAN HOCKEY RIOTS AND THE SOVIET NEXT GENERATION

From January until August, 1968, Soviet-controlled Czechoslovakia enjoyed new freedoms under the new leader Alexander Dubcek. Dubcek pushed for the removal of some state control which led to greater freedom of arts, press, culture, and speech. This period in 1968 became known as **the Prague Spring**. This was unacceptable to the ruling Soviet government in Moscow. They felt Czechoslovakia's freedom undermined their socialist agenda and reputation worldwide. During the night of 20 August, around 200,000 troops and 2,000 tanks entered Czechoslovakia from four Warsaw Pact countries (the Soviet Union, Bulgaria, Poland, and Hungary), and occupied the country. Dubcek was ousted and the Prague Spring was halted.

Hockey wise, the Czechoslovakians saw the Soviets as the enemy. The occupation helped solidify the reputation of Soviet hockey players as cold robotic communists. The fact they were seemingly unbeatable in world competitions, coupled with their oppressive cold war government, made them the enemy ideologically and on the ice. **Especially for the Czechoslovakians**.

The 1969 World Hockey Championships, originally to be held in Prague, with the invasion were moved to Sweden. The extremely motivated Czechoslovakian National Team would produce two of the most memorable wins in international hockey history.

On March 21st, 1969, the Czechoslovakian National Team outplayed, out hustled, out skated the Soviet National Team, defeating them 2-0. As this was the first World Championships that allowed hitting in all three zones, the Czechs played physical and aggressive. Future star of the 1976 Canada cup Vladmir Dzurilla shut out a Soviet team that had many of the players who would play in the Summit Series. On March 28th, they did it again, this time with **a grinding 4-3 victory**. Foreshadowing the events in Moscow during the Summit Series, the unbeatable Soviets had been defeated twice by the same team within a week. Defeated by a very motivated group of players who were defending their country in their own manner. Defending their way of living against an oppressive opponent. **This would be the original War on Ice**.

The Czechoslovakian players would refuse to shake the hands of the Soviet players. They would wear black tape over their country's logo, symbolizing the Soviet oppression. Historian Jan Kalous recalls how the players formed a unique sign of protest:

> *"Some hockey players put black tape over the red star of the Czechoslovak state symbol on their jerseys. In the end, the entire team refused to shake hands with their Soviet opponents. The trainer Pitner, at a press conference, apologised ironically saying normally the losers do congratulate the winners."*

After the March 28th victory, an estimated half a million people took to the streets. In Prague and elsewhere, gatherings quickly turned into anti-Soviet protests. With the celebration lasted two nights, the Soviets had military forces in the squares. Eventually, protestors confronted some of the Soviet military units. The office of Soviet airline Aeroflot was ransacked. **For the first real time in hockey history, hockey games were the background and catalyst for political action.**

Unfortunately for the Czechoslovak team, they couldn't maintain the same level of motivation against Sweden, losing to them twice, 2-0 and 1-0. This would cause a three-way tie for first place with Sweden, the Soviets and the Czechoslovakians. The Soviets would win their seventh straight title on goal differential. The Canadian National Team with Ken Dryden in goal would fare poorly, finishing in 4th place, their only victories over the US and Finland.

While the Soviets would go home with another championship, the Czechoslovakian players and people would look at the 1969 World Championship as a significant moral victory. These were the first championships to allow hitting in all three zones. Previously hitting had only been allowed in the defensive zones. This would change European hockey forever, preparing them for the much more physical North American game that they would encounter a few short years later. Alan Eagleson attended the 1969 World Championships, with the goal of getting a buy in from the major European hockey nations to either allow professionals to play in the World Championships or organize a round robin tournament of three or four countries against the best Canadian players, a prelude to the 1976 Canada Cup. He was unsuccessful getting an audience with the Soviets.

The Czechoslovakian team would remain a thorn in the side for the Soviet National Team for the next ten years, upsetting them at the 1972 and 1976 World Championships. Czech player **Jaromir Jagr would be known by number 68**, which he wore to always remember the occupation.

The Soviet National Team looked quite different in 1969 than it had ever looked before. A wealth of riches had bestowed the Soviet hockey program. Young players, fast, skilled, and exciting had been dominating the Soviet league. As a result, the greatest group of young players in Soviet hockey history were now entrenched on the National Team. On defence Vladimir Luchenko had made the national squad in 1967. He would not give up a roster spot for 13 years. His Summit Series teammate Yevgeny Paladiev joined him in 1968 adding to the veteran nucleus of Davydov, Ragulin and Kuzkin. Yuri Lyapkin would join the team in 1968, with Summit Series workhorse Yevgeny Tsygankov making his debut in 1971.

Upfront, the Soviets had an abundance of new stars. Alexander Yakushev, Vladimir Petrov, Yegeny Zimin, Yevgeny Mishakov and Vladmir Vikulov all now had roster spots, at least periodically, on the national squad. They were joined by probably the best young forwards in the world in 1969, Alexander Maltsev, Boris Mikhailov and a small, immensely talented Russian of mixed Spanish background named Valeri Kharlamov. **This would like a modern-day NHL team getting 10 first round draft picks, with several being talented enough to be first overall picks.** The hockey growth in Soviet Union from the 1950's through the 1960's had produced a group of players that would dominate the hockey world for the next ten years.

This group combined with aging superstars Firsov, Starshinov and Davydov to form a team that had grown up playing the Tarasov inspired brand of Soviet hockey. The majority had already played with Tarasov or been developed through the Central Red Army program. This would allow them to use their considerable skills of skating, puck control, passing in a group setting, a team first concept, forming a disciplined, fit, group of uber talented forwards that overwhelmed teams offensively. They had a strong, steady group of defenders who played positionally very textbook defensive hockey and were able to headman the puck to the swirling forwards with devastating regularity and efficiency.

The Soviets felt they had all the parts. It was why Tarasov would proclaim his team the best in the world in 1968. However, Tarasov knew, and the other soviet hockey coaches knew there was a gap. **What was required was a goaltender**. On Canadian tours they had seen the great NHL goalies, Terry Sawchuk, Glenn Hall. They had faced Gump Worsley and the goalie they considered the best of them all, Jacques Plante. They had been awed by the brilliance of Seth Martin. They needed a Soviet goalie who could match the greatness of the Canadian goalies. They found him in a very young, tall, rangy, extremely athletic, handsome young man named **Vladislav Tretiak.**

On December 3rd, 1969, a skinny 17-year-old made his debut at the Moscow Izvestia tournament against Finland. A 5-1 win was the first in a legendary career for Vladislav Tretiak. The Soviets had previously had efficient goalies, smaller, capable of winning, but not able to be considered the backbone of the team. Tretiak was all that and more. He was tall with lightning quick reflexes. An excellent skater, athletic with excellent positional awareness, confident, driven, and competitive, he possessed the focus and discipline needed to succeed in the authoritative Tarasov environment. This was proven by the countless hours he would put in to develop his weaknesses, including his glove hand. He had the necessary drive. He was the potential missing link.

Tretiak would go on to have a Hall of Fame career, shocking the Canadian hockey world with his superlative play in the Canadian games. He would continue to frustrate his Canadian opponents with performances in the famous New Year's Eve game against the Montreal Canadians in 1976 and winning the 1981 Canada Cup MVP award. He would win best goaltender at the World Championships four times and from 1971 -1984 Tretiak would be on the Soviet League All-star team every single year. A testament to his consistency, if not a statement of the lack of Soviet elite goaltenders as well, he would also win the League MVP award an unprecedented five times.

Vladislav wasn't without his off days. Like all goaltenders Tretiak did have moments of less than great play. The young Tretiak would end up losing the last three games of the Summit Series, lose to a powerful Canada Cup team in a must win game at the 1976 Canada Cup, lose to the Philadelphia Flyers in the 1976 Super Series and would be infamously pulled after the first period in the 1980 Miracle on Ice game, a move coach Viktor Tikhonov would later regret. Those blips are more testaments to the great opponents he faced, opponents who were motivated to win. The reality is, the Soviets had no idea on December 3rd, 1969, that 17-year-old Vladislav Tretiak would become not only the greatest goaltender in Soviet hockey history, but the most famous player of the great Soviet squads.

The first Soviet player inducted into the Hockey Hall of Fame.

As Tretiak matured and solidified his spot on the Soviet National Team, the team went through a transition period for Soviet hockey. The 1970 World "helmet mandatory" Championships were originally to be held in Winnipeg and Montreal. Canada was to be allowed to use seven non-NHL professionals. However, when Canada pulled out of international hockey due to the debate over using professional players, the tournament was moved to Sweden. The Soviets struggled to beat perennial weak sister Finland 2-1. The improved Finns would also upset the Czechoslovakian team 5-3. A few one-sided victories against East Germany and Poland would seemingly get the Soviets back on track as they then avenged the 1969 losses to Czechoslovakia with a hard fought 3-1 victory. Shockingly, to the delight of the Stockholm crowd, the Soviets then lost to Sweden 4-2. The Czechoslovakian loss to Finland, coupled with a tie against Sweden would give the Soviets another world title, their eighth in a row. This tournament was Alexander Maltsev's coming out party. He led the tournament in scoring with 15 goals and 21 points, getting named the top forward as a result. Veteran Anatoli Firsov would show he was still a forced to be reckoned with by coming third in tournament scoring and being named to the tournament all-star team. Vladislav Tretiak at 18 was not yet the starter, with goalie Viktor Kovalenko making the tournament all-star team.

The absence of Canada, while certainly a hit for the IIHF financially as Canada was always a great draw, would not have been a concern for the Soviets. After the Carl Brewer/Seth Martin led Canadian National Team almost defeated the Soviets at the 1967 World Championships, **the Canadian National Team was no longer a threat**. From that game in 1967, until the disbanding of the National Team program in 1970, the Soviets had a record against the National Team of **20 wins, 4 losses and 1 tie**. They outscored the Canadians 133-61. This was an average of over 5 goals a game. It should also be noted that three of those Canadian victories came at the end of the Soviet/Canadian tour in 1969, the same time the Gilbert Perreault led Montreal Junior Canadians defeated an exhausted, young, Soviet group. The Soviets looked at the Czechoslovakians as the only real threat in international hockey. The possibility of matching their skills with the mythical professionals of the NHL seemed like a fantasy. The NHL certainly didn't view them as a threat.

Despite the new Soviet amalgamation of talent, the North American hockey world barely noticed. The one-sided blowouts over second tier nations such as Poland and East Germany at the World Championships seemed to make the tournament non-competitive and a lower level of hockey to the few north American hockey 'experts" who even took notice. Father David Bauer's Canadian National Team was not considered NHL level, so as the Soviets began to dominate them in exhibition tours, they only seemed to notice the Canadian victories and other blips in the Soviet armour such as the Montreal Jr Canadians defeating them at end of a very long Canadian tour. **If they could lose to a National Team full of amateurs, or a bunch of juniors, how could they possibly claim to be world champions?** The NHL arrogance continued oblivious to the more than legitimate challenge the Soviets presented.

The Soviets would win their 9th straight World Championships in the spring of 1971, but a disturbing pattern was starting to show. In the 1970-71 season, as Phil Esposito tore the NHL apart with 76 goals and 152 points, something new and disturbing was happening to the vaunted big red machine across the ocean. The Soviets, perennial winners of the World Championships and Olympics, kept losing to the highly motivated, highly talented Czechoslovakians.

On December 9th, 1970, at the Izvestia Tournament in Moscow, the Czechoslovakians would defeat the Soviets 3-1. Things wouldn't be better for the Soviets a week later as the two teams would travel to Pardubice, Czechoslovakia. A heated exhibition game resulted in a sound 5-2 thumping over the Soviets. The Soviets would rebound with a 6-0 victory two days later in Ostrava, Czechoslovakia, but the tone had been set. The Soviets wisely avoided any more games versus the Czechoslovakians until the 1971 World Championships in Bern, Switzerland. In the tournament as the Soviets went for their 9th straight title, they tied their rivals 3-3. However, in a rematch on April 1st, 1971, they got beaten again 5-2. **This led to a less than stellar one win in five games in 1971 against the Czechoslovakians.** While the Soviets still won the World Championship, the Czechoslovakians seemed to have **a singular focus** and it wasn't winning the Worlds: it was defeating their oppressors from the hated USSR.

Until the rise of Soviet hockey, the Czechoslovakians had traditionally been the strongest hockey playing nation in Europe. A small country geographically and in population, they always produced strong teams internationally. Their National Team would be at its historical peak from the late 1960's until the end of the 1970's. The Czechoslovakians played a different style than the Soviets, while they possessed much of the small skill talents of skating, stickhandling, and passing, they played a more Canadian style of straight ahead, physical, intense, hockey. Those teams had possibly the best goalie not in the NHL in Juri Holecek, and a streaky but very talented partner in goal named Vladmir Dzurilla.

The Czechoslovakian defence was probably the best in Europe during that time, with a physical, talented, mobile group. **Josef Horesosvky** was a big, physical, mobile defender who would have fit in nicely on any NHL team. Other notables on the back end were **Juri Bubla, Oldrich Machac**, and probably the best defenseman of that era not in the NHL, **Frantisek Pospisil.** An all-around defenceman who equal parts offense and defence was, Pospisil would be named Czechoslovakian player of the year in both 1971, 1972. He would also win best defenceman at the World Championships in 1972, 1976, and 1977.

Their forwards were led by future Hockey Hall of Fame inductee **Vladislav Nedomansky,** a big strong smooth forward who would defect to North America in 1974. He would score 56 goals in the WHA for the Birmingham Bulls, and another 38 goals one season with the Detroit Red Wings, despite being at the end of his long career. Nedomansky was joined by outstanding talents **Ivan Hlinka, the Holik brothers Jaroslav and Jiri, Vladimir Martinec, and Jan Klapac**. They were a deep, talented team who could not only beat the Soviets on any given night, would prove to be a match for Team Canada 1972 when the two teams met and played a spirited 3-3 tie after the Summit Series. **They were the real deal**.

The 1971-72 season would include the Summit Series in September, but the Soviets would firstly be focused on the Olympic games in Sapporo, Japan. The Soviets would win their 4th Olympic gold (3rd straight) by going undefeated throughout the tournament, their only blemish a 3-3 tie against the improving Swedes. The tournament's big surprise was the 5-1 upset by the young American entry over the Czechoslovakians. This helped land a silver medal for the American team, who had a 16-year-old wonderkid named **Mark Howe**. Canada, sticking to its 1970 withdrawal from international hockey did not have an entry.

The Soviets were led by the dynamic Valeri Kharlamov who had 9 goals and 16 points in 5 games. Anatoli Firsov was still a factor on the National Team, playing on the top line with Kharlamov and Maltsev, but the youth movement had won out and Kharlamov was now entrenched as the top Soviet star. The gold medal would be the final victory for the Soviet coaching duo of Arkady Chernyshev and Anatoly Tarasov who both been forced out or as they proclaimed, retired, from coaching the National Team.

The duo had guided the development of Soviet hockey, with their respective club teams of Moscow Dynamo and Central Army and by being the coaches of the National Team off and on for 18 years. It would start in 1954 when Chernyshev took over as head coach. His first stint lasted until 1957. Tarasov would have his own turn at the head coach from 1958-1960, before the two men would form an extremely successful coaching partnership from 1961-1972. Chernyshev was the head coach during this time period, with assistant coach Tarasov focusing on practices and fitness training. Players who found the bombastic, often demanding Tarasov difficult and relentless, would look to Chernyshev for a calmer, more understanding presence. They were a very successful tandem with Chernyshev finishing with 11 World Championship titles and 4 Olympic golds as head coach. Tarasov contributed to 9 world titles and 3 Olympic golds. **It could safely be said that they were the fathers of Soviet hockey, and very instrumental in the style, discipline,**

and success of the program. The veteran coaches would be eventually replaced by Vsevolod Bobrov and Tarasov's protégé and assistant at the Central Red Army club, Boris Kulagin.

Boris Kulagin, "Chuckles" as Phil Esposito referred to the stoic coach, was a respected member of the Soviet coaching fraternity. He had worked with Tarasov closely at CSKA throughout the 1960's and was probably added to the coaching staff to ensure the balance between the Tarasov/Chernyshev style and Bobrov's style. Kulagin had been responsible for Tarasov to give the small dynamic Valeri Kharlamov a second serious chance to play on the Red Army club, as Tarasov felt Kharlamov was too small. Kulagin had left the Central Red Army Club in 1971 to take over the smaller, less notable Krylya Sovetov team, known at the Soviet Wings or Wings of the Soviet club. Kulagin proved to be an excellent judge of talent and coach, recruiting the highly regarded "Kid Line" of Anasin, Lebedev and Bodunov to the Wings club, as well as other less known players who had been less regarded by the other Soviet clubs. **Kulagin's squad won a surprise Soviet League Championship in 1974, when the pupil out did the master and the Wings upset Tarasov's Red Army team for the league title**. This led to Kulagin being named the Head Coach of the Soviet national squad in 1974.

Kulagin would coach the National Team against the WHA Team Canada, coach the Wings in the 1976 Super Series, including the 12-6 blowout loss to the Buffalo Sabres, win the 1976 Olympics, lose the 1976 Canada Cup, when the Soviets failed to send their full team. Even more shocking was a 6-4 loss to Poland at the 1976 World Championships, allowing their rival the Czechoslovakians to grab another World Title.

Unfortunately for Kulagin, these losses, and a growing feeling within Soviet hockey that wholesale changes were needed in their style and approach led to the dismissal of

Kulagin and the dawn of the Viktor Tikhonov era.

The last major tournament for the Soviets before the Summit Series was the 1972 World Championships. This was Bobrov's and Kulagin's first big test, and they failed to deliver. The Soviets would put in one of their worst World Championship performances after defeating the Swedes 11-2, they would tie the swedes in the next round 3-3. They would continue to struggle against the Czechoslovakians, tying them 3-3 in the first meeting before losing 3-2 to them in the medal rounds. The bright light would be in their young offensive stars as Alexander Maltsev would win best forward and the Soviets would sweep the forward spots on the All-star team with Maltsev, Kharlamov and Vikulov (who was having his career season) all being named.

At this time, it was quite possible the Czechoslovakians were the number one team internationally, and Hockey Canada could have been negotiating with them instead of the USSR. However, Czechoslovakia didn't have the long history of winning, as the Soviets had just completed an unprecedented run of World Championship titles. The Soviet Union was also one of the world's superpowers, and the cold war rivalry, while not with Canada specifically would have added for much greater appeal than small, oppressed Czechoslovakia. The Soviets had risen to be the best international power in hockey in just 26 years. It had to be them.

While the Soviet players didn't realize it as they played the 1972 World Championships, the next challenge would be the most impactful, important moments of their hockey careers. **The Summit Series**.

PART 8 GAME 4 VANCOUVER;

ROCK BOTTOM

CHAPTER 36: VANCOUVER MILLIONAIRES TO VANCOUVER CANUCKS

Vancouver, British Columbia, is a unique city in the Canadian landscape. Located on Canada's West coast, bordered by mountains and the Pacific Ocean, it's a beautiful location. Its' great distance from the eastern hockey centres of Toronto, Montreal, New York, and Boston help to separate it from any other major North American hockey city.

In 1972, it was a city new to the NHL, having obtained a franchise in 1970 after missing out in the first NHL expansion in 1967. There was still some underlying bitterness in the city towards the NHL. Many in Vancouver felt they should have been awarded a franchise in 1967. They had missed out because of a back door deal for the St. Louis Blues franchise instead. The belief was that the bid was hindered by Toronto Maple Leafs president Stafford Smythe; after a failed Vancouver-based business deal, he was quoted as saying that the city would not get an NHL franchise in his lifetime. Additionally, along with the Montreal Canadiens, Smythe purportedly did not wish to split Canadian Broadcasting Corporation (CBC) hockey revenues three ways rather than two. There were reports that the St Louis group made a weak proposal with the expectations Vancouver would surely be awarded one of the new franchises. That didn't happen. **The seeds of Vancouver bitterness were sowed.**

In 1968, the (1967) expansion Oakland Seals were already in financial difficulty with poor attendance. An apparent deal was in place to move them to Vancouver, but the NHL did not want to see one of their franchises from the expansion of 1967 moved so quickly and nixed the deal. In exchange for avoiding a lawsuit, the NHL promised Vancouver would get a team in the next expansion. Another group, headed by Minnesota entrepreneur Tom Scallen, made a new presentation, and was awarded an expansion franchise for the price of $6 million, **three times the cost in 1967**. The new ownership group purchased the WHL minor pro Canucks and joined the league with the Buffalo Sabres in 1970.

Despite the difficulty getting a franchise, in 1972 Vancouver had a long professional hockey history, going back to **the Patrick brothers, Lester and Frank**, establishing the Pacific Coast Hockey League in 1911. This led to the first artificial rink being built in Vancouver, the Denman Arena, the world's largest at the time. It became the home ice of the vaunted PCHL's **Vancouver Millionaires**. The Millionaires were the flagship franchise of the fledging PCHL and needed a star to draw fans. The Patricks, who had played for several years in Eastern Canada, used those connections to lure one of the best players in early hockey, **Fred "Cyclone" Taylor,** to come west and play for the Millionaires. This move helped make them the top team in all hockey, combined with the only Stanley Cup victory in the city of Vancouver's history. The 1915 Millionaire team swept the best of the East, the mighty Ottawa Senators in three straight games all held in Vancouver. Incredibly, Cyclone was still around on

September 8, 1972, attending the fourth game of the series at 88.

As far as international hockey, Vancouver, and the province of British Columbia had some relevant, interesting international hockey history prior to the Summit Series. A quick summary of these games allows for the recognition of the province of British Columbia's place in Canadian international hockey history.

The foremost of these might have been the previously mentioned Penticton Vees reclaiming the World Hockey Championship in 1955 from the Soviet Union. The rural BC Senior A team named the Vees (after a type of peach) reclaimed the World Championship with a 5-0 victory over the Vsevolod Bobrov led Soviet Union team. This was the same Bobrov who was the coach of the Soviets in the Summit Series. This was big news in Canada at the time as the upstart Soviets had shocked the hockey world by defeating Canada's representative the Senior B East York Lyndhursts the year before. Led by former New York Rangers Grant and Bill Warwick, plus brother Dick, the Vees temporarily restored Canada's pride with their robust victory at the Krefeld Arena on the outskirts of Dusseldorf, West Germany. This was the first-time former NHL players, the Warwicks, played the Soviets.

The Kimberley BC Dynamiters represented Canada in the 1937 World Championships winning gold as did the Trail BC Smoke Eaters who represented Canada successful in 1939, 1961 and unsuccessfully in 1963. Trail's 1939 team barnstormed Europe to enthusiastic crowds, helping to kick start and develop European hockey pre-World War II. Trail's victory in 1961 was the last time a Senior A Team won the Gold Medal for Canada. The competition was simply too strong for the Senior A teams to compete successfully by the early 1960's. In fact, the 1963 Trail team was the last Senior A team to represent Canada at the World Championships, finishing out of the medal standings. Moving forward after that was Father David Bauer's Canadian National Team who would take the battle to the European nations for the next six years.

The Canadian National Team had a link to Vancouver as it was established in 1963 and located at the University of British Columbia (UBC) until 1964 when they relocated the program to the University of Manitoba in Winnipeg. During their short period in Vancouver, they went by the Thunderbirds nickname of UBC and lived in the campus dormitory.

While teams from the province of British Columbia had the previously mentioned successes representing Canada in international hockey, up until **December 20th, 1969**, the city of Vancouver lacked a historically significant international hockey game. That would change with a one sided 9-3 Soviet blow out of the Canadian National Team at the brand-new Pacific Coliseum. Why? **This game had the Canadian debut of the same two legendary goalies that would face each other in Game 4 of the Summit Series. Ken Dryden and Vyacheslav Tretiak.**

The Soviets had played the Canadian National Team in British Columbia the year earlier. The Soviets won both games easily, 7-0, on January 21st, 1968, in Vancouver, and then 8-3 the next night in Victoria. While these games were one sided, the Canadian National Team was far from a Washington Generals style patsy for the Soviets. They were able to beat the Soviets on occasion, and despite a large talent gap, **they usually gave them tough games**. For an interesting comparable, the same Canadian National Team defeated the expansion St. Louis Blues in two straight games that September in Winnipeg. Those same Blues would go to the Stanley Cup final later that season and had been the most successful team from the 1967 NHL expansion, at that time.

The 9-3 blowout was a confidence shattering game for the 22-year-old Dryden. His glory days on the Montreal Canadians were ahead of him; on this day, young Dryden was exposed as the inexperienced US college goalie he was. The Soviets had a wealth of young stars in that game including future Team Canada nemesis Valeri Kharlamov, fellow young forwards Mikhailov, Petrov, Shadrin, and Maltsev as well as the legendary veteran Anatoli Firsov up front. Summit Series veterans Kuzkin and Ragulin were two of the stalwarts on defence. In goal, a 17-year-old who was debuting in Canada and the future of Soviet goaltending for the next 15 years, Vladislav Tretiak.

As the game went on, Dryden became overwhelmed, stopping 44 shots by the Soviets, and having to make a great save with 10 seconds left to prevent the score from hitting double digits. Vladimir Petrov had two goals and two assists, but it was the slick Alexander Maltsev who got into Dryden's head the most. As author Todd Denault describes in his book, "The Greatest Game", Maltsev, only 20 years old himself seemed to delight in taunting the beleaguered Canadian goalie:

"For the beaten Dryden there was one moment that stuck in his memory. After the Soviets had put a fifth or sixth goal in the Canadian net, one of the Soviets best players, Alexander Maltsev slowly skated by the dejected goalie who wearily looked up at him. The two made eye contact, Maltsev looking every bit the conqueror winked at the vanquished Dryden". Todd Denault the Greatest Game.

Dryden himself recounts the terrible experience:

"I was never so tired after a game. They fired 45 shots on me, not an incredible amount by NHL standards, but an indoor record for the Russians. As I've said the Russians rarely shot unless they have the perfect shot. They had 45 perfect shots that night. I'm not trying to defend my reputation either. I felt like the ball in a pinball machine. All night long I got ready for a shot, moved, when down, got up, got ready and fished the puck out of the back of the net. Once I got so frustrated, I yelled out "damn it shoot the thing!"

To say this game shattered the young goalie's future confidence would be an exaggeration as he would go on to be a rookie sensation after stunning the favoured Orr and Esposito led Boston Bruins in the 1970-71 playoffs. However, this Vancouver experience **had to play on Dryden's psyche**, as Harry Sinden informed him, he would be starting the pivotal game four at the same Pacific Coast Coliseum, against the same powerful Soviet team. If Sinden and Ferguson knew of his past, they either ignored it or decided Dryden would want revenge. However, with Dryden's shaky play in game one and returning to the scene of his greatest humiliation, it was a **major gamble** at best for the Canadian coaches.

CHAPTER 37: SINDEN'S FOLLY PART II

Despite being undefeated in the last two games of the Series, and dominating long stretches of those games, Sinden and Ferguson decided to make wholesale changes to Team Canada's line-up. Stan Mikita who had played well in game two and sparingly in game three was scratched from the line-up. Mikita was possibly injured in game two when he crashed into the boards, potentially further aggravated his ongoing back issue; he wouldn't play again until the second exhibition game in Sweden and finally in the homecoming game against Czechoslovakia, where Mikita was born.

In the first of several shocking decisions, **Jean Ratelle** was also not dressed for Team Canada in game 4. Ratelle had played in game one, but the New York Ranger GAG line was inconsistent and ended up minus 3. This seemed to weigh on the coaches' minds as the entire line was scratched in game two, with only Ratelle dressed for game three. Ratelle had an excellent game in Winnipeg, showing he was close to regaining the form that won him the Lester Pearson award as the NHL's best player the season before. He skated well, scored a great goal, and teamed nicely with Yvan Cournoyer. However, **despite all of this**, the coaches decided to again bench the NHL's second-best centre, and then inexplicably dress his wingers Vic Hadfield and Rod Gilbert **without their**

regular star centre.

Vic Hadfield added a physical presence to the game and was certainly the muscle on the GAG line with the gentlemanly Ratelle and Gilbert. Hadfield was a big strong winger, who wasn't a great skater but could score goals, including 50 the season before. Up to that point in his career he had been a solid 20 goal scorer but playing on the GAG line with Ratelle as his centre elevated Hadfield to an all-star. Rod Gilbert was a good player, skater, and a consistent offensive threat. He had been a top Ranger forward since the 1963-64 season. As part of the GAG line, he had a career high 43 goals and 97 points, he led the entire league for right wingers. The line itself had finished 3rd, 4th and 5th in league scoring the season before as the Rangers went to the final. Sinden was seemingly set against any further reunification in the Series. Starting the wingers without the centre who was the glue of the line but had played well in game three seemed illogical.

Replacing Mikita and Ratelle at centre was the young, talented Buffalo Sabres forward **Gilbert Perrault**. Perrault was a beautiful skater, a slick stickhandler and one of the most talented players in the world, at the age of 22. As a star for the Montreal Junior Canadiens, Perrault led them to back-to-back Memorial Cups in 1968-69 and 1969-70 seasons, before being picked 1st overall by the expansion Buffalo Sabres. Perrault had faced the Soviets in a game before and achieved a remarkable upset when they beat the Soviets 9-3 in Montreal, a game where Perreault scored two goals and had three assists.

The second controversial decision the Canadian coaching duo made for the fourth game was to drop the **highly effective duo of Wayne Cashman and JP Parise**. Both players had caused the Soviets issues with their tenacity, corner work and in Cashman's case, a bit of intimidation to boot. The two had formed a strong line with Phil Esposito that led to crucial goals in both games two and three. Esposito and Cashman had years of experience together on the two-time Stanley Cup champions Boston Bruins. That chemistry had been obvious on the ice so far in the series. However, with Cashman getting a ten-minute misconduct in game three, Sinden felt Cashman was targeted by the referees and decided not to dress him. Cashman's effectiveness against the Soviets and his effectiveness with Esposito should have overshadowed any concern about the officials. JP Parise seemed **to be omitted without reason**. The dynamic Minnesota North Star had shown he had the energy to skate and compete with the fitter soviets, and his passion level was a great benchmark for the rest of Team Canada to work towards. It was very strange to omit him.

Replacing Cashman and Parise were Minnesota North Star right wing Bill Goldsworthy and Chicago Blackhawk left wing Dennis Hull, the younger brother of Bobby Hull. Hull was a good skater, had a huge, booming less than accurate slapshot with a funny, boisterous personality. Goldsworthy, on the other hand, was a big strong prototypical NHL power forward, a winger who could score goals and play with an edge. Sinden's hope was that Goldsworthy, "Goldie" as he was known. could replace the edge Cashman brought. Harry Sinden instructed Goldsworthy accordingly as told in Richard Bendall's book The Summit Series: Stats, Lies and Videotape:

> *"I don't want you going out of your way to take a cheap shot at these guys. Just make sure that every time you go into the corner with one of them that you come out with the final word. Get that last lick in so they know you are around."*

The last forward omitted for the Vancouver game was another surprise. Montreal Canadiens forward Peter Mahovlich had played in the first three games and played well, especially in a penalty killing role. He scored the classic goal in game two and like Parise, Cashman and Ratelle, **he was omitted despite his fine play**.

On defence, the Montreal Canadiens duo Serge Savard

and Guy Lapointe were scratched. Savard had suffered a hairline fracture after taking a shot off his foot in Winnipeg. Lapointe was all banged up and had been inconsistent in his own end, trying to do too much. They were replaced by the game one tandem of Don Awrey and Rod Seiling. This was a defensively minded duo from opposing teams with Awrey being from the Bruins and Seiling on their arch-rivals the New York Rangers. Both had struggled in game one with the speed and fitness of the Soviets, especially Valeri Kharlamov who victimized both players on two separate goals in game one.

Sinden's options were limited on defence. His only other options were two young, inexperienced Vancouver Canucks defensemen, **Jocelyn Guevremont**, and **Dale Tallon**. With the game being in Vancouver, it would have been a nice touch to have them playing, and if Canada had won the first three games, he might have done so. However, considering the importance of this game, the coaches were certainly not confident enough to put a pair of inexperienced 22-year-olds out there.

Jocelyn Guevremont wasn't inexperienced. He had played against the Soviets with Gilbert Perrault as a member of the Montreal Junior Canadiens team that had the surprise 9-3 victory over the Soviets. Guevremont was a big strong defender, a 3rd overall pick by Vancouver in the 1971 draft. He would have a short NHL career, due to a shoulder injury, but was a solid defender for the years he was in the league. After being traded to Buffalo in 1974, he would help them reach the Stanley Cup final in 1975 and played in the 1974 All Star Game. Guevremont would also play well against the Wings of the Soviet club team using his heavy slap shot to open the scoring in the famous 12-6 Sabres rout.

Strangely, Sinden and Ferguson would remark to Guevremont as stated in Brian McFarlane's "Team Canada 1972 Where Are They Now" book that they didn't even want him on the original 35-man roster.

"We don't really want you here, but you are going to be here, so just get along with everyone and have a good time".

Guevremont had been a top draft pick, so it seems a little strange that Sinden would make this comment. There appears to have been some politics involved in the Guevremont selection. Perhaps for Vancouver to host the game they wanted local players? The reasons have never been revealed but Sinden mentions it in his book "Hockey Showdown",

"Guevremont was a political choice. When we got down to our last defensive spot, we had a list of 10-15 guys who were all about the same. We took Guevremont because we were going to play one game in Canada, and we only had one player from out that way on the squad Dale Tallon."

He then further tarnished Guvremont's reputation by adding the following jibe:

"Next time there won't be any political or geographical choices. Next time, character will mean as much as ability".

This was most likely in reference to Guevremont leaving the team in Moscow despite playing in both exhibition games in Sweden.

Dale Tallon seemed to be a valid selection for the team by Sinden. Tallon had been a highly touted prospect since he began playing junior hockey at the age of 16. He had an outstanding junior career. His value was so high that he was traded from Oshawa to the Toronto Marlboroughs for five players! He was also Canada's top junior golfer, winning the Canadian junior championship in 1969 and seemingly having a dual career choice in sports.

Tallon would end up the number two pick in the 1970 NHL draft. This may have tarnished his image in Vancouver, as the Canucks lost the draft lottery to the fellow expansion team the Buffalo Sabres and a chance at the vaunted Gilbert Perrault. Tallon did have very good rookie and sophomore seasons, making the NHL All-Star game in 1971 and 1972. This led to his apparent legitimate selection to Team Canada on the expanded roster. Tallon would go on to play in the second Sweden exhibition game and the final game against the powerful Czechoslovakian team, both times paired with Brad Park.

The Vancouver Canucks of the early 1970's were poorly managed, with equally poor results. Like his counterpart Guevremont, the Canucks would give up on their draft pick, trading Tallon to the Chicago Black Hawks in 1973. Like Guevremont, Tallon would have a fairly short career in the NHL as a player, retiring by 1980. He did have a long and storied career as a broadcaster and General Manager, with Chicago and the Florida Panthers.

With Team Canada's numerous line-up changes set by Sinden, the Soviets were also tinkering with their line-up for this critical game. The first three games for the USSR had been a mixture of good and bad. They had outplayed Canada in the majority of game one and exposed several Canadian flaws both tactically and individually. Game Two had been a turnaround for them, as they had to adapt to NHL playoff style aggression and a realization, they were playing an opponent with sublime and explosive skills. Game three continued the pattern of game two, until about halfway through when the young Soviet Kid Line scored the quick goals and the fitness level of the Soviet team started to wear the Canadians down. If they had lost game three, Bobrov and Kulagin may have changed the line-up more drastically, but they had pulled out a tie. **A win in Game four would put the Soviets in the driver's seat going to Moscow.**

On defence, **the inconsistency of Alexi Gusev** was noticed by the coaching staff as he was dropped from the line-up. In a bit of surprise, **Yuri Shatalov** wasn't dressed, despite a strong game in game three paired with Valeri Vasiliev. Combined with the Soviet Kid Line, they had formed a young energetic group of five that caused the Canadian players fits. Shatalov was also responsible for getting Wayne Cashman riled up, and in the penalty box, after drilling the

Bruins winger with a clean hard hit at the Soviet blue line.

Replacing Gusev and Shatalov would be Soviet veterans Alexander Ragulin and Evgeny Paladiev, players who were victimized on the two spectacular goals in game two by Yvan Cournoyer and Peter Mahovlich. Ragulin was one of the veteran leaders of the Soviets and played a physically strong, composed, NHL style of defence. His skating was weak, especially for the speed of the series to date, but the coaches obviously decided they needed his physical presence, experience, poise, and leadership out there.

On forward, the seldom used Vyacheslav Solodukhin was replaced by revered Soviet star, **Vladimir Vikulov**. Vikulov had injured his shoulder in game one but was deemed healthy enough to return. This must have been a real boost to the Soviets as prior to the series Vikulov was one of the stars of the Soviet team, its leading scorer from the 1971-72 Soviet Elite League season with 34 goals in 31 games. The final line-up change was a swapping of wingers **Evgeny Mishakov** with **Yuri Blinov**. Mishakov had done well killing penalties in game 3 and was a physical player, but Blinov was a semi-star in the Soviet Elite League scoring 25 goals in 31 games in the 1971-72 season. He played game one with Petrov and Mikhailov and would be reunited with the same linemates for game four. The Soviets would be icing a similar line-up to their successful game one. With the additions of Vikulov and Blinov, this was a line-up that was expected to be offensively focused with some veteran presence on defence to deal with the expected counter attacks by Canada.

With the line-ups for both sides set, it was time for one of the **most dramatic, bizarre games in international hockey history.**

CHAPTER 38: GAME 4 VANCOUVER. PERIOD ONE. THE TALE OF GOLDIE AND BORIS

As the teams line up at their respective blue lines for the traditional introductions and gift exchange, the Soviet players had decided to exchange Matryoshka "Nesting Dolls". These are small wooden dolls, almost perfectly cylindrical, painted to resemble a peasant woman in traditional sarafan dress holding a rooster. The biggest doll opens to reveal a smaller doll, which opens in turn to reveal another doll, and so on. In total, there are seven dolls in addition to the mother doll; the dolls consist of five girls dressed in similar fashion, a boy doll, and a tiny baby at the centre. The dolls symbolize the traditional representation of the mother carrying a child within her and can be seen as a representation of a chain of mothers carrying on the family legacy through the child in their womb. The Canadian players seem genuine in receiving the gifts, as these were quite common Russian gifts at the time. In hindsight, the dolls, with their multiple layers, seemed a fitting gift for what was to be an extremely poor game four performance for the inconsistent, disjointed team

Canada in game four, after two solid games.

Canada starts the Clarke-Henderson-Ellis line with Park and Bergman. The Soviets counter with Maltsev-Kharlamov-Vikulov who had played well together in game one. Tsygankov and Ragulin start on defence. Canada quickly gets trapped in their own end as Vikulov takes Park out against the boards. The puck bounces out to Ron Ellis who makes a lazy play up the boards on the other side of the ice. Maltsev is there and intercepts. With an early panic for Canada, Henderson finally strips the puck off Kharlamov and uses his speed to rush up the ice. The puck goes to Ellis who makes a second poor pass, a failed attempt to Bobby Clarke, who was trailing behind. Canada is quickly back in their own zone, Park once more gives the puck up to Maltsev and in a déjà vu moment, Henderson rags it out of his end again, this time taking it himself deep into the Soviet end.

During this rush, **big Alexander Ragulin can be seen coming across centre and knocks Bobby Clarke down in what should have been a blatant interference or elbowing call.** Clarke's head had been turned watching Henderson and obviously did not see Ragulin coming. It's a brutal elbow. Clarke is flattened, out of the rush, yet no call is made on the play. Henderson gets the puck deep behind the Soviet goal and makes a nice centring pass to Park in the high slot. Park takes too long to set up his slap shot and drives the puck wide.

Both teams change lines on the fly, Petrov and linemates Blinov and Mikhailov both come on as does the newly formed Canadian line of Esposito with Goldsworthy and Dennis Hull. Blinov takes the puck deep into the Canadian zone, and Goldsworthy tracks him down **slashing him violently** across his back, **crosschecking him** in the head from behind and giving the falling Blinov a shove at the end for good measure. A penalty is quickly called. Goldsworthy then decides to give Boris Mikhailov **a shot to the head** as he skates by after the whistle. Boris is not one to back down and waves his stick menacingly. The Vancouver crowd is booing loudly as Goldsworthy skates off to the penalty box.

Petrov's line stays out for the power play with Luchenko and Kuzkin. They are up against Phil Esposito, Frank Mahovlich with Bill White and Pat Stapleton.

Goal 1: Boris Mikhailov. Soviet Union 1 Canada 0

It's difficult to fully understand why Bill Goldsworthy started his first shift in game four with such aggression. He wasn't the only Canadian player who played reckless and undisciplined this game, but he was certainly the most noticeable right off the bat. It would have been somewhat understandable if this had been his first shift in the series, but it wasn't. He played sparingly in game two. With Sinden not dressing Parise or Cashman, he had taken Goldsworthy aside and suggested that he "let them know he was around". While he obviously wanted aggression, Sinden would not have meant for Goldsworthy to go out and take a quick unwarranted penalty. Blinov was not in a scoring position, nor had he done anything previously to Goldsworthy that might have warranted the attack. It seemed to simply be a case of an undisciplined, ramped up player misreading the coach's instructions, and taking a needless penalty as the result.

In the NHL, Bill Goldsworthy was not an overly aggressive player for the Minnesota North Stars. In the 1971-72 NHL season, he scored 31 goals with 59 minutes in penalties. In his career he only went over 100 minutes in a season once, in his 1968-69 breakthrough season in the NHL where he was assumedly showing an aggressive side of his game in order to stick in the NHL after several seasons of bouncing around the minors. Goldsworthy was more of a proven goal scorer after three straight seasons of 30 plus goals despite playing for a weak team in the 1967 expansion North Stars. 'Goldie" had teamed well with another Team Canada player, JP Parise on the North Stars top line with Jude

Drouin at centre. Whether this was known by Sinden, or Ferguson is unknown, **but it was another puzzling decision by Team Canada not to play the two North Stars linemates together**. Goldie was a big man for that era, as he stood close to 6'2 and was a solid 190 pounds. As a result, it could have been perceived that Goldsworthy had the size and muscle to compete against the strong, fit Soviets. Goldsworthy was also a former Boston Bruin prospect and teammate of one Harry Sinden in the 1965-66 season for the Central Hockey Leagues Oklahoma Blazers. Harry Sinden knew Bill Goldsworthy, knew his abilities and temperament and made the decision to insert him into the game four line-up. **This fateful decision would lead to the first of two reckless penalties by Goldsworthy and two key powerplay goals by the clever Soviet forward Boris Mikhailov.**

Boris Mikhailov was one of the greatest Russian players of all time, one of the greatest who played during the Soviet era. Born in Moscow in the later stages of the devasting Soviet- Germany war in World War II, Mikhailov was born as his country was undergoing terrible loss and economic conditions. As Boris survived during the rebuilding years, he suddenly lost his father at age 10. These circumstances may have helped shape his tough, determined and, at times, nasty hockey style. Not an overly big man at 5'10 and 180 pounds, he was quick, extremely mobile and a very clever goal scorer. A unique combination of Bobby Clarke and Mike Bossy, **Boris was also an antagonist**. Of all the Soviet players in the 1972 Summit Series, Boris was the most "Canadian-like" in style. Soviet hockey guru Anatoli Tarasov recalled Mikhailov's aggressive play against Canada in the 1970s as follows:

> *"Mikhailov really went after the Canadians the way they went after our players and beat them all over the rink... Canadians became much less aggressive every time he was on the ice."* www.SI.com

After learning to play the game in Moscow, Boris

joined the Soviet B division club Avangard Saratov in 1962, at 18, a team based in Saratov, 900 kilometres from Moscow. Boris thrived in his first season there, scoring 20 goals in 26 games and 23 in 36 games a season later. He was then moved to the next level, the first division team of Lokomotiv Moscow. Back home in Moscow with his family, he continued to show his goal scoring ability with 20 goals in the 1966-67 season. This earned Mikhailov a final promotion to the Central Red Army club the next season where he played for the next 14 seasons, retiring in 1981. Boris would retire with **a record 429 goals in just 579 Soviet Elite League games.** This goal scoring pace of .74 per game is comparable to New York Islander great Mike Bossy who had a career .76 goals per game average in the NHL. Internationally, Mikhailov joined the National Team in 1969 and immediately made an impact scoring 9 goals in 9 games at the 1969 World Championships. By the time the 1972 Summit Series came around, Boris had already been a top producer on the National Team with 36 goals in 41 games at the World Championship and Olympics. Kharlamov may have gotten the glowing press and admiration on this Canadian side of the Summit Series, but **Boris Mikhailov was about to show Team Canada that his unique skill set was no less devastating.**

With Goldsworthy in the box, Canada puts out Phil Esposito and Frank Mahovlich with Stapleton and White on defence. The Soviets counter with Petrov, Blinov and Mikhailov up front and Luchenko and Kuzkin on the points. Early in the penalty kill, the Canadian forwards apply some pressure, but with that quick passing game, the Soviets successfully get into Canada's end. Petrov takes the puck just over the Canadian blue line where he stops and looks to set up the power-play. Esposito is watching him closely, shutting off Petrov's ability to put the puck deep into Canada's zone.

Frank Mahovlich, on the other hand, does not set up the Canadian 4-man box for penalty killing. For some reason, he sees Petrov but turns his back on the play, going for a skate all the way into the Canadian slot area, where Bill White is residing. The Big M has created an immense amount of distance between himself and Luchenko on the point. Petrov sees his teammate wide open and makes a nice dump pass to the blue line where Luchenko picks the puck up. The Soviet defender is now on a straight angle to the Canadian goal. White and Mahovlich are jumbled in the slot area, no doubt restricting Dryden's view of the puck. Mahovlich continues to skate going to the right side of the ice, where not a single Soviet player could be found, leaving a clear space for Luchenko to fire the puck.

While this was going on, Boris Mikhailov was at the far goalpost, to Dryden's right. With White watching Luchenko fire from the point, Boris cleverly sneaks in behind the Chicago blue line and deflects Luchenko's low hard slap shot past an unsuspecting Dryden. Tip in goals were nothing new in hockey in 1972 but the great goal scorers could disappear and appear back into the play at will. Mikhailov's goal was a true goal scorers' goal similar to Mike Bossy's deflection of a Paul Coffey slapshot in the 1984 Canada Cup semi-final match against the Soviets.

Canada's poor positional play by Mahovlich allowed the Soviets to have an open lane for the shot. The Big M needed to be up at the blue line to either block the Soviet defenders shooting lane or limit his options. Instead, Luchenko had both time and space to fire his shot. Mahovlich's poor positional play also handicapped Bill White. White had the Big M in his area. This could have distracted him from noticing or tying up Mikhailov at the post. That also would have potentially left the slot area open for a rebound for Yuri Blinov who was lurking to the left of Dryden. **Canada's inability to set up the 4-man box certainly allowed for the Soviet set deflection play, but full credit to Boris Mikhailov for reading the play, anticipating the shot, and getting his stick on the puck for the deflection.** Canada would have to adapt to the Soviet style of the wingers staying at the sides of the net near the posts, rather than the typical Canadian style of loading the slot area for shots. One final note on this opening goal of the game was that Luchenko's point shot was low and accurate, allowing for the Mikhailov tip in. At this stage in the series, the Soviets' ability to shoot the puck quickly and accurately was another advantage they had over Team Canada. The Canadians were still blasting the puck at Tretiak from bad angles or missing the net entirely. The Soviets had been better so far in the series at getting the puck on net, and from more effective areas.

On the faceoff after the Soviet goal, Phil Esposito can be seen mouthing the words "come on" and shaking his head at Bill Goldsworthy, assumingly for taking the unwarranted and costly penalty. Coach Sinden has Goldsworthy back on the ice, where perhaps a bench bound lesson would have been a better choice.

The Soviets have changed to their Kid Line, hoping they continue their success from game three. Goldsworthy makes a nice move at the Soviet blue line, but then receives a vicious slash from Anisin that knocks the stick out of Goldsworthy's hands. As they are tied up after the slash, the North Star player kicks with his foot at Anasin in frustration. Goldsworthy then skates around fuming, holding his forearm where Anasin had slashed him. No penalty on the play. In hindsight, this non call and the non-call interference by Ragulin earlier on Bobby Clarke had a direct impact on this game. If even one of those two infractions had been called, it might have stifled the early Soviet momentum.

Esposito stays on the ice as his wingers change to Gilbert and Hadfield with Awrey and Seiling on defence. The Soviets have their top line of Vikulov, Kharlamov and Maltsev out, and almost immediately Awrey gives up the puck at the Soviet blue line, leading to sustained pressure in the Canadian end. Gilbert makes a terrible cross ice pass to Hadfield that is a good ten feet ahead of him. Tsygankov intercepts and lugs it back into the Canadian zone before attempting a long slap shot that is blocked by Awrey. Canada doesn't get the puck out however, as Ragulin pinches in at the blue line. Rod Gilbert goes to hit the smaller Valeri Kharlamov against the boards, but he bounces off the Soviet winger, falling to the ice. Humiliated and frustrated, **Gilbert proceeds to cross check Kharlamov from behind**. Finally, Hadfield attempts a long breakout pass to Phil Esposito who misses it. Canada is called for icing. As the whistle blows, Gilbert hits Kharlamov again from behind with a dangerous, reckless high stick. Kharlamov seems bewildered by this anger, and probably even more so at the lack of a call against Gilbert. **This behaviour was completely out of character for Rod Gilbert.** Embarrassing for Gilbert and a difficult, embarrassing shift for the Canadian team.

Canada's answer to the Soviet Kid Line is the extremely talented, former Montreal Junior Canadiens star Gilbert Perrault. The same Perrault who lit up the Soviet National Team as a junior player. Perrault comes on the ice, making his debut in the series on a line with Frank Mahovlich and Yvan Cournoyer. Off the draw the play goes to centre ice where Perrault gets tied up with Mikhailov, dumping the Soviet antagonist to the ice. Almost immediately, Perrault's brilliant skating ability sets the Soviets on their heels. He flies behind the Soviet net and pressures Luchenko into a giveaway. The Soviets try to get control with Blinov making a cross ice pass while being nastily high sticked by Frank Mahovlich without a call. As a result of the high stick, the pass goes astray, and Perrault recovers the puck deep in the Soviet end. He shifts and makes a nice pass to Frank Mahovlich in the slot area, however, the Big M bungles the puck and fails to get a shot off.

Boris Mikhailov recovers the puck, slows the pace down behind his net and lugs the puck up the ice to teammate Blinov. This quickly develops into a two on one on Brad Park, who is almost standing stationary in his own end. Blinov makes a nice give and go to Mikhailov as they pass it easily around Park. Boris then has a clear shot on Dryden who makes a nice pad save. Park looked terrible defensively on the play but is able to recover the puck and make a nice outlet pass to Perrault. The slick Buffalo centre flies across the Soviet blue line as he attempts to stick handle past Kuzkin. The steady Soviet veteran has no part of it and easily stops Perrault, stripping him of the puck. The play goes back and forth with both teams skating well. Paul Henderson comes out and after missing the net from a clever corner pass from Perreault, he makes a nice feed to Cournoyer who one hands an attempt directly on Tretiak. Perrault has skated to the bench slowly exhausted. It was a definitive first shift for the 21-year-old Buffalo Sabre star, as he brought much needed energy to the Canadian team. However, his Canadian teammates seem more intent on taking their frustrations out on the Soviets than anything else.

The play continues with Clarke forechecking hard on Anisin behind Tretiak's goal. The puck pops out to Kuzkin who gives Cournoyer a spearing jab with his stick. The Roadrunner completely overreacts to the jab and **viscously swings a one-handed slash to the Soviet defender's arm. No call.** The puck pops back out to Stapleton at the blue line, who takes a wild slap shot wide of Tretiak. Kuzkin gets the puck again, and this time **Cournoyer slashes him with the same one-handed swipe as Henderson cross checks him in the head.** The tough Soviet Captain shrugs off the attacks, and headman's the puck out of his end zone. No calls on the play, but with normally clean players like Rod Gilbert, Frank Mahovlich, Cournoyer and now Henderson taking multiple cheap shots at the Soviets, Canada is out of sorts, angry and frustrated. At this early stage in the game, a couple of blatant incidents should have resulted in penalties to the Soviets, but **multiple penalties could have and should have been called against Canada**. That would change.

Esposito comes back out with this game's linemates

Dennis Hull and Bill Goldsworthy. Rather than taking a typical long shot at Tretiak, Esposito goes back to the long-angled dump in. It works as Dennis Hull shows his skating ability as he whirls around the Soviet goal, curling in front, finding space in the Soviet end. With Hull wheeling around looking for an open teammate, he comes into the slot area where he makes a quick low shot. Tretiak makes a good save. The puck goes into the Soviet corner to the right of Tretiak. Goldsworthy was already bumping with Vasiliev and then Paladiev as the Canadian forward looked to set up himself in the slot area. When the puck goes into the corner, Goldsworthy leaves the slot following the Soviet defender Paladiev. The North Star winger slams Paladiev hard into the boards, with his elbow impacting the Soviet defender's head so fiercely that his helmet comes flying off. After letting several Canadian cheap shots go, this one was perhaps too blatant to ignore. The referee signals a penalty to Goldsworthy for elbowing. For the first time in the game, boos could be heard from the Vancouver crowd. Whether it was because of a perceived bad call or because it wasn't the style of play, they expected from the best players in the NHL is unknown, but it **becomes hauntingly loud** as Goldsworthy makes his way to the box for the second time.

Goal 2: Soviet Union. Luchenko to Mikhailov Déjà Vu

Vladimir Luchenko was never known in North America as a top-level offensive defenceman as future Soviet-Russian players like Slava Fetisov and Sergi Zubov would be. His name is rarely mentioned amongst the Soviet greats of his era, nor as a candidate for the Hockey Hall of Fame. Soviet defenders in his era were taught to play solid, yet cautious defence. A player like Luchenko leading an offensive rush or jumping deep into the offensive play was saved for those moments when success seemed assured. **Control was key**. The Soviet defensemen's priority in their own end was the headman pass to the circling forward.

Another option was hitting a breaking forward with a longer pass. As defenders, they were expected to defend, to be responsible positionally, physical, when necessary, but always with the intention of puck recovery. This is where Vladimir Luchenko shined. He was a big man at a reported 6'1 and 205 pounds. Soviet reporting of size and weight for the Summit Series was inconsistent at best, as the players appeared to be larger than reported. A good example is Alexander Yakushev who was reported at 6'1 but was closer to 6'3. Luchenko was strong physically, calm, composed, a very solid rear-guard who made few mistakes.

Born in a small village outside Moscow in 1949, Vladimir's father left the family when he was 7. As a result, the family was quite poor with his mother working long hours at a local factory. Left with a lot of free time, young Vlad embraced multiple sports including the new and extremely popular sport of hockey. A large athletic boy with immense potential, his maturity was noticed by Anatoli Tarasov who moved him directly to the Central Red Army club in 1966 at age 17. This was exceedingly rare for any player in the USSR at that time, to find a spot on the CSKA without time on other teams or lower division teams. This would be the only club team Vladimir would play for, until his retirement in 1981. Luchenko would play well enough to earn a spot on the Soviet National Team in 1967 at 18. He would continue to be a fixture at the national level until 1980. Luchenko's consistency and durability were his trademarks, but he also possessed an extremely hard, accurate slap shot. This weapon was used in 1974 to score four goals in a game against Sweden, still a Russian international hockey record, and to hit a career high of 10 goals in the 1974-75 Soviet League season in 33 games. He retired, coaching throughout the 1980's before starting a long second career in scouting the New York Rangers, a role he does to this day.

In the Summit Series, Luchenko would log a ton of ice time, playing all 8 games. He would end up the third highest scoring defenceman in the Series with 1 goal and 3 assists. His Series play was analysed in the Soviet Newspapers as follows:

> *"Vladimir Lutchenko played very well defensively. He showed that even against the Canadians a defenseman can use clean bodychecks effectively. He played the real style of Soviet hockey - smart, elegant and clean. "*
>
> *Vladimir Dvorstov, TASS Agency*

Luchenko was also intimately involved in the first two goals of this game.

The leadup to the second goal had some exciting action. Bobby Clarke and Ron Ellis are out for Canada for the penalty kill, with the steady duo of Stapleton and White on defence. The Soviets have Vikulov on right wing with Maltsev and Kharlamov. Tsygankov and Ragulin are the point men. Clarke sends the puck deep into the Soviet end, where Tysygankov recovers the puck. He rounds the Soviet goal and quickly hits Vikulov with their patterned long breakout pass. This frees Vikulov on a sudden semi-breakaway, until Pat Stapleton catches him and plays him nicely off the puck. Canada sends the puck deep in the Soviet end a second time, where Ragulin spots Petrov and headmans the puck to the streaking forward. Petrov gets over the blue line and launches a hard slap shot that Dryden has trouble with. The crowd moans as Dryden struggles with the puck, giving it away to Petrov.

The Canadian penalty has only been only 30 seconds, yet the Soviets have already changed the forwards to the Petrov, Mikhailov, Blinov line. They seem to sense blood and ramp up their game. At the faceoff outside the Canadian zone, Ellis and Mikhailov have started battling with their sticks, waiting for the puck to drop. When it does, the puck goes to the boards, where Ellis gives Boris a bit of a high stick. Undeterred, the Soviets circle back into their own zone, quickly moving the puck up ice from Luchenko to Petrov, back to Mikhailov and finally over to Kharlamov on the far-left side of the Canadian zone. Kharlamov is being watched by Clarke but is able to make a nice flip pass across the ice to Luchenko on the left point. Ellis makes the same mistake that Frank Mahovlich made on the Soviets' first goal by **not covering the point** or forming a tight 4-man box in the Canadian zone. Instead, Ellis went after Petrov in the far corner, leading a wide-open lane not only for Luchenko to fire his shot, but giving Mikhailov time and space to move into the slot area for the deflection. Luchenko strategically seems to take a bit off his slap shot, instead making it a half shot-half pass that is cleverly directed right at Mikhailov's stick. Ken Dryden for some reason flops to the ice, overreacting to the shot. If he had just stayed tall, the deflection would have hit his pads. Similar to game one, Dryden needed to be better.

This second goal in Game 4 was almost a duplicate of the game's first goal. Like the first goal, Luchenko's hard, accurate shot from the point was deflected by Boris Mikhailov. **On both goals, Canadian penalty kill coverage was sloppy and disjointed**. Yet Team Canada's best penalty killer, Peter Mahovlich was not dressed. That is where the similarities end. This goal was much more than just a well-timed, slapshot deflection. This goal was a testament to Soviet quick puck movement. A better comparison would actually be Game Ones first goal of the Series. This was where Canada used quick, accurate passing, combined with constant movement to score a deflected goal that stunned the Soviets. Three games later, the Soviets do one better. From the time Luchenko circles in his own zone, they have the puck for a **full 18 seconds**. During that possession they pass the puck 5 times before it's in the net. What is more shocking is during those 18 seconds, Canada does not touch the puck once. **Not once.** The Soviets moved the puck effortlessly against two of the best penalty killers in the NHL in Clarke and Ellis, as well as White and Stapleton, the NHL's 1971-72 Second team all-star pairing on defence. This had to be disheartening for Team Canada. Just like the 9-3 blowout over the Canadian National Team in 1969, the Soviets had brought their **A game** to Vancouver and Team Canada was struggling to compete.

Phil Esposito is back out after the goal, centring Hadfield and Gilbert. As play starts, Anisin gives the puck away to Esposito, but Esposito's pass to Gilbert is quickly intercepted by Valeri Vasiliev. One of the key differences in this game compared to the first three for the Soviets was the play of their defence. **They had added a new aspect to their game, one of instant counter attacks against turnovers.** As soon as the Soviet defender has possession, they have been immediately turning up ice at full speed. This had a dual effect of catching Canadian forwards deep and behind the play, as well as changing the speed of the game. The Soviets are playing at a counter attacking speed that Canada seems either unwilling to match or cannot match at this stage in the series. Whether this was a strategy implemented by coaches Bobrov and Kulagin or a case of the defenders seeing open ice is unknown, but it was certainly working in the Soviet favour. Vasiliev continues this strategy, counter attacking to mid-ice before hitting Bodunov with a pass. Bodunov uses his big slap shot to fire a long one at Dryden who wisely covers up, slowing the pace back down.

Esposito again wins the draw and Canada breaks up ice on a 3 on 2. However, Esposito decides to fire a long slap shot at Tretiak rather than feeding the breaking Gilbert or Hadfield. Tretiak easily catches the long shot, but a whistle is called as Valeri Vasiliev and Rod Gilbert joust behind the net. While Gilbert is much smaller than Vasiliev, he is the aggressor with a bemused Vasiliev pushing back. The crowd murmurs loudly at Canadian poor decisions and chippy play. Play starts again, comes to centre ice where Hadfield dumps the puck back into the Soviet end. Rod Gilbert shows absolutely no hustle going after the puck, stopping before he gets to Tsygankov who easily plays the puck over to Bodunov on the boards. With Gilbert's lack of effort, and the defence pairing of Awrey and Seiling backing up all the way into their own end, as they did constantly in game one to poor results, Bodunov is able to skate unencumbered all the way into the Canadian Zone. He feeds Anasin for yet another slap shot blast at Dryden, who makes a panicky stop. An interesting sidenote after this play. Canadian Series announcer Foster Hewitt makes the statement on the broadcast about the Soviet slap shots.

"They weren't supposed to know anything about the slap shot when they arrived."

The fact that Soviets had come to Canada for multiple tours, as recently as 1969, the statement exemplifies **the complete ignorance and arrogance of the Canadian hockey establishment**. Soviet great Anatoli Firsov was known throughout the 1960's as having one of the best slap shots in the world. Yes, the Soviets often preferred to use the quick wrist shots close in, but this was not 1957. They weren't in Canada learning how to take them. They knew, and as Canada was finding out game after game, the Soviet slap shots were just as good and often better than the best players in the NHL.

The puck gets dumped into the Soviet end, where Paladiev turns, falls, and slams into the boards with Vic Hadfield. While this play was an accident, it looked very dangerous as Paladiev's head slams against the boards for the second time in the period. The referees ignore the crash and play moves on. Don Awrey gets the puck behind his net and does a nice impression of his Boston teammate Bobby Orr, using his left hand to fend off the forechecking Kharlamov and then blowing the speedy Soviet away before making a cross ice pass to Frank Mahovlich, who typically fires a bad angle slap shot wide of Tretiak. Awrey looked excellent on this rush, showing that if the Canadian players start skating to match the Soviet game pace, they could be successful. This play also had to have Team Canada (and Canadians across

Canada) wishing for a healthy Bobby Orr to be able to play. Kharlamov recovers the puck after the Big M slapshot but makes a terrible decision to stickhandle in front of his own goal, crashing into Tsygankov. This frees the puck up for the opportunistic Phil Esposito who has a dangerous chance close in on Tretiak.

Gilbert Perrault is out for his second shift of the game, with the Big M and Cournoyer. Mahovlich does a nice back check on Vikulov, stripping him of the puck and then barrels down the ice, stickhandling wildly until making a blind pass to Perrault. What is noteworthy on this play is the Soviet defence (Tysygankov/Ragulin) play him at the blue line, before angling him to an area of the ice where his options were limited. Simple, positional defending that the Canadian forwards are having trouble penetrating with their long individual rushes. Perrault fails to get a shot away, loses the puck to Tsygankov, who takes off down the ice at full speed, using that new strategy of the defence instantly counterattacking. He hits Mikhailov with a quick pass. Mikhailov is on the right-wing boards, then cuts across the Canadian zone feeding a wide-open Alexander Maltsev on the left side. Maltsev now has a clear break on Dryden. Perhaps digging into his memory from the 1969 humiliation, Dryden reads Maltsev's deke and makes an excellent save. **Brad Park had left Maltsev wide open on this play**. He had backpedalled at the Soviet counterattack all the way into the Canadian zone. **However, his positioning was awful as he was almost right beside partner Bergman when Mikhailov received the puck**. This left the speedy Maltsev completely wide open on the other side, a blunder that easily could have put Canada down 3-0 early in the game. This was the second time in the period that Brad Park gets burned in his own end. Park's defensive positional play was truly shocking for a player who was often considered the 2nd best defenceman in the NHL at the time. Park follows up on the play by high sticking Mikhailov in the corner.

Canada counter attacks with Cournoyer flying up the ice into the Soviet zone before making a clever drop pass to the trailing Perrault. The Soviet are caught in a rare moment of standing still, as Perrault takes a couple of strides before releasing a rocket slap shot that Tretiak barely kicks out. While Cournoyer makes a nice play on the rush, he had the slow footed Ragulin turning his back to the play and easily could have beat the Soviet veteran to the outside. The Canadian forwards are not reading the game or playing to their capabilities. Perrault gets the puck back at centre ice and for the **second straight time tries to beat the Soviet Captain Viktor Kuzkin one on one**. The result is the same as the first try, Kuzkin easily stops him, counter attacks, feeding the puck back up to Mikhailov. The crowd grumbles at the Canadian individual play. The lines change with Henderson hitting Ellis with a long cross ice pass. Ellis flies into the Soviet zone, unleashes a slap shot that Tretiak comes out to the slot area to cut off the angle and easily stop.

Clarke's dogged trio continues to pressure the Soviets, with Petrov giving Henderson a bit of an elbow behind the net. No call, play continues, as the Soviets decide they had seen enough of the Canadian forecheck and slow the game down by circling and passing. The Vancouver crowd voices its displeasure as the Canadian forwards simply watch the Soviets slow the game down. The puck comes to centre ice where Pat Stapleton does the same ineffective play that Phil Esposito had done a few shifts earlier, taking a long, useless, slap shot at Tretiak. No dump in, not trying to set the play up, just a long slap shot at the Soviet tender. As expected, Tretiak easily stops the shot, plays the puck to Vasiliev who quickly gets it up ice to the streaking Kid line. Luckily, the ultra-steady Bill White is back there, playing Bodunov to the boards, stripping him of the puck with some textbook defending. The Soviets keep it in, as Stapleton gives the puck away, until finally Dennis Hull is able to get the puck up ice, despite being hooked on the play by Bodunov. Canada gets a moment of pressure as Vasiliev gives the puck away to Esposito, but the puck is shot into the crowd.

The faceoff is to the left of Tretiak where Phil Esposito, who has been dominating the faceoff circle all game, takes Maltsev to school by bulling his way off the draw, right to the soviet goal. This play obviously shocks the Soviets who were seemingly unprepared for the move, and it almost works as Tretiak falls desperately on the puck. Tsygankov can be seen patting the back of Esposito in a moment of sportsmanship almost saying, "Well played, big Phil, you fooled us", before berating his teammates on their lack of positional acuity.

On the following faceoff, Esposito gets it back to White for a shot, but as soon as Tysygankov gets the puck he again counterattacks, lumbering up the ice at full speed. The puck gets into the Canadian zone, where Stapleton continues to struggle, giving the puck up to Vikulov. Finally, the cagey veteran White wisely freezes the puck in his corner getting a faceoff. The Perrault line comes back on, with Sinden hoping his young thoroughbred can pick the pace back up in Canada's favour. Instead, Frank Mahovlich makes a similar blind pass in his own end to the one in game two where Petrov blasted a short-handed goal. Maltsev keeps it in the Canadian end as a result of the giveaway, until a besieged Rod Seiling covers up the puck in the Canadian corner. Canada is trying to hang on at this point, to not give up a devastating third goal.

Off the faceoff, the puck goes around the Canadian goal where Don Awrey picks it up, spins so quickly he causes the forechecking Blinov to fall. Awrey flies behind his own goal and, for the second time this period, the Boston defenseman rushes the puck up the ice. He blows by Petrov before dumping the puck deep while getting hit by Luchenko at the Soviet blue line. Perhaps spurred on by the sudden burst of energy by Awrey, Cournoyer flies into the Soviet end, intercepts a Kuzkin clearing attempt and feeds the Big M in front of the net. The puck pops back to Cournoyer, who wastes all that effort by blasting a bad angle slap shot through the maze of players in front of Tretiak. The shot deflected into the crowd.

Perhaps giving Esposito a rest or looking for chemistry, Perrault is out with the Ranger duo of Hadfield and Gilbert. However, this is not the Gilbert Perrault of the previous shifts. He is barely skating this time, slowly going after the puck in the Soviet corner, with zero sense of urgency, setting the disgruntled crowd off into a series of murmurs and whistles. Hadfield does some forechecking work keeping the puck in the Soviet end, but a couple of Canadian slap shots at the point are blocked as the Soviets regroup defensively. Petrov intercepts a poor Hadfield pass and then does some nice neutral zone stickhandling before passing it off the Blinov. Blinov gets it deep in the Canadian zone, getting it to Mikhailov who subsequently drops it in the corner for Petrov. As Petrov goes for the puck along the boards, the big Centre gets absolutely crushed by a dual bodycheck from both Awrey and Hadfield. Petrov takes the hit, passes it back to Mikhailov behind the Canadian net who throws it out front to Blinov. The Soviet ability to take hits and still make the plays is not something the NHL players are used to. In the NHL, hitting is used to remove a player from the puck, or wear them down physically throughout the game. Neither result is happening at this stage for Team Canada.

As the first period winds down, the Soviets seem content with just slowing the pace passing the puck around, running out the clock. Phil Esposito who has come on replacing Perrault, tracks Mikhailov down behind his own goal, strips him of the puck and gets a decent backhand off on Tretiak. This seems to wake Team Canada up, as Goldsworthy knocks Anasin of the puck, feeding it back to Awrey. Awrey makes a nice pass to a circling Hadfield who carries the puck into the Soviet zone. Hadfield crosses the blue line before giving it to a streaking Esposito on the left wing. Esposito fires a tricky long wrist shot that surprises Tretiak, but just misses the far post. The Soviet Kid Line are struggling a bit this shift, as they lose the puck with a rare blind pass that goes directly to Dennis Hull. Hull flies through centre ice before taking a wild long slap shot that is nowhere near the net, hitting the high part of the glass in the corner. The Soviets recover and quickly counterattack into the Canadian zone. **During this play, Brad Park can be seen blatantly tripping Bodunov who is driving to the net.** Esposito falls on Bodunov, but gets up, skates hard out of the Canadian zone, where he gets the puck from Brad Park. Espo crosses the blue line at full speed, causing the Soviet defensive duo of Vasiliev and Paladiev to back up deep in their own end. Espo passes back to Dennis Hull who, despite having tons of space between himself and Paladiev, decides to unleash yet another slap shot from an angle at Tretiak. Tretiak makes a shoulder save on the shot, and the Soviets fire the puck around the boards out of their end. Brad Park gets the puck at his blue line and decides to try and stickhandle at centre ice through two Soviet forwards. He loses the puck, as he has done numerous times so far in this series by stickhandling in the neutral zone, and the Soviets get several chances before Dryden covers the puck. During this pressure in Canada's end, Bill Goldsworthy trips Lebedev in the slot area. No call. Dryden covers up forcing a whistle.

The Clarke line is out against the Soviet top line of Maltsev, Kharlamov and Vikulov. Team Canada gets trapped in their own end, where Pat Stapleton accidently passes the puck directly back to Dryden. Luckily for Canada, the Canadian netminder was aware enough to cover up the puck. At the faceoff, Stapleton redeems himself with an explosive rush up the ice. He spots Henderson breaking between Tsygankov and Ragulin and attempts to hit Henderson with a pass. The play almost works but the Soviet defence is too tight, and Henderson tries a failed back pass to Ellis. Ragulin recovers but makes a poor, long pass that is intercepted by

Stapleton. The puck goes up the left side, where Clarke breaks in free on Tretiak. Clarke is on a bad angle from the wing, but gets a good shot off, but Tretiak makes a quick glove save.

Vladimir Petrov and Yuri Blinov were both having excellent first periods. Petrov was everywhere, using his size to create turnovers, and leading the rush on numerous occasions. Blinov was skating well, forcing the Canadian defence to retreat on several rushes. With the Perrault line trapped deep, Petrov and Yuri Blinov find themselves coming down on Rod Seiling as they cross the Canadian blue line. Blinov goes wide and passes to Petrov who is trailing on Blinov's right. Seiling goes to poke check the pass or knock Petrov off the puck, but Petrov does a wonderfully creative play at that moment. Instead of receiving the pass from Blinov, he shovels it right back to him in one motion. Blinov is now well past the bewildered Seiling and can cut to the net on Dryden. Dryden for the third or fourth time this period is forced to make a good save. Blinov kicks the puck up to his skate in one motion, as he cuts in on Dryden. **A unique play between the two Soviet forwards, showing off their high-level dexterity and skill.**

Perrault tries another one-man rush but is taken out of the play nicely by Luchenko. There were four Soviet players focused on the Buffalo speedster, giving him zero room for manoeuvrability. Perrault loses the puck, and seemingly his interest in pursuing the puck as he simply stops skating and watches Kuzkin immediately skate the puck out of the Soviet zone. He makes a nice pass to a circling Blinov, who then flies into the Canadian zone before hitting Boris Mikhailov with a picture-perfect pass in the slot. While Seiling and Awrey flop and attempt to block Mikhailov's shot, he wires a hard dangerous wrist shot at Dryden who barely makes the save. The entire play from Kuzkin to Mikhailov takes 5 seconds before the puck is shot at Dryden. Canada does not come close to touching the puck on this sequence.

Esposito and the GAG line wingers are back out on the

ice. Luchenko gets a chance to unload his heavy shot from the point, but fans on it. Rod Seiling intercepts and takes a page from the Soviet playbook by immediately rushing the puck up ice. He hits Vic Hadfield on the wing, but Hadfield kills the play by unleashing another long, ineffective slap shot at Tretiak. Hadfield makes up for this play by skating hard on the backcheck and knocking Blinov off the puck in the Canadian slot area. The puck goes to Esposito who carries it into the neutral zone, but like Perrault on the previous shift, finds himself with four Soviet checkers on the puck. Esposito gets another chance as he recovers the puck in his own end, but under Soviet pressure and with no one open to pass to, he fires it down the ice for an icing.

Off the ensuing draw, Brad Park makes two more poor plays. The first is where he fires it aimlessly around the boards where Anisin picks it up and fires a direct hard shot at Dryden. Park gets the rebound and attempts to stickhandle out of his end once more, with the same result. **He loses the puck to the forechecking Bodunov**. Dennis Hull recovers and for what must be the tenth time of the period, fires a long slap shot at Tretiak. The Soviets ice the puck with a missed long break out attempt, as the final minute of the period is announced. After a Goldsworthy dump in, the Canadian forwards apply some pressure. This leads to Tsygankov responding with a vicious, yet clean, rubout of Dennis Hull along the boards. The puck comes out to Kharlamov in the corner. He attempts to stickhandle past Phil Esposito, jumping over Espo's stick, falling, and drawing a tripping penalty. The crowd hates this call and boos the referee's decision relentlessly.

The Soviets put out Maltsev, Kharlamov and Vikulov at forward against Clarke and Ellis for Canada. After Clarke knocks the puck off Vikulov, the puck makes it way into the Canadian zone. Clarke then knocks Tsygankov down with a clean hit that lays out the big Soviet defender, knocking him spinning to the ice. Canada is doing a better job on this penalty kill, playing in a tight box formation, but they are leaving the points wide open for their heavy slap shots. As expected, Tsygankov unleashes a howitzer that Dryden makes a good skate save on. The buzzer goes to end a very one-side period of hockey.

Game 4: First Period Analysis

It would be easy to blame Canada's poor first period performance on Bill Goldsworthy. In his first two shifts of the game, he took two unnecessary early penalties that the Soviets capitalized on. Without those infractions, Canada wouldn't have been behind early, and a different result might have been possible. Or, if the referees (USA officials Gordon Lee and Les Gagnon who had officiated games 1,3 and 4) had made calls on Ragulin or even Anasin early in the period, things might have been different. Or would they? **Canada seemed woefully unprepared for this game, and to make things worse they played with a sense of misplaced anger.**

The reality was that Canada could have been called on numerous penalties early on, from Goldsworthy to Rod Gilbert, Yvan Cournoyer, even Frank Mahovlich. The other reality was that Canada played very, very poorly almost to a man in the first period. The effort was sporadic, and the positional play was disjointed and at times almost non-existent. Failed individual rushes, a lack of creativity offensively, and a lack of team chemistry all contributed to the performance. Match that with the Soviets playing their best period of the series and you had a one-sided romp that really could have ended with the Soviets ahead by 3 or 4 goals. While Ken Dryden appeared shaky on a couple of long slap shots, he could not be completely faulted on either of the power play goals. They were defensive breakdowns. Dryden in fact, made several saves that kept the period closer than Canada deserved.

There are very few bright spots on Team Canada in this period, but Phil Esposito was by far their best player. He was skating, winning draws, forechecking and leading rushes. Paul Henderson continued his strong play in the series, using his speed and tenacity to keep the Soviet pinned deep a few times. The Clarke line had few shifts this period, as Sinden rolled four lines, limiting their effectiveness. Vic Hadfield had a decent period, working hard in the corners and backchecking, but his linemate Rod Gilbert seemed focused more on attacking the Soviet players than playing his usual game. Gilbert Perrault was a positive addition at centre, but his effort was inconsistent, and his individual rushes led to turnovers against the stellar Soviet defence. Canada's top defensive players like Brad Park and Pat Stapleton struggled with poor positioning, but a surprise was the strong play of Don Awrey. Awrey was much maligned in game one for his play, especially against Kharlamov, but in the first period of this game he was skating and led several counterattacks out of his end.

The Soviets had an excellent period of hockey. Their defence was pristine, playing superb positionally, and giving very little space for the disjointed Canadian forwards. They were physical when required, but it was the new strategy of immediate counter attacks from the back end that really set the pace for Soviet domination. **Tsygankov had a wonderful period of hockey**, using his size and physical strength to win battles and then surprisingly leading several attacks down the ice. The big Soviet was not a great skater in comparison to some of his teammates, but he didn't let that stop him as he made several individual rushes out of his own end and away from any forecheckers. Luchenko of course contributed to the two goals with his shots from the point and Valeri Vasiliev kept up his strong play from game three.

Up front, **this was the period of Boris Mikhailov**. He was everywhere, flying all over the ice, battling with Ron Ellis and others, and scoring two clever deflection goals. As previously mentioned, Yuri Blinov was skating really well and combined with Vladimir Petrov on several offensive opportunities. Maltsev was becoming more engaged in the games, using his speed to create some open space but his linemates Vikulov and Kharlamov had very quiet periods. **Another question was, where was Alexander Yakushev and his centre Vladimir Shadrin?** They didn't see the ice for the entire period. Why? Well, they had a poor performance in game three, and lacked a regular right winger after Zimin's disappearance. Or perhaps it was an internal discipline issue? The Soviets were very tight lipped on these sorts of decisions. To sit two of their best forwards and still have a dominant period showed the Soviet team depth and team play. The Kid Line was still causing Canada issues, especially Anisin who was often leading his lines forays into the Canadian end. Overall, the Soviet forwards were playing as a team, skating non-stop, and backchecking with an intensity that helped their defence corral any Canadian incursions. A great period of hockey for the Soviets, resulting in very little work for Tretiak besides the repetitive long slap shots from outside the blue line that he easily handled.

How would Canada respond?

CHAPTER 39: GAME 4 PERIOD 2. SITTING ON TRETIAK

As the second period started, Team Canada was still shorthanded for one minute, thirty-one seconds. It had to have seemed much longer for the Canadians. If Canada could start the period with a successful penalty kill, it might help kick start a comeback. This was also a crucial powerplay for the Soviets, as a third goal would further deflate the Canadian spirit, perhaps even putting the game out of reach.

The Soviets start the period with Petrov centring Kharlamov and Mikhailov with Kuzkin and Luchenko on the points. Canada has the duo of Clarke and Ellis out with Park and Gary Bergman. The Team Canada coaches have unrelenting faith in the Park-Bergman duo, playing them as Canada's go to pairing. Off the draw, the puck goes back into the Soviet end where it is recovered by Boris Mikhailov. Mikhailov, perhaps boosted in confidence by his first period duo of goals, decides to make various stickhandling moves in the feet of Bobby Clarke. Having successfully dangled through the Philadelphia Flyer, Boris fires a cross ice pass to Kharlamov. Kharlamov enters the Canadian zone, but the game one star gets a stick in the head from Gary Bergman. An obviously annoyed Bobby Clarke pushes Petrov out of the way, allowing Bergman to dump the puck deep into the Soviet zone. Luchenko picks it up, fires their traditional long break out pass to centre, but Valeri Kharlamov is still out of sorts this game. He is stationary as he receives the pass and then makes a rare blind pass into a group of Canadian players. Ron Ellis intercepts but gives it right back to Kuzkin at the Soviet blue line. Kharlamov gets the puck again, skates at half speed into the Canadian zone and then as Brad Park angles him into the boards, Kharlamov makes a drop pass to absolutely no one. Strange to see the Soviet star out of sorts.

Once more, Ron Ellis recovers and throws the puck deep into the Soviet end. Mikhailov takes it himself this time, moving at a good speed into the centre ice area, where he tries to hit Petrov open on the right side. The pass is behind him, so Petrov knocks it back to Kharlamov **who loses it for a third time,** having his stick lifted by Bobby Clarke. It's déjà vu yet again, as Ron Ellis recovers and dumps it once again deep into the Soviet zone. **A very poor, unorganized powerplay by the Soviets, and a terrible shift for Valeri Kharlamov.**

The Kid Line comes on against a makeshift Canadian group of Esposito, Rod Gilbert, and Frank Mahovlich. After Lebedev is bumped off the puck by Rod Gilbert, the puck goes to Bill White who makes a nice pass under the stick of Bodunov, freeing Gilbert with some skating room in centre ice. Gilbert gets it over to Frank Mahovlich on the left wing, but the Big M makes a poor pass to Esposito that its easily intercepted by Anisin. **One has to wonder why Mahovlich is on the ice, as Rod Gilbert of course plays regularly with Vic Hadfield.** With Jean Ratelle not being dressed, and Hadfield getting minimal playing time watching the Big M make poor play after poor play, an anti-New York Ranger bias by the Canadian coaches seems a real possibility.

Gil Perrault gets Canada's first chance of the period. Flying into the Soviet end after receiving an outlet pass from Pat Stapleton, Perrault takes a slap shot that goes at least five feet wide of Tretiak. The Soviet top line of Maltsev, Vikulov and Kharlamov line up for a faceoff, which forces Canada to scramble to match lines with the Clarke line finally coming on. The shift is somewhat scrambly for both sides. The highlight being Bill White twice breaking up rushes into his zone. On a third rush, Maltsev cleverly gets one through the wily veteran's feet, jumping around White and wiring a hard snapshot that whipped past Dryden's head.

Off the faceoff, Kuzkin gets the puck over to Luchenko on the right point. Luchenko moves in as Seiling backs up, and then fires a hard high wrister at Dryden. **Dryden drops to his pads, catches the shot in his glove and then inexplicably drops the puck, causing it to almost over the goal line**! With the crowding screaming in abject fear at a third Soviet goal, Don Awrey is there to push the puck under the shocked Canadian netminder. Dryden gives his future Montreal Canadiens teammate a thank you pat, as does Phil Esposito who gives his Boston teammate a couple of enthusiastic pats on the back. Off the faceoff, Goldsworthy twice gives the puck up along the boards in the Canadian end to some boos and moans from the crowd. Goldsworthy does show some real hustle forechecking in the Soviet zone, but the damage is done. Even with some slight Canadian pressure, the crowd is mumbling and moaning loudly. Canada seems off. The hockey world seems off.

Things quickly change for Canada as Luchenko pinches up, causing Seiling to give it up in the neutral zone. The puck goes to Petrov who hits a streaking Blinov just over the Canadian blue line. Blinov stick handles against a retreating Don Awrey, buying time for his Soviet linemates to join the rush. Awrey is standing still, frozen, having backed up to the slot area in front of Dryden. On cue, opportunistic Boris Mikhailov appears, and fires a wicked wrist shot over the flopping Rod Seiling, just missing the top corner of the Canadian goal. Petrov recovers, tries a wrap around on Dryden who stops it with his big pad. The puck goes back to Mikhailov who appears to be everywhere. He passes it back to Kuzkin who fires a low snapshot that Dryden wisely covers up with (who else but) Boris Mikhailov lurking for a rebound.

Goal 3: Canada Gilbert Perrault. Soviets 2 Canada 1

In the history of hockey, there have been very few players who could skate and stickhandle at the level of Gilbert Perreault. A 1970's version of Connor McDavid, when Perrault was dialled in, he had moments of unstoppable brilliance. He had a bow legged, powerful skating stride, slick moves, and a powerful shot. **He also had the very rare ability to do all of this at full, blazing speed**. When he was a junior with the Montreal Junior Canadiens, Perreault helped his team to back-to-back Memorial Cups. With teams drooling over his talent, Perreault was the unanimous #1 overall pick in the 1970 draft by the expansion Buffalo Sabres. He scored 38 goals in his rookie season to win the Calder trophy as the NHL's top rookie, but he dipped in his second season to 26 goals. This was still good enough to get selected for Team Canada 72, but it was a testament to Perreault's career of unfulfilled expectations. He never quite seemed to bring the results his prodigious talent warranted. He was outscored by the younger Marcel Dionne in OHA junior, and never came close to Guy Lafleur's 104 goals with the Quebec Remparts (although to be fair the OHA was a stronger league than the Quebec Junior A loop at that time). It was Lafleur's team that won the Memorial Cup in Perreault's last year of junior hockey with Montreal.

In the NHL, Perreault jumped ahead of his two French Canadian junior rivals by taking the expansion Sabres to the Stanley Cup final in 1975. However, that season was also Guy Lafleur's first of six straight 50 goal seasons. One year later, Lafleur was the league's dominant player, going on to winning every award possible and enjoying multiple Stanley Cups with Montreal. Dionne became a point machine with Los Angeles and won his own scoring title in the 1979-80 season. Even lesser skilled players like Bobby Clarke and Daryl Sittler were often able to put up larger numbers than

Perreault while playing much more physical, two-way games. Although he was extremely talented, Perreault was never a strong player defensively nor had a real physical aspect to his game.

Through the rest of the decade, Gilbert Perreault's Buffalo Sabres became the image of their talented leader, never quite living up to expectations. This was despite possessing one of the NHL's best lines, the French Connection line of Perreault, fellow Team Canada teammate Richard Martin and Rene Robert. Perhaps the NHL grinding style combined with the small ice dimensions in the Buffalo Auditorium didn't mesh well with the temperamental superstar. He seemingly needed space for his individual rushes, and he wasn't the type of centre iceman who made his wingers successful with sublime passing like Wayne Gretzky or Adam Oates. He could, and would, pass, of course, and his linemates certainly benefitted from playing with him, but his rushing, individual style may have limited his production. **At least in the NHL**.

It was in international hockey that Perreault seemed to shine brightest. He feasted on Soviet teams for his entire career, starting with his 5-point game as junior in 1969. He had a goal and an assist in two games in the Summit Series, before leaving the team after game five. He also had a goal and an assist in the 1972 second exhibition game vs Sweden. In the 1976 NHL Super Series, his Buffalo team gave the Soviet Wings a terrible 12-6 trouncing, a game in which Perrault had a goal and 2 assists. Wings coach Boris Kulagin called him (and Richard Martin) the best professional players he had ever seen after watching his players struggling to stop the duo The following summer, Perreault played what might have been the best hockey of his career at the inaugural Canada Cup 1976 Tournament. He scored 8 points in 7 games, including a goal and an assist in Canada's 3-1 victory over the Soviet team. He also outplayed Lafleur and Dionne in the tournament.

His superb play in international games flowed into the next decade. In 1980, the Buffalo Sabres with Perreault as their leader, continued their astounding play against teams from the Soviet Union by pounding the stacked Central Red Army club 6-1. Gilbert played for the ill-fated Team NHL in 1979 that lost to the Soviets in the Challenge Cup, but he was dangerous throughout the series. In 1981, he starred with Team Canada in the Canada Cup; in that tournament, he had an incredible 11 points in only 4 games on a dream line with Wayne Gretzky and Guy Lafleur, before getting injured. The team would lose in the final to the Soviets, never seemingly recovering from losing Perreault. **From 1969 Gilbert Perreault played a team from the Soviet Union nine times, and was often a nightmare for the Soviets, scoring 16 points with 6 goals and 10 assists in those games**. Overall, in international play, Gilbert Perreault was one of the greatest ever. From 1969 to 1981 he played in 20 international games. **In those games, the Victoriaville, PQ native scored an unbelievable 12 goals and 20 assists for 32 points**. Those were against some of the best teams in hockey and Perreault absolutely owned them. His international hockey game was completely different than his NHL career, and the results spoke volumes.

Gilbert Perreault had made several individual rushes in game four to this point. Two of those had been stopped by Victor Kuzkin, leading to quick turnovers against Team Canada. The next one would end up with Canada making it a one goal game. With the faceoff deep in the Canadian end to Dryden's right, Perreault is out there with Frank Mahovlich and Cournoyer. Park and Bergman are on defence. They are matched up against the Soviet Kid Line of Anisin, Lebedev and Bodunov with Paladiev and Vasiliev on the back end. Perreault cleanly wins the draw against Anisin. The puck goes behind the Canadian goal, where Brad Park attempts to get control before being bodied off the puck by Lebedev. The puck springs loose around the end boards, and Perreault picks it up. He picks up speed in a couple of powerful strides and blows by Bodunov easily with a sweet deke. Perreault weaves into the centre ice zone, where Anisin is skating backwards, as are the two Soviet defenders. Perreault is at full speed now and flies by Anisin to his left, then continues to cut to the left past the Soviet blue line and teammate Yvan Cournoyer. Perreault goes by Paladiev, who hasn't even turned completely before Perreault is suddenly cutting in on Tretiak. In blowing by Paladiev, Perreault has gone a little wide and can't quite cut directly to the goal. He instead goes to the side of the net where he either tries to take a quick bad angled attempt at Tretiak's right pad, or a pass out front to the Big M. Valeri Vasiliev dives in front of Tretiak, trying to prevent the pass, but ends up knocking the puck into the Soviet goal. Perreault continues moving at Mach speed behind the Soviet net, until he realizes the puck has gone in. **From the time Perreault had picked the puck up along the boards to the time it goes behind Tretiak, 8 seconds had passed**. End to end in the net in 8 seconds. Pure speed and skill on full display for the disgruntled Vancouver fans.

The Soviets seemingly did everything right here. They had a forechecker deep who was able to get the puck loose, and his two linemates were both in positions to stop the rush. The problem was, they couldn't. The Buffalo star flew right by Bodunov and Anisin. Paladiev and Vasiliev, much like Seiling and Awrey on Kharlamov's goals in game one, had backed up into their own zone, probably in pure panic seeing the French-Canadian player coming at them at full speed. Playing closely together, Paladiev turns correctly, tries to play the Canadian forward wide, but is too slow in reacting to make any difference. Vasiliev's mistake is similar to one plaguing Team Canada's defence, falling to the ice trying to stop a play. Vasiliev either falls or flops to the ice trying to block either Perreault's shot or pass out front. When he does this, his momentum and big body allows for the deflected puck to accidently be carried into the net. **An own goal for**

the Soviets, but this goal was all Gilbert Perreault at his international hockey best.

Canada keeps the same group out after the goal, but the Soviets send out Maltsev, Vikulov and Kharlamov. The change pays dividends immediately as Kharlamov wires a long snapshot, similar to his second goal of the game in game one. Dryden stops this one however, but just barely, as he falls to the ice making the save. The crowd jeers now every time Dryden stops the puck, difficult save or not. Perreault picks the puck up again behind the goal and attempts another one-man rush, but this time he gives the puck away in the Canadian zone to Maltsev, who drops it to Kharlamov. Kharlamov cuts to the slot area, where Gary Bergman inexplicably falls to the ice. Kharlamov easily skates around him and feeds a wide-open Alexander Maltsev at the far-right corner of the goal net. Dryden was prepared for this common Soviet play and makes a great two pad save, covering the puck.

Seeing the sudden pressure, Sinden switches all five players, sending out the Bobby Clarke checking line with Stapleton and White. After a moment of scrambly play for both sides, Bill White makes a perfect thread the needle pass through Tsygankov and Ragulin at the Soviet blue line, freeing Bobby Clarke on a semi break away. Clarke gets tied up by Tsygankov and drops the puck to a trailing Ron Ellis. Ellis goes to his backhand and fires a shot that Tretiak makes a desperate save on. The puck trickles free across the goal crease, where Tsygankov gloves it back under Tretiak. If Tsygankov had covered the puck at that moment it would have been a penalty shot. Luckily for the Soviets, shovelling it over to the goalie wasn't penalty worthy. Good chance for Canada to tie the game up.

In game one, Canada's second goal was a quick Paul Henderson shot right off the faceoff that surprised Tretiak. Clarke won that draw and pulled it cleanly back to Henderson for the quick shot. Canada has an identical set up on the faceoff leading to an *almost* identical result three games later. Clarke cleanly wins the draw off Petrov and pulls it directly back to the top of the face circle where Henderson awaits. In game one, Henderson drilled the puck almost instantaneously, but this time he slightly hesitates before firing a hard low snapshot. Tretiak handles the drive, dropping to the ice to cover the puck. Two good chances in a row for Team Canada, and the crowd come to life. No longer jeering the Canadian players, the crowd noise amplifies with hopeful anticipation that Canada will soon be tying the game up at 2-2. Their hopes would quickly be shattered.

Goal 4: Yuri Blinov Soviets 3 Canada 1

If Team Canada's Mickey Redmond had a counterpart on the Soviet side, it would be Yuri Blinov. Both players were fast, explosive wingers, both had the ability to score goals. Their careers were short lived, and for both players the Summit Series was their last, in Redmond's case his only, opportunity to play for their respective countries. Like Redmond, Blinov's career had moments of success, with some excellent goal scoring numbers. In the 1968-69 season Blinov had 20 goals in only 28 Soviet Elite league games. Playing for the Red Army club, Blinov followed up that breakthrough season with 25 goals in 43 games, dipped off to 14 goals in 37 games in 1970-71, but rebounded with 25 goals in only 32 games in the 1971-72 season. This earned him a spot on the Soviet National Team for the 1972 World Championship. Blinov, playing on a line with Petrov and Mikhailov had a solid tournament scoring 10 points in 10 games. The tournament was a very political one, based in Prague Czechoslovakia, and the thusly motivated Czechs won the championship, ending the Soviet run of 9 straight wins. **Blinov's fine play kept him on the National Team for the upcoming Summit Series versus Canada.**

Born in 1949 in Lublin, a Moscow suburb, Blinov started playing soccer aged three. He had a natural athleticism that led to his becoming a renowned youth soccer star. Young Yuri was a top striker as a boy and won scoring titles in the highly competitive Moscow region. He started playing hockey late, as a way to stay in shape for the summer soccer season. He took to the game immediately, showing strong skating ability, combined with a natural athleticism. It became apparent that he had long term potential in both sports. The Soviet sports establishment took notice, as Blinov graduated in his early teens to playing both sports with the Central Red Army youth sports club. Former Soviet soccer and hockey star Vsevolod Bobrov spent time with Yuri, training him, working on migrating him to hockey as Blinov's prime sport. However, by 17 Blinov was still focused more on soccer than hockey. It wasn't until Anatoli Tarasov intervened after having several conversations at Blinov's family home that Yuri was finally convinced to switch full time to hockey.

Blinov joined the Soviet under 18 squad in 1967, winning gold for the first ever European Junior Hockey championships. The tournament was considered an exhibition, with the first official one in 1968. In the 1967-68 season, Blinov played on the Army junior team but was also promoted to the Central Army top team, scoring an impressive 8 goals and 12 points in 10 games. The next season he was on the top team full time. He would stay with CSKA for 7 more seasons, before being demoted to the Second Division SKA Mov Lipsek, where he would reunite with Summit Series teammate Yevgeni Zimin. Blinov would finish his career in the 1976-77 season playing only six games with Kristall Saratov before retiring at the young age of 28.

Fifty years after the Summit Series, Blinov is one of many forgotten Soviet stars, a footnote in hockey history. Yuri Blinov would play five games in the Series, scoring two goals and one assist. Blinov certainly contributed to the series and played very well in game 4. However, he appeared to start to struggle as the games became more intense and physical. It could also be surmised that as Soviet hockey evolved after they started playing professional teams in 1972, Blinov's overall game did not survive the transition, leading to his early exit from competitive hockey. Vladimir Dvortsov's editorial comment for the Tass Agency seemed to reflect on these struggles:

"Against the Canadians our players had to play over their heads, otherwise they were

over-matched. Some did not play to their potential. One was Yuri Blinov."

Blinov himself seemed to agree that he struggled against the NHL players, especially

Gary Bergman.

"It was uncanny. Gary Bergman was always between me and their net. He seemed to know all of my moves. I had the feeling we had played a hundred games against each other before."

Blinov certainly didn't struggle in game four, as he and centre Vladimir Petrov were two of the Soviets best forwards. They would combine on a picture perfect two on one strike to restore the two-goal lead for the Soviets.

The goal begins with a second straight face off in the Soviet zone. After the Henderson shot on goal, the faceoff returns to the Soviet left circle. Vladimir Petrov is again facing Clarke, with Boris Mikhailov on the right boards. Blinov is hanging far out on the left side of the Soviet zone, which was not the usual defensive positioning for a winger in a defensive zone. Clarke wins the draw again, but this time it doesn't go directly to Henderson. Henderson has to completely turn to get the puck behind him, and this gives Boris Mikhailov time to poke at the puck with his stick and knock it off the boards. **Pat Stapleton is not having a good game for Team Canada.** It gets worse as he pinches at the boards, takes a swipe at the puck, but misses and the puck bounces out off the boards to a breaking Vladimir Petrov.

Petrov carries the puck at full speed through the neutral zone, with Blinov matching him on the far-left side of the rink. Bill White is the only defenseman back for Canada, as Stapleton is caught behind the play. White hustles to get himself in good positioning, spacing himself between the two Soviet players. Petrov does a very clever little fake shot, and then slides the puck beautifully under White's stick, landing right on the tape of Blinov's stick. Ken Dryden has reacted too late to the pass, as Blinov instantly hammers a hard low shot through Dryden's feet.

It should be noted that Petrov's pass was almost the equivalent of a basketball "no look " pass. Petrov was looking right at Dryden when he makes the pass across the ice to Blinov. Tarasov had long integrated other sports to add to the Soviet hockey skillset, with Basketball being one. Blinov is visibly happy to score the goal, as the Soviets rejoice in another lightening quick strike on Team Canada.

While it would be easy to blame Pat Stapleton for the goal, it was a normal move for a defenseman to attempt to keep the puck in the offensive zone, especially as it was right within his reach at the blue line. **Stapleton's job was to ensure the puck stayed in the zone, but it unfortunately hopped past him.** Mikhailov was the catalyst, with the aggressiveness and wherewithal to get his stick on the puck after the faceoff. Petrov and Blinov jumped to the attack, as the Soviets tended to do, and in this circumstance, it paid off. Petrov makes a fantastic rush, showing some decent speed to burst up the ice and make a picture-perfect pass over to Blinov. Yuri showed why he was able to put up some good numbers in the Soviet league by finishing the play off with a hard shot through Dryden's feet. Dryden was too slow to react, possibly fooled by the Petrov fake shot and no look pass, and that was all it took for the puck to go in. Bill White played the two on one with good positioning, with no chance to stop such a perfect pass underneath his stick.

The timing was ideal for the Soviets. Canada had

looked like they were going to tie the game up, and this quick strike would break that momentum. While it was a great goal, difficult for any goalie to stop, **Dryden needed to make a save**. This was similar to the third period in game one, where Canada was pressuring late, down 4-3 and the Soviets would go down the ice for a quick strike. Dryden needed to come up with a big save in both those crucial moments, to hold the fort when the counterattack happened, but in both game 1 and 4, **Ken Dryden failed**.

After the goal, both teams do wholesale changes. Esposito is back out with Hadfield and Gilbert, with Awrey and Seiling backing them up. The Soviets have Shadrin and Yakushev out for their first shift of the game, with Anisin on the right wing. Paladiev and Vasiliev are at the points. The puck goes all the way into the Canadian zone, where Dryden plays the puck out to Rod Seiling. Seiling misses the puck, it goes to Vasiliev at the point, and he pinches in, moving the puck over to Yakushev. Seiling has moved towards the blue line, putting himself out of position. The dangerous Yakushev is deep in the corner with the puck. Don Awrey continues the Canadian defensive practice of dropping and sliding to the ice, but this time he is successful in taking the puck away from Yakushev. Yakushev had tried to pass it out front to the trailing Anasin, but Vic Hadfield made a good defensive play in covering the trailing Soviet winger, limiting Yakushev's options. The puck ends up under the flopping Don Awrey for a faceoff.

Canada gets control off the faceoff. Hadfield makes a crisp breakout pass to Rod Gilbert. Gilbert motors into the Soviet zone, spins around and then makes a terrible pass that is easily intercepted by Shadrin. The Soviets try and get set up in the Canadian zone, but Yakushev is bodied off the puck by Seiling. The puck comes around to Hadfield on the left wing, and the Ranger winger brushes off a slash and hook from Anisin to motor up the ice with the puck. On the rush, **Vasiliev takes out Phil Esposito in what should have**

459

been called as blatant interference, since Espo was nowhere near the puck. However, it does take Vasiliev out of the play, leaving Paladiev alone against the New York Ranger duo of Hadfield and Gilbert. Hadfield gets it over to Gilbert who fakes a slap shot before throwing it back to Hadfield in front. **Tretiak makes a fantastic save** by coming across the crease, stopping the Ranger fifty goal scorer with a two-pad stack save. As Hadfield is skating out of the Soviet zone, Paladiev can be seen holding the Rangers stick preventing him from backchecking, until an annoyed Hadfield rips it away from him.

The game picks up pace as Vasiliev leads the puck up ice, passing it to a streaking Yakushev who then drops it to Vikulov. Vikulov dekes around Esposito and rifles a high wrist shot that just misses the net. The puck comes all the way back to the Soviet blue line where Shadrin circles and throws it over to Paladiev. Since Evgeni Paladiev never played a moment in the NHL, he was probably aware that a player like Hadfield would remember his stick being held and exact a form of revenge later in the game, or even several games later. This was commonplace in the NHL player mindset in the original six era, it carried over into the 1970's for seasoned players like Hadfield. **As Paladiev makes a pass, he gets absolutely crushed by Hadfield with a clean bodycheck.** The crowd loves it.

Canada seems to get a boost from the hit and picks up the pace. The result would be a couple of moments of wide-open, end to end hockey with two great chances for Canada to score. Firstly, as Rod Seiling brings the puck out of the Canadian end, he hits Yvan Cournoyer **with a beautiful long pass** springing the Roadrunner free in the Soviet zone. Cournoyer flies in on a breakaway, but Tretiak comes out of his net, cuts the angle down and makes a kick save. No repeat of the game two Cournoyer goal here. The Soviets come right back down the ice, firing the puck wide of Dryden. Tsygankov gets the puck stolen from him at the Canadian blue line by

Phil Esposito. **Esposito hits Cournoyer for a second great chance** as the Montreal Canadians star flies down the right side. Vasiliev is unable to catch up to the speedy Canadian forward, allowing Cournoyer to fly in on and attempt to pull the puck past him to the left. Tretiak comes out of his crease, reads the deke, stopping him with his outstretched right skate. Cournoyer flies headfirst into the net. These were two straight failed chances by Cournoyer that could have made a real change in the game's outcome.

The Soviets try to slow the pace down with some passing, but the puck bounces out in centre ice to Frank Mahovlich, who meanders to the blue line before passing it off to Esposito on left wing. Esposito hammers a slap shot that seems destined for the top right corner on Tretiak, however, the athletic netminder is too quick and snags it out of the air with his glove. Tretiak wisely freezes the puck for a whistle, ending a chaotic few minutes.

With the faceoff again in the Soviet zone, Perreault flips it over to Yvan Cournoyer. As Cournoyer is about to fire a backhand from the slot area, Viktor Kuzkin pulls the feet out from under him, resulting in a two-minute tripping penalty. Perreault stays out for the power play, with Frank Mahovlich, Cournoyer, Park and Bergman. The Soviets have the dangerous duo of Mikhailov and Petrov, with Luchenko and Ragulin. Off the draw the puck goes to Frank Mahovlich who is on the left boards. For some reason, Frank passes it directly onto the stick of Boris Mikhailov, who says thank you very much, skates uncontested to centre ice, where he dumps a long shot at Dryden. Dryden catches the high shot, and the Vancouver crowd cheers in mock appreciation.

Esposito and Rod Seiling come out replacing Perreault and Gary Bergman. Brad Park gets the first chance of the power play when he rifles a hard high shot over Tretiak's shoulder, but the shot was too high, missing the net. The Soviets are extremely aggressive on the penalty kill, chasing the puck in a two-man unit, preventing Canada from getting any free ice or time to set up the power play. Espo stays out with the Ranger duo of Hadfield and Gilbert coming on. The Soviets do a full-scale change, bringing on Paladiev, Tsygankov, Shadrin and Valeri Kharlamov. In Soviet hockey, even the top players killed penalties.

The puck goes around the Soviet net where Paladiev is able to dump it deep into the Canadian end. Brad Park recovers the puck, brings it up to mid-ice where he hits Phil Esposito with a crisp pass at the Soviet blue line. Esposito passes it over to Vic Hadfield on the left side, just as Vladimir Shadrin brings Esposito down with an uncalled trip. Hadfield cruises in on Tretiak but is at a bad angle so he goes slightly past the left post and throws it out front to Rod Gilbert. Gilbert has gone into the goal crease area to get the pass, but in stopping suddenly, his skates turn towards Tretiak, and the puck bounces off his skate blade into the net. The Soviets immediately protest, with Tsygankov shaking his hands to say no goal, quickly joined by Tretiak in protesting. **The referee Gordon Lee immediately calls no goal, with the decision being that Gilbert directed into the net**. Canada protests loudly but the call is final.

In reviewing the play, two questions arise. Did Rod Gilbert purposely direct the puck into the net? Was it the right call either way? It appears in close analysis that Gilbert was stopping, which takes place with both skates pointed sideways in one direction. The puck caromed off his skate into the net. **Using the rules of hockey, this was actually a legal goal**, as there was no kicking motion, nor did Gilbert purposely turn his skate to score. He was stopping and had the good fortune of the puck bouncing off his skate into the goal. In hindsight, it was a bad call for Canada, as the goal should have counted. To compound matters, a second mistake by the referees was missing the blatant trip by Shadrin on Phil Esposito. A double whammy against Canada. Harry Sinden, in the book "Hockey Showdown" felt this moment was **the turning point in Game 4**, taking away

Canada's momentum.

With the decision of no goal finalized, the faceoff takes place for some unfathomable reason outside the Soviet zone. Team Canada gains control in the Soviet zone, but a pass from Rod Gilbert gets misplayed by Brad Park, and the Boris Mikhailov takes off through the neutral zone. Rod Seiling is still backing up too far and allows Boris to enter the Canadian zone all the way to the top of the faceoff circle. Mikhailov then whips a hard high wrist at Dryden. The shot is seemingly harmless as it goes right at Dryden's pad, but the Canadian goalie is still completely out of sorts and doesn't even seem to know where the puck is. Luckily for Dryden it slides out of harm's way and is recovered by Rod Seiling. Kuzkin comes out of the box and the Soviets ice the puck, having dodged a bullet with the disallowed goal and no call on Shadrin tripping Esposito.

Shadrin, Yakushev and Anisin go out against the Clarke line. The Soviets dominate the matchup, with Yakushev firing the puck from all angles, seemingly sensing that Dryden is off his game. The poor shift by team Canada culminates where Pat Stapleton continues his struggles by misplacing a pass to teammate Bill White that goes all the way back to Ken Dryden. The crowd roars in mock cheer as Dryden stops the misguided Stapleton pass attempt. As the lines change, Dennis Hull swings his stick at Yakushev in mid ice, hitting him in the face, but again **the referees see nothing, call nothing**. The game is in a bit of a lull halfway through, as both teams play some sloppy hockey, missing passes. Kharlamov puts on a brief moment of sublime artistry, fighting through some stick work by Phil Esposito and putting the puck through Dennis Hull's legs, then dancing around him. The Vancouver crowd murmurs in appreciation.

Goal 5: Vladimir Vikulov, Soviet Union 4 Canada 1

In 1972 Vladimir Vikulov was one of the top players

in the Soviet Union. When the Summit Series began, Vikulov had just finished a stellar 1971-72 season in which he had a (Wayne Gretzky like) Soviet league high, 34 goals in 31 games. This would be an 87-goal pace over an 80-game season. In fact, Vikulov dominated the goal scoring race that season, scoring 8 more goals that the 2nd place finisher, Valeri Kharlamov who had 26 goals in the same 31 games. Vikulov scored another 12 goals in 10 games in the World Championships, making the tournament all-star team. He added another 5 goals in 5 games in the 1972 Olympics. In total the sniper snipped **51 goals in 46 games**, a legendary season for anyone.

Why didn't Vikulov dominate the Summit Series in the same manner? In the six games he played, he only had 2 goals and 1 assist for 3 points. **He was playing hurt.** In game one, he suffered a partially separated shoulder. He returned in game four, playing the rest of the series, but his impact was minimal except for the two game winning goals he scored in games 4 and 5. **The second reason may have been playing against the aggressive professionals from the NHL may not have suited his game**. He was not a big man, standing at 5'9 and weighing 175 pounds, a similar size to Valeri Kharlamov or Stan Mikita. Unlike those two players, however, Vikulov did not possess the added edge to his game that was needed against seasoned pros. Pros who played hockey with such an edge 80 times a year and ramped that up in the NHL playoffs. Finally, Vikulov seemed throughout his career to be an inconsistent, somewhat streaky player.

Vladimir Vikulov was born in 1946, making him one of the older Soviet forwards in the Series. He was fast, with quick hands, and he possessed the ability to score goals in bunches. Another product of the Central Red Army Sports program, he was called up to the top club a few times aged 18. He cracked the CSKA line-up full time at the ripe age of 19 during the 1965-66 season. Despite only scoring 12 goals that season, National Team coaches Chernyshev and Tarasov obviously saw great potential in the speedy youngster, playing him in the 1966 World Championships. Vladimir played well, scoring 4 goals in 7 games. This success propelled Vikulov to a top line on both the National Team and CSKA, often playing with veteran stars Victor Polupanov and the Soviets best player in the 1960s, Anatoli Firsov. Those linemates helped propel Vladimir to seasons of 27 and 29 goals, as well as 24 points in only 14 games at the 1967 World Championships and 1968 Olympic Games combined. By 1968, he was a mainstay on the National Team, seemingly one of the top players in the USSR.

The next season, Vikulov's numbers inexplicably crashed to only 13 goals and then a dismal 2 goals in 9 games at the 1969 Worlds. His numbers slightly improved the next season with 19 goals in 39 games in the 1970-71 season but the days of his playing on the top line and producing large goal totals seemed over. As a result, there could have been no way to predict Vikulov's explosive 1971-72 season. He scored at a rate that hadn't been seen since Summit Series teammate Alexander Yakushev scored 50 goals in 42 games in the 1967-1968 season. Vikulov found that elusive chemistry again, this time playing with new Soviet stars, the very talented duo of Maltsev and Kharlamov.

He would play in the 1974 Summit Series against the WHA stars, going scoreless and being dressed in four of the eight games. He seemed to be finished internationally, especially against the professionals. Vikulov would resurrect his career once more though. In the 1976 Canada Cup, Vikulov was the Soviets second leading scorer, playing wonderfully putting up 7 points in 4 games. He would also play in the 1976 super Series as a member of CSKA, and then join the National Team playing 11 games against WHA clubs over two tours. In the 1977-78 season, at age 30 he would rebound with 22 goals and 40 points in 35 games. This gave him one more crack at the NHL pros as Moscow Dynamo added him for their 1978 NHL tour. Vikulov would score 2 goals in the 6 games.

Vladimir Vikulov was never able to transfer his goal scoring ability in the Soviet league to those games against the North American professionals. **In total, he would play 31 games against NHL or WHA pros and only score 8 goals**. A very talented player, one who simply did not produce against the pros. Vikulov played his entire career from 1963 to 1979 with the Red Army club, before joining Ska Leningrad for 9 games in his last season. After retirement, Vikulov was the Head coach for the Soviet under 18 team in 1984-85. Sadly, like so many of his Summit teammates, he passed away at the relatively young age of 67 in 2013. Vikulov's main contribution to the Summit Series? Scoring two key, eventual game winning goals in games 4 and 5.

The fourth goal for the Soviets was a backbreaking goal for Team Canada. The Canadians had shown some life for the previous few moments, with several good chances and a waived off goal. A 4-1 Soviet lead halfway through a game in which Canada had been badly outplayed would have seemed almost insurmountable. It was also the natural result of such a mundane, inconsistent effort by the Canadians, combined with a superbly executed Soviet game to that point.

The play leading to the goal begins with Don Awrey controlling the puck behind his own net. Valeri Kharlamov gives the Bruins defenceman zero time to set up, quickly coming behind the net and forcing Awrey to throw the puck up the left side. Dennis Hull is waiting on the hash marks, but the Soviet game is built on puck pressure. Kharlamov has followed the puck to the left side, linemate Vikulov is right there in front of Hull, and big Tsygankov pinches in off the blue line. Under pressure, Hull decides to throw the puck back around the Canadian net. The puck travels to the right corner of the Canadian zone, where Rod Seiling skates to recover the puck. Vladimir Vikulov has followed the puck and quickly harasses Seiling in the corner. Seiling turns, but Vikulov pins him against the boards. Seiling turns again, allowing him to escape Vikulov's dogged checking. Defenseman Alexander Ragulin has pinched into the fray along the boards, bodying Goldsworthy, who has come to Seiling's aid. Seiling pokes the puck past Ragulin, but right onto the stick of Alexander Maltsev, who is standing on the hash marks. Seiling bodies Maltsev against the boards, but **the puck is already gone**, as Maltsev took the hit as he passed to Valeri Kharlamov.

If Valeri Kharlamov had a sleepy game to that point, he was about to make up for it. He is just above the faceoff circle and does a little spin to give himself some space, but also trying to draw a defender towards him. The ploy works as Don Awrey leaves the slot area and goes towards Kharlamov. For the second straight time, the puck moves quickly, as Kharlamov plants a beautiful backhand pass to the sniper Vikulov who is wide open at the right side of the Canadian net. Dryden comes across and drops to his pads, but he is too late as the Soviet League goal scoring leader snaps the puck past him into the net. **There are smatterings of applause from the Vancouver crowd, who seem to be appreciating the Soviet hard work and execution.**

This goal was a result of the **Soviet swarm** at its finest. Canadian defenders Rod Seiling and Don Awrey had their time and space taken away from the Soviet swarming forwards and the pinching Soviet defence. In sequence, Don Awrey **gets pressured** behind the net by two forecheckers and throws it up the boards. Dennis Hull **gets pressured** by the same two Soviet forwards and gets bumped from behind by the pinching Tsygankov. Rod Seiling is battling Vikulov but as Bill Goldsworthy attempts to help, Alexander Ragulin **pinches in** off the point, taking him out the play. Canada simply is getting smothered by the nonstop skating, buzzing Soviet players.

Where were the other Canadian players? Phil Esposito was late to the play, waiting at the blue line for the puck. He comes back slightly, giving Kharlamov a half-hearted hook, too little too late. Dennis Hull was on the left side, also awaiting a breakout that never came. One positional mistake made was when Don Awrey left the slot area to chase the puck, but Dennis Hull needed to see that opening and cover Vikulov. Instead, he and Phil Esposito are standing away from the action, watching the puck go in the net.

This goal is a prime example how the Soviet fitness allows them to outskate and outwork the Canadian defence with predictable results. At this stage in the series, Canada needs to learn that the Soviets tend to score goals two ways. The first is with a fast break capitalization of a foes mistake either in the Soviet end or neutral ice with the Blinov goal as an example. The second is where they use their two-man forechecking/swarming offence to outnumber the defence, breaking them down, until a player is open for the quick and usually effective strike. Canada will have to somehow become fitter and play more intelligent, positional hockey to compete.

After the goal, Perrault, Cournoyer and Frank Mahovlich faceoff against Petrov, Blinov and Mikhailov. The Soviets immediately get possession, passing it several times with it ending up on the stick of Yuri Blinov. Blinov has continued his strong play from the first period, as his confidence seems boosted by his earlier goal. He circles at his own blue line, then jumps over an attempted check by Perreault. Blinov shows great athleticism as he maintains both his balance and control of the puck. He then easily skates around a disinterested Cournoyer who makes almost no attempt to stop him. Finally, Blinov flies around Park, who times his check poorly. **Park is quickly two strides behind Blinov as he vainly chases the Soviet winger down the boards.** While Blinov eventually makes a poor drop pass, **his rush is an unsettling display of skill**. The Canadian fans watching live and across Canada had to have been in shock watching one of the Soviet's lesser-known players making the NHL stars look slow, lazy, and inadequate. **This was bad, but Canada is about to look even worse.**

After Blinov's failed drop pass, Yvan Cournoyer makes a terrible cross ice pass to no one. The puck goes trinkling into the Soviet zone, where Vladislav Tretiak comes out of his crease to play the puck. **Suddenly, he is bulled over by Frank Mahovlich in full flight.** The duo slide to the far side of the goal net, close to the corner. **Frank then holds the Soviet goalie for 8 long seconds, refusing to allow him to get up, sitting on him, holding him down.** When Mahovlich does finally let the goalie up, he gives him a final unsportsmanlike shove before skating back down the ice.

Frank Mahovlich is considered by many fans as one of the best left wingers of all time. While that might be a bit of exaggerated praise for a beloved player, there is no doubt that when Frank was in the right state of mind, he could do things on the ice that few players in hockey could. Frank was an extremely talented natural athlete. He was a big man for that era, yet one of the fastest players in the NHL. When he wound up for one of his swooping rushes, he could blow by players easily. **Matching that talent was his on-ice charisma.** He had jet black hair, a handsome boyish face, and a shy 'aw, shucks' demeanour that endeared him to fans across Canada. As a result, the Big M was one of hockey's biggest stars throughout the 1960's and early 1970's. Mahovlich wasn't all show, producing some excellent seasons for three different NHL teams. He would beat out Chicago's Bobby Hull to win the Calder Memorial Trophy with the Maple Leafs as the NHL's top rookie in 1957-58, and after three solid but disappointing campaigns, he exploded for 48 goals in the 1960-61 season. That year Frank had been placed on a line with Red Kelly and Bob Nevin, two cerebral two-way hockey players who would help settle Frank down and help focus his talent. Frank needed that guidance from a successful veteran like Red Kelly because Frank was a quiet, sensitive man, who found the pressure difficult, pressure placed on him by coaches, management, and expectations to live up to his massive talent.

That 48-goal season would be the highest goal total Frank had with the Leafs. Despite the team winning four Stanley Cups in the decade, Frank would constantly get picked on by coach/GM Punch Imlach who looked at Frank as a talented, lazy underachiever. Instead of motivating Frank, it caused him to slip into a frustrated, depressive state. Frank would average 30 goals a season for the next five seasons but by the 1966-67 season, the stress of playing for Imlach had impacted Mahovlich to the point where he scored only 19 goals. Even a surprise Stanley Cup win that spring failed to elevate Franks production as he had only 3 goals in 12 playoff games. His time seemed over as a Leaf.

The next season, the enigmatic Mahovlich was dealt to the Detroit Red Wings. This was a huge trade, a seven-player package that brought Team Canada teammate Paul Henderson to the Leafs. Mahovlich was reborn on the Red Wings. Playing on a line with another veteran centre, future Hall of Famer Alex Delvecchio and the great Gordie Howe on the right side, Frank had 49 goals in his first season as a Wing, following it up with a strong 38 goal campaign in 1969-70. With Gordie Howe around, Frank no longer felt the pressure to be the best player on the team, and his veteran linemates were able to keep him positive and focused. Frank was also able to briefly play with his younger brother Pete which added to his joy of being released from his stressful time as a Maple Leaf. The Red Wings were a team on the decline and after two seasons they traded Frank to the Montreal Canadians for another future Team Canada teammate, Mickey Redmond.

Frank's brother, Pete, had been traded to Montreal a year earlier, so it was a reunification for the brothers, a lifelong dream of Frank's to play for the fabled Canadiens. For the third time in his career, Frank was placed with a strong two-way intelligent centre, this time with Jacques Lemaire.

Lemaire was an excellent passer and defensive player, which allowed Frank to play his freewheeling game to perfection. The results showed, as Frank would have a fantastic playoff performance in 1970-71 scoring 14 goals and 27 points in 20 games as the Canadians shocked the league by winning the Cup after knocking out the heavily favoured bruins in a 7-game quarterfinal. Frank would continue his strong play the next season, scoring 43 goals and a career high 96 points at 34 years old. This led to Harry Sinden happily choosing him for Team Canada, making him one of the co-captains and **placing great faith that Mahovlich would be one of his go-to players**. That of course never happened. Frank's performance in the series got increasingly worse. He struggled so badly that he was eventually pulled from the line-up in games 6 and 7.

What happened to Frank that made his play so disappointing in the Summit Series? Firstly, he lacked the right centre with which to play. Frank was successful when he was in the right surroundings, the right mix of players with whom he could gel. **Sinden and Ferguson made a mistake when they overlooked Jacques Lemaire in the selection process**. Lemaire was not only a sound two-way player, but he was a solid skater who had centred a line with both Frank and Yvan Cournoyer in Montreal. Stan Mikita centred the duo in training camp, and they performed well. Sinden however didn't dress Mikita for game one, instead putting the Montreal Canadians duo with Phil Esposito. That was a terrible mix as Phil was a centre who needed the puck. He also had a big, vocal personality that probably wasn't a good fit with sensitive Frank. Mikita joined the line in game two and they produced, scoring two goals including Frank's only goal of the series. Mikita however played sparingly in game 3 and was dropped from the line-up afterwards. **Gil Perreault centred the duo in game four and like Espo, Perreault was a player who needed the puck**. Another reason for Frank's poor play was he became increasingly paranoid about Soviet espionage and cold war propaganda. He felt the Soviet KGB agents were following him everywhere and even ingesting him with pollen. This excerpt from blogger Nitzy's Hockey Den seems to confirm that:

"Watch it, Harry," Frank Mahovlich keeps telling his coach. "Watch it. Be prepared for anything. This is a cold war, you know. A cold war. I've had hay fever for a week now. In Toronto, Winnipeg and Vancouver. How can the pollen count be so high everywhere I go?"

"Maybe," Eddie Johnston suggests in jest, "they're following you around with a powder in a spray can, just to upset you."

"Ha, ha," Sinden chuckles.

"Don't laugh," Frank says. "They'd do anything."

The interesting thing is Frank also poorly played two years later in the 1974 Series for Team Canada WHA. Despite wanting to make up for his poor 1972 play, he underperformed in the 1974 series just as badly, scoring only one goal and eventually being dropped from the line-up. **The reality is Frank's game did not seem suited for international hockey.**

When he was in the WHA with the Toronto Toros, they went to Europe to play some exhibition games against Swedish and Finnish club teams. These teams were obviously not the level of the Soviet National Team, yet Frank scored 2 goals in the 6 games. In total he played 18 games against European competition and scored 4 goals. On the Canadian side there seems to have been three types of forwards who thrived against European competition. The greats of the game, players who produced no matter the opposition. Legends like Wayne Gretzky, Phil Esposito, or Bobby Hull are prime examples. The second type were great skaters and solid two-way players. Paul Henderson, Ralph Backstrom who was fantastic in the '74 Series, Mark Howe and Mark Messier are all good examples. Finally, big strong aggressive forwards who could chip in offensively. Players like John

Tonelli, Brent Sutter, Clark Gilles, or even Wayne Cashman fit that mould. All three types played well against the Soviets at varying times. Unfortunately, Frank Mahovlich was different than those style of players. While very talented, his was an individual game. Mahovlich wasn't overly physical, nor had fantastic hockey sense. **While his individual skills gave him success in the NHL, that style did not translate well to the international game**.

Perhaps it was Frank's growing frustration with his own play that led to the infamous mugging of Vladislav Tretiak. Perhaps it was his paranoia about the Soviet KGB players or the fact that for four straight games Tretiak had been easily handling all of Frank's heavy slap shots. He may have felt it was just a good hockey play. Whatever the reasons, these 8 seconds in game four triggered the Vancouver crowd to a chorus of nonstop jeers and boos. **They had seen enough**. They had seen Bill Goldsworthy's needless penalties. They had seen Yvan Cournoyer slashing wildly at Soviet players. They were shocked when the clean playing Rod Gilbert was hitting Kharlamov from behind. They had seen that and more. This was bigger. None of those players were Frank Mahovlich. Frank was one of the most respected, admired, loved players in Canada. He was *the Big M*. He was Casey at the bat. Yet there he was sitting on Tretiak, holding him down. The Vancouver faithful, and those across Canada, saw their hero sitting on the Soviet goalie refusing to let the young netminder up. They saw **desperation.** They saw their NHL stars losing to a team from another part of the world. They saw a Canadian team that was shouting out to the hockey world, *we can't beat them, so let's cheat. Maybe a goal can be scored if I just hold him down.* **They saw the myth of Canadian hockey supremacy gone in that moment**. Deceived. *I thought we were the best.* They saw themselves in the players, frustrated and desperate and sad. So, they booed. They booed loud and strong. They rained down their anger and frustration on Frank Mahovlich. They rained down their emotions on a beleaguered, outclassed Team Canada.

With the second period winding down, the Soviets appear in complete control of the game. The Canadians respond with vicious stick work. Off a faceoff **Clarke hooks Maltsev** who shoots the puck in. Pat Stapleton recovers, passes the puck, and then gives V**ikulov a two-hand slash** across his ankle. A moment later **Henderson trips Maltsev, before Clarke spears Tsyganko**v and follows that up by whipping his stick around for a slash attempt at Vikulov. The Soviets just slow the game down and pass the puck, oblivious to the Canadian stick work. Mikhailov makes a solo rush around Awrey for a quick shot that Dryden is able to stop, as the Soviets keep on pressing. It gets to a point where Vic Hadfield swings his stick like a golf club (Vic would end up owning a successful driving range in Oakville Ontario) and fires a long wedge shot to Tretiak. Its Canadas only shot on goal for several moments and **the Vancouver crowd roars in sarcastic approval**.

On one rare counter strike, Gilbert Perrault makes a rush using his speed he makes a rush into the Soviet zone. He dishes over to Frank Mahovlich who decides to wind up for a big slap shot. Frank takes too long to shoot so his slapper is stopped by a textbook sliding shot block from Paladiev. A quick wrist shot might have been a goal. As the play comes out of the Soviet zone, Cournoyer hooks Shadrin from behind, and then skates into Anasin with his stick held face high. **Neither the hook nor the cross check is called by the officials, nor was the Mahovlich hold of Tretiak**. The Soviets press as Yakushev makes another slick back door play to Anasin, who has recovered from his face full of Cournoyer's stick. **Ken Dryden makes his best save of the night, when he rockets across the crease and makes a two-pad stack save on Anisin**. A final Dennis Hull giveaway in the Canadian zone has Shadrin setting up behind the Canadian goal before the bell signals the end of the second period.

Game 4: Period Two Review

The second period of game four was immensely dramatic. There were multiple near chances, world class saves, boggled pucks, a disallowed goal, and a legendary player sitting on a goaltender refusing to allow him to get up. This period was also the turning point for the Vancouver crowd who had seemingly had enough of Team Canada's unsportsmanlike, unorganized play. The fans displeasure with Team Canada's poor sportsmanship and rough play also included goaltender Ken Dryden who was mock cheered every time he made a save. To add to the Canadian players' frustration, the Vancouver crowd began to appreciate the Soviet style of play, acknowledging their artistry with applause.

While it appeared that Team Canada hit rock bottom in the second period, they had several close calls to tie the score at 2-2. Gilbert Perreault's goal had energized the Canadian players, leading to very close chances for Ron Ellis, Cournoyer and Hadfield. Tretiak held them all at bay, until the quick strike from Blinov put the Soviets ahead 3-1. Canada almost made it 3-2 on the Rod Gilbert disallowed goal, but they were soon deflated by the fourth Soviet strike, ending the period down 4-1. **It was a justified result for the Soviets**, as they may have had some lapses, but they were out skating, outworking and out thinking Team Canada. In similar circumstances in game one when Canada got to 4-3 halfway through the third period, this Soviet team showed again that **they would simply not wilt under pressure**. In fact, more often than not, they would come back with a devastating counter strike. If Ken Dryden had not made two excellent pad stacking saves on Maltsev and Anasin, or if Don Awrey had not intercepted the puck crossing the goal line after Dryden bobbled Luchenko's shot, **Canada could have been easily down 7-1**.

On the Soviet side, Tretiak had another strong period.

He smothered any long shots, read the plays perfectly and gave his team clutch save after clutch save. Kharlamov started out poorly, but quickly returned to form. He was dancing everywhere, and he made two wonderful passes in the period, the second resulting in the crucial Vikulov goal. For the second straight period Boris Mikhailov was the best player on the ice. He was forechecking, creating offense and skating nonstop every shift. Alexander Maltsev also stood out for his sublime skating and puck handling. Yakushev and Shadrin were certainly impactful when finally inserted into the game. The Soviet defence were a bit less impressive this period, they were sloppy at times, perhaps pinching too much, getting caught positionally, which led to some dangerous chances for Canada. However, they continued to be aggressive offensively, leading some rushes and giving their forwards quick accurate passes out of the Soviet zone. Overall, the Soviet team was playing their strongest game of the series, **a high speed, constant movement, puck control game that had the dual effect of both frustrating and exhausting Team Canada.**

Those watching the game, in Vancouver and across Canada, had to wonder what was wrong with Team Canada. Their play was erratic, sloppy, often recklessly dirty. Passes were too far ahead of a teammate or well behind them. They weren't consistently skating hard, they were losing battles on the boards, and they didn't seem to have any creativity to their game. The dump ins were often without a forechecker, ending up easy turnovers for the Soviet defence. The angled dump in from earlier games seemed to have been ignored or forgotten. Defensively, the effort was inconsistent, as they made bad plays under the forechecking pressure, or dropped to the ice for shot blocks that never materialized. Ken Dryden was terribly shaky, dropping one shot near the goal line and completely losing a Boris Mikhailov shot later in the period. While he did make several good saves, he never seemed settled down or composed, the opposite of his counterpart at the other end of the ice.

There were very few standouts for Canada this period. Yvan Cournoyer used his speed to get two excellent chances to score, but he was still playing an angry, high sticking game that was out of character. The same could be said for the usually clean playing Ron Ellis who was also running Soviet players with his stick face high, or even Paul Henderson who was clutching, grabbing, and hooking at every moment instead of using his notable speed. Bobby Clarke seemed exhausted from overuse, and actually spun and fell towards the end of the period to the derision of the Vancouver crowd. Phil Esposito made some good plays, but he was not skating hard or getting involved enough in the game. Vic Hadfield had another good period of hockey, always the first man back, making some good passes, setting up a disallowed goal and getting a clean big hit on Paladiev. Combined with Gil Perreault who was periodically skating and creating some offence, they were Canadas best forwards. Defensively, Bill White and Gary Bergman had good periods, but Pat Stapleton was struggling to regain his form he showed in games 2 and 3. While Canada had shown some spark to try and get back in the game, after the 4th goal they collapsed into an exhausted, disjointed, angry state. They were joined by an angry, shocked, dissatisfied Vancouver crowd.

CHAPTER 40: GAME 4 PERIOD 3. BOOS AND MORE BOOS

The crowd doesn't seem to have cooled during the second intermission, as the grumbling noises rumble during the opening faceoff. The Soviets, not taking anything to chance, start their top line of Maltsev, Kharlamov and Vikulov. As per usual to this point in the series, Canada counters with the Clarke line, Bergman and Park. The Soviets quickly get the puck into the Canadian zone, harassing the Canadian players with relentless pursuit of the puck. Ron Ellis makes a nice spin-o-rama behind the Canadian goal helping Canada relieve the pressure. Tsygankov makes a bad pass at the Soviet blue line which Clarke recovers, then feeds Henderson who is breaking in on Tretiak. Henderson gets a shot away from a bad angle on Tretiak who stands up and makes the save. Tsygankov attempts to going back to his earlier success in rushing the puck but gives the puck away at his blue line with a bad pass that Henderson intercepts. Henderson breaks in on Tretiak but takes too long to set up a half slap shot. Suddenly, an intensely backchecking Vikulov slides, knocking the puck away before Henderson could shoot. The Soviets get possession and put on a clinic with their circling and extremely accurate passing. Canada seems resigned to let them do it for a few moments, until finally play is called for a two-line pass. **It's amazing to watch how**

the Soviets work in unison, moving the puck around in a soccer style format, regrouping until they can spot an open team mate up ice.

Canada wins the ensuing faceoff, but Pat Stapleton takes another long slap shot at Tretiak from outside the blue line. Tretiak handles the easy shot, yet Luchenko has trouble getting control of the puck in the left corner. The puck slips out to a pinching Bill White who gets a good low shot off at Tretiak. The Soviet defence is being a little sloppy so far in the third period, either because of the large lead, or the unfamiliarity with leading the rushes out of their zone.

Vladimir Petrov had the difficult task in the Series of going up against Phil Esposito. Esposito was incredibly strong on his skates and a big, heavy-set man for that era. As Esposito drives to the Soviet net, Petrov is hanging all over him, finally bringing Esposito down to the ice. **In a moment of genuine sportsmanship**, Petrov smiles at Espo, pats him, holding up his gloves in a shrug seemingly saying, "Sorry, big Phil, I had no choice".

One of Harry Sinden's mistakes in the games in Canada was a stubborn refusal to change up his power play lines. Despite a lack of both chemistry and success, Sinden puts his usual powerplay group of Esposito centring Frank Mahovlich and Cournoyer. The only position that Sinden can't seem to decide on is who should play with Brad Park on the point. The coaches have tried at various times Rod Seiling, Red Berenson and even Phil Esposito. In a 4-1 game, where Canada badly needs a goal, Sinden decides to try Rod Gilbert on the point, **hoping for some sort of magical success**. What Team Canadas coaching staff seems to miss, is that it has been the Soviet buzzing, high pressure penalty killing that has been stifling the power play more so than anything else. Canada's group of five struggle for any sort of cohesion. Cournoyer makes two bad passes, both are intercepted. **The crowd moans in united derision.** Boris Mikhailov easily carries it into Canada's end, wasting time off the clock. Phil

Esposito does a modern-day style neutral zone drop pass to a streaking Rod Gilbert, but the play fails as Gilbert fails to set up the powerplay in the Soviet end, finally giving the puck away to Shadrin. The number of bad passes by this Team Canada group is astounding. They are completely out of sync.

Canada finally gets a good chance on goal as Esposito carries it himself into the Soviet end. Esposito moved well for a big man and was an underrated stickhandler. **He easily goes around the immobile Ragulin, cutting directly towards Tretiak**. Tretiak makes a quick pad save, his first serious save in several minutes. Esposito goes after the puck in the corner and tries to poke it to Frank Mahovlich on the boards, to ideally start a cycle of some sort. **Frank misses the easy play and shows complete disinterest in pursing the puck any further.** This allows Luchenko to fire the puck down the ice, wasting Esposito's efforts. Mahovlich picks up the puck in the Canadian end and decides to do a long individual rush into the Soviet zone. Predictably, he loses the puck.

As Canada again restarts the power play in their own end, Vic Hadfield comes onto the ice. He gets the puck just over the centre ice line where he fires a beautiful pass to Cournoyer who is breaking into the Soviet zone. The problem was the Montreal Canadiens speedster was called offside on the play. It doesn't deter Cournoyer from firing another useless slapshot directly at Tretiak's pads. The young Soviet goaltender makes the save and bats the puck away **in obvious derision** at the late shot.

The officiating in this game has been odd, missing numerous calls. After the offside, the officials decide to drop the puck not at a faceoff dot, but instead about 10 feet behind the red line on the Canadian side of the ice. There has probably never been a face off held in that position on the ice again in the history of hockey. Perrault has come on to centre a makeshift line with Hadfield and Cournoyer.

It should be noted that Cournoyer played the entire two-minute powerplay, made two poor passes, went offside, yet is still on the ice going into his third minute of the shift. **Much like game one, Sinden seems to lose track of his players and their ice time, to the detriment of the team**.

As the play goes into the Soviet zone, Cournoyer continues his less than stellar play by bowling over Kharlamov, who was nowhere near the puck. Again, no call. In an impressive moment of skating, Alexander Maltsev speeds across the ice, hammering a long shot at Dryden, then as Canada counter attacks, it's Maltsev who strips Cournoyer of the puck in the Soviet end. In contrast to the Canadian forwards who are playing in spurts, **the Soviet forwards never stop skating. Forechecking and backchecking at full speed, the Soviets play textbook two-way hockey.**

One of the areas where the Soviets have truly struggled so far in the series is in the faceoff circle. Canada has dominated to the point where defenseman Valeri Vasiliev is taking the draw in the Soviet end against Gil Perreault. The Soviets get possession and quickly move the puck down the ice. In a typical Soviet rush, Yakushev gives it to Anasin who weaves into the Canadian zone. He drops it Shadrin, who gives it back to Anasin. Anasin has now pulled the Canadian defenders Seiling and Awrey to one side of the ice. Seeing this, Anasin lands a beautiful pass back on the stick of Shadrin, who is now alone in front of Dryden. Dryden makes a good save. Perreault gets the puck in the corner and then commits one of the cardinal sins of hockey, **he stickhandles in front of his own goal**. This is basic hockey as predictably Perreault loses it to Anasin, right in front of Team Canada's goal. Dryden had seen enough and covers the puck. As he does, Awrey decides to cross check Anasin. Anasin gives him a "come on, there's no need for that" look and skates away. **The crowd sees the difference in the two teams' sportsmanship and cast loud, intense, ongoing boos of derision down on the Canadian players.**

Canada does a whole scale change putting out the Clarke line with White and Stapleton. Clarke wins another draw. The puck goes back to Pat Stapleton, who rushes the puck up ice. He one hands a pass to Ron Ellis who flies over the Soviet blue line. Ellis is poke checked off the puck, and then stood up at the blue line by Valeri Vasiliev. **This was another beautiful textbook hockey play.** Vasiliev then angles the trailing Stapleton to the boards and delivers a clean, hard hit. Vasiliev wasn't dressed for the first two games, but he has been the Soviets' best defenseman since. Young and aggressive, he had good size and played a mobile two-way game. He was also a devastating hitter.

The Canadians regroup, starting with a nice Bill White pass to Henderson from the Canadian end. White was a big man for the era, and looked like an awkward skater, but he was deceivingly mobile and beat young Anasin the puck to start the rush. Henderson gets the puck over to Clarke who then makes a slick no look backhand pass to a speeding Ron Ellis on the right wing. Ellis has Henderson open on the left side, and a pass would have certainly ended up with a goal for Canada. Ellis shoots from the angle, but Tretiak gets his pad on it. The three on two rush was something Canadian teams often practiced, with quick passes to the breaking wings. However, the difference between the Soviet game and the Canadian one at this stage, was **the Soviets would have made that final cross crease pass** instead of shooting. They also would have probably scored doing so. One final note on this play. Clarke's pass is a thing of beauty as he actually leans towards Henderson on his left, moving the Soviet defence in that direction, before dishing off to Ellis on the right.

The play gets a bit scrambly for both sides for a few moments until Paul Henderson fires another long slap shot from outside the blue line at Tretiak. Tretiak holds the puck for faceoff. The break allows for both teams to fully change players. The quick and talented trio of Maltsev, Kharlamov and Vikulov are out against Phil Esposito, Dennis Hull and

Bill Goldsworthy. Hull gets a chance for a slap shot at the Soviet blue line but fires it several feet wide and high of the Soviet net. One of the obvious skill differences between Dennis and his brother Bobby is in shot accuracy. Dennis has fired a couple of shots this game that ended up nowhere near the Soviet goal.

After the ensuing faceoff, Kharlamov makes a quick rush down the right side, trying to free sniper Vikulov for a shot on goal, but is foiled by Gary Bergman. Goldsworthy awkwardly carries the puck for a moment behind the Canadian goal before getting pressured by Vikulov. Goldsworthy drops the puck back to Brad Park who makes a poor pass that is intercepted by Tsygankov at the Canadian blue line. The Soviets dump it back into the Canadian end, but Gary Bergman fires the puck up the boards as he flies out of the Canadian zone. Phil Esposito intercepts the puck just over the red line. Phil Esposito often gets historically categorized as a big man who wasn't overly fast on his feet. **In reality he was deceivingly fast,** and he shows it on this rush as he flies down the right side of the ice into the soviet zone. Tsygankov struggles to catch up to him, which allows Esposito to make a nice backhand pass over Tsygankov's stick, to a streaking Gary Bergman.

While Brad Park was the top NHL point producer for Team Canada before the series, generally known as the second-best offensive defenseman in hockey behind Bobby Orr, the fastest skater for Team Canada on defence was indisputably Gary Bergman. Bergman was known primarily as a tough defensive defenseman, but he could move when he wanted to. He shows it here, as he catches up to the play and gets rewarded with a great chance to score on Tretiak. Tretiak makes another stupendous save; a sliding two pad save that had him barely kicking his pad in time to stop Bergman's attempt. Tretiak's quickness and athleticism is on full display as he stifles yet another Canadian chance. His save has the crowd murmuring in appreciation as the play continues back into the Canadian zone.

Brad Park struggled defensively the first four games of the Summit Series. He seemed out of sorts positionally and wasn't playing the airtight one on one defence needed against the slick Soviets. As Don Awrey found out in game one, the Soviet forwards were much more than just pass first players. They were excellent and devastating one on one players. Alexander Maltsev was one of the top Soviet forwards both on the National Team and in the Soviet league. He was mobile, fast, and like his teammate Kharlamov, could stickhandle and make quick moves while in full flight. As Vikulov brings the puck into the neutral zone he heads mans it to Maltsev who is in full flight on the left wing. Maltsev crosses the blue line, now in a one-on-one situation against Brad Park. Park is skating backwards and attempts to poke check the puck. Maltsev however leans to his right and in one quick motion **puts the puck between Park's legs and goes around him**. Park looks at the puck instead of Maltsev, something young defensemen are taught not to do. Luckily for Canada, Maltsev's shot is right at Dryden's pads. A move like that is just not seen at the higher levels, it's more of a move in kids' hockey or even shinny hockey. The fact that this happened to a player of Park's stature was truly embarrassing moment for the New York Ranger all-star.

Goal 6: Bill Goldsworthy (Phil Esposito) USSR 4 Canada 2

Phil Esposito was one of the greatest pure goal scorers in hockey history. He wasn't exactly like a Mike Bossy or Alex Ovechkin who feasted, still feasting in Ovechkin's case, on goalies with quick one-timers from side angles. Nor did he have the dramatic end to end rushes of a Rocket Richard, or the devastating slap shot of a Bobby Hull. Esposito was a different sort of goal scorer. **He used a devastating combination of strength, timing, and spatial awareness** to catch goalies unawares or unable to stop the sudden strike. He also possessed a powerful set of wrists that could fire a puck almost instantaneously before a hapless goalie could get set up. Esposito of course had a plethora of other skills, including great stickhandling, superior hockey sense and emotional leadership that was a handful for any team on the planet in 1972. In the case of the second goal of the game for Team Canada it was Phil Esposito's devastating shot that seemingly went in and out, but was called as being off the crossbar, that showcased his ability to handcuff goalies. The subsequent rebound by the beleaguered Bill Goldsworthy gave Canada a faint glimmer of hope for a late third period comeback.

In some sense, the goal was redemption of sorts for Bill Goldsworthy. After his antics in his first shift that led to a powerplay goal by the Soviets, he went out on his next shift and took another senseless penalty. This of course led to a second straight powerplay goal by Boris Mikhailov. Canada never recovered from the early deficit and the Vancouver crowd took their anger out on Goldsworthy the few times he got on the ice afterwards. This affected Goldsworthy deeply. His Minnesota North Stars teammate JP Parise felt Goldsworthy never recovered from the effects of this game. Goldsworthy himself seemed to be deeply distraught after the game.

> *"I may not say it after I've slept on it, but right now I'm ashamed of being Canadian. You have one bad shift and they're on you. We're playing for our country and that's the kind of support they give you? You're so nervous that you can hardly hold onto the puck after that. There was a time when a guy was proud to play for his country. Not it's a shame. Not just here tonight. It was the same in Montreal, and in Toronto and in Winnipeg...I'm glad the next four games are in Russia, we will probably get a better reception there" Nitzyshockeyblogspot.com*

Much like Goldsworthy's performance in this game, a contradiction of reckless play coupled with goal scoring ability, Bill Goldsworthy's career and life had similar peaks and valleys. Goldy had been a junior star, winning a Memorial Cup with the Niagara Falls Flyers in 1965. While he struggled to find a roster spot on the Bruins in the later 1960's, he thrived once he joined the expansion Minnesota North Stars, in many ways becoming the star attraction and face of the franchise. He had a little dance after he scored a goal that the Minnesota faithful dubbed the "Goldie shuffle". He did that dance 48 times in the 1973-74 season. This would be his career high in goals and the peak of his hockey life. Unfortunately, Goldsworthy battled alcoholism, which no doubt contributed to his rapid decline in production after this career season. He would be traded to the New York Rangers in 1976-77 after only 2 goals in 16 games with the North Stars. He floundered with the Rangers, eventually being sent to the Rangers AHL farm team. Goldsworthy would try to revamp his career in the WHA, with little success, before retiring at age 34 with the Edmonton Oilers. A life of promiscuity and alcohol caught up to Goldsworthy. He died of Aids in 1996. On February 15th, 1992, the Minnesota North Stars retired Goldsworthy's number 8, a tribute to a troubled, beloved player.

The goal itself results from a quick, Soviet-like counterattack after the Maltsev undressing of Brad Park and subsequent shot on Dryden. To Brad Park's credit, he recovers instantly from the Maltsev rush, gathering the rebound off the Maltsev shot and immediately skating the puck out of the Canadian zone. The Soviet forwards are now caught deep as the Soviet defenders Tsygankov and Ragulin backpedal. Park makes a pass to the streaking Goldsworthy who carries the puck over the centre red line. At this stage Ragulin has stopped skating and is almost stationary inside the Soviet zone. This allows Goldsworthy time to make a pass into the high slot area to Phil Esposito who has joined the rush. Tsygankov has backed up almost to the slot, where Brad Park has skated directly into him. This may have blocked Tretiak's sightline to the puck. Esposito drills the puck over Tretiak's shoulder, and while Ragulin watches the play, Goldsworthy knocks the puck back into the net. Video replays are inconclusive as to whether the puck first went in for Espo's shot or if the goal was scored on the rebound. Either way, the final decision was to award Goldsworthy the goal. Poor defensive work by the Soviet players, especially Alexander Ragulin certainly contributed to the goal, but it was also Canada's ability to strike quickly that gave them a chance to come back in this game.

After the goal, the Canadian players get an energy boost but still seem to be more focused on stickwork and intimidation. Yvan Cournoyer gives Valeri Vasiliev a two-hand chop that goes uncalled, and then the diminutive Montreal Canadian gets into a tangled shoving match with Shadrin as the play heads up ice. Cournoyer does get a good chance on goal as he intercepts a stray Kuzkin pass, steps around Luchenko and gets a close shot on goal. Canada begins to apply some pressure as Cournoyer, then Perrault get point blank shots on goal. The Soviet group seems exhausted as Rod Seiling does the angled dump in, allowing the puck to bounce out to Cournoyer. Perrault and Frank Mahovlich cycle the puck with the Big M suddenly coming to life. He lugs the puck in a big swooping circle, around Kuzkin who desperately hooks and stabs at the Big M, before delivering a hard wrister at Tretiak. It's testimony to just how good Frank Mahovlich could be when he decided to turn it on. **The flurry also showcased the talent of Vladislav Tretiak, who was everywhere stopping the onslaught and keeping Canada from crawling back into this game.**

Clarke's line is up next against the Maltsev/Kharlamov/Blinov line. Kharlamov loses the puck twice, once to Bill White at the Canadian blue line and then moments later to Bobby Clarke at the Soviet blue line. The latter turnover resulting in Clarke feeding the speedy Henderson for a dangerous shot off the wing that Tretiak snags with his glove. With the first 10 mins gone in the third period, the teams switch ends. Esposito Hull and Goldsworthy are back out, facing Shadrin, Yakushev and Anasin. The Canadians continue to press, with Goldsworthy doing some aggressively borderline forechecking on the puck in the Soviet end. Unfortunately, the pressure is negated as Dennis Hull gives the puck away carelessly.

The puck goes into the Canadian zone, where the Soviets cycle the puck effortlessly until its ends up in the Canadian net, ending any remote chance for a Canadian comeback.

Goal 7: Shadrin. Soviets 5, Team Canada 2

Since the beginnings of the sport, there have been hockey players who have "flown under the radar". Players who were undervalued, underrated or unappreciated. This mindset tended to be towards defensive players, whose ability to shut down the opponents would get lost in the glory of their flashier or more offensively productive teammates. The trend also included well rounded centremen who both fed the puck to their high scoring wingers and remained the defensive conscience of the line. Milt Schmidt, Dave Keon, Jacques Lemaire, Bryan Trottier and in recent times Patrice Bergeron are all good NHL examples. During the period when Vladimir Shadrin was on the Soviet National Team, he was one of those versatile, somewhat undervalued, underrated, unappreciated players. Bobrov in fact had benched Shadrin and Yakushev for the first half of game four, looking at them as extra players on the bench, certainly not go-to guys at that stage in the Series.

In the summer of 1972 as the Soviets prepared to face Team Canada, Vladmir Shadrin had only been on the National Team as a part time player. He had been called up for a game in the 1969-70 season and had a great game with 5 points. That still wasn't enough for him to land a permanent spot. In 1971, he had 6 goals in 5 games at the World Championships but was not dressed for several games.

Finally, in the important Olympic year of 1972, Shadrin was taken to the games, but only participated in 3 contests, scoring one goal. He was kept on the roster for the 1972 World Championships scoring at a point a game pace with 10 points in 9 games. Soviet Newspaper TASS would remark on Shadrin's Summit Series impact:

"it can be deducted that Shadrin was considered a role player before the Summit, one of the many superbly talented Soviet forwards who were having a hard time getting playing time on the star-studded line-up. That would all change during the Summit Series, as he and his long-time partner Alexander Yakushev would become key contributors to the Series.

When Vladimir Shadrin died in the summer of 2021, having battled cancer and Covid 19, the accolades started pouring in for his cerebral, well-rounded game. Anatoli Tarasov who was on the National Team coaching staff when Shadrin was first called up in 1969.

"He was incredibly useful both for Spartak and the National Team," Tarasov said. "First and foremost, we must look at Shadrin's brilliantly developed sense of the pass. He gave his partners the puck subtly and skilfully, and most of all, at the right time – precisely in line with their high-speed 2 moves. He valued the puck, and it was rare that Shadrin's stick sent it to an opponent. It must be said that he was fluent in the art of passing, but he also mastered the game's other techniques – shooting, stickhandling, checking. Shadrin's game was always consistent. He was a cultured individual who never needed to be forced into practice. Nobody needed to worry about Vladimir's behaviour off the ice – he was a man who valued his reputation."

A rarity in Soviet hockey, Shadrin played his entire career with Moscow Spartak. His first full season with Spartak came in the 1966-67 season, the same year he joined fellow Summit Series teammates, Blinov, Solodukhin and Luchenko on the Soviet entry in the European Junior Championships. Spartak was often known as the "People's choice team" as they were perennial underdogs to the stacked Central Red Army club. Led by star Vyacheslav Starshinov's 47 goals in 44 games, Shadrin's first full season with Spartak was a championship one. The coach that successful 1967 season? None other than Summit Series coach Vsevolod Bobrov.

In 1968-69 Alexander Yakushev scored 50 goals playing on a line with Shadrin, and the Spartak team won a second championship in three years. Shadrin had his best goal scoring season in 1968-69, with 28 goals in 31 games, but this production failed to secure himself a place on the National Team. With a renewed focus on his defensive game, Shadrin's numbers in subsequent seasons went down, but his respect in Soviet hockey circles went up. His greatest season was the 1975-76 season, where Spartak won a surprise Soviet championship against a Central Red Army club that was stacked with National Team players. Shadrin's Spartak line of himself, Yakushev and Solodukhin was added to the Krylia Sovetov (Wings of the Soviet) club for the NHL Super Series, where Shadrin played well scoring 4 points in 4 games. However, it was at the 1976 Winter Olympics where Shadrin had his career defining game.

The Czechoslovaks were a team that went on to win the 1976 World Championships, and make the final of the 1976 Canada Cup, handing the powerful Team Canada squad its' only loss of the tournament. They were primed to win the 1976 Olympics in Innsbruck, leading the Soviets 2-0 mid-game and on a 5 on 3 power-play. Shadrin was put out to kill the penalties and he delivered a legendary performance. **The Spartak centre won three straight crucial faceoffs while killing the entire two-minute penalty.** He then scored the first Soviet goal of the game on route to hard fought 4-3 victory and the gold medal. **Shadrin led the Olympic tournament in scoring with a fantastic 10 goals and 14**

points in 6 games.

The 1972 Summit Series was a coming out party for Shadrin and his linemate Alexander Yakushev. Shadrin would get more and more responsibility in Moscow, his two-way game instrumental once Team Canada raised the Series intensity to a level the Soviet players had not experienced. As he would prove in the 1976 Olympics, Shadrin was a big game player who thrived on the competition. He ended the Series as the fourth leading point getter with 8 points in 8 games. What was even more impressive was that he had the top plus minus on either team in the Series, ending at plus 7.

Alexander Yakushev thrived as the Series went on, but Author Yuri Lukashin from Sports life in Moscow **credited much of Yakushev's success to his centre ice man**.

> *"The excellent performance of Alexander Yakushev can in part be attributed to Vladmir Shadrin. Aside from averaging one point a game, Shadrin was the best Soviet defensive forward in the Series " Chivoldski.net.*

Vladimir would finish out his career with Spartak in 1978-79 leaving after being rewarded by the government with being allowed to go play in Japan for four seasons. After retiring, the intellectual Shadrin, with an advanced degree in Mathematics, coached junior hockey before becoming the Vice President of Operations for his beloved Spartak, retiring in 2010. A fitting tribute to a great, yet unheralded player was made by former National Team teammate Boris Mikhailov:

> *"He was a true Spartak man to the tips of his fingers," Mikhailov told Sport-Express. "He was a Spartak man all his life, and never hesitated to talk about it. Having grown up with the club, he wore the red-and-white jersey with pride and throughout his life he spoke with pride about his connections with that club. He was a wonderful player, in my view he was often underrated. He was one of the best centers of his era, anywhere in the world. And he was smart off the ice as well, he graduated from the*

Institute of Oil and Gas in Moscow. "Volodya was just a good guy. I don't remember him ever being involved in any dispute with anyone, causing anyone problems. He was an approachable, even-handed, highly disciplined man."

The fifth, final goal of the game for the Soviets was a result of more textbook hockey from the USSR. **This time, the lesson delivered to the scrambling Canadians, was one of puck cycling.** "Cycling" is a modern-day term, certainly not on the Canadian coaching radar in 1972.

Nowadays, the term is used at almost all levels of hockey, in reference to the offensive team constantly moving and passing the puck around the offensive zone, generally around the boards or "the wall" as they are oddly known as today. The goal is to break down the defensive players into a state of chasing the puck, leading to an eventual opening which becomes an opportunity to score.

The play leading to the goal starts with a blind pass by Dennis Hull in the Soviet zone. As per usual the Soviets capitalize and transition the puck quickly. Alexander Yakushev carries the puck up ice, then does a nice give and go at the Canadian blue line with Shadrin. Yakushev enters the Canadian zone where he fakes a slap shot which causes Brad Park to drop to the ice on his knees. Yakushev of course walks right around Park and drops it back to Shadrin. Yakushev then starts the cycle by going deep into the Canadian corner, where he receives the puck back from Shadrin. As Park and Phil Esposito go after the puck, Canada is now starting to chase. The puck goes out to the right point, where Paladiev dumps it back around the boards to Shadrin who has taken Yakushev's spot in the Canadian corner. **This is the Soviet pattern of constant movement at work.**

Shadrin tries to pass out front to Yakushev, but Bergman has him tied up. The puck goes to Brad Park behind the Canadian goal, but Park gives the puck away by throwing it blindly up the boards. As they have been doing all game, the Soviet defenceman Vasiliev reads the play, aggressively pinches in, and beats Bill Goldsworthy to the puck. Goldsworthy takes him out along the boards, but Vasiliev has already dumped it deep again behind the Canadian goal. In a moment of poor decision making, **both Canadian defencemen go behind the net.** Park has his back turned to the play, which allows the puck to go by him straight behind the Canadian net to Alexander Yakushev. Park goes to hit Yakushev along the boards, but just like Goldsworthy a moment earlier, the body check is fruitless as the Big Yak has already thrown the puck out front to Shadrin. Since Bergman made the cardinal sin of going behind the Canadian goal when his defence partner was already there, **the front slot area is wide open.** Shadrin drives a backhand shot that is stopped at first by Dryden, but the clever Spartak player stays with it and switches to his forehand to flip the rebound over the prone Dryden into the open net.

Canada's defensive zone coverage is an absolute mess on this goal. The Soviet passing and cycling cause the Canadian defence pairing of Park and Bergman to make several key errors starting with backing up into the Canadian zone, allowing Shadrin and Yakushev to enter the zone unencumbered. Brad Park makes multiple mistakes including dropping to the ice, allowing the cycle to get set up, throwing the puck away and allowing Yakushev to make the final, fateful pass out front. Gary Bergman leaves the slot area vacant, where Shadrin gets two chances to score. The Canadian forwards are lackadaisical in skating and re-establishing control of the puck. Dennis Hull lazily allows Paladiev to throw the puck deep around the boards, continuing the cycle.

On the Soviet side, Vasiliev reads the play and does a key pinch along the boards. Vladimir Shadrin and Alexander Yakushev show why Spartak won two Soviet championships in the late 60's with their synergy and teamwork. It was impressive work by the duo. The Soviet coaches had to take notice of this chemistry, and consistent domination of the

Canadian players, for the remaining games in the Series. This game seemed out of reach.

After the goal, Canada goes back to Perreault with Cournoyer and Mahovlich, but the line fails to generate any offense. A Mahovlich bad pass leads to a dangerous Petrov rush. Petrov centres out front to Mikhailov for the hat trick, but Dryden gets a pad on it. The soviets do a full change to the Maltsev, Kharlamov, Vikulov line, but Canada only changes the wingers. This leaves Perreault out centring Rod Gilbert and Vic Hadfield, with Awrey and Seiling staying on for a long shift. Awrey makes some composed plays with the puck, but his partner Seiling struggles with some bad passes and stickhandling attempts. The puck does get picked up by Vic Hadfield in centre ice, who makes a move around Tsygankov getting a good solid snapshot off from the wing at Tretiak.

Clarke comes out to replace a tired Perrault, and Canada's energy increases. The Soviets decide they had seen enough and decide to start passing the puck around effortlessly, slowing the game down, making Canada look somewhat foolish in pursuit. The Vancouver crowd responds to this display of puck control with cheers, clapping and a horn tooting. **No longer satisfied with polite applause for the Soviet players, they now cheer them on, boldly, loudly, openly**.

To the Canadian players' credit, they continue to try to put pressure on the Soviet defence. As each attempt is an individual effort, they are less than successful. The Soviet defence does what the Canadian defence has failed to do in most of the Series so far; they stand up at the blue line, minimizing any individual rushes into their zone. With five minutes left in the game, Canada pressures a bit more, with Phil Esposito stealing the puck at the Soviet blue line and bulling his way into the slot for a quick shot. Dennis Hull gets the rebound, but again Tretiak is up to the task, foiling him with an off balance save. On the next shift Perreault gets some skating room as the Soviets go into a bit of a lull, perhaps sensing the game is won. Perrault flies through Ragulin and then Tsygankov before getting a one-handed shove on the puck towards Tretiak. **His speed is impressive as he bursts through the traffic at the blue line.** Canada continues to pressure, as the Soviets seem content with dumping the puck out of their zone, sending only one forechecker after the puck.

Valeri Kharlamov and Boris Mikhailov were fierce competitors who caused team Canada all kinds of problems in the games in Canada. Kharlamov comes on the ice with only three minutes left in the game. He spins at the Soviet blue line, bursts away from Bobby Clarke and speeds into the Canadian zone unleashing a slap shot. The shot is wide, but Anasin and Mikhailov go back to the two-man forecheck and pressure Pat Stapleton in the Canadian corner. The Soviets recover the puck and begin cycling the puck for a few moments with Mikhailov putting on a weaving and circling display in the Canadian end. Canada is forced to ice the puck. **The crowd boos in frustration**. The icing is waived off as the puck goes directly to Tretiak. The Soviets make a long pass to Anisin who takes a Canadian style slap shot from just over the blue line. Bill White drops to his knees to successfully block the shot. With just over two minutes left in the game, the crowd starts to leave the building, all hopes of a Canadian comeback gone.

In another odd moment of officiating, the faceoff is in the Canadian end, but the puck is dropped about two feet above the face off dot. The Canadians get control, as the Soviets suddenly stop forechecking and let Gary Bergman stand stationary behind the Canadian goal. Canada attempts to breakout with some speed, but Dennis Hull makes a bad pass stopping all momentum. Canada regroups with Hull passing up to Esposito, who then misses a pass to Goldsworthy at the Soviet blue line. Blinov recovers the puck and is skating along the boards when Bill Goldsworthy attempts a heavy bodycheck. Blinov speeds up, evades the hit as Goldsworthy slams into the boards, his prey gone. The crowd comes to life with the murmuring and booing, hitting a fever pitch when Dennis Hull fires another useless mid-ice slap shot at Tretiak.

The Soviets slow the pace down, leisurely chasing the Canadians' puck possession, even throwing it back into their own end. Esposito forechecks without any real intent but it does cause a turnover to Dennis Hull. Hull immediately throws the puck right back to the Soviets, as the remaining spectators rain disgusted Boos down on the Canadian squad. This seems to motivate Phil Esposito who springs to life, taking the puck off the weaving Boris Mikhailov and fires a shot away at Tretiak. In a short sequence, Dennis Hull makes three straight failed attempts to either pass the puck or shoot it, until he finally gives it away again by firing it blindly around the Soviet net.

If the Soviets had decided to run out the clock at this stage in the game, no one told Boris Mikhailov. In an unexpected strike, Kuzkin passes it to Blinov, who is stationary at the hash marks in the Soviet zone. Blinov one times a long pass up the middle to spring Mikhailov on a sudden breakaway. Gary Bergman however is able to catch up to him, hooking Mikhailov who ends up getting a weak shot away at Dryden. Dryden tries to shovel the puck behind his goal, but the fierce Soviet Mikhailov is all over him, hooking Dryden to the ice, holding the Canadian goalie slightly as the Soviets recover the puck. The puck slides out to Petrov at the faceoff circle who takes a slap shot. The shot hits Mikhailov as he battles with Park in front of the Canadian goal. Vikulov recovers the errant shot but then does a poor pass out front that is intercepted by Gary Bergman. The pass is rushed as Vikulov sees he is about to be hit behind the Canadian goal. The puck gets to Phil Esposito who slowly carries it through the neutral zone. Espo would make **a clever play** leading to the final goal of the game, and making the score look closer than it really was.

Goal 8: Dennis Hull. Soviet Union 5 Canada 3

Dennis Hull has spent a lifetime being overshadowed by his talented, famous brother Bobby and, to a lesser degree, his goal scoring nephew **Brett Hull**. Despite that, Dennis has made a name for himself as a much-publicized speaker, using his potent, self-depreciating sense of humour to entertain audiences with hockey stories. While not as good as his brother, Dennis was a fine hockey player, with a solid career in his own right. Dennis certainly didn't start off as a junior level player when he joined the St Catherine's Tee Pees of the Ontario Hockey Association in the 1961 season. Hull scored a meagre 6 goals his first two seasons of junior hockey. Dennis' struggles were not helped by a self-awareness that he was not the same player as his brother. Finally, after being told several times by his parents to be himself, Dennis started to blossom. In his fourth season of junior hockey, Hull scored 48 goals in 55 games and started to look like he might have the potential to play in the NHL. The Chicago Black Hawks agreed, giving him a shot to make the line up several times in the 1964-65 and 1965-66 seasons. After some time in the minors, Dennis cracked the Chicago roster for good in 1966-67 scoring an impressive 25 goals in the last year of the six team NHL. Bobby was delighted to have his brother on the team,

> "I'm just delighted that Dennis has made it this year. I sure as hell wouldn't want to be in his shoes, to have that comparison constantly on your neck. In the same position I'd have likely done worse." Maclean's The Other Hull Susan Decker 1967.

The brothers would fit into their roles for the next five seasons, with Bobby being the glamourous star and Dennis being the solid role player who could score goals. Since both were left wings, they would never play together on a line. Dennis instead played on a line called the MPH (miles per hour line) with Pit Martin and Jim Pappin. Dennis flourished on this line scoring 40 goals in 1970-71 and a high of 90 points in the 1972-73 season. Hull was fantastic in the playoffs that season, scoring 24 points as the Hawks lost in the Stanley Cup final to Montreal. As a tribute to his great year, Dennis was named to the NHL's 2nd team all-star team. Unfortunately, Hull's career went downhill after that season, and he finished his NHL career in 1977-78 at age 33 with Detroit.

Dennis, like many others, would be surprised to be named to Team Canada 1972. **When his brother was precluded from remaining on the team after signing a contract with the WHA, Dennis wanted to boycott the series in protest.** It was actually Bobby who convinced him to play. Dennis followed his older brother's advice and had a good series with two goals and two assists in four games. When Vic Hadfield left the team in Moscow, Dennis joined with Rod Gilbert and Jean Ratelle on a revised GAG. The line gelled and provided some solid 3rd line play for games 6, 7 and 8. Like the majority of his teammates, Dennis struggled in game four. He took useless long slap shots, wasn't skating as well as he could and made some poor passes. However, Hull did have one redeeming moment with the final goal at end of the dramatic game.

As Boris Mikhailov gets sprung on his semi breakaway, linemates Vikulov and Petrov join in on the pressure deep in Team Canada's zone. When Vikulov makes an errant pass to the slot area straight to Gary Bergman, the Soviet forwards were caught deep behind the play. With the score 5-2 and only thirty seconds left in the game, they were more than likely not concerned about any Canadian counterattack. Bergman headmans the puck to Phil Esposito who leisurely skates through the neutral zone with the puck. Vladimir Petrov is backchecking, but he seems to be satisfied just watching Espo carry the puck. Esposito gets to the Soviet blue line where Tsygankov reaches out with a poke check. Esposito stickhandles in Tsygankov's feet and then delivers a what might seem like nice little backhand flip pass onto the stick of Dennis Hull. **In closer view, Esposito actually has the puck back in his skates and kicks the pass up to Hull with his skate!** The Soviets were masters at kicking the puck with their skates, especially due to the soccer background many of them had, but it was rarely seen in North America. **Esposito was in full flight, with a defender on him which make the play even trickier and more impressive.**

The recipient of the skate pass had been cruising down the left side wide open. Hull is now completely alone on Tretiak and snaps a hard shot up top over Tretiak's blocker. Tretiak backs up into his net, leaving the top corner open for Hull's shot. Tretiak's teammates seemed content to let the clock run out, showing no real sense of urgency to stop the rush. Even the usually defensively focused Petrov only makes a half stab attempt at backchecking Esposito, getting involved just before Esposito makes the pass to Hull. This is a goal that had no real bearing on the game, and only made the score appear closer than it was. What was the key result from the goal? **It would cement Phil Esposito as the Canadian player of the game.**

Game 4: Third Period Review

The game was seemingly over at the start of the third period. It was 4-1 for the Soviets, who had completely owned the play for the majority of the contest. It's hard to know what was said in the dressing rooms between the second and third periods, but Canada showed more energy, while the Soviets seemed somewhat comfortable to just let the game play out. The Soviets began by abandoning the aggressive two-man forecheck that had caused so many issues for the Canadian defence.

Instead, they were content to play a single forechecker harassing the puck carrier, while the other four teammates waited in the neutral zone. Also minimized was the new Soviet strategy of the defence immediately either carrying the puck or giving a quick headman pass to a circling forward. Defensively they went back to playing their standard zone style defence, eliminating any real chances defensively and making simple outlet passes out of trouble. **One thing about the Soviet hockey team in 1972, they would suddenly change tactics on their opponents.** Whether this was coach instigated or simply a case of players acting on the moment, it was a common theme throughout their history. They did this a couple of times in the third, suddenly springing a long pass to a breaking player, or as per the Shadrin goal, cycling the puck deep in the Canadian zone. **Canada on the other hand, really lacked any formal strategy.** Any attempted incursion into the Soviet zone was generally an individual one. Canada did score two goals, both on semi-two on one situations, but besides a 3 on 2 rush by the Clarke line, it was generally one player rushing the puck, or shooting from a bad angle or distance.

Strong players for the USSR in the third period were Boris Mikhailov, who would be named the Soviet player of the game, and fellow forwards Petrov, Maltsev, Shadrin and Yakushev. Blinov continued his fine game, while Tsygankov was the best defender for the Soviets, although he carried the puck less in this period. For Canada, this was certainly a good period for Phil Esposito, who directly caused both Canadian goals, led several rushes and was skating hard. Bobby Clarke made some brilliant passes after stealing the puck, Bill Goldsworthy scored a goal, and was working very hard in the corners and adding a physical element. **It wasn't enough to redeem himself as the fans continued to jeer him, but he certainly put the effort in.** Don Awrey capped off a decent game with some individual rushes, and his partner Rod Seiling also had probably his finest period of the series, settling down and making some good outlet passes. Otherwise, it was more of the same weak defensive play by Brad Park, and some scrambly play by Stapleton and even Gary Bergman. Overall, for the Canadian defenders it was better, but still nowhere good enough to defend against the wave after wave of Soviet forwards and it was much too little too late.

CHAPTER 41: GAME FOUR IN REVIEW. ROCK BOTTOM

Looking at the 1972 Summit Series from a Canadian viewpoint, Team Canada seems to follow the traditional "heroes' journey" upon which so many novels, movies and folklore have been based. They were unaware of their opponent, encountered hardships, hit rock bottom, and began a long arduous road back to final redemption and victory. Using that storyline, the Vancouver game was certainly **rock bottom for Team Canada**. The line-up changes that Coaches Sinden and Ferguson resulted of a double whammy of poor team chemistry, combined with poor team discipline. The Canadian players started the game with such seemingly misplaced anger.

Why were they so frustrated and determined to focus on intimidation more than playing fundamental, high-level hockey? Was this the directive from the coaching staff? It was not only Bill Goldsworthy's two penalties, but players like Yvan Cournoyer and Rod Gilbert, small skilled players, who were swinging their sticks, or hitting players from behind, in comical fashion. Early in the game, the Canadian poor positional penalty killing encountered the slick Soviet passing, and two quick Soviet power play goals were scored by Boris Mikhailov. Canada never seemed to recover. They were rarely able to match the Soviets speed, discipline, skill, defence, or goaltending.

Why did this happen? How could a group of top NHL players play so poorly? To start, fitness wise, the Canadian players seemed to have hit the proverbial wall. The emotional boost they used in game two seemed to have fizzled out. The team played with shocking lethargy. The Canadian forwards played a game of skating in spurts, far too often standing around, watching the play happening around them. The players inserted into the line-up, Gilbert, Goldsworthy, Hadfield, Perreault, Dennis Hull made for a lack of chemistry between the lines. There was very little cohesive passing, instead there was a plethora of failed individual rushes. Those rushes were against a Soviet defence that shut them down, play after play. This resulted in very little offensive opportunity, with Team Canada often just taking long useless slap shots at the Soviet goal. Neither strategy worked. In fact, Perreault's goal was an individual effort that was really an own goal by the Soviets. It was a pattern for Perreault, and he caused turnovers with his rushes more than he provided offensive opportunities. The other two goals were Phil Esposito led, with Hull and Goldsworthy just being in the right place to finish the play. Those were one-time successful rushes down ice for Canada, lacking the seamless synergy the Soviet forwards had in spades. The Canadian forwards seemed to also forget what made them successful in games 2 and 3. Dominating play along the boards, angled dump in plays, quick transition passes to their linemates mixed with strong defensive play, the forwards backchecking hard. Those were infrequently seen in game four.

The Canadian lines never seemed to gel, and the use of three centres with four sets of wingers greatly contributed to that unfamiliarity. As the Clarke line was still playing as a unit, it meant that Esposito and Perreault found themselves playing with duos of Frank Mahovlich/Cournoyer or Hull/

Goldsworthy or on infrequent cases Hadfield/Gilbert. It just didn't work. Esposito and Perreault were centres who needed wingers to get them the puck, and to finish the plays. The young Buffalo Sabre Richard Martin had excellent chemistry with Gil Perreault and may have been a better alternative than Frank Mahovlich on the left side. However, the coaching staff were not ready to admit that the Big M was hurting the team. While Phil Esposito had another strong game, his linemates Goldsworthy and Hull seemed to be the beneficiaries of Esposito's offensive forays, rather than adding to the consistent cycling and corner work that Parise and especially Cashman had been adding in the previous two games. Finally, dressing the Ranger duo of Hadfield and Gilbert without Ratelle simply didn't make any sense.

The Canadian defence pairing had greater familiarity, but poor positional play, the chasing, the dropping to block shots that never came, and the inability to stop the Soviets one on one, just seemed to showcase a lack of fundamental skill. Bill White continued his steady play, but Brad Park was not playing anywhere near his capability. His mind and game seemed to be elsewhere. Pat Stapleton also struggled this game, while Rod Seiling with partner Don Awrey played somewhat inconsistently, although certainly improved from game one.

Gary Bergman was Canada's best offensive defenseman this game, using his skating ability to jump into a few rushes, a role that wasn't his speciality. Ken Dryden turned out to be a very poor choice in goal. Whether it was because of his humiliating 1969 loss in Vancouver with the Canadian National Team, or just a poor performance amplified by his team's poor play, Dryden was shaky and out of sorts. The crowd's jeers at every save no matter how minuscule only added to the spectacle. Much like game one, the big netminders game seemed to not fit the Soviet style and, like Brad Park, his mind seemed elsewhere. Overall, the game was a mess for Team Canada, a lacklustre, undisciplined performance. Adding the embarrassment of Frank Mahovlich sitting on Tretiak and the angry, jeering Vancouver crowd, Vancouver was Team Canada's rock bottom. The hero story became one of comeback and redemption.

The Soviets must have left Vancouver in good spirits. They had come to Canada unsure of their opponent's true ability. They were told the mythic NHL professionals were the best players in the world, and they were leaving the country ahead in the Series after four games. Their performance in Vancouver had been their best in the series, and it came after two games of being somewhat outplayed. Coach Bobrov's and Kulagin's decisions had paid off. The line-up changes worked out at forward. Vikulov and Blinov had excellent games and were two of the best players on the ice. On defence the two players added weren't as outstanding, but overall Paladiev had been solid, while Ragulin seemed a step behind the play, and was his lack of foot speed was exposed in the Goldsworthy goal. The decision to bench Shadrin and Yakushev for whatever reason seemed to invigorate the duo. Adding young Anisin onto the right side paid off as in just over half a game the line dominated play, scoring the crucial fifth goal of the game. If Bobrov had put in a new strategy for the defence to counterstrike immediately, it was very successful. Team Canada was often caught deep in the Soviet zone, as they were getting used to the Soviet long pass to the middle as the transition game. The Soviets still had that weapon, but in this game, they added another dimension of defensive puck carrying, with a full speed outlet pass instead. Canada was too often caught flat foot as a result.

This had been the finest game of the series for the Soviet team. Boris Mikhailov was the best player on the ice, a nonstop ball of skill, feistiness, and energy. The Soviet forwards as a group were skating relentlessly, showing extreme versatility in both style and strategy. They had used their fitness, skills, and a savage mix-up of strategies from lightning-quick transition to the two-man weaving forecheck to modern style cycling of the puck to completely overwhelm Team Canada. To make matters worse, in what must have been a terrifying concept to the Canadians, the Soviets seemed to have an abundance of individual stars up front, all capable of being game changers. Maltsev, Petrov, Kharlamov and Mikhailov were as skilled as any Canadian forward at that stage in the series. Making it worse, there was still Yakushev, Shadrin and even players like Blinov, Vikulov or Anisin to contend with. When the Canadian forwards were able to make any forays into the Soviet zone, the Soviet defence played them with some textbook defence, watching the puck carrier's chest, angling the play to boards, and taking them out of play. This happened repeatedly to the Canadians, even to a player as skilled as Gilbert Perreault. When Tretiak was required to make a big save, he did. He handled all the long Canadian slap shots with ease, smothering the puck when pressured. The young netminder did his job, shutting down the majority of Canadian chances. He was a revelation to the Canadian people. Who was the young, handsome, athletic goaltender? He and flashy Valeri Kharlamov would leave Canada as new hockey stars. Their previously unknown ability a topic of discussion amongst the hockey world in North America.

The fans started to cheer and appreciate the new Soviet stars, while simultaneously showing their newfound disdain of the NHL stars. This negative reaction shocked coach Harry Sinden,

"I was upset as the players over it. We didn't expect any of it. I guess that's why it seemed worse than it was. We had played a poor game, a very poor game and there it was. Our reaction to it, including my own, was embarrassment that we had performed so poorly. In some ways we magnified it to case blame on the crowd". How Hockey Explains Canada, Paul Henderson and Jim Prime.

Bobby Clarke felt the team deserved the scorn from the Vancouver fans. He also felt his team understood the fans' reaction.

"I think everybody was mad. They were mad at themselves, not the fans. I can speak only for myself, but there was anger at the way I'd played and way we as a group had played. It wasn't the fans. We deserved what we got".

How Hockey Explains Canada 2011

The drama and impact of this fourth game in the Series cannot be understated. The score flattered Team Canada, but the viewing public, in person and on TV, knew better. They had all grown up with the belief that the best hockey in the world was being played in the NHL. It was being played by Canadians, who had mostly grown up in small towns, playing outdoors in the cold Canadian winters, developing skills that would take them to the NHL. In every Canadian's mind, those skills made them the world's best players. It was more than admiration of athletic ability. These were the Canadian heroes, they had skills that no one else had, and represented rightly or wrongly all that was good in the 1972 Canadian psyche. In the book 'How Hockey Explains Canada', CBC announcer Ron MacLean summed up the Canadian mindset that was prevalent at the time of the Summit Series:

"Figure skaters might take issue with that, but the fact remains that even though lacrosse and football and baseball and soccer all have had rich histories here, hockey seems to be the one that just epitomized what we thought was great about ourselves. We admired our own pluck, pure and simple. That seemed to be a representative of what it takes to live in a place where the winter is as harsh as it is."

Now, the Canadian public saw those players being outplayed by a team from another part of the world. That was the first shocking event. During the Vancouver game, they saw those same Canadian heroes handle adversity by slashing, hitting from behind, taking undisciplined runs at Soviet players, throwing tantrums, showing poor sportsmanship. They saw a revered player like Frank Mahovlich sitting on the Soviet goaltender, preventing him from getting back to the net. They watched poor passes, individual play, lazy backchecking, useless long slap shots, and a player they thought was the second-best defenceman in the world get the puck put through his legs and spun around as if he was learning to play the game. They saw their heroes running all over the ice, without strategy, making common hockey mistakes. The damage? Slowly, play by play, shift by shift, the Canadian public was seeing the destruction of the myth that these were the best players, playing the best brand of hockey.

The most lasting, impactful legacy of the third period of game four would be one incredible moment that took place after the game. A series changing rally cry from Team Canada's best player and emotional leader Phil Esposito, it's known today as simply **"The Speech"**.

CHAPTER 42:
THE SPEECH

If Team Canada lacked a real leader at this point in the series, they soon had one.

When Phil Esposito skated to the post-game interview and shook Soviet player of the game Boris Mikhailov's hand, he was visibly frustrated, angry, and hurt. He was frustrated with the way the Series had gone. He was likely frustrated with his teammates' play. He might even have been frustrated with his own play to date in the Series. He was certainly angry at the Vancouver crowd for the jeers and negative reactions. He was angry at the media who steadfastly predicted an easy series win for the Canadian team. The same media who told the Canadian players how great they were, over and over. As Esposito spoke, the anger migrated to passion which showed the most impactful aspect of Phil Esposito's interview. How hurt and disappointed he was and how he was determined he was to lead a change. He was hurt by the Canadian people who were booing the players. Hurt and let down by the booing of the Team Canada players. Hurt by the fans putdowns and cheering for the Soviets. Hurt by the lack of support for their own fellow Canadians.

These feelings came through in Esposito's post-game interview with Johnny Esaw. He was a bundle of pent-up emotions; it all came out in is one of the defining moments in Canadian history. He spoke passionately, honestly to commentator Johnny Esaw. Esaw certainly eschewed one of the reasons for the Canadian fans discontent with his questions alluding to underestimating the Soviet team and overestimating the NHL players but sensing that Esposito had some real passion for what he was saying, led the Team Canada player onto further discussion.

> Phil Esposito *To the people across Canada, we tried, we gave it our best, and to the people that boo us, geez, I'm really - all of us guys are really disheartened, and we're disillusioned and we're disappointed at some of the people. We cannot believe the bad press we've got, the booing we've gotten in our own buildings. And if the Russians boo their players, like some of the Canadian fans, I'm not saying all of them...then Ill come back and apologize to each one of the Canadians...but I don't think they will. ......
> I'm really really ....really disappointed. I am completely disappointed. I cannot believe it......Some of our guys are really, really down in the dumps. We know, we're trying like hell. I mean, we're doing the best we can and they got a good team and let's face facts. But it doesn't mean that we're not giving it our 150 percent, because we certainly are.*
> Johnny Esaw: "I think Phil, the disappointment is a natural thing, because the whole thing was an unexpected thing. ...They...we all live with the National Hockey League; we have all be so proud over the years of how great they (NHL players) are."
> Phil Esposito: "Its unexpected because of the press said that we were so good, not one of us said ever we were good".
> Johnny Esaw: "No no this is the thing, this is the thing that I'm, on behalf of the fans, I must say that , ah, probably since everything is relative, we know how good you people are, the people didn't realize how good the Soviet team was and we found how good they are. I think we can appreciate how good both teams are".
> Phil Esposito : "But I'll tell you, we love....I mean, every one of us guys, 35 guys that came out and played for*

Team Canada, we did it because we love our country and not for any other reason, no other reason. They can throw the money for the pension fund out the window. They can throw anything they want out the window. We came because we love Canada. And even though we play in the United States, and we earn money in the United States, Canada is still our home and that's the only reason we come. And I don't think it's fair that we should be booed."

Johnny Esaw: "Well Phil I'm sure that the people can see from your sweat just pouring off your face that you and all your players have given 100% and we look forward to some great games from you and the rest of your gang when you get over to Moscow and we can wish you the best of luck. Keep working hard."

Esposito ended the speech on a positive note to Canada. *"Johnny We are going to get better".*

To this day, there is a myth that this speech united the players as they left for Europe. Everything would change. Phil Esposito was now the undisputed team leader, and the players would unite under this rallying cry as a team. That wasn't the case. The players on either team never actually heard the speech and were completely unaware of it. Esposito himself didn't realize the importance of that moment in the history of the game or in that series until 10 years later when they gathered for a reunion and finally watched it. Even at that stage, Esposito was the best player and the leader of the team, and the players didn't need to hear the speech to rally around the big Bruin. That would happen moment by moment as the Series progressed. They certainly felt his passion, his anger in the room, his determination on the ice. Despite his reluctance in originally playing, this was now Phil Esposito's team.

The Soviets of course had no idea what was going on, or that through their excellent play they had awakened the NHLs top scorer, and what would follow for the rest of the series would be one of sports greatest examples of leadership.

"I was embarrassed," Esposito said. "I came as close as you can come to swearing on the air and caught myself. Which is unusual because I was in the kind of mood where I could have said anything. The truth is, I had nothing to lose. I was playing in the States. If we lost that series when I got up to Montreal or Toronto, they might have booed a little bit, but I got booed anyway. What right do I have to say something like that? Then I realized after, the best way to make a speech is emotionally if you want to get your point across."

Esposito made his point. Where the impact was felt, where his words truly resonated, was throughout the Canadian public. In a short interview, Esposito had managed to shame the millions of Canadian people watching the game as well as the media, while at the same time uniting everyone in a common cause. All in one speech. Perception changed. These were not overpaid hockey players who should be chastised, these were our boys, who were in deep. Shame on us for not supporting them. Shame on us for booing them. Shame on us for not realizing how good the Soviets were. As Canadians we need to support these guys. Our guys.

This support would show in multiple ways, including the 3000 fans who travelled to Moscow and out cheer the Soviets, to those who sent thousands of telegrams in loving support. This would be the true legacy of Esposito's speech, rallying a country to support the beleaguered players as they ventured into the unknown. Changing the external nature of the Series from player versus player, or NHL versus the USSR, to country versus country. People versus people. Us versus them.

Even more than Montreal, the Vancouver game changed Canada's perceptions after 100 years of smug superiority. Suddenly, the players aren't what the Canadian people thought they were. It was a shocking reality, a bitter pill to swallow for a country and a people that based so much value on being the best at the game off hockey. Now?

Canadian hockey might not be the best, Canada might lose this series. If that realization started in Montreal, it was cemented in Vancouver.

For the country of Canada, nothing would ever be the same.

PART 9: REVIEWING THE TEAMS.

WHAT DID THE GAMES IN CANADA MEAN?

CHAPTER 43: TEAM USSR, THE CONQUERING HEROES

While the Canadian games in the series was impactful in opposite ways, in two differing countries and cultures, the four games also exposed players, coaches and styles on both teams. **For the USSR, Vladislav Tretiak was the star of the team.** The young, athletic goalie was consistently strong all four games. When Team Canada pressed, whether behind or ahead, he kept his team in the game, Examples of this would start with Game one. Instead of folding under the pressure of giving up two quick goals, Tretiak rose to the occasion, keeping his team in the game in the first period, and then holding the lead at 4-3 in the first ten minutes of the third. Those were crucial moments where the Soviets could have been down two or three goals, or as per the case of the third period, let the lead slip away. Despite the original feeling from Team Canada that Tretiak would fold under the heavy offense, especially the supposed greater slap shots on the Canadian team, the young netminder had no issues with the shot. Although he did let in 14 goals in the 4 games, he was a rock in goal. A rock star, as Canadian fans were soon enchanted by the talented, handsome young netminder.

On defence, the Soviet defence had inconsistent

performances both individually and as a group. On the positive side, they were often successful at head manning the puck out of the zone and stopping the consistently individual rushes of the Canadian players. Individually it was a mixed bag as well. **Valeri Vasiliev** was an excellent addition to the group in game three, adding more mobility and physicality. **Gennady Tsygankov** played a physical, smart game, including rushing the puck at times in Vancouver. Team captain **Viktor Kuzkin** led by example, showing a fiery physical side, and matching that with some very solid defensive play. Kuzkin was often (or trying to) making up for his playing partner(s) mistakes. **Vladmir Luchenko** was inconsistent. While he made some smart offensive plays, especially with the two shorthanded backbreaking goals in Vancouver, he was also sporadically weak defensively, giving the puck away under pressure or being caught out of position.

Another veteran, **Alexander Ragulin** struggled with the speed of the game in the smaller rink. His lack of mobility and quickness meant he lost foot races to younger, faster Canadian forwards such as Yvan Cournoyer, Paul Henderson, and Ron Ellis. A big man, he was badly victimized by Cournoyer's speed on the second goal of game two and subsequently benched for game three. Overall, the veteran player failed to use his size and considerable strength to his advantage and seemed unwilling at times to battle in the corners with tenacious Canadian forwards such as JP Parise and Wayne Cashman. Ragulin was a smart player, composed and a leader, He would be back in the line-up for game four after being benched for game three, and put in a calm, respectable performance. This would bode well for when he would get back on the more comfortable larger ice surface in Moscow. The other player victimized in game two was **Evgeni Paladiev** who was unfortunately the scapegoat for Peter Mahovlich's spectacular goal. Paladiev had played well up to that point, showing some offensive ability in games one and two despite limited ice time. He would not be dressed for game three but played a solid, not overly physical game four.

Finally, fringe national player (in 1972) **Yuri Lyapkin** had a good game in Montreal, being on the ice for two goals for, but as the seventh defenceman did not receive a lot of ice time. He was less effective in game two, seemed a bit overwhelmed with the Canadian assertive style, finishing -1 despite getting an assist on the only Soviet goal. He would not be dressed for games 3 or 4. Another fringe player was **Yuri Shatalov**, who only dressed in game three, but played quite well. He teamed with Vasiliev and the Anasin kid line to form a young energetic group. He had some physical moments and made some good plays from the blue line. It was certainly surprising to see him not dressed for game 4.

A player who was not a fringe player on the National Team was **Alexander Gusev**. He had played all the games in the 1972 World Championships and was considered one of the top defencemen on the National Team. A large man for the times, at least 6'1 and 195 pounds he was considered a somewhat physical player in the Soviet Union. **Gusev however would really struggle in Canada.** He was often out of position and seemed to not be overly interested in the physical play, a choice that cost his team in a few situations. He gave up on the play in game two after taking a penalty, a shocking act for a National Team player. He forced passes up the middle trying to spring teammates that weren't open, and despite some good offensive pinches, he really struggled in the first three games. Coaches Bobrov and Kulagin seemed to notice Gusev's play, finally not dressing him for game 4.

At forward the Soviets were led by the dynamic **Valeri Kharlamov**. If Tretiak was the most valuable player for the USSR in the four games in Canada, Kharlamov was the runner up. As soon as he stepped on the ice in game one, his speed and skill set were immediately noticeable. Kharlamov's first goal was memorable as he blew around Don Awrey, showcasing his great speed and skill. If that display didn't catch the Canadian hockey fans attention (and Team Canada's) his second goal a few minutes later did. He added another spectacular goal in Game three and made a fantastic pass to Vladimir Vikulov for a goal in game four. On the downside, Kharlamov did have quiet games in Toronto and Vancouver, as he dealt with strong experienced defencemen like Bill White & Serge Savard and was beginning to feel the pain of playing against the tight checking Clarke, Henderson, and Ellis line. Valeri also showed his temper, getting a ten-minute misconduct in game two that certainly hurt the Soviet momentum. Despite all this, Kharlamov was a definite force in the four games, and the best skater on the Soviet team.

The second Soviet forward that had a very significant impact in the four Canadian games was **Boris Mikhailov**. Boris was fantastic in the four games, the most consistent forward on the USSR. He scored the backbreaking fifth goal in Game one, where he demonstrated some high-level edging and athleticism moving laterally on Rod Seiling, something that was rarely seen in the NHL. Boris would set up Valeri Kharlamov for his breakaway goal in game three and then dominate game four in Vancouver with two goals and an assist. He would be the leading scorer in the four games, with five points, but in Richard Bendell's book "Stats, lies and Videotape," Richard's detailed analysis of the games gives Boris another assist for an impressive six points in four games. Mikhailov was also the key forward on the Soviet swarming forecheck, he was relentless on the puck and not shy about sticking his stick into Canadian midsections as he forechecked. He was a handful.

Despite the Soviet victories in two of the four games, the rest of the forward group was somewhat inconsistent. **Vladimir Petrov** had the difficult task of matching up against Phil Esposito and his revolving door of linemates. While at times he seemed a bit overwhelmed with the task, Petrov put in a workmanlike performance. He backchecked hard, did a great job killing penalties and scored the very important second goal of game one. His big slapshot goal in game three was shorthanded and painful to Team Canada. His linemate **Yuri Blinov** had two good offensive outings as he dressed for games one and four. Blinov was a little-known player coming to Canada, but often showed excellent skating ability and agility as he contributed to a goal and an assist in his two games. Another stand out penalty killer was the tank like **Evgeni Mishakov** who did an excellent job harassing the Canadian puck carriers and battling hard in the corners. Mishakov's game was limited however, as he lacked the finesse required to contribute offensively at that level.

Alexander Maltsev was an extremely talented forward. His skating speed, agility and slick puck skills were as good as anyone in hockey, but for the four Canadian games, Maltsev was inconsistent. His rushes with the puck were often ineffectual and he lacked the appetite for the physical game that was needed. With that being said, he was still a threat every time he was on the ice and contributed to three goals in the four games, but otherwise failed to be an impact player. He was certainly an underachiever considering his vast talents.

Perhaps the biggest threat to Team Canada in the first two games of the series was the line of **Vladimir Shadrin**, **Alexander Yakushev** and **Yevgeny Zimin**. This was the trio that started the scoring in game one, and ended up scoring three of the seven goals, totalling seven points as a line. They continued that success into game two, scoring on the powerplay, but by game three they were starting to be lackadaisical defensively. This led to less ice time throughout game three and a benching for half of game four. This could have been because of the absence of Zimin who was either injured or a defection problem. Zimin's speed and goal scoring had made his surprise selection to the team to be validated. Adding 22-year-old **Vyacheslav Solodukhin** to the line in game three didn't pan out, but once **Vyacheslav**

Anisin was moved to the line for several shifts in game four, Yakushev and Shadrin came back to form, which was bad news for Team Canada. The line certainly had some success in the Canadian games. Yakushev was devastating at times, using his size, reach, and skating ability to overwhelm the Canadian defence core, who simply had no answer for him. Using Richard Bendell's revised statistics, Yakushev would end up with five points in the four games, Zimin, and Shadrin three each. Anasin of course was the centre for game threes pivotal Kid lines performance when they shocked Team Canada with two quick goals in the second period. His linemates **Yuri Lebedev** and **Alexander Bodunov** were secondary players despite those two goals, and the kid line was not overly effective for the remainder of game three or game four.

The final two forwards had to be considered disappointments for the Soviets. **Vyacheslav Starshinov** was one of the great stars of the Soviet 1960's dynasty. A great goal scorer, leader, and an intense clutch performer, he was only dressed for game two. The Soviet coaches gave him every opportunity to impress however, as he centred the two most talented forwards on the team, Kharlamov, and Maltsev. Starshinov also had power play and penalty killing time, but unfortunately at 32 his game was no longer at the level it needed to be. Starshinov seemed a step behind the play for much of the game and was subsequently dropped from the line-up for the remainder of the games. **Vladimir Vikulov** was a major star back in the Soviet Union. The top goal scorer the previous season in the Soviet league. However, in the two games he played in Canada, games 1 and 4, he was unnoticeable except for a goal in game four on a beautiful pass from Kharlamov. To be fair, Vikulov had been injured in game one, and was indubitably playing game four in discomfort. A small slick player, he seemed unable to find open ice against the professionals, and not used to the physical play. This had to be a disappointment for the coaches knowing the goal scoring ability Vikulov possessed.

The Soviet coaches **Bobrov** and **Kulagin** were either extremely prepared, or very lucky in the four Canadian games. One of the main changes they imposed after the more restrictive previous coaching regime, was to allow the players freer will for individual play.   This became obvious with the great individual efforts on several of the Soviet goals in Canada. The game one strategy of using seven defensemen worked out wonderfully for them as the expected Canadian offensive onslaught was absorbed by the group of seven. Despite the omissions of Firsov and Davydov, the team performed better than expected in Canada. If that had not happened, those player omissions would have come back to haunt them. The selection of full lines helped greatly in cohesion as the Shadrin Yakushev Zimin Moscow Spartak line performed well, and the gamble to insert the young Anasin Bodunov Lebedev line paid off in game three. Adding Valeri Vasiliev in that same game was another move that paid off, as he added a needed physical element to the Soviet back end. **Unlike their Canadian counterparts, when player performances declined, Bobrov and Kulagin acted on it**. Ragulin and Paladiev were removed from the line-ups for game three, and Alexander Gusev for game four. Strategically, it's impossible to determine how much of the Soviet play was based on the coach's game plans, or on years of symmetry between the players, most who were developed in the Tarasov regime. However, there were certainly some obvious subtle adjustments implemented such as the long break out pass, the aggressive penalty kills, the swarming offence, and the game four change with the defence rushing the puck. These strategies must have had some coaching influence.

The Soviet coaching staff had to have been ecstatic after game four. They had come to Canada unsure as to whether their team would be competitive against the NHL stars, yet they would only lose once on Canadian soil. It was a great success for Bobrov and Kulagin. They would leave Vancouver as the conquering heroes, perhaps too confident as history would show.

CHAPTER 44:
TEAM CANADA,
A SPAGHETTI
WESTERN

To use the title of the great Clint Eastwood western, the performance of Team Canada could be summed up as **the good, the bad and the ugly**. Canada was ill-prepared for the Soviet abilities, game style and fitness level. It often showed. This led to a frustrated group, who took irresponsible penalties and didn't seem to adjust their games to the new style they were encountering. During these four games, Team Canada was not yet a team, they were a group of frustrated individual stars. Yet, Team Canada was an extremely talented group of seasoned professionals. That talent, grit and ability was also present during the four games, with moments that were spectacular in execution. While many players struggled, some who were elite stars in the NHL, new and unexpected contributors emerged. Despite all this, Team Canada only won once in four games. They felt the pressure of a fan base and media that had suddenly turned on them, and that pressure led to an edgy, high strung group that bottomed out in Vancouver. This wasn't helped by the coaching decisions, that were as inconsistent as the team, damaging their hopes for success.

Ken Dryden was not an overly experienced goalie

in the fall of 1972, having just completed his rookie season on the Montreal Canadiens, after leading them to an unexpected Stanley Cup in 1971. He did have some international experience with the Canadian National Team, and despite his short professional resume, he was considered a clutch, playoff goaltender. This resume, combined with the first game being in Montreal, most likely led to Dryden being chosen the starting goaltender for game one. It was a poor choice. The big man was inconsistent at best, making some solid saves, but he simply did not provide the clutch goaltending required, especially when his teammates needed that big save to keep them in the game. The save that just never appeared. Dryden was even shakier in Vancouver, bobbling the puck, looking very out of sorts, lacking in confidence. This was not the Ken Dryden the hockey world knew or expected. **Tony Esposito** on the other hand played a wonderful game in Toronto. He brought stability, poise and a quick athleticism to the position that allowed Team Canada to take the lead. Esposito made several clutch saves throughout the game that sealed the only victory of the Canadian games. He played well again in Winnipeg, not letting in a bad goal, and preserving the tie when his teammates hit the conditioning wall and tired in the third period. In hindsight, the coaches made a terrible decision to not continue with Esposito for game four.

It's a fair statement that in the first four games of the series Team Canada's defence faced styles and skill sets that were completely foreign to them. These were experienced NHL defencemen, the best of the best, who had spent their careers adapting to the NHL style. A shoot first, up and down, crash to the net style that as defencemen they learned the best ways to negate. Suddenly, without any preparation, these same defencemen were now required to face, and shut down a completely different style of opposing forward, and team. They now had to deal with opposition that was extremely talented, very strong, with a fitness level that was beyond anyone in the NHL, playing a unique, high speed, high skill offensive game. They also had to deal with that despite being in any sort of mid-season form or fitness level. With the weight of an entire nation and hockey culture on their back. With a starting goalie that was struggling through issues of his own. Team Canada's defence was swimming up a waterfall. Because of these factors, it was surprising in hindsight they performed as well as they did.

Brad Park was the alpha dog on Team Canada's defence core. Without Bobby Orr, Park was the top defenceman in the NHL and the go to guy for Harry Sinden's squad. Park was a very confident player, with sublime stickhandling and passing skills. These skills were on display through the Canadian games as Park made numerous fine outlet passes, his most memorable a laser onto the tape of Yvan Cournoyer that led to the crucial second goal of the game. Despite his numerous offensive skills, Park was also a decent defensive defenceman in the NHL. He was a good body checker, especially the hip check, a skill he displayed in game one as he threw Boris Mikhailov for a ride off a textbook hip check. He could also block shots, a frequent skill for NHL defencemen of that time period, but one that required the defender to drop to the ice. This became an issue for Park, and other Team Canada defencemen as once he was on the ice, the Soviet forward wouldn't shoot as expected. The player would simply walk around the prone defender or make a pass, taking the prone defenceman on the ice out of the play. In the NHL Park was able to lead more individual style rushes, able to stickhandle his way out through traffic, as he progressed up the ice. Against the Soviets, this was less effective for Brad, as his stickhandling through the neutral zone led to costly turnovers. The Soviets were relentless back checkers through the neutral zone, quick skaters and Park found himself making one move too many. His positional play was also suspect defensively at times, and his one-on-one play was inconsistent, leading to the shocking and embarrassing puck through his legs by Maltsev in game four. Despite these inconsistencies, Park's effort was always top notch, and he seemed to bounce back instantly from a bad moment. After the Maltsev opportunity in game four, Park quickly recovered and led a rush up ice. His confidence, work ethic and skill set somewhat equalled out some poor play in the Canadian games, but it was still not the performance he was capable of, or what Team Canada needed from their defensive leader. Despite all of that, Park would end up a solid +4 in the four games.

Brad Park's partner on defence, **Gary Bergman** performed very well in the four Canadian games. He would finish with a team high + 6. Bergman was more physical and a better skater than Park, and he used that to his advantage in dealing with the Soviet swarming offense. Bergman rarely found himself overmatched in one-on-one situations, and his skating ability allowed him to be able to get the puck out the Canadian zone quickly. Bergman still had some issues with positioning and the Soviet style, including one goal in game four that had both he and Park behind the Canadian net, a basic faux pas for defensemen, but overall, he was a surprising and valued anchor on the Canadian defence core. A player who played a steady defensive game like Bergman, but with less of an edge, was **Bill White**. When Team Canada inserted White and Chicago Black Hawk defensive partner **Pat Stapleton** into the line-up for game two, it gave the Canadians much needed defensive steadiness. White was fantastic in the three games he played. He was virtually impossible to beat one on one, and despite not appearing to be a smooth skater, he was able to handle the Soviet speed and team play quite well. He played textbook defence and it worked. He was Team Canada's most consistent defenceman. His partner Pat Stapleton was small, a quick skater with decent but not outstanding offensive skills. He was an energetic player, quick and used that energy to stay on the Soviet forwards and counterattack out of Canada's zone quickly. He had some off moments in game four, but overall, he and White were an excellent second pairing for Canada.

Guy Lapointe was one of the five defensemen selected for game one. For whatever reason his ice time was minimized for the first period as Team Canada rolled two sets of defence pairings. When Lapointe finally came out for his first shift, he was a bundle of energy, skating around chasing the puck, out of position, a mistake that heavily contributed to the first Soviet goal. Lapointe settled down with a good game in Toronto, but he and partner Serge Savard struggled a bit in game three. They were victimized for both goals in the second period by the Anasin Kid Line. Lapointe was a good skater, with some natural offensive assertiveness that led to some good plays offensively, but that same wayward assertiveness made his positional play lacking in discipline. This was his single biggest issue in the three games he played. As a result. Lapointe would end up a terrible -6 in the two games he played. Lapointe's Montreal Canadien teammate **Serge Savard** was a wise insertion for Team Canada in game two. Savard had a multifaceted game. He was big, strong, surprisingly mobile, very strong defensively and a superb puck carrier. Combined with Bill White, Savard helped to settle down Team Canada's defence after game one, forcing the Soviet wingers to realize they could no longer go wide or have an easy time getting to the net. Like Lapointe, Savard a few poor moments in game two, but generally was always one of the best players on the ice. He was badly missed in games one and four.

The other two Team Canada defencemen that played in games one and four were the unlikely pairing of Boston's **Don Awrey** and New York Ranger **Rod Seiling**. These well-respected veterans had great chemistry in training camp, leading to starting roles in game one. While Seiling had played against the Soviets before with the Canadian National Team, their style and game were new to Awrey. Unfortunately for both players, the tandem failed to repeat their training camp performance. Awrey and Seiling played very hesitant in game one, seemingly overwhelmed by the speed of the Soviets. They consistently backed up deep into the Canadian zone, allowing the slick Soviet forwards to use their quick movements successfully against them. After Kharlamov victimized Awrey on the third Soviet goal in game one, Awrey's ice time was minimized for the remainder of the game. This led to his partner Rod Seiling, a player who was already uncomfortable playing at that level to become exhausted. That exhaustion hurt his performance for the rest of the game, as Seiling would finish a horrible -6 for the game. The duo was subsequently not dressed for games two or three, but injuries to the Montreal duo of Savard and Lapointe, and a lack of choice for the coaching staff led to Awrey and Seiling dressing for the disastrous game four. The duo performed a bit better this game, especially Awrey who used his decent skating ability to rush the puck out of the Canadian zone. He still seemed a bit out of sorts defensively, as his shot blocking, defensive style that worked well in the NHL failed to suit the Soviet game, but it was a much-improved performance for Awrey, his last in the series. Seiling also had slight improvement from game one, but he just did not seem capable of playing at that level. His reaction times were always a half second slow, and he seemed uncomfortable with the puck and decision making. Only an average skater, he simply did not seem to have the skill set required for success. He would again be a minus player, leaving him with a dreadful plus minus of -7 for the two games in the series.

At forward, and overall, Team Canada was led by Boston's **Phil Esposito**. If the hockey world felt Esposito would be less effective without Bobby Orr, they were quickly proven wrong. From the opening ceremonial faceoff to scoring the opening goal, Esposito was dynamite in game one. As the four Canadian games unfolded, a new Phil Esposito emerged. Obviously extremely motivated to be representing his country, the big man was skating harder than seen before, backchecking, winning faceoffs, being physical and of course scoring goals. Phil easily could have had three or four goals in Montreal but was either stymied by Tretiak or didn't receive a pass from linemate Frank Mahovlich. In the tighter checking game two, Esposito again opened the scoring, and looked more comfortable with new linemates Wayne Cashman and JP Parise. This synergy carried into Winnipeg, where Phil would score for a third straight game, and have several other chances. A final change of wingers in game four didn't deter Esposito's production. The NHL's top scorer would finish the four games with a dominant seven points. He was proving to be more than a handful for the Soviet team. On the negative side, Phil would be on the ice for as many goals against as goals for. Phil was never a fitness fanatic, and was certainly motivated by patriotism in these games, but was also most certainly not in mid-season shape. He did have incredible stamina that would allow him to take very long shifts on the ice, but with the frantic pace the Soviets played at, combined with the pressures of playing for Team Canada, and not being in mid-season form, a fatigued Esposito was victimized a few times by being either late on the backcheck or outworked in the Canadian zone. A good example of this was the third goal in game three where Esposito and Cashman were outworked by the young relentless Anasin Kid line. These moments didn't tarnish Esposito's massive impact in the four games, an impact that cumulated in his dramatic and powerful speech in Vancouver. He was Team Canada's best player, leader, and a force to be reckoned with every time he was on the ice.

Frank Mahovlich was Team Canada's biggest disappointment. The Big M started out well in game one, skating hard, getting involved in the offense, and having several chances on goal. The problem was his decision making was poor. He often took long windups for his slap shot, allowing Vladislav Tretiak to get set for a shot that was typically right at him anyways. Frank also had several opportunities to pass to an open linemate but didn't, nullifying the opportunity. Part of this was as a result of a lack of chemistry with Phil Esposito, and the change to Stan Mikita in game two was a much better fit. Frank had his best game of the four Canadian games, scoring his only goal of the series in the third period. Game three in Winnipeg was a repeat of the poor decision making, as Frank was now almost completely off his game. His terrible giveaway to Vladimir Petrov for a shorthanded goal was a perfect example of Franks lack of focus. Frank's defensive game was non-existent, and there were periods where he looked lost without effort. He would end up -3 in Winnipeg. As his game slipped away from him, it all came crashing down in game four where Frank was completely ineffective. His decision to sit on Vladislav Tretiak will forever go down as the symbol of Team Canada's bottoming out in Vancouver.

The third forward on Canada's starting line in game one was **Yvan Cournoyer**. The Roadrunner as he was widely known, was one of hockey's fastest players. He would use that lightening like speed to have constant chances on Tretiak all four games. Unfortunately, only one of those chances ended in a goal, the beautiful full speed strike in game two. Game two was Cournoyer's best, he was everywhere, working and skating hard at both ends of the ice and with a goal and an assist, easily could have been named Canada's player of the game. The Roadrunner made a beautiful pass to Jean Ratelle in game three, but with the rotating centres and Mikita getting less and less ice time, Cournoyer would end up -2 on the night. In Game four, the hockey world saw a completely different Cournoyer. Gone was the classy gentleman of the Montreal Canadiens, a role that would make him captain and instead Yvan was extremely irritable, throwing his stick around like a machete, playing with what would seem to be unprovoked anger. Despite this, the Roadrunner would still use his speed to have a couple of semi breakaways on Tretiak. But was unable to convert. He was certainly one of Canada's better forwards, ending up with three points in four games, but truly could have had many more.

Bobby Clarke was Team Canada's player of the game in game one. From the opening shift where he got cross checked by Maltsev, to the end of a game when he not only got vicious revenge, cross checking the prone Maltsev after tripping him, but had played a very strong Bobby Clarke style game. Clarke would set up linemate Paul Henderson off the faceoff for Team Canada's second goal, and score one himself in the third period, making the game a tight 4-3 lead for the Soviets. He would set up Henderson again in Winnipeg, having continued his relentless two-way game in both games two and three. Overplaying Clarke as Team Canada's coaches struggled to find synergy with their centre ice men, led to Bobby appearing exhausted for game four in Vancouver. He too would finish with three points in four games, but what was more telling was his plus 2 rating, despite lining up against the top Soviet players each shift. Clarke's two linemates **Paul Henderson** and **Ron Ellis** also performed well. The line had instant chemistry from the first moment of training camp, and that carried over into the four Canadian games. While neither player had dominant performances, their speed, defensive acuity, and tenacity made them very difficult to play against. Ellis had been injured in game one, but persevered and put in a solid, workmanlike four games. Henderson was more of an offensive threat, scoring two goals in the four games, showing hints of what was to come.

Peter Mahovlich was as surprising in performance as his brother Frank was disappointing. Pete was part of a makeshift line with Red Berenson and Mickey Redmond for game one. This line did not perform well, lacking cohesion and tenacity. Pete was fantastic on the penalty kill, ragging the puck through the neutral zone, knocking important seconds off the penalties. Pete's shorthanded goal in game two was one of the greatest in hockey history and shocked the Soviet team with its skill and execution. Peter would have limited ice time in games two and three, primarily being used as a penalty killer. Despite performing well in that role, the coaching staff did not dress Peter for game four. **Red Berenson** and **Mickey Redmond**, Mahovlich's game one linemates, were only dressed for the one game. Both players had poor games, with Redmond getting little ice time, and not really adding any offensive input during his limited time on the ice. Berenson had more opportunity, including being put on the point on a power play, but like Redmond, was not impactful in the game. His forte was as a defensive forward, and that would be how he would be used later in the series.

The New York Ranger trio **of Jean Ratelle**, **Rod Gilbert** and **Vic Hadfield** were pigeonholed by the coaching staff after game one as not being able to play against the Soviets style wise. While their game one performance was certainly not up to the expectations that were had for the NHL's best line the previous season, they were somewhat unfairly blamed for the three Soviet goals that occurred when they were on the ice. The reality was those three goals were a result of the highly skilled Soviet team overwhelming the Canadian defence. The real problem was the Ranger line failed to generate any substantial offensive pressure that game. As a result, all three players were not dressed for game two in Toronto. This was the beginning of Vic Hadfield's discontent, as he was from Oakville, just outside the city and wanted to perform in front of friends and family. After game two began a series of strange line-up decisions involving the Ranger stars. Centre Jean Ratelle was dressed for game three in Winnipeg, scored a beautiful goal, and played well despite limited ice time, often the best player on the ice. Ratelle's smooth skating and cerebral game seemed perfectly suited for international hockey, however, the coaching staff obviously disagreed, benching the previous seasons Lester

Pearson winner for game four. Gilbert and Hadfield were dressed for Vancouver, but without their star centre. A very unfamiliar position for the wingers. Hadfield had a solid game in Vancouver, skating hard, backchecking, delivering a solid bodycheck to Paladiev, and setting Gilbert up for a disallowed goal. Hadfield also set up Yvan Cournoyer for a breakaway that was called offside. Gilbert on the other hand had a similar game four to Yvan Cournoyer. Normally a classy player with the Rangers, Gilbert was running all over the ice in the first period, playing reckless, undisciplined hockey including crosschecking Valeri Kharlamov, agitating him for no apparent reason. Gilbert was also guilty in the two games he played of stickhandling through the neutral zone, causing turnovers, a malaise that also effected Ranger teammate Brad Park. Gilbert did score a goal in game four that would have made the score 3-2 for the Soviets, but it was disallowed. This was certainly not the style or production of the Rod Gilbert who was the NHL's top Right Wing the previous season.

Phil Esposito played with six different wingers in the four games in Canada. The most successful pairing was that of his regular Boston Bruins linemate **Wayne Cashman** and Minnesota's **JP Parise**. Once inserted into the line-up in game two, the dynamic of the games shifted. Team Canada was more aggressive on the puck, started, then continued, to rule the battles in the corners and along the boards, and in Cashman's case added a bit of mental intimidation. The Soviets seemed flummoxed in dealing with both players, Parise a bundle of energy, hounding the puck, manically battling for the puck and Cashman cleverly using his size, air of menace and skillset to feed Phil Esposito the puck. This resulted in Esposito opening the scoring in game two, breaking a tight scoreless struggle early in the second period. Parise would open the scoring himself in game three, and then a classic Cashman to Esposito strike in the second period would give Canada a two-goal lead. Both players were extremely impactful, with both Cashman and Parise getting two points and +2 in their two games. Despite their success, Team Canada coaching staff decided to bench both players for game four in Vancouver. Esposito's new wingers in Vancouver would be Minnesota's **Bill Goldsworthy** and Chicago's **Dennis Hull**. Goldsworthy had played in game two, but received little ice time, but when he did, he was aggressive, with borderline play such as kneeing Vladimir Petrov in the head. This didn't deter the Canadian coaches, who proceeded to watch Goldsworthy sabotage Team Canada's early momentum with two unwarranted, undisciplined penalties. Those penalties led to early Soviet goals by Boris Mikhailov, putting Canada down 2-0 early on. Goldsworthy settled down afterwards, scored a goal on a Phil Esposito rebound, and did some good forechecking work, but the damage had been done. He would be forever linked with Team Canada's undisciplined play in Vancouver. Hull was a different style of player, not a physical force like Goldsworthy, but possessed good skating ability and a dynamic, wild shot. Hull didn't provide much impact in game four, taking long slapshots that were either off target or easily stopped by Tretiak. He did score a very late goal after a wonderful play by Phil Esposito, but by then the game was pretty much completed. Replacing the very effective Cashman/Parise duo with Hull and Goldsworthy was one of the many line-ups mistakes the Canadian coaches made for the disastrous game four.

The final two forwards that played in the Canadian games were transplanted Czechoslovakian legend **Stan Mikita** and future Hall of Famer **Gilbert Perreault**. Mikita centred Frank Mahovlich and Yvan Cournoyer in game two, a line that played well together and contributed two of the four Team Canada goals. Mikita would set Mahovlich up for his only goal of the series, and played a feisty, intelligent game that at times looked like the Stan Mikita of the mid-1960's. Whether it was through injury (either latent or new) or the coaches trying to work four centre icemen through the line-up in Game three, Mikita's ice time was minimal, and he was dropped from the line-up for game four. The veteran had played well when called upon. Perreault's single game in Vancouver was as enigmatic as his career. He certainly added immense speed and skill to the game, showcasing his puck carrying abilities and speed in his end-to-end goal, the first of the game for Team Canada. The problem was, he continued to try the same play, making individual rushes that were ineffectual, and caused turnovers. At other times he seemed disinterested and lacked tenacity. Whether that was because of his youthful temperament, it felt like it was only a glimpse of what this incredibly talented player could have delivered.

When evaluating Team Canada coaches **Harry Sinden** and **John Ferguson**, there is always the caveat that this was an entirely new experience for anyone in North American hockey in 1972. They had the unenviable role of taking a group of NHL stars, who played on different clubs, with zero intermixing of players due to intense rivalries, in an age where the majority of professional players did not train in the summer and form them into a team that was capable of defeating the very unified, very fit, very skilled Soviet National Team. This was to be achieved in three weeks, with an unfortunate promise from the coaches that all the players would play in the games.

The duo would do their best to prepare the players, putting them through what could have been considered a fairly hard camp in 1972, showing them video of the Soviets playing Whitby in 1959 and trying to drive home a message that the series would be harder than expected. This was consistently at loggerhead with a media and adoring public who kept telling the players they would win easily. Unfortunately for the coaches, their strategy of only going with five defensemen, mixed with horrible bench management, directly affected game one's outcome. Decisions such as using the soon to be beleaguered duo of

GRANT DOUGLAS PENNELL

Rod Seiling and Don Awrey, two journeymen defensemen as your shut down second pair, or playing Phil Esposito with Yvan Cournoyer and Frank Mahovlich, a trio that had very poor chemistry in camp, were in hindsight very poor ones. As was the offense first strategy, telling Team Canada to shoot on every opportunity, hoping to overwhelm the young Soviet goalie Vladislav Tretiak.

They certainly rectified the line-up situation and should receive full kudos for changing the team outlook and strategy for game two, a successful win. They would continue that general line-up for game three, with the only new insertion being Jean Ratelle who scored a goal and played a strong game. The revised strategy of making the Soviets adjust to NHL style checking, tenacity paid off, as did the option of the wingers playing deep in the Canadian zone, helping the overwhelmed Team Canada defence out man the Soviet swarming forecheck. These decisions helped Team Canada go undefeated for two games.

However, it would come crashing down in Vancouver. If game one player decisions, strategy and bench management were directly impactful to the loss, the game four decisions repeated the process. In hindsight the player selections were almost completely baffling. Tony Esposito had been a rock for Team Canada in goal. He was undefeated and was not to blame for any of the well-executed goals by the Soviets in game three. Ken Dryden had been shaky in game one, misplaying several goals, and not coming up with the clutch saves required. Ken had a terrible history with the Canadian National Team against the Soviets including a 9-3 shellacking in Vancouver in 1969. Ken's goaltending style of coming out to challenge the shooters and being a very large man, he lacked the mobility of Tony Esposito that was required with the constant down low passing plays used by the Soviets. Despite all this, the coaches decide to not go with the undefeated goalie and instead put Dryden back into the net, rolling the dice that Dryden would rebound from his

536

game one performance. This would fail miserably as Dryden was again out of form, even bobbling the puck on easy shots, and drawing the ire of the Vancouver crowd.

Up front the choice to replace Cashman and Parise with Goldsworthy and Dennis Hull would be a very strange one. As mentioned, Cashman and Parise were very effective in the two games they played and seemed to fit quite cohesively with Phil Esposito. Cashman especially had seemed to get into the Soviets heads, always a good thing for a long series like this. Despite that, both players were dropped, forcing Phil Esposito, Team Canada's best player to play with two wingers he had never played with before. If the coaches knew that JP Parise had played many times on a line with teammate Bill Goldsworthy in Minnesota, they ignored that potential pairing and instead went with the less physical Dennis Hull. Another odd decision was to drop the NHLs second best forward Jean Ratelle, who had just come off a very fine game in Winnipeg, and insert his wingers Rod Gilbert and Vic Hadfield, whose success was always as a trio in New York. This would mean that Gilbert and Hadfield would play with a rotating group of centres instead of the one centre they were used to, as part of the best line in the NHL. A tough task.

Finally, dropping Peter Mahovlich, Team Canada's best penalty killer so far in the series, was a terrible decision. The Soviets were renowned for their devastatingly effective powerplay, and the result was two quick power play goals to start the game in Vancouver. Whether those goals happen with Peter in the line-up is impossible to tell, but since both were partially a result of poor coverage by Team Canada players Frank Mahovlich and Ron Ellis, Peters benching made zero sense from a hockey perspective.

While the coaches obviously made the line-up decisions that they thought were giving them the best chance of success, the results were mixed at best. It was a very difficult task for them to make the right choices, deal with the large number of players chosen another mistake Sinden would regret, and find the right mix to battle a unique, unified, highly skilled opponent. These decisions would turn out to backfire on Team Canada. If you added the very poor bench management in game one, a reluctance to pull Ken Dryden (in either games) mid game to hopefully stop the bleeding, or bench players like Bill Goldsworthy after taking unneeded and costly penalties, then the coaches unfortunately greatly contributed to Team Canada's losses. **They would need to get the right line-ups, strategies and discipline needed for their team to have any success in Europe.**

CHAPTER 45:
CONCLUDING A
CONCLUSION

The impact of these four games in Canada was immense. Knowing Canadian international hockey history, or the North American media and hockey establishments view of European hockey, the four games in Canada became a shockingly huge comeuppance for Canadian hockey. For much of the games in Canada, the Soviets seemingly skated better, passed better, and played better positional hockey. They showcased their own unique style that was mixed with fundamental hockey but better fundamental skills. They used those same skills in a unified, energetic, relentless, and unique team style. It worked, and at times seemed to overwhelm Team Canada. This was completely unexpected to the Canadian fans, media, and players themselves.

These games exposed Canada to a new reality. Canada was not the only country who could play this game, **and they might not even be the best at it**. Phil Esposito's passionate speech made this new realization even more impactful. It was a cry for help, for the country of Canada to unite behind their heroes. To understand that the players are in deep.

Why did Canadians not take the European game seriously? Why the shock and anger?

As discussed in detail in previous chapters, in 1972, Canada as a nation had been playing hockey for almost 100 years. Teams representing Canada had been playing internationally for over 50 years. While Canadian teams had dominated early on, especially teams like the Toronto Granites, European hockey improved rapidly. By the mid-1930's, however, Canadian victories were not always guaranteed, as countries like Czechoslovakia and Sweden became legitimate threats. Of course, the two World Wars delayed international hockey competition, but once play resumed, teams from Canada were still hard pressed to defeat a team from Czechoslovakia. Sweden took longer to rebuild and develop a program that was competitive but by the late 1950's they were certainly a considerable opponent for a Canadian Senior A team. Once the Soviets came on the international hockey scene in 1954, there became three countries that could challenge Canadian amateur teams at the worlds and Olympics. By the mid-1960's, those teams were beating the Canadian teams regularly and consistently. Canadian teams had faced top players, international stars like Rudi Ball, Vladimir Zabrodsky, Vsevolod Bobrov, Tumba Johannsson and Anatoli Firsov. Great players with great stories.

Despite all of this, international hockey was always dismissed by the Canadian media and hockey establishment as lesser. **That prevailing attitude never left the Canadian conscious**. To be fair, it was a different time in society. Canadians couldn't go on YouTube to watch a Soviet Czechoslovakian game, nor was there any television or media coverage of events like the World Championships. The newspapers and Canadian press were focused on the NHL or even local amateur hockey. It would be rare for an international hockey game, even one with a Canadian team to be front page news, If a reporter was even sent overseas to cover the tournament. **The NHL was the only hockey that mattered.** Families would gather around the radio to listen to the Leafs or Canadians play, and once television became the norm, the NHL was broadcast coast to coast. Any rare occurrence of an international game being broadcasted, such as the Whitby-Moscow selects game in 1957 was a novelty. Even then it was just a senior team playing the Soviets, not the NHL despite having former Maple Leaf star Sid Smith in the line-up.

The NHL certainly didn't perceive international hockey as equals, and for many years they were correct. In the 1950's, the Soviets had trouble consistently beating the top Senior A level Canadian teams, those teams were still quite strong but were probably comparable to a mid-lower range American Hockey League or AHL team. **Where the disconnect happened with the Canadian public, media and hockey establishment was in failing to understand or acknowledge that the Europeans, especially the Soviets, had improved to an NHL level a decade later**. This is the single main reason for the extreme disappointment in the results of game one, and the results of the Canadian end of the series. If somehow the media, or the NHL had given the public the impression that the Soviets were a real significant challenge for the NHL, good enough to challenge even a team of NHL all-stars, then the resulting emotional distress Canadians went through would have been lessened.

A couple of reasons stand out in that failure to acknowledge the European playing level before the series. Firstly, they had no basis of comparison. Europeans were not playing in the NHL, and the few that came over didn't make an impact. The competition that the Soviets, Czechs, and Swedes were playing had been amateurs, either Senior clubs or the Canadian National Team. Despite the National Team briefly having outstanding NHL player Carl Brewer or the National Team being competitive against NHL clubs in exhibition games, they were not NHL teams. As a natural assumption that meant they were not equal. Yes, the Soviets were beating the Father David Bauer's squad, but they were not the NHL, so the victories were meaningless. The NHL was the only true test.

Secondly, the hero worship of NHL players was deeply ingrained in Canadian culture. Since the dawn of professional hockey, the star players had become bigger than life in the minds of young Canadians. Sitting around a radio listening to names such as Howie Morenz, Eddie Shore or Rocket Richard made those players legendary figures in people's minds. Television only enhanced those thoughts as Canadians could now watch Howe, Hull, Beliveau and Orr fly across their screens. Even if Canadians felt the Soviets were an actual threat, they had decades of believing in their own Canadian hockey heroes could and would vanquish them. It was a deeply ingrained, full on belief. Canadian players were the best. Yet that belief would shatter in the four games in Canada. From Montreal to Vancouver, shift after shift, a new reality set in. The emotional crash that realization caused was significant, it was felt universally across Canada.

Can an entire country suffer from grief? The Mayo clinic, one of the world's most well-known and revered medical facilities refers to grief as:

"Grief is the natural reaction to loss. Grief is both a universal and a personal experience. Individual experiences of grief vary and are influenced by the nature of the loss."

While grief is usually associated with overcoming the loss of a loved one, important relationship or even job loss, there can be an argument made that in 1972, during the four games in Canada, millions of Canadians went through some of the stages of grief. Who? Well, it was those millions of people that loved hockey, that felt hockey represented them **as who they were as Canadians.** The games in Canada would have such a dramatic impact on those people, that they would go through grief related stages: denial, anger, bargaining, depression, and eventual acceptance.

In only seven days, in four games, things that Canadians had thought were true, had truly believed in, changed. That change began with the loss of the Canadian belief in their hockey superiority, thus a belief in themselves.

That change was also a belief that the NHL, a league that was almost exclusively Canadian in its player content, was the top league in the world, with the top players. There was a loss in a belief in the Canadian way of life, that the freedoms, the society they loved produced not only the best hockey players, but players who played hard, tough but classy. These things were now being questioned or already determined false. In just seven days.

The stages might not be in exact order. **Denial before and after game one.** European hockey is not equal to Canadian. The Soviets are not as good as our players. They are frauds. Then the loss. The players are not in game shape. It was hot in the arena. They were unfamiliar with the Soviet tactics. **It's one game**. It doesn't mean anything. Denial became stronger after game two when Team Canada would rebound, showing the great skill set of the NHL stars, defeating the Soviets. Setting things right again. However, anger would start to creep in after Team Canada would lose a two-goal lead twice in Winnipeg, being dominated by a group of young kids to tie the game, almost losing the game as fatigue and Soviet talent came inches away from stealing another win. A tie was like a loss to Canadians. Now the bargaining came in. If only Bobby Hull had played in Winnipeg, or if Bobby Orr could play, things would be better. The players just need to get in game shape, but bargaining wouldn't last. **Anger took over in Vancouver**. We have been duped. These players are not as good as the Russians. Our players are taking cheap shots, stupid penalties, playing poor hockey. They aren't acting with dignity or class. They are letting us down. As Canadians. Is this who we are? Our players lazy, overpaid, with poorly developed skills? Have we (Canadians) been living in denial? Can a communist system create better players? Should we be ashamed to be Canadian now? **Anger.**

Finally, **acceptance**. Maybe it's true that Europe has really good players. Excellent players. That Kharlamov is a wonderful player, that Tretiak as good as any NHL goalie. Maybe there are other ways of playing hockey that are different than ours but still very effective. They are great to watch. Let's appreciate the differences and respect the Soviets. Cheer them on. We might lose this series, but we can appreciate how good the Soviets are.

Phil Esposito's Vancouver speech helped ratify some of those emotional stages. His passionate verbal beat down of the Canadian fans and press was shocking in its bluntness. It was also extremely effective. Anger was slowly replaced by awareness. Awareness that the Canadian players were trying hard. Trying their best. Awareness that their opponents were very good. Much better than anyone realized. Awareness that by not being supportive, by booing the players, or insulting them or questioning them as Canadians, they themselves were not acting "Canadian". Now those very same people had to look internally, to change that anger and disappointment to acceptance. They had to dig deep down, look at themselves, question themselves. Why were they so angry? Why did they feel deceived? Why weren't they more supportive of their Canadian hockey heroes? The speech forced those questions, forced Canadian self-reflection. Once answered, those same people would be able to finally support Team Canada, and by doing so, supporting Canada as a nation, as a people, **united in a single cause.**

Yes, the four Canadian games had major emotional impact on Canadian society, but what about the reactions in the Soviet Union? The Soviets were much newer to the game, but within fifteen years they had become the dominant nation in international hockey. Soviet society was a much more closed society than in North America, but as the teams had success internationally, and the Soviet hockey league grew in popularity, a similar thing happened in the USSR that had happened in Canada, **teams and players became part of the culture and self-identification**. Fans cheered for their local teams, their local stars. With the best players often lumped onto the CSKA or Central Red Army club, fans of Moscow Spartak or Dynamo or the Wings became underdogs, hoping to defeat the hated Army club. The league stars became household names. Children skating on outdoor rinks in Moscow or on ponds outside the cities, pretended to be Anatoli Firsov, or Starshinov, or Alexandrov. While they didn't have the ability to see the players on promotional items or hockey cards, they still had their own version of hockey hero worship. The question on many minds in the Soviet Union was, were these heroes truly the best?

The Soviet players, fans and hockey bureaucracy had always heard the same retort from Canada, our best players are professionals. In the NHL. You are only winning championships because you haven't played our best. This caused some consternation to the Soviet hockey fan. Without direct comparison, or an ability to watch games in North America, the NHL players became mythical figures. As a result, the series became a big event in the USSR. Despite the time differences, the games were televised to millions of viewers, who sat in their small state apartments glued to the drama. **The Soviet win in game one was probably as shocking to the hockey fan watching the game in an apartment in Moscow as it was to a Canadian fan.** Soviet fans had to be nervous before the game. How would their team do? After a terrible world war, the fear of the west during the Cold War, and living a bureaucratically controlled bleak life in Communist Russia, validation of their players would be impactful. Their pride and self-worth were represented by their players.

After game one in Montreal, to the Soviet viewer, the myth of the NHL superiority, of Canadian hockey superiority was shattered. After game four in Vancouver, the Soviet players were validated. They were not only as good as the Canadian mythical superman, but they are also seemingly better. With the series going back to Moscow for the final four games, there appeared to be little concern for worry.

It was a time for pride, celebration, and excitement. Soviet hockey was the best after all. **While Russian pride was being validated, Canadian pride and self-worth was being tested as never before**.

How would Canada as a nation respond to these four games? What would happen to Team Canada as they would venture into Europe? What was the history of great international games in Moscow? How would the players on each team do in the four remaining games? The second half of the greatest series in hockey history would be told in Volume II.

These would be the most dramatic games in the history of hockey.

ABOUT THE AUTHOR

Grant Douglas Pennell

Born and raised in Winnipeg Manitoba Canada, Grant Douglas Pennell has had a lifelong love for the game of hockey. Raised in a hockey family, he has been playing and involved in the game for over fifty years. He has always had a keen awareness and passion for Soviet Hockey and international hockey history.

Grant currently resides just outside the City of Toronto Ontario with his family and two dogs. He spends his days playing shinny, oldtimers hockey, golfing and writing his next book!

COMING SOON

The Summit Series Play by Play.

*Volume 2: Waving at Brezhnev-
The European Games*

As Team Canada 1972 headed to Sweden, they were a team in disarray. They had lost the series in Canada, only winning once out of four games. Their own country had turned on them, booing them mercilessly in Vancouver. Now the beleagured Canadian players had to travel to a hostile, foreign environment, play on unfamiliar larger ice surfaces, with international officiating that had seemingly different standards and potential bias. How would they adapt? What obstacles would they face? What about the internal dissent amongst the players? Could the coaches actually bond this group of all stars into a team capable of defeating the Soviets on home ice? Were the Soviets overconfident? What players would rise to the occasion? Who would falter?

Stay tuned for book two in the 1972 Summit Series Play by Play Series! "Waving at Brezhnev: The European Games".

Made in United States
North Haven, CT
21 December 2023

46388371R00303